D1167725

THE POLITICAL ECONOMY
OF NORTH AMERICAN
FREE TRADE

THE POLITICAL ECONOMY
OF NORTH AMERICAN
FREE TRADE

Edited by
Ricardo Grinspun
and
Maxwell A. Cameron

St. Martin's Press
New York

PUBLIC LIBRARY, PLAINFIELD, NJ

382.71
POL

[TK]For Doris, Eitan, and Yuval
For Fabiola
with love

© Ricardo Grinspun and Maxwell A. Cameron 1993

All rights reserved. For information, write:
Scholarly and Reference Division,
St. Martin's Press, 175 Fifth Avenue,
New York, NY 10010

First published in the United States of America in 1993

Printed in the United States of America

ISBN 0-312-07599-5

Library of Congress Cataloging-in-Publication Data
The political economy of North American free trade / edited
  by Ricardo Grinspun and Maxwell A. Cameron.
       p.   cm.
  Includes bibliographical references and index.
  ISBN 0-312-07599-5. — ISBN 0-312-09534-1 (pbk.)
  1. Free trade—North America. 2. North America— Economic
integration. I. Grinspun, Ricardo. II. Cameron, Maxwell A.
HF1746.P65   1993
382'.71'097—dc20   93-14764
                                                             CIP

Fig. 7.1, on p. 108, is reproduced with the permission of the Minister of
Supply and Services Canada, 1992.

TABLE OF CONTENTS

I. Framework of Discussion

II. The Political Economy of Canadian Integration

III. The Political Economy of Mexican Integration

LIST OF ACRONYMS

AFL-CIO	American Federation of Labor–Congress of Industrial Organizations (United States)
ALADI	Latin American Integration Association
ALTEX	Program for Advanced Exporters (Mexico)
BCNI	Business Council on National Issues (Canada)
CAC	Canadian-American Committee
CAW	Canadian Autoworkers
CBI	Caribbean Basin Initiative
CEA	Council of Economic Advisors (United States)
CONCAMIN	Mexican Confederation of Industrial Chambers
CUFTA	Canada-U.S. Free Trade Agreement
CVD	Countervailing duty
EAI	Enterprise for the Americas Initiative
EC	European Community
ECLAC	UN Economic Commission for Latin America and the Caribbean
EEC	European Economic Community
EPA	Environmental Protection Agency (United States)
EPZ	Export processing zone
ESPRIT	European Strategic Programme for Research in Information Technology
FDN	National Democratic Front (Mexico)
FEI	Fragmentary export industrialization
FMS	Flexible manufacturing systems
GATT	General Agreement on Tariffs and Trade
GDP	Gross domestic product

GNP	Gross national product
GSP	Generalized System of Preferences
JESSI	Joint European Semiconductor Silicon Project
ILO	International Labour Organization
IMF	International Monetary Fund
IMSS	Social Security Institute of Mexico
ISI	Import-substitution industrialization
MERCOSUR	Southern Common Market
MITI	Ministry of International Trade and Industry (Japan)
MMPA	Marine Mammal Protection Act (United States)
NAFTA	North American Free Trade Agreement
NDP	New Democratic Party (Canada)
NEB	National Energy Board (Canada)
NEP	National Energy Program (Canada)
OAS	Organization of American States
OECD	Organization for Economic Cooperation and Development
PAN	National Action Party (Mexico)
PEMEX	Mexican Petroleum Company
PMI	Mexican International Petroleum
PRD	Party of the Democratic Revolution (Mexico)
PRI	Institutional Revolutionary Party (Mexico)
SECOFI	Ministry of Commerce and Industrial Promotion (Mexico)
TNC	Transnational corporation
UAW	United Autoworkers
UN	United Nations
UNCTAD	United Nations Conference on Trade and Development
USITC	United States International Trade Commission
USTR	United States Trade Representative

ACKNOWLEDGMENTS

Most of the chapters in this volume were initially presented in draft form at a December 1991 workshop held in Toronto and organized by York University's Centre for Research on Latin America and the Caribbean (CERLAC). CERLAC provided an ideal environment for developing a project of this nature, and we acknowledge the institutional support offered by CERLAC throughout the life of this project.

Naturally, during this book's gestation we have accumulated a huge debt to friends, supporters and colleagues. We would like to acknowledge the helpfulness of the following individuals and organizations. Seed funding for this project was provided by the Ministry of Colleges and Universities of the Government of Ontario and the Social Sciences and Humanities Research Council of Canada (SSHRC) through CERLAC's Canada as an Hemispheric Actor (CHA) project, directed by Edgar Dosman. CHA project funding allowed Ricardo Grinspun some much needed release from teaching duties. His research was financed in part by York University's Faculty of Arts and Small SSHRC research grants. Maxwell Cameron's research was financed in part by a research grant from SSHRC. He acknowledges the encouraging research environment at the Norman Paterson School of International Affairs at Carleton University in Ottawa, as well as the Center for U.S.-Mexican Studies at the University of California-San Diego for a visiting research fellowship in 1991 which allowed him to work on this book.

Meyer Brownstone, director of CERLAC, had a key role in securing the funding for this project and provided ongoing encouragement and support. Liisa North and Louis Lefeber provided continuous encouragement. Liddy Gomes, administrator of CERLAC, assisted in the organization of the workshop and handled the finances of the project with her usual efficiency. Edgar Dosman personally encouraged us to engage in this project. Lizeth Alvarez, Zarina Alloo, Laura Eustace, Susan Rainey, Tracy Reid, Diane Pantelle, Grace Baxter and, in particular, Carol Duncan provided secretarial support. Patricia Landolt translated the chapter by Edur Velasco Arregui. Jim Gronau copyedited the complete draft and helped make this a much more readable and accessible book. We appreciate the support and patience of Simon Winder and Laura Heymann of St. Martin's Press, as well as the sharp pen of the copy editor Clifford D. Thompson. We also thank Phillip Cerconi at McGill-Queen's University Press for his encouragement of the project. Robert Kreklewich and Viviana Patroni wrote an excellent rapporteurs' report of the workshop, which is available through CERLAC. Patti Smith provided research assistance for Maxwell Cameron. Participants in the workshop who did not contribute chapters provided key feedback and enriched the discussion. They include: Diana Alarcón, Duncan Cameron, Stephen Gill, Ma. Teresa Gutiérrez-Haces, Joan MacNeil, Robert O'Brien, John O'Grady, Morris Miller, Richard Roman, Michelle Swenarchuk, Ken Traynor, and others. We also gratefully acknowledge receiving permission to reproduce an updated and revised version of an article by Steven Shrybman, "Trading Away the Environment," *World Policy Journal,* Winter 1991/92, from the journal's publishers. Scott Sinclair wrote parts of the glossary. Other parts of the glossary were reprinted from *The Canadian-U.S. Free Trade Agreement: Commentary and Related Documents,* 1987, with permission from the publishers, CCH Canadian Ltd. We acknowledge the Ministry of Supply and Services, Canada, for permission to reproduce Figure 7.1. Theresa Healy and Richard Rothstein, as well as two anonymous referees, provided valuable feedback on an earlier draft of the volume.

Two individuals played especially key roles in this project. Thomas Legler, a doctoral candidate in political science at York University, excelled as organizer of the workshop at CERLAC, making possible what was a highly fruitful intellectual exchange. In addition to contributing a chapter and coauthoring the rapporteurs' report, Robert Kreklewich was essential in the final stages of preparation of the manuscript. He assisted in the editing and revision of chapters and prepared the glossary, the list of acronyms, and the index.

The contributors to this volume deserve a special acknowledgement. Their unswerving support, collaboration, and enthusiasm transformed what at first seemed like an overwhelming task into a very pleasant and encouraging experience.

Our last word goes to our families. Yuval, Eitan, and Doris Grinspun and Fabiola Bazo lived through the ups and downs of this project, supporting us with patience and love. It is simply right that we dedicate this book to them.

R.G. and M.C.

FOREWORD

Robert Kuttner

The North American Free Trade Agreement (NAFTA) has sparked an essential debate about the benefits and costs of liberalized trade in North America. The open outcry against NAFTA in the United States and Canada, and the muted skepticism in Mexico, are all really part of a more fundamental debate about political economy. The larger debate concerns what sort of economic and social systems are desirable as well as politically sustainable at home and how such systems can be reconciled with global economic pressures.

Many advanced capitalist democracies maintained a crude consensus on this question from the end of World War II until the oil crisis in the early 1970s. The consensus held that a sustainable market economy is necessarily a mixed economy. It matured out of the excesses of the ultra-capitalist 1920s, the depression and chaos of the 1930s, and the dictatorships and global war of the 1940s. The conviction deepened that a pure market economy produced intolerable costs both in equity and in efficiency, which in turn generated social unrest and political conflict.

Interventionist governments quite literally saved capitalism from itself. The mixed economy of the postwar era combined a mild form of Keynesian demand management with a welfare state, tolerance of trade unions, labor legislation, pegged currencies under the Bretton Woods system, and gradually expanding—but not perfectly free—trade. It was relative stability and growth at home that made possible relatively open trade abroad, not vice versa.

Even the more conservative industrialized nations regulated their economies. Large oligopolies with stable market shares and profits plowed their profits back into productivity-enhancing capital investments, which, in turn, contributed to higher living standards. Policies had a social democratic tone in some nations and a conservative or Christian-democratic cast in others, but in all cases capitalism was managed and national. Successful policies, in turn, generated the political constituency for their continuation.

The global postwar system depended on U.S. hegemony. Whenever the World Bank and the International Monetary Fund (IMF) faltered in their role as suppliers of development capital and stabilizers of currencies, the immense economic reach of the United States filled the vacuum. The U.S. dollar, not the "bancor" John Maynard Keynes intended, became the global currency; the Marshall Plan, not the World Bank, became the font of European recapitalization after the war. The conservative United States accepted social democratic allies—of whose domestic policies it disapproved—to present a common front against communism.

The postwar entente between capital and labor in the wealthy capitalist nations produced an unparalleled era of sustainable growth and almost full employment. However, the political basis of this historic compromise was always shaky, for labor had never quite been accepted as a full social partner, except perhaps in Sweden. The compromise was pragmatic and contingent, not ideological and permanent, and it started to disintegrate as a result of the slowdown in economic growth after 1973. Many wage earners, frustrated by diminished economic prospects, supported conservative governments that promised a reverse course during the late 1970s and the 1980s.

This political and ideological reversal of the last fifteen years coincided with technological shifts that accelerated the conversion from national capitalism to global capitalism. Technological advances in areas such as computers and telecommunications made the deregulation of finance and commerce more encompassing than ever before. It became easier to locate advanced production anywhere in the world. With portable technology and capital it was suddenly possible to combine advanced production from the North with cheap labor from the South. This situation led to a new dilemma involving the practical impossibility of "global Keynesianism"—the ability to manage and regulate the world economy in order to produce high demand and rising wages.

Hitherto, the combination in one country of aggregate demand management by the state and a high wage strategy enforced by the trade unions produced a virtuous circle. Expensive labor made it rational for industry to substitute capital for labor. As labor was shredded through increasing capital intensity, it was absorbed elsewhere in the growing and fully employed economy. Capital investment yielded real productivity growth and rising living standards, which were shared more or less equitably due to the power of the unions. High wages, in turn, created consumers with the purchasing power to buy the products.

Through the globalization of production and finance, an underemployed labor force in the South undercut the high-wage social contract in the North. Transnational corporations' easy recourse to cheap labor overseas also undercut their incentive to invest at home. Stagnant wages in the North undermined the domestic markets needed for economic growth. As elites in the South competed to industrialize and to win preferred access to the markets of the wealthy North, the common strategy was to let wages lag behind increases in productivity.

The new centers of advanced production in the South inevitably produced more than they consumed, for the development strategy was predicated on chronic export surplus and low wages. In the rich countries, imports enjoyed a price advantage over domestic goods, which were produced with higher-cost labor. Only a few rapidly industrializing countries, such as Japan and South Korea, were able to export enough unemployment through chronic trade surpluses to maintain some semblance of the high-wage/high-growth strategy in their own economies.

The effort to increase wages and consumption in many newly industrializing countries was undercut not only by even cheaper labor in poorer countries, but by another legacy of the 1970s: the Southern debt. Pressure from the creditor countries, the IMF, the World Bank, and the private commercial banks to repay the foreign debt led to belt-tightening measures, which further depressed wages and consumption in those countries.

Thus, accelerating globalization during the 1980s undercut the domestic social contract in the advanced industrialized countries. What was required—and absent—was a social contract on a global scale. There was no global counterpart to a national fiscal policy, since there was neither a single hegemonic nation—the United States was slowly losing its power—nor a global government. Nor was there a global monetary policy, since the U.S. dollar was losing its status as universal currency and the financial and foreign currency markets proved to be increasingly unstable and speculative under deregulation. As there was no global labor ministry, there could be no floor to buttress global labor standards, let alone a global minimum wage. Laissez-faire had returned, via the back door of trade and corporate investment, with the inequalities and instabilities that it implies.

Once again capitalism needed to be saved from itself. But Ronald Reagan, Margaret Thatcher, and their champions did not appreciate that reality. Instead, large corporations took advantage of the situation to weaken the power of trade unions and welfare states of which they had never entirely approved. The various conservative regimes that held sway during the 1980s insisted that the cure for the malady was privatization, deregulation, and ever purer free trade. As the state was weakened, industries deregulated and "rationalized," and wages undercut, the crisis of the capital-labor entente deepened.

In the financial realm, the end of the Bretton Woods regime after 1973, the abolition of capital controls, and the advances in telecommunications and computers combined to create a monetary system of wildly fluctuating currency values, all too reminiscent of the 1920s. Under Bretton Woods, currencies could fluctuate only within very narrow bands, whose margins the central banks were sworn to defend jointly. Revaluations were rare. There was little opportunity for speculative profit, and most currency transactions went to finance real commerce and capital investment. Today, after 20 years of currency deregulation, most cross-national currency transactions are purely speculative.

In the realm of trade the laissez-faire crusade has produced schizophrenic moves both for global free trade and for preferential regional trading arrangements, which are, of course, inconsistent. These arrangements act as a battering ram against what is left of the high-wage/high-growth mixed economy in countries such as the United States and Canada. The European Community (EC), the one effort to replicate the social contract on a continental scale, has suffered serious adversity. The collapse of communism has caused Germany to turn inward, contributed to high interest rates that wrecked the European Monetary System, created a refugee crisis, and set back this promising experiment in regionalizing a mixed economy.

In North America regional economic integration has proceeded under entirely conservative auspices, rejecting high wages and continental regulation. Free trade undermines what is left of the mixed economy, which is seen as archaic and "protectionist" rather than deliberate and economically functional. NAFTA lacks even the embryonic safeguards of the EC: no regional development funds, no common regulations to prevent a "race to the bottom" in labor or environmental standards, and no movement toward democratic political and governmental institutions on a continental scale.

Yet NAFTA should not be seen as the source of the problem. The shift of manufacturing jobs and investment capital to Mexico—the *maquiladoras,* the combination of high technology and low wages—have all occurred even without the added stimulus of NAFTA and will keep occurring even if NAFTA is not implemented. Even without NAFTA, laissez-faire in the United States will continue to undercut a slightly more social-democratic economy in Canada.

NAFTA is merely one element of a larger problem: the disintegrating effects of globalization on our mixed economy and on our social contract.

We face four possible courses of action. First, we could give in to laissez-faire and promote declining living standards and political chaos. Second, we could return to the elements of the postwar system: national regulation, pegged currencies, relatively high tariffs, and a domestic mixed economy sheltered from trade. (Some nations, such as Japan and South Korea, have continued this strategy into the post–Bretton Woods era, combining trade barriers against imports with fierce local product competition in their domestic markets; but for many countries the insulation from foreign competition has led to inefficiency and stagnation.) Third, we could attempt to create the instruments of a mixed economy on an international scale, which seems improbably (a world central bank?), although one could imagine global labor and environmental standards. Or, fourth, we could attempt to create them regionally, as the EC has valiantly attempted and as NAFTA has not.

The last path may be the most realistic course in our region, although it requires a wholesale rethinking of the premises of North American economic integration. Happily, the authors of *The Political Economy of North American Free Trade* have cleared important ground in analyzing NAFTA's economic assumptions, its ideological and political dimensions, and its institutional consequences. Indeed, NAFTA makes for a superb case study of the larger issues confronting the global economy. The growing North American integration under laissez-faire auspices is compelling proof of the failure of the free trade model. The authors of this volume make a very significant contribution to the study of the North American continental economy and to the larger issues, which involve nothing less than the reinvention of an economy with a human face.

I

FRAMEWORK OF DISCUSSION

Chapter 1

The Political Economy of North American Integration: Diverse Perspectives, Converging Criticisms

Ricardo Grinspun and *Maxwell A. Cameron*

Prior to 1990, few observers believed a comprehensive free trade agreement between the United States and Mexico was likely.[1] In June 1990, the United States and Mexico announced their intention to negotiate such an arrangement, and in October 1990 Canada joined the consultations. A year later, in June 1991, formal trilateral negotiations commenced, following the "fast-track" approval of negotiations by the U.S. Congress. Fourteen months later, on 12 August 1992, a deal was reached, and the North American Free Trade Agreement (NAFTA) text was signed by the leaders of the three countries on 17 December 1992.

A number of international research projects initiated during 1990-91 sought to demonstrate the mutual economic benefits that would accrue to the three trade partners under a trilateral free trade arrangement. This research focused on the expected macro- and microeconomic gains from liberalized trade and investment, as well as on related aspects such as investment regimes, rules of origin, legal implementation, and intellectual property rights.[2] Significant effort was spent analyzing key industrial sectors, such as automobiles, petroleum and petrochemicals, financial services, and agriculture. Such research was valuable to policy makers in Ottawa, Washington, and Mexico City because it both prepared the background for the negotiations themselves and molded public opinion in favor of NAFTA.[3] However, this research agenda failed to adequately address the social, labor, environmental, and political implications of NAFTA, as well as some of the economic costs and possible alternatives. NAFTA negotiations were concluded before this significant research gap could be closed.[4]

Much of the early work on NAFTA could be regarded as what Robert Cox has called "problem-solving theory." Problem solving

> takes the world as it finds it, with the prevailing social and power relationships and the institutions into which they are organized, as the given framework for action. The general aim of problem-solving is to make these relationships and institutions work smoothly by dealing effectively with particular sources of trouble. Since the general pattern of institutions and relationships is not called into question, particular problems can be considered in relation to the specialized areas of activities in which they arise (Cox, 1986, p. 208).

Cox juxtaposes problem solving against critical theory. Critical theory

> stands apart from the prevailing order of the world and asks how that order came about. Critical theory, unlike problem-solving theory, does not take institutions and social and power relations for granted but calls them into question by concerning itself with their origins and how and whether they might be in the process of changing. It is directed toward an appraisal of the very framework of action, or problematic, which problem-solving theory accepts as its parameters (Cox, 1986, p. 208).

Since the 1970s, critical theory has gained influence within international political economy (Cox, 1987; Gill & Law, 1988; Murphy & Tooze, 1991). The collapse of the Bretton Woods monetary regime, global stagflation in the late 1970s, the debt crisis and recession in the early 1980s, the growth of protectionism in the industrialized economies, and, most recently, the formation of regional trading blocks, have created a sense of crisis and uncertainty in the international order (Gilpin, 1987). Change and uncertainty have, in turn, led to greater awareness of the relationship between politics and economics and to a renewed interest in the interplay of domestic social forces and the international system.

This volume, written as NAFTA was negotiated and updated upon release of the actual text of the agreement, contributes to this political economy tradition by addressing diverse themes and debates that unfolded in the three North American countries in the early 1990s. The analyses are often historical and focus on change; they deal with both domestic and international aspects of economic integration; and they reject an artificial separation of politics and economics.

This introductory chapter provides a synthesis of the major themes of North American integration based mainly, but not exclusively, on the chapters that follow.[5] We wish to highlight debates among the contributors to this volume that sharpen different perspectives on the issues. However, we also wish to underline the tendencies toward convergence that have emerged from these debates. This convergence indicates the type of intellectual framework that will support a critical analysis of the drive for free trade restructuring across the Americas.

Although the book reflects a variety of viewpoints, there is a unifying perspective in all the works presented here. The contributors agree that the questions raised here are important. Although they do not, in general, oppose economic integration per se, they are disturbed by the particular way in which this integration is unfolding in North America. The book seeks to stimulate further debate on the social, political, economic, and environmental costs and benefits of freer trade under NAFTA.

The overview is divided into eight parts. The first part discusses four areas of tension in the social democratic perspective on NAFTA; the second part discusses the neoconservative underpinnings of free trade; the third part suggests that free trade can serve as a neoconservative structural adjustment program; the fourth part addresses the possible negative impact of free trade on economic development; the fifth part analyzes the implications of economic integration for domestic political institutions and processes; the sixth part considers how asymmetries of power are reinforced by hemispheric trade liberalization, and explores the role of NAFTA within the "New World Order"; and the seventh part analyzes the role of the transnational corporation (TNC) as a force for globalization and regionalism. In the conclusion we evaluate NAFTA from a social democratic perspective.

DIVERGENT PERSPECTIVES, CONVERGING CRITICISMS

The effort to reach agreement among a disparate group of scholars was both exciting and challenging. It is clear, for example, that the perspectives of labor differ from country to country. Indeed, one important theme in the book concerns the position of labor on access to the U.S. market. Canadian and Mexican labor see enhanced access to that market as a legitimate policy, although they may be doubtful whether NAFTA will achieve that goal. In contrast, representatives of U.S. labor tend to be cautious about increasing imports of goods and services from Canada and Mexico; some are concerned that such increased access to their domestic market will take jobs from U.S. workers.

Stephen Diamond argues (Chapter 16) that a protectionist attitude pre-vailed in many U.S. labor organizations during the "fast-track" debate in Congress prior to NAFTA negotiations. This attitude is not surprising: the loss of highly paid industrial jobs in the United States due to recent deindus-trialization and the relocation of plants to cheap-labor havens overseas suggests that labor's fears are well founded. However, Diamond feels that U.S. labor should not fear expanded trade, as long as there is proper regulation of the social costs involved.

One positive outcome of NAFTA negotiations has been closer contacts between labor (as well as grassroots and environmental) organizations in the three countries. This in itself contributes to the search for common interests between labor movements in the North and in the South.[6]

Second, there are differences in the way social democrats evaluate the benefits of trade liberalization. One view sees significant benefits to the South from access to Northern markets but is concerned with the social impact on weaker groups in the industrialized societies. Underlying this position is the belief that protectionism in the advanced industrialized countries has hindered development in less developed ones. A beneficial aspect of NAFTA for Mexico is the increased access to the U.S. market. As Gerald Helleiner aptly points out:

> Free trade is an issue that makes social democrats [in the North] uncomfortable. The Third World has long been demanding "trade not aid." However, trade liberalization is most likely to hurt precisely the groups in society that are most vulnerable—women, the elderly, and immigrants who work in labour-intensive manufacturing (NSI, 1990).

An alternative position raises doubts about the benefits of free trade for the average person in both the North and the South. They argue that "trade not aid" is a false dichotomy for the South. The South needs to trade, but it also needs explicit developmental initiatives such as debt relief, better terms of trade, and compensatory financing, as well as significant environmental and technical assistance. Trade policy implemented through NAFTA-like initia-tives, in their view, can be inimical to the interests of less developed countries. NAFTA is seen as a mechanism that inhibits such developmental initiatives.

Third, national perspectives also differ because the likely impact of NAFTA will be different in each country. Differences in expected social costs and benefits of free trade lead to diverse cleavages of support and opposition. Canadian perspectives are shaped by the experience of the Canada-U.S. Free Trade

Agreement (CUFTA), implemented in 1989. Difficult economic conditions in Canada between 1989 and 1991 created widespread skepticism regarding the benefits of expanding CUFTA to include Mexico. However, it is clear that the discussion of NAFTA cannot be a revisitation of the 1988 Canadian free trade debate: there is a different set of issues and dynamics involved because the negotiations include a Third World country.

The Mexicans also have a different perspective. On the one hand, Mexicans temper their criticism of the trade-enhancing aspects of NAFTA due to the widespread conviction that the "old" model of import substitution was exhausted as a viable economic strategy for Mexico. By the late 1970s and early 1980s this strategy had resulted in inflation, balance of payments difficulties, a bias against exports and agriculture, and an inefficient industrial plant. On the other hand, Mexicans are weary of the effects of a decade of structural adjustment that has resulted in widespread impoverishment and a massive transfer of resources out of the country. Moreover, the reorientation toward a market-oriented and open economy directly affects the groups—peasants, workers, middle sectors, domestic enterprises, the public sector—that supported the traditional system, and hence threatens social and political stability. NAFTA's implementation may be accompanied by significant polarization in Mexican society.

A fourth debate concerns whether NAFTA should be used by foreigners to influence the domestic political process in Mexico. One view is that NAFTA's negotiation, ratification, and implementation should be used to pressure Mexico to make progress toward democracy and respect for human rights. Those who voiced this view were willing to use NAFTA to place democracy and human rights on the political agenda. However, many free trade opponents in Canada and in the United States preferred to influence Mexican domestic politics through direct collaboration with independent labor unions and popular organizations in that country. They did not want to legitimate the NAFTA process by participating in it.

Such divergences were a point of departure for the analyses commissioned for this book. Yet despite major differences in the background of the contributors to this volume, a large degree of consensus emerged as the book took shape.

NAFTA, ECONOMIC THEORY, AND NEOCONSERVATIVE IDEOLOGY

A recurring issue in this volume is the role of the social sciences (particularly neoclassical economic theory) in policy debates. Those who stress the role of ideas believe that neoconservative policies promoted by mainstream economists played a prominent role in the creation of NAFTA.[7] Others emphasize the role of concrete economic forces and powerful material interests in promoting economic integration.

The book reflects a consensus that highly abstract economic modeling divorced from an understanding of political, social, and ecological issues and institutional arrangements is of questionable value for empirical analysis and policy prescription. Stephen Clarkson (Chapter 4) examines the powerful policy role that neoclassical economics plays by giving neoconservatism theoretical coherence and winning acceptance for policies that represent a radical change from previous interventionist strategies of economic development. An alternative view would be that neoclassical economics has been adapted to serve powerful economic and social forces that stand at the root of neoconservative restructuring. Indeed, the extent to which neoconservatism has a solid foundation in neoclassical economics is problematic (see Bresser Pereira, Maravall, and Przeworski, forthcoming).

Mainstream economics views any preoccupation with the "winners and losers" of economic integration as revealing ignorance of the notion of gains from trade. NAFTA is seen as a positive-sum game. Trade negotiators repeatedly argued that there are no losers in trade liberalization. According to their view, NAFTA is a win-win situation and those who see free trade as flawed are ignorant of economic theory, irrational, or motivated by special interests.[8] Unfortunately, when opposition is dismissed as misguided or politically motivated, the substance of questions raised by critics is often left unanswered.

Some contributors to this volume felt that the paradigm of rational decision making upon which arguments in favor of NAFTA rested was itself vulnerable to criticism both in terms of its assumptions and its empirical basis. Judith Adler Hellman (Chapter 12) focuses on what Mexicans knew about free trade and how they would fare under NAFTA. She found that one group of Mexicans' expectations about NAFTA—either positive or negative—were often driven more by ideology than by rational analysis of available information. A second group tried to make rational predictions, but failed because they lacked adequate information or the analytical tools to process that information.

The idea of automatic gains from freer trade is part of a larger ideological package—what former U.S. president George Bush called the "new era of open doors, open minds, and open trade" (Bush, 1991). Bruce Wilkinson (Chapter 2) deals with the social impact of the spread of this ideology, the different roles that it plays in a hegemonic power such as the United States and a smaller economy such as Canada's, and the contrast between this ideology's rhetoric and reality. This set of beliefs has gained influence in policy and academic circles in the western hemisphere. One indication is the enthusiastic response to the Enterprise for the Americas Initiative from several Latin American governments, economists, a wide range of analysts and commentators, and multilateral organizations.

REDISCOVERING THE MEANING OF FREE TRADE

The belief that a free trade area like NAFTA will provide significant benefits to each one of the countries involved, and in particular to the smaller Canadian and Mexican economies, is based on well-known propositions on the gains from trade. In this view, enhanced access to the huge U.S. market will provide impetus for export-oriented industrialization for the smaller economies. Further, recent neoclassical analysis on imperfectly competitive markets and the gains derived from economies of scale rates the benefits from liberalized trade still higher.[9] These benefits are "objectively" estimated using highly abstract, computable general equilibrium models. Optimistic forecasts—based on such models—regarding the job, export, and production gains Canada would reap from the implementation of CUFTA played an important role in the Canadian public debate prior to ratification of the agreement.

Ricardo Grinspun (Chapter 7) argues that the economic arguments for free trade are seriously flawed. Most economic models do not incorporate intrafirm trade—trade between affiliates of TNCs—which accounts for much of the commerce among Canada, the United States, and Mexico. TNCs enjoy a growing ability to move capital and restructure production on a global basis in order to lower unit costs of production and maximize returns. The effects of "free trade" on movements of capital and investment diversion are more important—and less understood—than the effects on commodity trade. A key outcome of CUFTA and NAFTA—a significant shift of economic and political power toward U.S.- and Canadian-based TNCs—must be recognized and studied for its diverse and far-reaching implications.

Government intervention crucially affects the structure of markets and the pattern of international trade. As Scott Sinclair shows in Chapter 14, Mexican and Canadian exports are often affected by the application of U.S. trade-remedy laws. Contrary to expectations, CUFTA has not protected Canada from the political use of U.S. trade laws. Ongoing disputes over regional content in automobiles under CUFTA suggest that even the threat of U.S. harassment can inhibit foreign investment. Similarly, NAFTA leaves potent U.S. trade-remedy laws intact, while significantly restricting Canadian and Mexican policy options. NAFTA, like similar agreements, is another instrument to manage and shape trade and investment flows across North America. NAFTA shifts the decision making in these areas to big corporate capital, which is based mostly in the United States.

The Canadian experience suggests that neoclassical trade theory is poorly suited to predict the outcome of economic integration. Claims regarding the benefits of free trade that are derived from these theories must be treated with caution, since they understate key aspects of the integration process. These models discount the role of governments in economic activity as well as the role of intrafirm trade. They also tend to disregard other elements of economic integration such as: (a) changes in income distribution; (b) the effects of investment flows and increased capital mobility; (c) macroeconomic imbalances; (d) differences between countries and regions in the level of economic development and productivity; (e) differences between countries in the nature of institutional, social, and political structures; (f) the role of domestic markets, "human capital," and technological change in economic growth; (g) urban-rural and other regional links; and (h) the environmental impact.

Two major objectives of this book are to demystify the view of free trade presented by neoclassical economists and to reveal the implications of free trade from a political economy perspective. Without denying that free trade will affect trade and investment flows, the analysis in this book takes a different focus. Many authors in this volume share the view that free trade is closely related to economic and societal restructuring. In some cases, free trade can directly encourage this transformation; in others, it can contribute to consolidate past restructuring.

In particular, free trade is likely to: (a) promote domestic restructuring, so that the private sector—a euphemism for large corporations and transnational capital—takes the leading role in economic activity; (b) redefine the relationship between the state and civil society, weakening government intervention at all levels; (c) impose a neoconservative economic program of monetarist macroeconomic policies, privatization, and deregulation, in place of such Keynesian goals as full employment; (d) harmonize downward labor, occupational, social, and environmental standards (social dumping); (e) promote regressive, post-Fordist restructuring and weaken trade unionism; and, lastly, (f) weaken the provision of public services in the three countries. In essence, then, free trade can be seen, as Bruce Campbell makes clear in Chapter 6 of this volume, as a component in a neoconservative structural adjustment program for North America.

Campbell argues that CUFTA is an effective multipurpose device for advancing this neoconservative agenda in Canada. It has been used by the United States in tandem with the General Agreement on Trade and Tariffs (GATT) as a whipsaw to weaken interventionist Canadian laws and regulations. CUFTA has thus served the Conservative government as a key lever to facilitate the implementation of its policy program. Canada's experience should be taken seriously by other countries considering free trade arrangements with the United States.

Free trade can also play a role in consolidating the neoconservative restructuring model imposed on highly indebted countries such as Mexico. Judith Teichman (Chapter 11) analyzes the dramatic restructuring that Mexico underwent prior to NAFTA. Central to the new economic strategy has been a concerted effort to reduce the state's role through privatization of public enterprises. Domestic conglomerates and transnational corporations have been the major beneficiaries of both privatization and export incentives. This new economic model is reflected at the political level in a new understanding between big business and the state.

NAFTA AND ECONOMIC DEVELOPMENT

NAFTA is a fascinating topic partly because it inherently combines the issues of trade and development. The importance of the development question for Mexico and the rest of Latin America is obvious. However, this is a serious question for Canada and the United States also. Canada's industrial heartland, as well as certain regions of the United States, have undergone a process of deindustrialization in the post-free trade era due to the relocation of the industrial base to lower-wage areas.

The indirect pressures that CUFTA has created to shape public policies has become a major issue in Canada. Opponents of free trade argue that CUFTA and NAFTA constitute much more than trade agreements. Mel Watkins (Chapter 8) suggests that free trade constitutes an industrial strategy that forces an outward-oriented, natural resource-based, and TNC-driven model of development. Free trade affects a whole spectrum of economic and social policies. Important examples are regional development programs, which are vulnerable to challenges from the United States for being so-called unfair trade practices. Watkins considers abrogation of CUFTA and calls for a different model of development for Canada based on a social democratic cast.

On the question of Mexican economic development, proponents usually assume that there will be massive economic gains for Mexico from NAFTA.

They take the optimistic position that NAFTA will attract capital to Mexico, reverse capital flight, and provide jobs. This view leaves crucial questions unanswered:

(a) How much capital will be attracted to Mexico? How much will be directed to productive investment, and how much will go to speculation, financial intermediation, and to the purchase of existing assets? Are capital inflows going to reverse the debt-related outflow of resources that is crippling Mexico?

(b) What kind of jobs are going to be created in Mexico? Will these be more *maquiladora*-type jobs—without backward linkages to the rest of the economy, based on low wages, and producing social and environmental disruption? To what extent will this job creation compensate for the loss of the traditional industrial base that was the inevitable result of trade liberalization without adequate safeguards?

(c) What will happen to real wages and income inequality in a context of tremendous pressure to maintain "international competitiveness" (which in the case of Mexico is achieved mainly by compressing wages, coercing independent trade unions and avoiding environmental regulations)? How will the democratic process and labor rights be affected?

(d) What will happen to food self-sufficiency and to the quality of life in rural Mexico as a result of expanded agroexport operations?

(e) What effects will there be on "human capital": education, health, living conditions, training programs, occupational rights, occupational safety, and unemployment insurance?

(f) How will the Mexican economic and political system be affected by the increased capital mobility and heightened power of the economic elite and TNCs?

(g) What will be the results of NAFTA's restricting the ability of the Mexican government to apply independent domestic policies (regional and sectoral development policies; income redistribution policies; social programs; energy policy; and so on)?

There are no easy—and few pleasant—answers to most of these questions. Although there is no doubt that NAFTA will promote rapid economic growth in certain regions of North America (in particular, on both sides of the Mexican-U.S. border), the wider question of the nature of economic and social development implied by this growth is still open. Kathryn Kopinak (Chapter 9) raises the concern that the current phase of Mexican development is characterized by an extremely unequal, enclave-type growth in the *maquiladora* sector, with no prospects for a broader modernization of the economy and society. In fact, the "boom" of the Mexican economy in the early 1990s has strong components of financial and speculative growth, which may not be stable in the long term. Edur Velasco Arregui (Chapter 10) argues that the current industrialization strategy—which is intended to insert Mexico into the worldwide production strategies of TNCs—will be short-lived and subject to boom and bust cycles.

As Jeff Faux and Thea Lee (Chapter 15) point out, the danger for the United States is that NAFTA commits the country to a faulty response to the competitive threat arising from Japan and from a unified European common market. In particular, they see NAFTA as harmful to the long-term competitiveness of the United States, arguing that it will encourage lower wages and make it more difficult for governments at all levels to invest in infrastructure, training, and education. Robert Kreklewich (Chapter 17) foresees similar worrisome tendencies. He argues that Canadian and U.S. TNCs are short-sightedly taking advantage of CUFTA and NAFTA to accelerate a poorly conceived restructuring from Fordism to flexible manufacturing systems. This restructuring is characterized by regressive working conditions and increased social tension.

Environmental concerns have emerged in the course of the NAFTA negotiations. These negotiations were marked by intense opposition by environmental groups. There are good reasons for this, given the environmental disaster created by the *maquiladora* industry. Steven Shrybman (Chapter 18) insists on the necessity of designing trade and economic policies that are environmentally sound and at the same time provide a fast and energetic response to the development needs of Mexico and other underdeveloped countries. Unfortunately, the U.S. government pursued NAFTA (as well as the completion of the Uruguay Round) with the aim of limiting the use of trade policy to maintain environmental standards.

NAFTA, DEMOCRACY, AND THE POLITICAL PROCESS

There is an extensive debate in Latin America on the interplay between economic liberalization and political regime change. Most academic observers recognize that the process of economic reform affects the prospects for stability and democracy in Mexico. However, there is disagreement on whether economic liberalization contributes to the opening or the closing of possibilities for democratic reform. Optimists see the Mexican system moving toward greater openness and more competitive elections. Others are less sanguine about the governing party's commitment to democracy, pointing to the 1990 electoral code and electoral fraud in state elections in 1991 and 1992 as the basis for their pessimism. Adolfo Aguilar Zinser (Chapter 13) suggests that Mexico has insulated its authoritarian regime from international criticism by pursuing free trade with the United States.

A related consideration is the impact of trade treaties on state autonomy and sovereignty, a topic dealt with by Daniel Drache (Chapter 5). Advocates of freer trade are fond of observing that a NAFTA would "lock in" the current economic reforms in Mexico, so that regardless of who wins future elections, the market-oriented policy framework will remain intact. By increasing the cost of policy shifts, NAFTA aims to undermine more interventionist policy approaches in the future. This explicitly political strategy is part of the reason the debate on NAFTA in all three countries is widely recognized to be a debate about "more than trade" (as Drache puts it). The debate is about the basic framework for policy making in each country into the next century. The view that voters cannot be trusted to make such decisions implies either that the electorate is not rational enough to support a successful economic strategy or that the strategy is expected to impose such heavy costs as to be politically unviable and should be removed from the arena of public debate.

In Canada, NAFTA clearly has provoked sharp political divisions. The Canadian public has grown skeptical of the free trade promises made during the 1988 national election. This same public has been wary of negotiating a trade deal with a low-wage country in the middle of a deep economic recession—a recession that many see linked to free trade itself. The government was also distracted by a profoundly divisive constitutional crisis created by the failure of the Meech Lake Accord as well as by the failed October 1992 referendum on constitutional proposals.

The debate in the U.S. Congress for "fast-track" approval for NAFTA demonstrated the divisiveness of trade issues. Sharp divisions appeared between those corporate and political interests pushing for continental integration on the one side, and an unprecedented coalition of labor, environmental, and other grassroots organizations opposed to it on the other. This debate is part of a broader one about the increasing polarization of the U.S. political and social system in an era of global economic restructuring.

Although the negotiations took place behind closed doors, the governments of both the United States and Canada still have to pay attention to their political constituencies at home. Fast track legislation forces Congress to vote yes or no to the final legislation—without amendments. Yet, U.S. trade representatives are always extremely attentive to the views of Congress. The Canadian parliamentary system is less permeable to pressure groups. Parliament had little influence during the negotiation process, and as long as the prime minister controls the House of Commons, via traditional party discipline measures, legislation can be passed. Mexico, because it had a malleable Congress, did not have the same domestic political constraints preventing the leadership from agreeing to a deal that imposes harsh domestic costs. This was a weakness, not a strength, of the Mexican negotiators, since it made it more difficult for them to use domestic constraints to extract concessions from the United States and Canada.

Political restrictions on public debate of NAFTA is a recurrent theme of the book. The case is clearest in Mexico, as documented by Adolfo Aguilar Zinser. However, in a debate with such high stakes, it is not surprising that the corporate sector and governments in each country have used their enormous financial resources and influence to shape the public, policy, and academic debates on NAFTA.

ASYMMETRIES OF POWER

A key aspect of the debate on NAFTA is the regional dominance of the United States—not only economically, but also culturally, militarily, and politically. Asymmetries of power, wealth, technology, and cultural influence among Mexico, the United States, and Canada guarantee that the short- and long-term benefits and adjustment costs will be distributed unequally within and between the member countries. Moreover, these asymmetries transform NAFTA from a narrow trade and investment treaty into one that affects, directly and indirectly, the whole pattern of life in the smaller societies.

As Gerald Helleiner argues (Chapter 3), if a small country is bargaining for an agreement in which it will gain more market access than its more powerful partner will, that stronger partner will inevitably extract some compensating concession. Mexico's national product represents about 3 percent of the total North American economy; it will gain far more market access through trade liberalization than Canada or the United States will. However, enhanced U.S. access to the Mexican energy sector is one side payment that Mexico had to make to get a deal. Petroleum has enormous political and symbolic value in Mexico, for it is a major power resource that had been used to strengthen Mexico's bargaining position in relation to the United States in the past. John Dillon argues (Chapter 20) that U.S. access to petroleum was a key objective of the United States in the negotiations, as was access to Canadian energy resources in the CUFTA negotiations. The issue has potent implications for Mexico's future political sovereignty and political autonomy from the United States.

Finally, asymmetries of power affect how the legal text of an agreement is translated into actual policy at the implementation stage. According to several authors in this volume, a major lesson of CUFTA's implementation is that bilateral trade agreements do not insulate smaller countries from the political use of U.S. trade-remedy law. Harassment of Canadian exporters continued under CUFTA, discouraging third-country investors from investing in Canada as an export platform to the United States. Canada can threaten to retaliate, but will think twice before escalating a trade war with the country that absorbs most Canadian exports.

NAFTA, LATIN AMERICA, AND THE NEW WORLD ORDER

NAFTA is a strategic response by the United States to global trends such as the increasing economic threat arising from an expanded and unified Europe and a more assertive Japan. For many years, the strength of the North American economy permitted the United States to exercise a preponderant role in international institutions. The relative decline of U.S. hegemony during the last two decades—and, with it, the weakening of U.S. policymakers' commitment to multilateralism—has led to a new interest and vitality in regional and bilateral trade arrangements in the western hemisphere.

A diminished hegemonic role for the United States in the global economic order has brought about a more active U.S. hemispheric role. NAFTA and President Bush's Enterprise for the Americas Initiative (EAI) promised to reshape U.S.-Latin American relations and forced both Canada and Mexico to rethink their positions as hemispheric actors. For Mexico, this involved restricting that country's aspirations to be a major player in Central America and the rest of Latin America.

Free trade from Alaska to Tierra del Fuego as proposed in EAI, as well as deep neoconservative reforms throughout the hemisphere, were two crucial components in the Bush administration's vision of a "New World Order." This vision has been encouraged by the multilateral agencies (World Bank, International Monetary Fund, Inter-American Development Bank), which followed Washington's policies and conditioned credit flows to Latin American countries on their implementation the "right" policies. A number of Latin American countries have signed framework agreements (with the

United States in the case of Chile, or on a regional basis in the case of the MERCOSUR[10]) and have considered comprehensive free trade agreements with the United States, perhaps through use of the accession clause in NAFTA. NAFTA provides a substantive example of what the "New World Order" means. Although several countries have already faced the pain of neoconservative reforms, Mexico was the first Latin American country to undergo the double treatment of neoconservative policies and a free trade agreement with the United States. How Mexico responds to the process of economic and political integration promoted by NAFTA is of importance to those countries contemplating a similar course.

The Canadian example is also telling for these countries, since Canada starts from a more advanced stage of economic development and has undergone severe and painful restructuring as a result of free trade, as several authors argue in this book. It is not surprising that there is an acute interest among Latin Americans to learn more about the Canadian experience.

GLOBALIZATION, REGIONALISM, AND TRANSNATIONAL CAPITAL

The current era is one of seemingly opposed forces: globalization and regionalism. Increasing capital mobility, accelerated technological change, the remapping of political and economic regions, and revolutions in transportation and telecommunications have contributed to the creation of what some are calling a single world economy. These global competitive pressures affect us in our daily lives. They have turned the national economy into a much less secure economic environment for business and labor. The fact that workers in Hermosillo, Detroit, or Oshawa are productive by national standards does not mean they can assume that their jobs are secure.

A parallel, and apparently contrasting, trend is the movement in the global economy toward regionalism and away from multilateralism. Are we witnessing the formation of three regional mercantilist blocks in the international economy: the Triad of a unified Europe, a North American block, and a yen block? The answer is not yet clear. However, it is evident that multilateral institutions are being strained beyond their ability to provide the rules by which international economic relations are governed. The crisis of multilateralism—exemplified by the difficulties experienced in completing the Uruguay Round and by growing tensions between the poles of the Triad—is a manifestation of the lack of undisputed leadership in the international economy.

Can these seemingly opposed trends of globalization and regionalism be explained within a unified conceptual framework? We think they can. An important element of explanation has to do with the growing role of TNCs in the global economy. It is estimated that intrafirm transactions among TNC affiliates already constitute about 25 percent of global trade (*IMF Survey,* 1992). These TNCs tend to be regionally based, but compete globally, and their influence in world trade and investment patterns is growing. Tensions in the Triad represent, to a large extent, competitive tensions between TNCs based in different poles of the Triad.

Lorraine Eden and Maureen Appel Molot (Chapter 19) analyze the pressures for TNC-driven continentalization of the North American auto industry. They examine the pattern of auto trade and investment within North America and explore the effects of lean production on locational patterns of U.S. auto TNCs. They conclude that continentalization of this industry is inevitable whether or not NAFTA is implemented and that this may pose serious problems for the Canadian segment of the industry.

TNCs played a key role in the creation of NAFTA. Canadian critics have argued, with much reason, that NAFTA is a continental economic constitution.[11] This constitution solidifies a bill of economic rights for transnational business. TNCs gain continental citizenship, permitting them to restructure and rationalize their productive processes at a transnational level, lowering their costs and gaining competitive positions vis-à-vis Japanese and European capital.

Capitalist competition, then, transcends the nation-state and requires a continental, or regional, base. Continental citizenship is expressed in numerous measures that are part of CUFTA and NAFTA, including the "national treatment" clauses for foreign capital; the dismantling of control mechanisms on foreign investment; the legitimization of increased capital mobility; intellectual property laws that protect principally large TNCs; the drive toward deregulation and privatization; the diminished role for public initiative; and the continental restructuring of financial services. Yet, NAFTA, unlike the European Community, has not created supranational political and social institutions to manage economic integration on behalf of a larger political community.

CONCLUSION: NAFTA AND ECONOMIC INTEGRATION

The push toward economic integration on both a regional and a global basis corresponds with deep structural transformations in the nature of world capitalist competition. Should this trend toward economic integration be opposed by political parties and groups concerned with social agendas in the North and in the South? We do not argue it is necessary, or realistic, to oppose economic integration per se. A central point of convergence in this volume is the argument that *how* economic integration is institutionalized is enormously important. Cuauhtémoc Cárdenas, leader of the Mexican Party of the Democratic Revolution (PRD), has called for an alternative Trade and Development Pact in North America (1991). In sharp contrast to NAFTA, the pact would utilize managed trade as a tool of development, and would include labor mobility, compensatory financing for less developed regions, and a social charter that would promote harmonization of social, labor, and environmental standards to the *highest* common denominator. Although such a pact does not appear to be likely in the near future, it is useful as a critical standard by which to evaluate NAFTA.

It is useful to design general criteria to evaluate economic integration from a social democratic perspective. The first column in Table 1.1 presents a suggested, partial list of questions to ask. Whether the process of integration will fulfill these criteria depends on the particular actors and the institutional setting put in place to promote integration. The second column in Table 1.1 asks how well the August 1992 NAFTA agreement measures up to these criteria. A glance at the table shows that NAFTA gets a very low mark in this evaluation. The NAFTA performs poorly because the objectives of the negotiating governments were dictated by the geopolitical interests of each administration as well as by a deep commitment to a neoconservative agenda. This agenda, clearly, is largely inconsistent with an alternative social democratic one.

A comparison with the institutional setup of the European Community is enlightening, since it emphasizes again that a key question to ask about economic integration is not whether it should or should not be implemented, but rather how it is implemented. In sharp contrast to NAFTA, the European Community has developed a complex institutional framework to deal with issues such as decentralization (subsidiarity); labor mobility; compensatory arrangements; social, labor, and environmental standards; and supranational institutions. Even so, many Europeans are worried that these institutions are not adequately fulfilling their objectives.

Our interest in the wider social, economic, political, and environmental implications of continental integration leaves us with few illusions about the dimensions of the issues we are tackling in this volume.[12] At the very least, we hope that we have addressed key problems and uncertainties and have provided a better background for further inquiry. Should this book help crystalize a more sober, thoughtful, critical, and socially responsible analysis of the underlying processes of NAFTA, then it will have served its purpose well.

NOTES

This chapter draws from all the others in this volume. It also summarizes—without attribution—views expressed in a December 1991 workshop held in Toronto and organized by York University's Centre for Research on Latin America and the Caribbean (CERLAC), where most of the chapters were presented in draft form. We are indebted to the participants, who are too numerous to mention by name. We thank Teresa Healy, Robert Kreklewich, Louis Lefeber, Maureen Appel Molot, Liisa North, Judith Teichman, Mel Watkins, and Bruce Wilkinson for useful comments on earlier drafts of this chapter. The views presented herein, as well as any errors, are solely our responsibility.

1. See, among others: Weintraub, 1990a, pp. 15-23; Schott, 1989, pp. 45-9; Bueno, 1988, pp. 115-8; Diebold, 1988, pp. 160-3.
2. In Canada, see the work sponsored by the Fraser Institute (Globerman 1991; Waverman 1991) and the C. D. Howe Institute (Lipsey, 1990; Wonnacott, 1991). See also Hart (1990). In the United States, see Hufbauer & Schott (1992) of the Institute for International Economics. See also Weintraub (1990a, 1990b). In Mexico, see Vega Cánovas (1991) of the Colegio de México.
3. Significant research efforts have been directed toward showing the benefits of NAFTA using computable general equilibrium (CGE) models. For a compilation of related CGE work, see USITC (1992).
4. Books promoting alternative perspectives on NAFTA became available only in 1992. The book by Randall (1992) incorporates a broad spectrum of trilateral issues. Cavanagh et al. (1992) and Sinclair (1992) present compendiums of critical excerpts on various aspects of free trade in North America. (The term "North America" in this book refers to Mexico, the United States and Canada). The study by the Office of Technology Assessment (1992) was completed after the negotiations ended. Saborio (1992) is a useful introduction to issues of hemispheric integration.
5. Given that each chapter relates to the specialized literature and supports its arguments accordingly, in this introduction we have decided to relate only to general literature on NAFTA. We have made no effort to support specific claims treated in more detail elsewhere in the volume.
6. Regarding Mexican labor, we focus here on independent labor organizations in that country that have taken a different and more critical stance toward NAFTA than has the official CTM (Confederation of Mexican Workers), which is closely linked to the government and the ruling party.

7. Most authors in this volume use the term "neoconservative" ideology rather than "neoliberal" or "free-market ideology." This ideology calls for reliance on market forces and private initiative; a subsidiary microeconomic role for the government; monetarist macroeconomic policies (with an emphasis on anti-inflationary measures and shrinking government expenditures); privatization of state enterprises; deregulation of market activity; a strong antiunion drive; less state involvement in the provision of health, education, and welfare; trade and investment liberalization; a prominent position in society for large corporations; and lower tax rates. One should not confuse neoconservatism with political conservatism; neoconservatism is a movement for radical change, and not a call for maintenance of the status quo. For a different terminology, see Gilpin (1987); Gill and Law (1988); Murphy and Tooze (1991).

8. However, one must emphasize that the notion of gains from trade is based on the compensation principle, by which those who gain from liberalized trade will compensate those who lose. If there is no compensation mechanism, as is the case in NAFTA, one cannot argue that post-NAFTA societal welfare is superior to the previous one. It is rational behavior for affected groups, who know that there is no redistributive mechanism, to oppose free trade. For an articulate criticism of neoclassical economics and its irrelevance for current development problems, see Lefeber (forthcoming).

9. There is a broad literature on these issues. A simple introduction is provided in Krugman and Obstfeld (1991, chapter 6).

10. MERCOSUR is the acronym for the Southern Cone Common Market, encompassing Argentina, Brazil, Paraguay, and Uruguay.

11. Many of the criticisms of CUFTA presented in this chapter are elaborated in different chapters of Duncan Cameron (1988). See also Barlow and Campbell (1991).

12. Several key issues in the political economy of NAFTA were not adequately treated in this volume. Particular issues to mention are: the impact of economic integration on gender and race relations; the expansion of intellectual property rights; migration and border issues; and broader studies on environment and development. Clearly, this list is not exhaustive.

REFERENCES

Barlow, M., and Campbell, B. (1991). *Take Back the Nation.* Toronto: Key Porter.

Bresser Pereira, L.C., Maravall, J. M., and Przeworski, A. (forthcoming). *Economic Reforms in New Democracies: A Social Democratic Approach.* Cambridge: Cambridge University Press.

Bueno, G. (1988). "A Mexican View," in W. Diebold, Jr., (ed.), *Bilateralism, Multilateralism and Canada in U.S. Trade Policy.* Cambridge, Mass.: Ballinger Publishing Company.

Bush, G. (19 March 1991). Remarks at a White House Briefing for the National Leadership of the Hispanic Alliance for Free Trade.

Cameron, D. (ed.). (1988). *The Free Trade Deal.* Toronto: Lorimer.

Cárdenas, C. (8 February 1991). *The Continental Development and Trade Initiative: A Statement.* New York.

Cavanagh, J., Gershman, J., Baker, K. and Helmke, G. (eds.). (1992). *Trading Freedom: How Free Trade Affects Our Lives, Work and Environment.* San Francisco: Institute for Food and Development Policy.

Cox, R. W. (1986). "Social Forces, States, and World Orders." In R. Keohane (ed.), *Neorealism and its Critics.* New York: Columbia University Press.

———. (1987). *Production, Power, and World Order: Social Forces in the Making of History.* New York: Columbia University Press.

Diebold, Jr. W. (ed.). (1988). *Bilateralism, Multilateralism and Canada in U.S. Trade Policy.* Cambridge, Mass.: Ballinger Publishing Company.

Gill, S. and Law, D. (1988). *The Global Political Economy: Perspectives, Problems, and Policies.* New York: Johns Hopkins University Press.

Gilpin, R. (1987). *The Political Economy of International Relations.* Princeton: Princeton University Press.

Globerman, S. (ed.). (1991). *Continental Accord: North American Economic Integration.* Vancouver: Fraser Institute.

Hart, M. (1990). *A North American Free Trade Agreement: The Strategic Implications for Canada.* Ottawa and Halifax: The Centre for Trade Policy and Law and the Institute for Research on Public Policy.

Hufbauer, G. C., and Schott, J. J. (1992). *North American Free Trade: Issues and Recommendations.* Washington: Institute for International Economics.

IMF Survey. (20 July 1992). "Transnational Corporations' Expanding Role in Global Economy Described in UN Report." 21 (15), pp. 227-230.

Krugman, P. R., and Obstfeld, M. (1991). *International Economics: Theory and Policy* (2nd ed.). New York: HarperCollins.

Lefeber, L. (forthcoming). "What Remains of Development Economics?" *Indian Economic Review.* Special issue in memory of Prof. Sukhamoy Chakravarty.

Lipsey, R. G. (1990). "Canada at the U.S.-Mexico Free Trade Dance: Wallflower or Partner?" *Commentary* (whole issue, August). Toronto: C. D. Howe Institute.

Murphy, C. N. and Tooze, R. (eds.). (1991). *The New International Political Economy.* Boulder: Westview.

North-South Institute (NSI), Ottawa (October 1990). "Consultative Session on NAFTA," oral presentation.

Office of Technology Assessment, U.S. Congress. (1992). *US-Mexico Trade: Pulling Together or Pulling Apart?* ITE-545. Washington: U.S. Government Printing Office.

Randall, S. J., with H. Konrad and S. Silverman (eds.). (1992). *North America without Borders? Integrating Canada, the United States and Mexico.* Calgary: University of Calgary.

Saborio, S. (ed.). (1992). *The Premise and the Promise: Free Trade in the Americas.* New Brunswick, New Jersey: Transaction Publishers.

Schott, J. J. (1989). *More Free Trade Areas?* Washington D.C.: Institute for International Economics.

Sinclair, J. (1992). *Crossing the Line: Canada and Free Trade With Mexico.* Vancouver: New Star.

United States International Trade Commission (USITC). (1992). *Economy-Wide Modelling of the Economic Implications of a FTA with Mexico and a NAFTA with Canada and Mexico: Report on Investigation No. 332-317 under Section 332 of the Tariff Act of 1930* (USITC No. 2516 and 2508). Washington, D.C.

Vega Cánovas, G. (ed.). (1991). *México Ante el Libre Comercio con América del Norte.* Mexico City: El Colegio de México.

Waverman, L. (ed.). (1991). *Crucial Issues in North American Free Trade.* Vancouver: Fraser Institute.

Weintraub, S. (1990a). *A Marriage of Convenience: Relations Between Mexico and the United States.* New York: Twentieth Century Fund.

———. (1990b). "The North American Free Trade Debate." *Washington Quarterly* (Autumn), 119-130.

Wonnacott, R. (1991). *The Economics of Overlapping Free Trade Areas and the Mexican Challenge.* Toronto: C. D. Howe Institute, and Washington: National Planning Association.

Table 1.1

Evaluating NAFTA from a Social-Democratic Perspective

Criterion	How does the NAFTA measure up?
(a) Are significant redistributive mechanisms to be implemented to bridge the gap between countries at different levels of development?	At the national level, the major issue is the lower level of Mexican development and the negative transfer of resources through debt-servicing. NAFTA does *not* incorporate compensatory financing or debt relief. Moreover, there are serious doubts whether the current "trickle-down" model of economic growth, supported by NAFTA, can provide a decent standard of living for most Mexicans.
b) Are significant redistributive mechanisms to be implemented within each country to compensate displaced workers and communities?	NAFTA does not specify or require the implementation of programs such as worker retraining and relocation. Each country must decide separately on this important issue. In Mexico, the country with the largest social deficit, the recent trend has been to trim social expenditure. In Canada, the Mulroney administration is not planning new programs. The reasons raised in (e) below also constrain Mexico's and Canada's ability to implement new programs. The United States, under the Clinton administration, is likely to implement new initiatives in areas such as labor retraining but is constrained by the budget deficit.
(c) Is economic integration tied to a deepening of participatory democratic institutions?	The contrary seems to be the rule. NAFTA has all the characteristics of an elite-driven process, both at the economic and political levels. The key promoters are TNCs, for which NAFTA represents "a continental bill of economic rights." NAFTA implies a shift in the balance of power away from the state and toward TNCs. Trade unions are also weakened by unfettered capital mobility. NAFTA helps perpetuate an undemocratic political regime in Mexico, which continues to practice repressive policies toward independent labor unions and to manipulate electoral outcomes.
(d) Are substantial mechanisms implemented to promote *upward* harmonization of social, labor, and environmental standards?	The likely effect is some *downward* harmonization, as a result of social dumping. NAFTA does not set standards for social programs, occupational safety, or labor rights. NAFTA promotes deregulation, privatization and increased capital mobility, creating pressures that may erode existing social programs and make the implementation of new ones more

Criterion	How does the NAFTA measure up?
	difficult. Trade unions may see their bargaining power weakened as a result of labor segmentation, production restructuring, and increased capital mobility. The treatment of environmental issues is declaratory and lacks significant implementation powers.
(e) Is the ability of the regional and national governments to engage in developmental policies recognized and protected?	NAFTA is likely to hinder the ability of governments in Canada and in Mexico to promote economic development. NAFTA creates a conditionality framework for public policy that is market-oriented and emphasizes conservative macroeconomic policies. Fiscal, monetary, industrial, and trade policies are all affected by this policy framework. The lack of agreement on a common definition of allowable trade subsidies constrains the use of policies targeted to specific regions or sectors, since these can be challenged as "unfair" measures. For example, Canadian regional development programs are often challenged by the United States. Of particular concern in Mexico are constraints on the ability to implement programs for rural development.
(f) Is the unavoidable loss of political and economic autonomy and sovereignty at the state and regional levels compensated by the creation of truly representative supranational institutions?	No. As a consequence, there is a shift of power to the major national player: the United States. There is also a major shift in economic and political decision making to unelected, unrepresentative corporate and "technical" bureaucracies. (An example of technical bureaucracies are those that handle the dispute settlement mechanism.) Contrast this with the European Community, where the Commission and the Parliament represent efforts to create representative institutions.
(g) Is integration based on increased mobility for capital *and* labor?	Increased mobility is created only for capital, thus promoting a shift of power to corporations. The only labor mobility included in NAFTA is for business representatives.

Note: Our evaluation does not encompass the supplemental agreements on labor adjustment and the environment negotiated as this book went to press (March 1993).

Chapter 2

Trade Liberalization, the Market Ideology, and Morality: Have We a Sustainable System?

Bruce W. Wilkinson

Trade liberalization and market integration in North America, as manifested in the incipient North American Free Trade Agreement (NAFTA), as well as in the Canada-U.S. Free Trade Agreement (CUFTA), which has been in operation since the beginning of 1989, are really parts of a much larger phenomenon. They are pillars of an ideology in which acquiring income, wealth, position, and power is the appropriate focus of all human activity and the source of all well-being. NAFTA and CUFTA stress the importance of market forces and market objectives in such an ideology. The transnational corporation (TNC), foreign direct investment, and the general free flow of capital, supported by trade liberalization measures, are seen as the joint saviors of our Western economies. They are also the main manifestations of the above-mentioned ideology in the international economic sphere.

All too often we limit our discussions of free trade agreements such as the NAFTA to an examination of the costs and benefits of the trade provisions themselves, the strategies to be employed, the time horizon in which changes are to be made, and the economic effects of the provisions. Seldom do we step back and ask ourselves about the longer-run implications of what we are doing, or question the ideology that is driving the system.

Initially, this chapter will elaborate on the market ideology and outline its major manifestations and its apparent lack of any solid ethical base. Then it will briefly consider the role of the TNC in the evolution of this ideology vs. the roles played by the governments of the three largest units in the world economy—Japan, the European Community (EC), and the United States. The implications for smaller nations such as Canada will then be considered. Subsequently, questions about the sustainability of the world economic system will be addressed. The chapter concludes that we need to move beyond the analysis of global markets and begin asking some of the old questions about right and wrong, about ultimate values regarding the worth of individuals, and about the purpose of our lives. The chapter argues that we need to reaffirm certain moral-ethical principles if we are to have a world where humans can live in dignity with reasonable amenities. A NAFTA and an ideology dedicated to promoting the interests of the transnational corporation, without an adequate moral-ethical system, will not in themselves perform this task.

THE IDEOLOGY AND ITS MANIFESTATIONS

A main emphasis of this age is upon "the market" and "the bottom line." Popular buzzwords and phrases in business, government, and the interface between the two are "let the market work," "competitiveness," "globalism," "the global perspective," "being 'lean and mean,'" and "maximizing the bottom line." "The market" has been elevated to the status of a god that will, supposedly, administer the affairs of the world in an impartial and appropriate manner.

The TNC is seen as the chief vehicle of change, the means of moving capital and technology internationally, and the main source of new technology. Its activities, such as foreign direct investment, in whatever form that takes (new investment, takeovers, mergers, joint ventures, horizontal and vertical integration, and so on), are to be encouraged. The belief is that as TNCs prosper and profits are maximized, economic efficiency will be enhanced, product variety and quality will be increased, consumer choice will be enlarged, and the general well-being of society will thereby be maximized (Ohmae, 1990).

Another dimension of this ideology is the role of government. In this view, the best government is next to no government. The role of governments is to remove hindrances that obstruct the workings of the market. NAFTA, which entails a removal of trade barriers in North America, and the Uruguay Round of General Agreement on Tariffs and Trade (GATT) negotiations, are portrayed as key policy moves in this regard. So are the measures to privatize government-owned corporations and to deregulate business activities in North and South America, Europe, and many other places in the world.

Probing beneath the rhetoric, however, one finds that the reality is somewhat different. At the same time as the public is fed the virtues of minimizing government involvement, the corporate structure is energetically recruiting the support of government to protect its international interests. Witness, for example, the measures being taken to have international agreements protecting patents and copyrights for longer periods— measures that in turn greatly enhance the profits of the corporation at the expense of consumers. In places like Latin America, government pressures are brought to bear on the economy to produce structural adjustments in the interests of the TNCs. Government attitudes and actions toward education and the labor force are generally being geared more and more to meeting the needs of the corporation. I return to this issue in the subsequent sections, where I compare the application of these measures in the large economic units—the United States, the European Community, and Japan—to that in smaller nations such as Canada.

The final, and undoubtedly the most important, aspect of today's ideology needs to be emphasized. It is the significance assigned to wealth and power and prestige, with greed assuming the status of a virtue (unless it becomes a little too blatant, and then it is frowned upon). Ethical and moral considerations are all too often shunted aside or completely ignored in today's race for economic gain. The end apparently justifies any means deemed necessary.

The application of this attitude at the corporate level implies that what matters is not just whether a reasonable return on capital is made, but whether the corporation is growing as rapidly, or has as high a profit rate, as other corporations. Measures that enhance growth of profits are deemed acceptable regardless of their moral or ethical nature. TNCs are responsible for much of the world's environmental problems; some produce and promote breast milk substitutes that increase infant mortality rates in developing countries; others sell pesticides in developing countries even though they are banned in developed nations; still others sell armaments or components for weapons of war to almost any nation that will buy them; many fix prices so as to exploit the consumer and exploit Third World labor. More generally, corporations move their operations to where wages and employment benefits are minimal (often from industrial nations to developing countries), frequently with little sense of responsibility to the new workers they are hiring, or to those they have left behind. Other companies trim layers of management so that those remaining must work longer hours under more stress, to the detriment of family life and/or health—all in the name of "letting the market work" and achieving improved efficiency and greater profits, as if these were the only values in life.

Individuals, too, are caught up in an ideology that places "the market" and "the bottom line" at the center of human endeavor. The old idea of simply having "enough" for oneself and family is now deemed outmoded. What is deemed to matter most for individuals is "winning," "being a success," climbing the corporate or bureaucratic ladder, and having abundant material possessions. If people are shareholders in corporations, they want those corporations to act in whatever way is necessary to maximize the returns on their investments.

The value placed upon fellow human beings is all too often dependent upon such things as their position in the hierarchy; their income or wealth; their power; how fast they have climbed the ladder of success; or how profitably they can serve the interests of the corporation or bureaucracy of which they are a part. How they treat their wives or husbands; how well they rear their children; how they treat their fellow human beings; their integrity, faithfulness, humility, and compassion are all too frequently forgotten, ignored, or at least greatly downplayed.

Governments are generally no better. The well-being of society, which governments are supposed to enhance, and to which lip service is given, is often not their prime concern. Governments have, on many occasions, built up cumbersome bureaucracies, bribed taxpayers with their own funds, or borrowed heavily (which implies greater taxation at a later date) all to maximize their incomes, their pensions, the probability of their being re-elected. They may try to manipulate the media through selective release of information, even though it does not represent the truth, so as to enhance their own popularity. Promises are made and then the opposite is done—witness the federal government of Canada, which promised to make the tax system more equitable and to tax corporations more, but then did just the opposite. Or take the province of Alberta, whose government created pension schemes for politicians several times richer than anything allowed under either private pension plans or federal government rules, with minimal costs to the politicians themselves (Kenney, 1991).

On environmental issues, the government record leaves much to be desired as well. Consider, for example, that Ontario Hydro, a corporation of the province of Ontario, is the largest single atmospheric polluter in Canada. Brazil and Southeast Asia support the denuding of their landscapes, either to sell the timber or to make space for farmers, even though the ecological balance is destroyed or mountainous areas are made susceptible to mudslides in the process. In the United States, we have the spectacle of a debate on whether to use the CIA for industrial espionage to further the ends of U.S. corporations and ultimately the United States itself (Greenaway, 1991).

Obviously, this is somewhat of a caricature of what is happening, and there are shining exceptions in every walk of life—in business, at the individual level, and in government. But there is enough truth in the picture sketched above to give us cause for concern about the frequent absence of ethical principles in our economic activity and the consequent direction in which our economic societies are headed.

We shall return briefly to the moral-ethical issues in the closing section of this chapter. But first, let us examine how the market-oriented globalism is being worked out in the members of the Triad (Japan, the European Community, and the United States), and then consider the implications of this for smaller nations such as Canada and for the world more generally.

GLOBAL COMPETITIVENESS, THE MARKET, AND THE TRIAD

First, it is worth noting how the TNC has become the key actor on the world's economic stage. Foreign direct investment has been expanding far more rapidly than has international trade—34 percent annually versus 9 percent for the years 1983 to 1989 (GATT, 1990). In 1989 alone, the outward foreign direct investment from the G-5 nations (excluding Canada and Italy) was over $140 billion (Julius, 1991), and for all nations it was $215 billion (GATT, 1990). The expectations are that these huge flows will continue, so that by 1995 the stock of foreign direct investment will be double what it was in 1990 (Julius, 1990, p. 105), with Japan becoming the world's largest investor. This new investment has involved new plants, takeovers, mergers, joint ventures, technology-sharing agreements, and diversification into other industries—measures designed to lessen competition, circumvent possible new protectionist policies, protect existing markets, develop new markets, control and/or keep current with new technology, reduce the risks of potential exchange rate changes, and generally enhance the continuity, growth, and profitability of the firms involved (Julius, 1990, 1991; Stevens, 1990). To some extent, as with the Mexican *maquiladoras,* the TNCs have also gone where labor costs are lower and/or regulatory costs of doing business (such as with regard to pollution) are less.

Other international capital flows have been of even greater magnitude— about $400 billion in 1989 alone. These have involved multinational banks and, increasingly, other financial intermediaries, as well as TNCs generally. Their growth, like that of foreign direct investment, has been a function of the dominant laissez-faire ideology of the day. The deregulation of capital markets, the innovations in lending and borrowing instruments, and the internationalization of perspective and action by owners of capital have all been a part of this (Turner, 1991).

The rhetoric of letting global markets regulate economic decision making—which supports these massive capital flows—has emanated largely from the United States and, to a somewhat lesser extent, from the EC and Japan. Simultaneously, much support has been given to the negotiation of trade liberalization agreements such as CUFTA and NAFTA, ostensibly so as to free up the market. Deregulation and privatization have also been espoused as essential parts of the trade liberalization process.

What is all too often neglected, however, is that, as indicated in the previous section, it is not simply a matter of governments getting out of the way so as to let the market work. Rather, as evidenced by the active lobbying and other participation in governmental decision making by the corporate complex, the governments of the Triad are only interested in encouraging the unrestricted operation of the market, provided that the long-run interests of their corporations are being protected and extended. The view is that if these corporate interests are promoted, then national interests will also be advanced. Where the uninhibited workings of the market, especially via freer trade policies, might not result in their corporations' interests being achieved, then market forces are to be appropriately regulated, modified, directed—or whatever is necessary to ensure that national purposes are attained.

Japan

Most students would agree that this is so for Japan. The prominence of Ministry of Trade and Industry (MITI) in gathering intelligence and setting strategic objectives for industry is well known. Working with other government departments or agencies as appropriate, MITI has orchestrated a wide array of programs designed to encourage research and development, enhance technology transfer, and subsidize, protect, finance, or promote particular market structures to further the competitiveness and export potential of Japanese industry. A host of advisory committees exist as well, with membership including the very influential Keidanren (consisting of the biggest corporations in industry, finance, and trade). Even Japanese foreign aid policies involve the targeting of funding for infrastructure in a way that lets Japanese corporations in other parts of Asia produce and export particular products; this practice minimizes competition from the products of other Asian nations (Julius, 1991, p. 14). And for years Japanese interest rate policy has been one of keeping domestic rates low, much as Keynes advocated in his *General Theory* (1936), in order to stimulate domestic investment and employment, and provide Japanese firms a cost advantage over foreign competitors. Intense Japanese nationalism has made these policies not only possible, but, by and large, very effective, in serving long-run national interests.

The European Community

In the EC, with the possible exception of France, the role of governments in orchestrating the affairs of the business world to further national and community objectives has been, historically, not nearly as great as that in Japan. But the role has increased over the years and has become of vital importance. By far the best-known and farthest-reaching initiative has been that in which the European Commission, working closely with the large European corporations through their European Roundtable organization, brought about the move to Europe 1992. This was done as a means of encouraging and promoting the competitiveness of European industry as against the industry of Japan and the United States, both within Europe and in world markets.

The European approach also includes widespread protective and subsidy measures. Protection has been in the form of high import levies in agriculture; very active use of antidumping rules, so as to restrict imports and encourage domestic content of at least 40 percent; active utilization of rules of origin to encourage local production; and the like (Ostry, 1990, pp. 48-49).

Subsidies have been most notorious in agriculture. But a variety of other initiatives have been undertaken as well. Airbus Industrie, subsidized heavily by Britain, France, Germany, and Spain, and designed to provide Europe with a world presence in large-scale passenger aircraft, is one example. Others include ESPRIT (the European Strategic Programme for Research in Information Technology) and JESSI (the Joint European Semiconductor Silicon Project). These initiatives involve the major European electronics firms (but not foreign-owned firms), the European Commission, and national governments in the sharing of information, targeting of research projects, and joint industry-government funding. These projects were undertaken to ensure that the EC would be a major player in the world information technology and microelectronics industries (Ostry, 1990, pp. 71-72).

The United States

The United States undoubtedly gives more lip service to the virtues of the "invisible hand" than any other nation. Yet beneath this veneer lies one fundamental objective: the furtherance of long-run U.S. economic and political power. The techniques have not always been the same as those of the other nations of the Triad, in part because the United States has been operating as the strongest country in the world, with a particular destiny in the world. But the purposes have been similar.

Recent U.S. measures include the elaborate structure of business-government cooperation that has been developed, whereby GATT negotiators consult with private industry advisory committees to define the goals for U.S. negotiations and work with Congress regarding the approval of results. The structure was initially established under the 1974 U.S. Trade Act for the Tokyo GATT Round and was also used in developing U.S. positions for the Uruguay Round and CUFTA. It was reconfirmed in the 1988 Omnibus Trade Act. Other high-powered industry lobby groups such as the CEO-level Business Roundtable (after which the Business Council on National Issues in Canada was modeled), the Emergency Committee for American Trade, and the Intellectual Property Rights Committee (which, by stimulating the interest of European and Japanese firms, was instrumental in getting intellectual property rights placed on the Uruguay Round agenda) have also been working closely with the U.S. trade representative's office and members of Congress to further U.S. objectives. As Ostry (1990, p. 25) has commented, "to the outside observer it presents an impressive and unusual image of 'U.S. Inc.'"

The U.S. emphasis has also been on developing more aggressive trade policies to further U.S. interests. This has involved changes in exchange rates (to U.S. advantage); a strengthening of the meaning of Section 301 of the 1974 Trade Act so that countries, not just practices, could be defined as "unfair" or discriminatory—from a U.S. perspective; the more active use of Section 301 provisions involving threats of retaliation; the more frequent use of U.S. trade-remedy laws; the inclusion of additional topics on the multilateral trade agenda (such as the intellectual property rights already mentioned, and trade-related investment measures—TRIMS) so that U.S. corporations would have more monopoly power and greater ability to extract higher profits from their technology and be able to operate to their own advantage in foreign lands; and the use of bilateral trade agreements such as that between the United States and Israel, CUFTA, and now NAFTA, in which U.S. bargaining power could be employed to maximum advantage against much weaker partners to achieve long-term

U.S. goals. The U.S. government has also been involved in the organization and financial support of Sematech, an organization of high-tech businesses formed to enhance U.S. technological advantage. Membership in Sematech is limited to U.S.-owned and -controlled firms (just as JESSI is restricted to EC firms). State and local subsidies (such as reduced taxes) to attract industries continue to be employed as well.

It has not just been business and government constituencies promoting U.S. goals.[1] A number of leading academic economists have, in one way or another, been doing so as well (Dornbusch, Krugman and Park, 1989; Krugman, 1990; Morici, 1991). Regarding the NAFTA negotiations, for example, Morici argues in a recent book that there will have to be controls over firms from the EC and Japan locating in Mexico to serve the U.S. market and upon labor-intensive clothing and similar products coming into the United States from Mexico under NAFTA. Or, to adapt an old phrase, discretion is the better part of free trade. He also envisages NAFTA eventually becoming not just a free trade area but an economic community, which "would necessitate the creation of a central governing body" (1991, p. 99).[2] In any such arrangement, he recognizes that the United States would, essentially, be in charge. He thus sees NAFTA as a means to increase U.S. strength and influence to counter the aggressiveness of Japan (and, to a lesser extent, the EC) and enhance the U.S. bargaining position in further "bilateral and multilateral negotiations" (1991, p. 98). He also believes that an agreement with Mexico is but the second step (CUFTA being the first) in bringing all of the Americas (North and South) into one giant block, with the United States at the helm.

IMPLICATIONS FOR CANADA AND
FOR THE WORLD ECONOMY

For Canada

In this international environment, the Canadian situation is a particularly tenuous one. This is partly because Canada is adjacent to the most powerful nation of the world and is about one-tenth its size, measured by GNP. Canada depends upon the U.S. market for about 75 percent of its exports. The United States, moreover, owns over 40 percent of Canada's manufacturing output (with another 25 percent owned by other foreign-owned firms) and engulfs Canadian culture via its television programs, movies, videos, and magazines.

It is not surprising, therefore, that the TNC community in Canada, both foreign and domestically owned, sees its long-run interests intimately linked with the U.S. economy and with U.S. interests generally. Through Canadian business organizations, the most powerful of which is the Business Council on National Issues, consisting of the chief executive officers of the 150 largest corporations in the country (both domestic and foreign-owned), the corporate community works closely with the Canadian government to enhance its own long-run interests. These two parties, along with a number of provincial governments, as well as many in the economic academic profession, strongly promote the current ideology.

The rhetoric of business and the government has been widely accepted. It is premised on the idea that Canada must privatize, deregulate, enter trade liberalization agreements, institute international as well as government-industry advisory committees based on the U.S. model, and spend millions on trade missions (far more than any other nation, in both absolute and relative terms). As a result, the largely private decisions of the market will automatically, and somewhat miraculously, produce economic growth, employment, and prosperity for Canada.

What is ignored, or at least carefully omitted, by the strong supporters of this ideology is that, unlike in the Triad nations, a large percentage of the multinational firms operating in Canada are foreign owned. With loyalties to their home countries in the Triad and with pressures from their home governments (which are much more powerful than Canada's) to ensure that their homeland's interests are protected, their natural inclination is, at best, to locate little more than assembly plants in Canada—as the United States and Europe are concerned that Japan is doing with them. At worst, these firms can locate in the United States or Mexico to serve the Canadian market. For them, Canada is primarily a market for the products of modern technology, not an important place to develop new technology for the enhancement of exports from Canada.

What also goes discreetly unmentioned by the Canadian corporate establishment and its supporters is that firms operating in Canada, even when Canadian-owned and/or -controlled, have (unlike their counterparts in the United States, the EC, and Japan, where loyalties to the homeland are strong), had little, if any, commitment to building the Canadian economy. These firms' prime concern is not the betterment of Canada, but their own continuity, growth, and profits (Grant, 1965; Kierans and Stewart, 1988; Shortell, 1991).

Also, little mention is made of the fact that Canada, because of its much smaller size, does not have the economic clout in international negotiations that the members of the Triad have, and has very little ability to influence the outcome of these negotiations or the behavior of TNCs (its own or those of the Triad) to its own advantage. This is evident in the fact that under CUFTA, Canada signed away its right to institute new measures to ensure that firms in Canada, whether domestic or foreign-owned, would undertake policies to promote or stimulate production in, and exports from, Canada. (The U.S. interpretation is that even *existing* Canadian policies of this type are outlawed by CUFTA.) Canada's relative powerlessness is also evident in the fact that the Canadian government has accepted and supported the U.S. international position on intellectual property, which is designed primarily to promote the profits of U.S. TNCs. Canada's interests, as primarily a user of technology rather than a large producer of it, would be best served in most instances by having minimal restriction on acquiring international technology and property rights. Again, under CUFTA, Canada is not an equal partner with the United States—even though there are dispute-settlement mechanisms that on occasion give the semblance of equality. The U.S. choice to disregard, with impunity, Article 701(4) of CUFTA regarding the commitment to take into consideration the interests of Canada when it subsidizes agricultural exports is but one example.

More fundamentally, Canadians, including those in the corporate, governmental, and economic establishment, have generally and naively bought the idea of Adam Smith's "invisible hand" maximizing societal welfare as businesses pursue their own interests, and have not even checked out the context in which Smith used this phrase. As I have noted elsewhere (Wilkinson, 1991), the phrase was employed only *once* in the 752 pages of Smith's *Wealth of Nations* (1776). Even then, the phrase was used with regard to the homeland benefiting from more investment and employment as its firms choose to invest at home, where they know the laws, customs, and markets, rather than in foreign lands, where their knowledge of markets is much less and uncertainties are greater. Quite a different situation from how this phrase is used today to justify foreign direct investment!

Of much greater significance is the fact that the world that Smith—as well as the neoclassicists of a hundred years later—envisioned was one of perfect or atomistic competition where firms, or individuals, either as sellers or buyers, were too small to affect the price in the market. It was not a world of oligopolistic companies, on the one hand, which are able to influence markets to their own advantage, or of large nations, on the other hand, acting in cooperation with their corporations to pursue their own economic and political objectives.

In summary, for a variety of reasons, Canada's uncritically accepting the market ideology, without carefully examining the reality of how the large industrial blocs are applying this concept, means that the nation may well be placing itself on a course that jeopardizes its long-run prosperity and political independence.

For the World Economy

Another set of issues arises as well. They are relevant to smaller nations such as Canada. But they also have a wider applicability for the world as a whole.

The concerns raised are of a variety of types. One type is whether, from either a theoretical or an empirical perspective, the growth of corporations via takeovers and mergers actually improves the efficiency of the economies involved, or whether these actions merely increase the concentration of economic power. Some studies certainly suggest that corporate performance does not, on average, improve (Scherer, 1988; Tarasofsky and Corvari, 1991). A second concern is whether the types of plants being built by TNCs in foreign lands are anything more than assembly operations involving little or no transmission of technology and little provision of sophisticated jobs ("screwdriver plants"). In this scenario, the bulk of the benefits in the form of technology, advanced employment, and profits are retained by the home countries of the firms.

This second qualm is aggravated where the rules and institutions of nations differ significantly and therefore the vulnerability of their domestic industries to takeover by foreign TNCs varies greatly. In Japan, for example, it is difficult for foreign firms to get much of a foothold—as evidenced by the fact that foreign investment in Japanese industry was less in 1986 than it was a decade before (1 percent in 1986 versus 2 percent in 1977 for all industry, and 2 percent versus 5 percent, respectively, for manufacturing alone). The cross-holding of stock by Japanese corporations, and holdings by banks of stocks as long-term investments, prevent, to a large degree, unfriendly takeovers in Japan—for both domestic and foreign firms. And the Japanese tradition of staying with traditional suppliers makes it hard for newly established firms to gain contracts (Julius, 1990, pp. 57-58). Similarly, within Germany and Switzerland, the cross-holding of shares by banks and other corporations makes foreign takeovers difficult. Thus, whereas TNCs from these lands can invest and increase their control abroad, their domestic operations are largely immune to foreign takeover. Their situation is in sharp contrast to that of nations such as the United States, the UK, and Canada, where foreign firms can easily take over domestic firms and gain access to new technology, which can then be moved to head offices in the homelands of the corporations.

Another set of issues arises with respect to the increasing interdependence of nations because of the ease with which funds and corporations can move among them. The TNC can borrow abroad and shift profits via transfer pricing to evade monetary and fiscal policies, and even alter international production patterns as may be appropriate in the light of exchange rate changes. Similarly, microeconomic policies relating to performance requirements for firms, industry taxation, subsidy policies, antipollution measures, anticombines regulations, and the like may be of limited effectiveness owing to the flexibility of TNCs' operations and their ability to play one nation against another to maximize their own advantage. They can always threaten to leave one nation that attempts to have strong antipollution laws, for example. Smaller nations may be particularly vulnerable to these types of problems.

The increased mobility of capital has generally also meant that "disturbances in one market have been more quickly transmitted to other markets, often irrespective of the underlying fundamentals" (Turner, 1991, p. 102), so that exchange rates often do not reflect the trading competitiveness of a nation. Often, too, the tendency for investors to "follow the leader" without analyzing the economic situation carefully (the bandwagon effect) has made the volatility of capital flows and exchange rates worse, while simultaneously permitting current account imbalances to continue longer than they otherwise would.

A related and much more serious issue is that, in many ways, the world economy, because of its increased interrelatedness through the international investments of TNCs of all types and because of trade liberalization measures, has become much more fragile. Hence a major economic disruption in one large nation could rapidly spread to other nations and conceivably lead to a collapse of the world economy.

Again, although the international trend is to eliminate restrictions on the operations of TNCs, there is also a widespread recognition that there has to be some common set of rules under which TNCs will operate. It is a major policy challenge to develop such a set. The extent of policy convergence required, given the diverse histories, institutions, and cultures of the nations involved, and the great time, energy, and patience needed to reach convergence out of this diversity, open the door for a wide variety of undesirable outcomes. A common position may not be achieved, at least not for an extended period, so that severe economic warfare could result—such as we have seen in the world agricultural sector.

Economic warfare is a struggle in which powerful nations gain and smaller nations are often greatly damaged. Most wars have been fought, and still are being fought, because of economic power struggles. This was the reason that Keynes desired much independence for nations for employment creation purposes—so that they would not have to focus on achieving favorable trade balances to attain their own domestic employment objectives (Keynes, 1936). From his perspective, the international trade that did occur would then be complementary for nations, based on more traditional views of comparative advantage, and not be of the adversarial nature followed today by nations like Japan, where the motive is not just to achieve domestic income and employment growth but to destroy the foreign competition entirely (Drucker, 1989). Another outcome may be that common rules are eventually agreed to, but the likelihood is that they will reflect the positions of, and be of advantage to, the most powerful nations.

Alternately, the resulting common denominator of regulations could be so watered-down that instead of promoting prosperity in markets, they could lead to a collapse of the market system, or a collapse of confidence in the system (Julius, 1990, pp. 95-96). For example, inadequate regulation of domestic and international banking could see the U.S. Savings and Loan debacle multiplied many times over. Or public safety, with respect to food products, the environment, and the like could be jeopardized. Or monopolies or collusive oligopolies could replace competition, so that consumers are disadvantaged as the TNCs maximize their profits and/or growth. Certainly, as TNCs expand and take over or merge with other firms, or engage in joint ventures, the opportunity for collusion in one form or another is increased. And even where intraindustry trade is occurring, collusion can still be taking place. In this situation, although trade may enlarge world welfare, for individual countries in weaker bargaining positions, some trade can be inferior to no trade (Fung, 1991).

In brief, what these various concerns suggest is that the current, naive ideology that emphasizes global markets, the maximizing of economic gain, and the eulogizing of the TNC—and the measures designed to promote these, such as NAFTA and the accompanying deregulation and privatization—in fact neglects many of the world-level problems created and/or augmented by this ideology and its supporting policies.

THE INADEQUACY OF THE MORAL-ETHICAL BASE

It is the contention of this chapter that one of the main reasons for the many difficulties discussed above, which we are only beginning to glimpse and understand, is that the policies being followed have no solid moral-ethical foundation underlying them. With the only guiding principle being the earning of greater incomes or profits, or power, or prestige, a real shallowness has occurred in the analysis of individual, corporate, and governmental activity.

The previous sections have outlined the types of behaviors that arise as the world moves toward greater liberalization of trade and other economic activities. In our enthusiasm for the decline of the tyranny of the extreme left, we have ignored that the right, the establishment, and the ideological principles it endorses, can, without an adequate moral-ethical base, be just as tyrannical as the left. As Francis Schaeffer (1970, p. 43) foresaw about 20 years ago, if the establishment comes to dominate, as it does now, and "give at least an illusion of what the people want concerning material well being," then the loss of our freedoms "will be much more gradual . . . for a while. But eventually it will be as total." The broader question, then, is, will we have a sustainable world society if we continue in the direction we are going, and with the approaches we are now taking? Can we continue to put profits above ethical principles, power and position above the needs of individual people, and "winning" generally above all questions of right and wrong? Perhaps it is time that we as Western societies slow down from pursuing our goals of wealth and power and ask ourselves about the appropriateness of having a narrow emphasis upon these goals while we neglect other vital human values.

Economists, of which I am one, have all too often been swept up with the ideology of the day, and in their analysis contributed to the emphasis upon market forces and free trade agreements such as NAFTA, to the neglect of ethical principles. The argument could be made that, in the process, economics has become separated from its roots, and slipped from amoral analysis to immorality. But that must be left for another paper (Wilkinson, 1992). Suffice it to say here that economists and other students of today's world need to move beyond the narrow focus on competitiveness and trade liberalization to consider the broader questions raised in this chapter. Unless we do this, we are likely to be continually disappointed with the long-term results of pursuing an ideology which has based its judgments on no criteria but profits, or winning.

I would argue, too, that answers lie not just in changing institutions alone, although some alterations are clearly warranted within our capitalistic system, but in changing peoples' focus and values as well. As Tawney (1931, p. 56) said sixty years ago:

> What matters to the health of society is the objective towards which its face is set, and to suggest that it is immaterial in which direction it moves, because whatever the direction the goal must always elude us, is not scientific, but

irrational. It is like using the impossibility of absolute cleanliness as a pretext for rolling in a manure heap, or denying the importance of honesty because no one can be wholly honest.

We need to at least address the problem today and do what we can. As Tinder (1989, p. 85) has recently said, may we, in this endeavor, be delivered "from a politically fatal fear and faintheartedness."

NOTES

1. See comments by Geza Feketekuty, senior policy adviser, United States Trade Representative, reported in *IMF Survey,* 15 July 1991, and by Richard A. Gephardt, majority leader of the U.S. House of Representatives, cited in *IMF Survey,* 30 September 1991.

2. Morici also admits that the CUFTA is not merely a free trade area, as government officials and most economists in Canada proclaimed. Rather, he says that it is essentially an economic union—as some of us have argued for a number of years.

REFERENCES

Dornbusch, R., Krugman, P., and Park, Y. C. (1989). *Meeting World Challenges: U.S. Manufacturing in the 1990s.* Rochester, N.Y.: Eastman Kodak.

Drucker, P. F. (May 1989). "The New World According to Drucker." *Business Month,* 133 (5), 48-59.

Fung, K. C. (1991). "Collusive Intra-industry Trade." *Canadian Journal of Economics,* 24 (20).

General Agreement on Tariffs and Trade. (1990). *International Trade 89-90: I & II.* Geneva: GATT.

Grant, G. (1965/1982). *Lament for a Nation: The Defeat of Canadian Nationalism.* Ottawa: Carleton University Press.

Greenaway, N. (31 October 1991). "Cold War Thaw Puts America's Spies on Ice." *Edmonton Journal,* p. D13.

Julius, D. (1991). *Foreign Direct Investment: The Neglected Twin of Trade.* Washington: The Group of Thirty.

———. (1990). *Global Companies & Public Policy: The Growing Challenge of Foreign Direct Investment.* New York: Council on Foreign Relations.

Kenny, J. (1991). "An Analysis of the MLA Pension Plan." Edmonton: Association of Canadian Taxpayers.

Keynes, J. M. (1936/1957). *The General Theory of Employment, Interest and Money*. London: Macmillan & Co.

Kierans, E., & Stewart, W. (1988). *Wrong End of the Rainbow: The Collapse of Free Enterprise in Canada*. Toronto: Collins.

Krugman, P. (1990). *The Age of Diminished Expectations: U.S. Economic Policy in the 1990s*. Cambridge, Mass: MIT Press.

Morici, P. (1991). *Trade Talks with Mexico: A Time for Realism*. Washington: National Planning Association.

Ohmae, K. (1990). *The Borderless World: Power and Strategy in the Interlinked Economy*. Scranton: Harper Business.

Ostry, S. (1990). *Government and Corporations in a Shrinking world: Trade and Innovation Policies in the United States, Europe and Japan*. New York: Council on Foreign Relations Press.

Schaeffer, F. A. (1970). *The Church at the End of the 20th Century*. Westchester, Ill.: Crossway Books.

Scherer, F. M. (1988). "Corporate Takeovers: The Efficiency Arguments." *Journal of Economic Perspectives*, 2 (1), 69-82.

Shortell, A. (1991). *Money Has No Country: Behind the Crisis in Canadian Business*. Toronto: Macmillan Canada.

Smith, A. (1776/1963). *An Inquiry into the Nature and Causes of the Wealth of Nations*. Homewood, Ill.: Richard D. Irwin.

Stevens, C. (1990). "Technoglobalism vs. Technonationalism." *The Columbia Journal of World Business*, 25 (3), 42-50.

Tarasofsky, A., and Corvari, R. (1991). *Corporate Mergers and Acquisitions: Evidence on Profitability*. Ottawa: Economic Council of Canada.

Tawney, R. (1931/1964). *Equality*. London: George Allen and Unwin.

Tinder, G. (December 1989). "Can We Be Good Without God?" *Atlantic Monthly*, Vol. 264 (6), 69-85.

Turner, P. (1991). *Capital Flows in the 1980s: A Survey of Major Trends*. Basle: Bank for International Settlements.

Wilkinson, B. (1991). "Free Trade, the Market and the Global Perspective: Some Reservations." *The American Journal of Canadian Studies*, 21 (2/3), 277-284.

———. (1992). "Economics and Ethics: Has Economics Forgotten its Roots?" (Mimeographed).

Chapter 3

Considering U.S. – Mexico Free Trade

Gerald K. Helleiner

This chapter seeks to set out some of the analytical considerations that should feature in the debate on a North American Free Trade Agreement (NAFTA) by discussing some relevant recent experience, notably that of the Canada-U.S. Free Trade Agreement (CUFTA). The chapter's perspective may be described as eclectic and skeptical.

The first section sets the stage by discussing Mexico's dramatic moves toward trade liberalization. In the second section, the different motives in Mexico and Canada for a free trade agreement with the United States are compared. The precedents of the European "enlargement" and CUFTA are drawn upon in the third section to shed light on the possible impact on Mexico of a free trade agreement. The fourth section presents the particular advantages of multilateral approaches for countries like Mexico. Mexico's relationships with its traditional friends in Latin America and elsewhere are considered in the fifth section. The final section briefly offers some alternatives the United States might pursue instead of signing a free trade agreement with Mexico.

THE BACKGROUND: MEXICAN LIBERALIZATION

The NAFTA negotiations must be understood in the context of recent Mexican trade policy experience. Mexico has undertaken a major drive towards trade (and other) liberalization over the course of the past five years. By the early 1990s, trade-weighted import tariffs averaged only 6.5 percent.

More important, import licensing was confined to only a very few sectors, and even in these, license requirements were eased.[1] Imports probably accounted for a higher share of gross domestic product (GDP) than at any time in the previous 40 years.

Severe adjustment difficulties that might have been expected from such pervasive liberalization were overshadowed by the dramatic macroeconomic adjustments occurring at the same time. Massive real exchange rate devaluation and real wage reduction eased the blow for import-competing industries while encouraging rapid expansion of nontraditional exports. It is difficult to assess either the immediate transitional costs or the likely gains in allocative efficiency, x-efficiency, reduced rent-seeking, and the like in the context of these other, quite radical changes.[2] Although the gains will probably be (though they were not yet at the time of writing) quite significant, they may well be far less important than the "signal" the broader changes convey, and indeed are intended to convey, to the international financial community.

The unilateral self-denial of the traditional instruments of trade and industrial policy may indeed have overshot what was necessary for the rebuilding of foreign confidence or desirable for future Mexican policymakers, who may have to resort to less direct and less efficient policy instruments in consequence. Mexico has, after all, implemented important industry-specific policy packages in the past—in motor vehicles, pharmaceuticals, electronics, and the *maquila* sector, for instance. Success has been variable but certainly not totally absent. Trade policy instruments have figured prominently in these industrial policies. Is it seriously intended that such policy efforts are broadly to be abandoned in the future? If not, can one be sure that policy packages that preclude the use of some of the traditional instruments will be more efficient? At this point, prudence alone would call for caution about further Mexican policy disarmament.

The interaction between trade liberalization and Mexico's balance of international payments has also been a matter of obvious concern. The growing deficit on current account reached the unprecedented level of $13.3 billion in 1991. Although massive inflows of capital covered this deficit, and even added $7.8 billion to the country's international reserves during the same year, the situation is not entirely stable.[3] A high proportion of the incoming capital is directed to the purchase of liquid assets, and, as Mexico has seen in the past, a surge of capital flight could create macroeconomic instability and another balance-of-payments crisis.

Premature and overenthusiastic import liberalization can bring stabilization and adjustment programs to grief. Mexican merchandise imports tripled between 1987 and 1991 (from $12.2 to $38.2 billion). Clearly, export performance will be critical to the success of Mexico's recovery program. During the late 1980s, Mexican nontraditional exports, particularly manufactures, grew rapidly; and most went to a U.S. market that was experiencing sustained expansion. Well over half this trade (the proportions vary markedly with the industry) was internal to U.S.-owned firms (Weintraub, 1988, pp. 16-17). However, the recession in the United States has contributed to a significant slowdown of Mexican merchandise exports (they grew by only 1.1 percent in 1991).

MOTIVATION FOR TRADE LIBERALIZATION
WITH THE UNITED STATES: CANADA AND MEXICO

As in Canada prior to the opening of CUFTA negotiations, there has been growing anxiety in Mexico over U.S. protectionist pressures, which are a serious threat to both Canada and Mexico, because they are so heavily dependent upon access to U.S. markets. Both countries have sought to insure themselves against existing and future U.S. protectionism. In other respects, though, Mexican and Canadian motivations for seeking free trade agreements with the United States are quite different; these differences may be more important than the similarities.

The fear of increasing U.S. protectionism (evidently more powerful than the long-standing lure of the U.S. export market) proved enormously helpful to domestic advocates of import liberalization in Canada. The most fervent advocates of CUFTA were concerned, above all, with liberalizing the Canadian import regime. Had they been able, they would long ago have undertaken (Mexican-style) unilateral liberalization, regardless of what the United States or other members of the General Agreement on Tariffs and Trade (GATT) were doing. It was not that they were indifferent to the problem of market access for Canadian exporters. On the contrary, they were most eloquent on the subject. But their principal objective was fitting the Canadian economy effectively into a competitive global marketplace: increasing domestic efficiency typically overshadowed the issue of market access in their perceptions of Canada's trading requirements (Winham, 1988, p. 44).

The current Mexican case is evidently very different. Mexico undertook massive unilateral import liberalization without expectation of any direct external quid pro quo. Such external returns as were gained were quite limited and indirect—a friendlier international financial community and U.S. administration. One could argue that if Mexico was prepared to undertake import liberalization it should have tried to achieve it, as Canada did, via trade negotiations with the United States and thus win reciprocal concessions from Washington as a reward for its own liberalization. But, it is possible that the strong anti-U.S. streak in Mexican politics would have made this even more difficult to achieve politically than unilateral liberalization was—a prime illustration of the differences between the Canadian and Mexican political scenes. In any case, Mexican liberalizers evidently do not need the problems of U.S. market access to achieve their domestic objectives, as their Canadian equivalents did.

The Mexican rationale for a NAFTA is best understood in terms of the country's need for external finance. Despite successful macroeconomic stabilization and major restructuring efforts, the Mexican GDP was stagnant until the early 1990s. Heavy debt-servicing obligations and a depressed world market for oil were among the chief factors responsible for investment levels that were too low to create robust recovery in the late 1980s.

The resumption of satisfactory rates of economic growth in Mexico is heavily dependent upon increased external capital inflow (including the return of Mexican flight capital). Having successfully undertaken massive macroeconomic adjustment and restructuring of incentives, Mexico seems ready for a major "leap forward"—if only there were sufficient investment to start it. It is undoubtedly, above all, Mexico's determination to acquire external private investment that accounts for its drive toward NAFTA. Such an agreement would bolster investor confidence not only by offering an important signal of future intentions, but also, more directly, by improving market access for export-oriented activities and by making concessions to U.S. capital. Indeed, some private capital flows have already responded to the prospect of an agreement.

Although the primary Canadian objective was import liberalization and the primary Mexican one is increased external finance, both countries also obviously see improved access to the U.S. market as another major objective. Both countries have been tempted to see advantage in discriminatory market access rather than in an across-the-board and nondiscriminatory opening of U.S. markets.

ASSESSING THE IMPACT OF NAFTA ON MEXICO:
THE EUROPEAN COMMUNITY PRECEDENT

Whatever the motivation, one must seek to predict the likely consequences of NAFTA for Mexico. In particular, what are the issues that arise when a relatively less developed country (or area) considers integration with a much richer one? The debates over the enlargement of the European Community (EC), which is a customs union rather than a free trade area, to include southern European countries (Spain, Portugal, and Greece) may be instructive. What I draw from those debates and subsequent experience is that the issues are not inherently so different from those in any other integration discussions. They hinge on the specifics of particular competing industries, the prospects for smooth reallocation between or inside industries and firms, and longer-term growth prospects; and they are very difficult to predict (Aktan, 1985).

European debates over such matters as the impact of capital market integration, the role of both internal and international labor mobility, the harmonization of economic policies, the contribution of financial assistance to the weaker members, and so on, are all relevant to the Mexican-U.S. discussions. Perhaps the most striking characteristic of recent research is the inconclusiveness of the results. An account of a recent conference on the EC's new southern membership concluded:

> it was difficult to foresee which of two divergent paths the new members would take. The double shock of accession and 1992 might drive their economies into depression or accelerate their modernisation. Unfortunately, economic principles do not point to a predetermined outcome. In fact, the degree of indeterminacy is so great that the outcomes may range between brilliant achievement and big difficulties (CEPR Bulletin, 1990, p. 7).

Mexico is actually considerably larger (in terms of GDP or population), relative to the United States, than Greece or Portugal is relative to the EC. The clearest difference between Mexico's case and that of the southern European nations is in per capita incomes: the U.S. per capita GDP is over ten times that of Mexico, whereas per capita GDP in the EC (excluding those three new members) is only two to four times those of the southern European countries. Mexico's proportion is in this respect roughly comparable to that of Turkey, which has not yet been accepted into the EC. Mexico's GDP is structured considerably more towards agriculture than is that of the rest of North America; in this respect, it is comparable to Portugal in the EC. Mexico is considerably *less* agricultural than Greece. Oddly, Mexico is more industrial in its GDP than is the United States, which has become so markedly a service economy.

BILATERAL DEALING WITH A STRONGER PARTNER: THE CANADIAN PRECEDENT

The presumption of simple-minded, "two-country two-good" neoclassical trade theory is that when a small country "opens" to trade with a large country, the resulting gains flow disproportionately to the small country.

This is basically because the large country's domestic price structure will dominate in the determination of prices and thus leave that country's structure of incentives essentially unchanged.

The small country, on the other hand, can expect a major change in its price structure and therefore, always allowing for greater adjustment costs, can also expect much greater gains from the reallocations of production and consumption that result from expanded trade opportunities. It is also presumed that the smaller country will benefit disproportionately from newly available economies of scale, since these will be relatively greater for that country than for its partner.

A more modern version of this basic proposition—often offered with a neomercantilist, export-oriented flavor—rests on the presumption that if one country's market is ten times the size of the other's, assuming both initially have roughly equal trade barriers, then reciprocal liberalization will provide (market) gains to the small country that are roughly ten times those of the larger country. These propositions, relating to the distribution of the gains from liberalized trade between two countries, one large and one small, obviously have to be adapted to the realities of particular cases. But the presumption that small countries gain more from trade liberalization—both their own and their prospective trading partner's—than do large countries is fairly universally accepted.

If the smaller partner in a bilateral trading agreement is expected to derive a disproportionate share of the gains from increased trade, then the obvious question is why the larger (and presumably more powerful) partner should permit this outcome to occur or, indeed, why it should participate at all (Dixit, 1987). It is possible that the positive-sum nature of the game leaves the larger country content with its gains even though a larger share of the "increased pie" is claimed by its smaller trading partner. But that is not how large countries' policy makers typically behave. It makes more sense, rather, to explore the possibility of other, nontrade gains accruing to the larger partner.

A better a priori hypothesis than that of "positive-sum contentment" is that the larger country will not consent to a game that is disproportionately beneficial to a smaller (weaker) trading partner unless it extracts a "side payment" from this partner that is roughly the size of that partner's disproportionate gain from trade alone. Certainly there must be something significant in it for the large country to want to play.

What, then, is the side payment that the United States requires as compensation for signing a trade-liberalizing agreement with a smaller partner? In the Canadian case, it had to do primarily with access for U.S. investors and agreements on services and energy supplies. Liberal Canadian economists obviously did not see these concessions to the United States as costly, any more than they saw reductions of trade barriers in this way. But the negotiators and the Canadian public certainly did.

Similar issues arise in the case of Mexican-U.S. free trade. It is critical to understand, at least as a first approximation, that a "profit-maximizing" United States is unlikely to agree to a trade deal with Mexico that generates disproportionate gains for Mexico unless Washington receives substantial compensating side payments. Alternatively, U.S. negotiators will withhold extra gains for Mexico by tightly limiting the coverage of the deal; if all of the "sensitive" Mexican exports (steel, textiles and clothing, agriculture, labor-intensive services and so on) are excluded from the agreement or subjected to special restrictive arrangements, the gains to Mexico can easily be "balanced" with those achieved by the United States. This may be the easier route for U.S. negotiators in terms of domestic U.S. political pressures (although it would obviously deprive the United States of significant gains from trade liberalization).

What, though, if the United States truly *is* prepared to liberalize Mexican market access in a serious way? What would Washington demand in compensation? Its demands of Mexico would probably look very much like those made of Canada before it.

As in the case of the Canadian agreement, the United States would seek national treatment for its investors, the elimination of maximum proportions for foreign equity, abandonment of trade-related investment rules (local sourcing and exporting requirements), increased protection for its firms' intellectual property, the emasculation of review procedures for external investors and technology purchases, and a liberal regime for services trade. U.S. pressure might also be expected in the sphere of labor and environmental legislation, and probably in competition and antitrust provisions and policies governing public ownership, the behavior of publicly owned enterprises, or both.

What did Canada achieve by way of improved access to the U.S. market in its bilateral bargain with the United States?[4] Sheer tariff reduction was never seen by Canadians as nearly as important as "getting under" U.S. nontariff measures and the rising battery of "process protectionist" measures deployed by the United States—notably countervail and antidumping duties, and 301 and "super 301" actions.[5] Although this was the top-priority Canadian objective, it was not achieved. Export subsidy issues could not be agreed upon and were deferred for later resolution. All relevant U.S. legislation therefore remains fully applicable. Canadian negotiators argued that they had achieved a binding dispute-settlement mechanism that would at least ensure that the letter of the (unsatisfactory) U.S. law would not be "bent" by political pressures.

Some argue that CUFTA's dispute-settlement procedures are among its major accomplishments. Similar legal procedures and a reasonably parallel evolution of trade-remedy laws probably made it relatively easy for Canadian and U.S. negotiators to agree on dispute-settlement arrangements. A quite different history and legal culture might make agreement with Mexico on such matters considerably more difficult.

Whatever the procedures agreed upon, there remains the question of how they actually work. There must always be anxiety over the degree to which powerful actors will actually submit to disagreeable developments, whatever they may have previously said, if they do not suffer greatly in consequence of failure to do so. Can the United States be credible in its commitments to comply with the terms of an agreement with a much smaller and weaker country? Must there not be a better balance of disadvantage from noncompliance—such as is approached in a multilateral system—for there to be hope that the U.S. political system will eventually comply with agreements Washington has entered into?

This is essentially the age-old issue of the consequences of economic dependence:

> A is dependent on B if the latter is in a position to inflict unacceptable damage on the former by dissociation, if B's threat is credible and it [A] is unable to retaliate . . . Two parties, A and B, are bilaterally interdependent in an economic sense when both derive substantial benefits from bilateral transactions and both will suffer unacceptable losses if the exchange is discontinued (Hirsch, 1987, p. 37).

Risks of dissociation can be lowered for a dependent A only by multi-lateralizing the relationship, thereby confronting B with the possibility of dissociations by a number of other countries as well. In alliances there can be trading strength. With or without a free trade arrangement, both Mexico and Canada are unquestionably dependent on the United States. It is therefore difficult to make bilateral agreements with the United States stick.

Experience with the U.S.-Canadian dispute-settlement procedures thus far does not inspire great confidence in this regard. A Canadian Senate monitoring report concludes that since the implementation of CUFTA:

> There appears to be no reduction in the use of U.S. trade remedy laws, nor of the threat of their use, on the part of U.S. business seeking protection (Canada, 1990, p. 19).
>
> It had been hoped that by judicialising the process, building in firm deadlines and timetables, and by placing the process in an international forum, the role of politics in the process could be reduced . . . [however,] there still is room for much political interference. An examination of the current cases

between Canada and the United States indicates that the delay, consultation, and negotiation that have been a feature of the past treatment of disputes will likely remain (Canada, 1990, p. 106).

This disappointing experience could be taken as evidence that the realities of international trade relations cannot be left to the naive models and approaches of liberal economists, who frequently know little of politics or law. On the other hand, one could interpret the disappointing outcome as vindication of the *super*sophistication of those same economists, who saw from the beginning that the real objective was not so much access to the U.S. market as the liberalization of Canada's own economy; for the latter is what they actually got.

In addition to tariff reductions on nonsensitive products, there are other gains that, based on the Canadian precedent, Mexico could expect from free trade with the United States. For instance, Mexico might, like Canada, obtain protection against "sideswiping" in U.S. global safeguard (Article 19) actions, although this was not achieved by Canada in respect of other nontariff measures. Only when a party to CUFTA is a substantial source of injury may it be targeted in safeguard actions and, even then, imports from that party cannot be reduced below their trend rate of growth. Similar preferential treatment could be quite helpful to Mexico. Mexico might also expect to benefit from the same asymmetrical treatment of foreign investment as Canada: exemption from any future U.S. foreign investment screening mechanism, even should some U.S. domestic investments in Mexico still be screened.

If, at the end of the day, all that Mexico acquires in the subsidy sphere is further U.S. commitments to consultations, review procedures, and an eventual harmonization of definitions (which is all that Canada got), it might be wiser for Mexico to pursue these matters in the GATT arena. In GATT there are allies (Canada among them) with similar doubts about U.S. interpretations of other countries' subsidies and the "fairness" of their trade. Indeed, the smaller countries' economic case for restoring some overall symmetry between export subsidies and import tariffs in the rules system has no prospect of receiving a serious hearing except in multilateral forums.

THE BENEFITS OF MULTILATERALISM

The protection offered to smaller countries by a multilateral rules system is far from perfect, but it is certainly greater than that available from the interplay among more powerful international actors pursuing their own interests in a world without rules. Would the United States have responded to Mexican or Canadian or even EC complaints against its discriminatory oil levy in 1987 in the absence of an international system of trade rules and the GATT panel's declaring the levy illegal? Is there any hope for reining in unilateral declarations by the United States of others' "unfair" trading practices in a world without a strong international trade authority? What hope can there be for a balanced and satisfactory outcome to future Canadian or Mexican negotiations with the United States on subsidies and countervailing duties in the absence of a multilateral agreement that sets out fair, transparent, and nondiscriminatory rules?

While it is true that all countries would benefit from a stable, transparent, and nondiscriminatory system of trading rules—and that all should therefore cooperate in its pursuit—it is not true that all would benefit from it equally. The importance of a strong multilateral system is much greater for smaller, weaker countries than it is for the strong. The strong, after all, will broadly be able to have their own way in a lawless environment. As an incentive to support a system of rules that disproportionately benefits the weak, the strong are provided with a side payment in the form of disproportionate influence in the establishment and management of the rules. Even after these concessions to the strong, however, the multilateral system is still likely to benefit the weak the most.

On the face of it, the U.S. commitment to the basic principles of GATT remains ambivalent. The bilateralism and unilateralism implicit in the Omnibus Trade and Competitiveness Act of 1988, the Structural Impediments Initiative and related measures with Japan, the renewal of steel quotas, and the like are not encouraging. Washington has deployed bilateral pressures (some of them in violation of GATT) most vigorously against some of the better-off developing countries, such as South Korea, Argentina, Brazil, and Taiwan. Is the prospect for an effective multilateral trading machinery better furthered by catering to the new U.S. approaches—knuckling under on pharmaceutical patents and other matters in return for special favors—or by joining a multilateral effort to bring the United States to heel? At present, Mexico may feel it has nothing to fear from the unilateral deployment of U.S. 301 or "super 301" procedures. It is a model performer just now, more likely to be singled out for rewards (like the Generalized System of Preferences [GSP]) and praise than for punitive measures. Mexico was the major beneficiary of the conversion of the GSP into another instrument of aggressive U.S. trade and other objectives: 209 Mexican products previously stripped of GSP status had that status restored in 1990. Yet to presume that Mexico is invulnerable to future U.S. pressures would be extremely foolhardy and myopic.

What is to prevent the United States from moving to further extraterritorial application of its own approaches, modified to suit its own interests where possible, in the "new" areas of services, intellectual property, and the like? Will Mexico do better in these spheres via bilateral negotiations with the United States or through multilateral alliances within a global system of checks and balances?

To ask these questions is to imply the obvious answer. Mexico and other small countries (including Canada) attempt to advance their interests exclusively or primarily in bilateral negotiations with larger countries only at their peril. They may win some concessions via special arrangements, but there is a high risk that they will, on balance, lose much more from their contribution to an overall disintegration of existing global rules and a failure to work sufficiently to build new ones. As a developing country with fairly limited retaliatory capacity on its own, Mexico could expect, in the longer run, to benefit greatly from an effectively functioning, nondiscriminatory multilateral system.

Developing countries have long been told that their gains from the GSP and their favored "special and differential treatment" may be more than offset by losses resulting from the breach in the fundamental GATT principle of nondiscrimination that the GSP represents. The recent use of these privileges as a source of bilateral rewards and punishments lends increased weight to such arguments. It is ironic that so soon after Mexico's accession to the GATT it should, in its newfound enthusiasm for outward orientation, be profiting from discriminatory arrangements and seriously considering further such arrangements that may contribute to the GATT's undoing.

What if, in frustration with GATT, those who want to move more quickly in some areas of agreement decide to proceed on their own in a "super-GATT" or, say, within the Organization for Economic Cooperation and Development (OECD)? Does Mexico's interest lie in membership or quasi-membership at the periphery of such "central" groupings? Or should it join with other "outsiders" in longer-term pressure for a more multilaterally acceptable set of arrangements?

These are highly "political" questions. How they are seen depends very much upon the political as well as the development strategies of the Mexican leadership. If that leadership wants to move to a highly liberal regime in the spheres in question—as in recent years it evidently has done—then it has little to lose and much to gain from joining. The leadership may even seek to bind future Mexican governments to such external obligations, thus achieving some irreversibility for their reforms.

But to move in that direction may be to submit the country's future policy possibilities to a mold that Mexico will always be unable significantly to shape. Is Mexico ready, at this stage of its development, to entrust so much

of its future to external decision makers who are concerned primarily with
the problems of quite different kinds of economies?

MEXICAN RELATIONSHIPS WITH
LATIN AMERICA AND THE CARIBBEAN

These considerations raise the question of the impact of Mexican-U.S. free
trade on traditional Mexican relationships with Latin America or, indeed,
with the rest of the Third World. Latin American economic cooperation has
not always gone smoothly and has been a source of great disappointment to
many. On the other hand, unexploited opportunities abound; and there is
fresh thinking about the emerging possibilities. President Bush's Enterprise
for the Americas Initiative has stimulated interest in the possibility of western
hemispheric free trade. Regional arrangements are developing or showing
fresh signs of life in Central America, the Southern Cone (MERCOSUR),
and the Andean Pact. The UN Economic Commission for Latin America
(ECLA) and the Inter-American Development Bank are both actively promoting new thought and action on Latin American economic cooperation.
Carlos Massad of ECLA, for instance, has called for a new "outward-directed
integration" effort in Latin America involving

> a systematic search for all possible forms of cooperation with a view to
> penetrating external markets, resolving financial problems, progressing in the
> technological field, taking advantage of economies of scale, joining up our
> external purchase and sales capacities, and thus confronting, united, the huge
> economic blocs whose formation is already under way. It [this proposed
> integration] consists in making the whole process of intra-regional liberaliza-
> tion negotiations, of approximations to a common external tariff, of coordina-
> tion of economic policies, functional to the objective of gaining a foothold in
> external markets (1990, p. 102).

He also notes, treading extremely carefully, that

> The common effort to penetrate into external markets may often mean renounc-
> ing the frequently fallacious belief that any one of our countries can obtain better
> terms from our financial and commercial partners in the exterior by itself than
> through any form of co-operation (1990, p. 102).

Could this have been written for Mexico?

U.S. discrimination in favor of Mexican manufactures is likely to be costly to other developing countries. Given the strength of U.S. protectionist interests in key sectors such as garments or steel, it is difficult to see any increase in market access for Mexican manufactures as likely to be "trade creating." Even Washington's Caribbean Basin Initiative (CBI), which allowed market access by much smaller and weaker manufacturers than those of Mexico, was hedged about with exceptions and restrictions sufficient to severely limit any impact upon the U.S. textile, sugar, and other industries. If Mexico is to be granted increased access to the U.S. market (and, as has been seen, it is quite possible that this access, like that for the Caribbean, would be severely limited) it is unlikely that it would be done at the expense of U.S. rather than third-country suppliers.

In the words of an editorial in London's *Financial Times*:

> The most immediate losers [from a Mexican-U.S. free trade agreement] would be other Caribbean and Latin American countries with whom Mexico competes. Since most of these rely heavily on the U.S. as an outlet for their exports, it is hard to see them viewing the prospect of a U.S./Mexican free trade pact with anything other than alarm (March 29, 1990).

However, in the principal area of recent growth in Caribbean exports to the United States—garments using U.S. material inputs and therefore subject to low tariffs on value added (Section 807)—trade is likely to continue to be controlled by quota arrangements. Even if, as many hope, the Uruguay Round of GATT negotiations manages to wind down the Multifiber Arrangement over the coming decade, it is difficult to imagine that the beneficiaries of the CBI would be treated any worse in the process than Mexico, in a NAFTA, would be. If there are to be U.S. import duties on textiles and garments, they will probably be similar for both duty-free supplying areas. In other spheres, as well, the Caribbean already benefits from the duty-free access that Mexico would achieve through a free trade agreement; Caribbean countries would lose the preferences they currently enjoy over Mexico if a Mexican-U.S. free trade deal were signed, but they would at least still compete on equal terms.

Much more likely to be anxious about a Mexico-United States special trade arrangement are the other (non-Caribbean) Latin American countries and the developing countries of Asia. The United States and Mexico might both find themselves discriminating against these countries. Latin America (not including Mexico) accounted for 8.9 percent of U.S. trade with countries other than Canada in 1988, more than Mexico's share of U.S. trade; and for

6 percent and 17 percent of Mexico's non-U.S. imports and exports respectively. Not only would a degree of trade diversion at their expense (as well as others') be likely, but aspirations for greater Latin American economic cooperation would suffer a major psychological blow with the "defection" of one of its major members.

Strictly speaking, the Latin American Integration Association (ALADI) treaty, to which Mexico is a signatory, actually prohibits it from offering trade privileges to a nonsignatory (like the United States) that are not equally offered to ALADI members. The other members of the agreement will be faced with a decision as to how to respond—treaty amendment, looking the other way, or Mexican expulsion—as soon as Mexico reaches an agreement with the United States (and perhaps, Canada). Those who actively seek U.S. agreements of their own—including Chile, Venezuela, and Argentina—will protect Mexico from being punished. Mexico has already also begun to soften the blow with new preferential trade agreements for Chile and Central America. But this illustrates the havoc that is created for traditional Latin American trade and other cooperative relationships by acquiescence to the U.S. "hub-and-spoke" approach to the hemisphere. If there are to be hemispheric trade arrangements and a retreat from global multilateralism, the interests of Latin American countries will surely best be served by collective negotiations with the United States rather than by a series of bilateral negotiations with so powerful a hub.

ALTERNATIVE U.S. APPROACHES TO MEXICO

What is the U.S. interest in a deal with Mexico? Strategic considerations and concern over illegal immigration from Mexico figure importantly in U.S. approaches to Mexico. Even firm U.S. proponents of the multilateral system used to consider Mexico as the "last exception" to the general rule that multilateralism is best for the United States (Aho, 1990, pp. xi-xiii; Morici, 1990, p. 141; Schott, 1989, p. 55). Now, however, the broader conception of a western hemisphere preferential trading and investment area—to be achieved, if necessary, via a series of bilateral deals—seems to have succeeded multilateralism as the instrument of choice in the liberal portion of the U.S. trade policy community.

Bilateralism and regionalism in trade relationships are still likely, however, to be disadvantageous to the United States as well as to the rest of the world. Proliferation of bilateral free trade arrangements would generate increasing bureaucratic complexity in terms of rules of origin, sequencing, dispute settlements, and the like, and would inevitably begin a succession of renegotiations with earlier partners (Schott, 1989, pp. 22-23, 50-54). The NAFTA negotiations provide only a glimpse of the complexities that may still be to come.

Free trade advocates always solemnly intone that the strength of the multilateral system is paramount and that bilateral and regional deals need not weaken the GATT. In the current global trading environment, however, the creation of NAFTA *would* constitute a further blow to the credibility of the multilateral system, a further step along the road to regional trading blocks. Even if the Uruguay Round were to fail, and (which does not follow) further efforts to make the GATT function better were stalled, preferential agreements like the proposed NAFTA agreement would still be inferior to multilateral ones among like-minded countries (Schott, 1989, p.55).

If the United States sees strategic or other economic advantages in having a stable and prosperous southern neighbor, or even a stable hemisphere, there are many ways in which it may act in pursuit of this objective. (If this is the case, the United States should not be "maximizing" in the manner described earlier: demanding side payments from Mexico and others in return for their gains. On the other hand, it may want, as it now says, to "reward" those who have chosen unilaterally to adopt policies of which it approves.) Actions in the financial sphere are, for the present, much more important than those in the trading arena; and there is more that a determined U.S. government could do in this sphere. The holding back of protectionist pressures, wherever they appear; strict adherence to existing GATT rules and panel findings; and strenuous efforts to strengthen the GATT system—these would suffice to protect Mexican and other hemispheric trading interests in the United States. It is not obvious that a preferential U.S.-Mexican trade agreement is in the best interest of the world in general, or that it is the best instrument for the pursuit of Mexican or U.S. objectives.

NOTES

An earlier version of this paper was prepared for a conference titled "Mexico's Trade Options in the Changing International Economy," Universidad Tecnologica de Mexico, Mexico City, 11-15 June 1990. I am grateful to Maxwell Cameron and Ricardo Grinspun for advice and assistance in its revision for this volume.

1. Import licenses were required in Mexico for 19.9 percent of tradeable output in June 1990, as compared to 92.2 percent in June 1985 (Hufbauer and Schott, 1992, p. 13).

2. Allocative inefficiency is the result of misallocation of resources due to price distortions, market failure, or other reasons. X-inefficiency is an increment in costs above their minimum possible level as a result of some unknown (usually managerial) cause. Rent-seeking behavior is the expenditure of scarce resources in capturing rents caused by government intervention in the economy.
3. All the data in this and in the next paragraph are from Banco de Mexico (1992).
4. For a detailed discussion, see the chapter by Sinclair in this volume.
5. See glossary for definition of trade-related terms.

REFERENCES

Aho, C. M. (1990). Foreword in Morici (1990).

Aktan, O. H., (1985). "The Second Enlargement of the European Communities: Probable Effects on the Members and the New Entrants." *European Economic Review,* 29 (2), 279-308.

Banco de Mexico. (1992). *Informe anual* (annual report). Mexico, D.F.

Canada, Senate of. (1990). *Monitoring the Implementation of the Canada-United States Free Trade Agreement.* Sixth Interim Report of the Standing Senate Committee on Foreign Affairs, Ottawa, March 27.

CEPR Bulletin (36). (January 1990). London: Centre for Economic Policy Research.

Dixit, A. (1987). "Issues of Strategic Trade Policy for Small Countries." *Scandinavian Journal of Economics,* 83 (3).

Hirsch, S. (1987). "The Political Economy of Interdependence." In J. Dunning and M. Usui (eds.), "Structural Change Economic Interdependence and World Development." *Proceedings of the Seventh World Congress of the International Economic Association,* 4, Madrid: Macmillan, 31-43.

Hufbauer, G. C., and Schott, J. J. (1992). *North American Free Trade: Issues and Recommendations.* Washington, D.C.: Institute of International Economics.

Massad, C. (1990). "A New Integration Strategy." *CEPAL Review* (37).

Morici, P. (ed.). (1990). *Making Free Trade Work: The Canada-U.S. Agreement.* New York & London: Council on Foreign Relations Press.

Schott, J. J. (ed.). (1989). *Free Trade Areas and U.S. Trade Policy.* Washington, D.C.: Institute for International Economics.

Weintraub, S. (1988). "Mexican Trade Policy and the North American Community." *Center for Strategic and International Studies: Significant Issues Series,* 10 (14). Washington, D.C.

Winham, G. (1988). "Why Canada Acted." In W. Diebold, Jr. (ed.), *Bilateralism, Multilateralism and Canada in U.S. Trade Policy.* Cambridge, MA.: Council on Foreign Relations.

Chapter 4

Economics:
The New Hemispheric Fundamentalism

Stephen Clarkson

Neoclassical economics has been the dominant intellectual belief system among the industrial world's decisionmakers since they became disillusioned with Keynesianism in the 1970s. The past decade's trend towards deregulation and privatization throughout the Americas indicates that the doctrine of laissez-faire is making converts even among the formerly state-centric elites in the less developed countries of Latin America. As a result, the movement toward hemispheric free trade, which began with Canada's request in 1985 that Washington negotiate what became the Canada-U.S. Free Trade Agreement (CUFTA) and continued with Mexico, Chile, Argentina, and other Latin American countries queuing for admission, is a phenomenon of both geopolitical and ideological significance. The formation of a regional trade block indicates that U.S. hegemony, if on the defensive globally, is ascendant regionally. It also suggests that the role of neoclassical economics is not merely academic but highly political, being linked to the strengthening of the United States's power as its ideological support.

This chapter proposes to first establish the ideological character of neoclassical economics, then to describe its impact on the main directions of Canadian public policy in order, finally, to reflect on the implications of its spreading dominance for the political economy of the western hemisphere.

ECONOMICS AS IDEOLOGY

For an intellectual theory to become an ideology—a body of ideas with the power to move adherents to political action—it has to meet three tests. To have intellectual appeal, it must first espouse an attractive goal and put forward a concrete program of action designed to reach the stated objective. To satisfy the emotional urges of its adherents, it must also offer a set of values and symbols that can meet their need for a faith, motivate them to high levels of commitment, and help them distinguish friend from foe. Finally, if it is to develop solid political support, such a doctrine must also express the material interests of a significant social class, sector, or group (Clarkson, 1978).

In Canada the latter-day disciples of Adam Smith and David Ricardo can be seen to meet these demanding requirements. The most prominent economists in English Canada have long had a goal for their homeland: "I believe that closer integration of the two [Canadian and U.S.] economies into one continental economy would be beneficial to both countries, and would involve no loss of any Canadian nationalist objectives worth pursuing," wrote Harry Johnson, the dean of his profession (1966, p. 16). The accompanying program of action consists on the one hand of achieving free trade and creating a single capital market with the United States and, on the other, of opposing interventionist government policies that attempt to limit foreign direct investment, to set the direction for industrial development, or to otherwise alter the country's comparative advantage.

As far as motivating values go, a missionary aura hovers over the economics literature on free trade for Canada. "A totally free trade situation has to be seen as the best answer to Canada's industrial concerns," intoned the Economic Council of Canada , since "*in a single step* our living standards would be raised *permanently* to a new level" (1975, pp. 82-83; emphasis added). The panacea for greater prosperity has overtones of a proselytizing zeal that is also manifest in the literature of Canadian economics in the form of attacks on the enemy, who are identified as the proponents of protectionism—"self-styled Canadian Nationalists" (Dales, 1966, p. 169)—and lampooned as "immature adults" whose thought processes are blighted by "emotional irrationality" (Johnson, 1966, p. 16).

Further evidence of the ideological status of mainstream economics lies in the coincidence between these writings and the positions of the organizations that have long spoken for transnational business operating in both the United States and Canada. Since the 1950s, the Washington-based Canadian-American Committee (CAC)—a group sponsored primarily by continental corporations—has advocated "a North American approach" (CAC, 1970, inside cover), a more highly integrated and specialized structure for Canada and the United States (Masson and Whitely, 1960, p. viii):

> For both countries, the continued dynamism of their economies depends in part upon maintenance of this North American common market for capital, and upon the expanding economic opportunities and the free flow of new technology and of managerial and technical skills which it automatically entails (CAC, 1963, pp. 1-2).

Like the economics literature, the CAC identifies "economic nationalism" as the enemy because it threatens to take "measures which involve sacrificing the benefits of economic interdependence" (CAC, 1964, p. ix). Whether represented by sectoral or specialized organizations, corporate Canada's material interests are directly expressed in a vast library of books, periodicals, reports, and studies that merge, with the academic economists' more scholarly output, into a virtually seamless ideology.

ECONOMICS AS PUBLIC POLICY

The radically simplified assumptions about human behavior, the biases against politics, and the ahistorical perspectives that inform the literature of the neoclassical school would be of no concern outside the profession were it not for the increasing presence of economists and their students in the corridors of power and the resulting impact of their advice on public policy (Watkins, 1978). For economists are not just theorists testing elegant theorems with ever more complex mathematical refinements. Many wear two professional hats. Under one hat, they are academics perfecting highly formalized models that have been set up on the basis of a logic that can, at the wave of a *ceteris paribus* disavowal, consciously abstract itself from the real world of confusingly complex causality. That "economic man" is a maximizer of pleasure or profit, that competition is perfect, that factors flow freely within (but not between) self-regulating markets—these propositions are necessary axioms in the discourse of theorists qua academics.

But a problem arises when theoretical economists put on their policymakers' hats without changing assumptions and offer advice based on unsupportable assumptions about human behavior and societal institutions. A graphic example of economists switching hats was offered Canadians in the mid-1980s by the Macdonald Commission inquiry into the economic and political problems of the country. A huge research operation was mounted to tap the best Canadian academic thinking in economics, law, and political science. Extensive efforts were made to consult not just business interests, but labor, citizens' groups, and the public at large. Ultimately, the commission managed to spend some $20 million and published 72 volumes of research studies covering a bewilderingly wide area of subjects. What determined the principal finding of the Macdonald Commission—that Canada should abandon attempts to pursue an industrial strategy of its own but opt instead for free trade with the United States— was less the thrust of the scholarly research or pressure from the public interest groups (which mainly advocated a reinforcement of the Canadian state) than the policy advice of a group of neoclassical economists whose theoretical studies favoring free trade were presented as a panacea for the country (Simeon, 1987).

Even though Canadian-U.S. trade had been growing at 15 percent per year since the early 1970s, the Macdonald Report argued that the Canadian economy, heavily dependent as it had become on trade with the United States, was facing a crisis due to the rise of U.S. protectionist actions against foreign imports. Dismissing the central role played by the state in stimulating development in most successful economies, including that of the United States, the report rejected out of hand the viability of state-led growth mounted with the cooperation of business and labor. Judging such industrial strategies to be futile, the Macdonald Report called for a market-imposed solution, the market in question to comprise the continental economy, in which entrepreneurs would be able to exploit economies of scale and specialization, thanks to the absence of trade barriers and the consequent free flow of productive factors (Macdonald, 1985). The commission's free trade recommendation was buttressed by macroeconomic modeling using data from the previous decade and making wildly optimistic assumptions about the security of access to the U.S. market that Canada would be able to negotiate for its firms (Grinspun, 1991). In effect, neoclassical economics took over the Macdonald Commission.

Although the antistatist position of the economic chapters of the Macdonald Report was contradicted by other sections of the commission's recommendations, which would have required the Canadian state to play an enhanced role, it was the free trade proposal to which the federal government, commanded since 1984 by the Progressive Conservative Party, responded with the greatest alacrity. Within a matter of days of the report's release, Prime Minister Brian Mulroney announced he had adopted its major recommendation. Declaring that the future well-being of the Canadian economy depended on its achieving access to the U.S. market that was "secure" from harassment by trade-remedy actions and "enhanced" by the abolition of all trade barriers between the two economies, Mulroney proceeded to ask the president of the United States to initiate a process for negotiating a free trade treaty between the two countries.

Although the actual free trade agreement fell far short of achieving even moderately secure access to the U.S. market for Canadian exporters (Doern and Tomlin, 1991), the economics profession appeared to rally to its defense. While most academic economists remained quiet, unwilling to dirty their hands in a public debate, the guild's star performers argued vociferously that, while far from satisfying the criteria of a true free trade agreement, CUFTA was the best deal that could have been achieved under the circumstances, that half a loaf was better than none, and that necessary industrial restructuring would proceed in such a way that the ultimate corporate rationalization would benefit both economies. "National treatment" for capital would encourage Canada's new generation of ebullient entrepreneurs to conquer the enhanced market now allegedly made secure by the magic of CUFTA. Foreign investment from overseas would stream into a Canada suddenly transformed into a peaceful, orderly, and well-governed platform from which to penetrate the U.S. market. Even workers who lost their jobs in declining sectors would further the process of economic adjustment by finding jobs in the more dynamic, technologically sophisticated industries that would spring up to exploit hitherto unavailable economies of scale. And if, unaccountably, this miracle did not materialize and the predicted economic gains were not quickly realized, then the exchange rate mechanism would come into play: the Canadian dollar would fall and stimulate Canadian exports, while reducing imports. As for the noneconomic issues, prospects were equally promising: in the new, wealthier Canada, the provinces would continue to develop their enviable system of social services while the federal government would play a more independent role on the world stage and get on ever more amicably with Washington, trade conflicts having been banished from bilateral politics (Crispo, 1988; Lipsey, 1988).

THE POLITICAL ECONOMY OF ECONOMICS

As this rosy free trade scenario bears little resemblance to the drastic deterioration in Canada of both economic and political conditions that followed the signing of CUFTA (Campbell and Dillon in this volume), we need to ask how neoclassical economics could have the power to cause a country to so radically alter its course of development to its own detriment. One answer lies within the sociology of knowledge.

The academic discipline of economics emerged in the late 18th century in response to a growing need to understand the nature of capital and markets in the first industrial society, Great Britain. The specific doctrine of free trade evolved during the 19th century as the intellectual rationale for the world's first capitalist system to extend its economic reach globally. It was in the economically dominant nations of the 20th century that highly formalized, free-market economics developed most fully, and it was in their universities that students from other countries came to learn its mysteries.

When expanding university faculties became ever more specialized and social science disciplines more differentiated, their adepts began to know more and more about less and less. The evolving academic guilds rewarded their members for communicating in jargon-laden formulas that could be understood only by other specialists. Not only did professors become less able to deal with general issues, they were penalized if they tried to engage with the general public by contributing to intellectual discourse outside the professional journals.

Of all the social sciences, economics became the most abstracted from social reality, the most entranced with mathematics, the most impenetrable for the average citizen. Economists could recommend free trade without realistically being able to conceive of its consequences for the nation's polity, culture, or social system, since they did not hold themselves responsible for what they considered nontechnical matters.

As long as economics was not dominant within the national community, its narrowness was counterbalanced by other intellectual forces. When the 1950s gave way to the 1960s, though, new conditions allowed for further advances by the "dismal science" into the apex of power. The postwar generation of generalists who ran the governments of industrialized nations had prided itself on being able to give strategic advice to its political masters in terms of the national interest. As the generalists retired, they were replaced by specialists who were more likely to have a Ph.D. in econometrics than an M.A. in history. To such technicians, the notion of the national interest had as little meaning as being able to integrate all the pieces of the policy puzzle into a coherent whole.

At the end of the 1970s, another shift took place. Good economics no longer made good politics, as it had when the Keynesian compromise was first struck and the market system coincided territorially with the nation-state's efforts to regulate it. By the 1980s, the market for Canada had become more and more continental in scope, as U.S. corporations matured in Canada and Canadian corporations expanded into the United States. Pierre Trudeau returned to power in 1980 as a born-again nationalist, and his government tried to strengthen the national economy by asserting the interventionist powers of the federal state with an unprecedented vigor; but his efforts quickly came to naught, because business revolted.

Inspired by resurgent neoconservatism in the United States and the United Kingdom, corporate Canada pushed onto the political stage with a sophisticated, multifaceted strategy. Business leaders felt the stakes to be too high for their interests to be left to the mercy of unreliable politicians and ineffectual bureaucrats. Whether in explicit lobby groups for business, big (the Business Council on National Issues [Langille, 1987]) or small (the Canadian Federation of Independent Business) the spokespersons of Canadian enterprise warmed to the task of instructing a government grown too intrusive and profligate for capitalist comfort. Their corporate peers in the media were persuaded to have their communications vehicles play on popular biases and take on the task of altering previously unfavorable public attitudes toward the market. Following another trend that had started south of the border, private sector firms started to provide major funding to encourage antistatist research and publishing in both private think tanks (the Fraser Institute) and public ones (the Institute for Research on Public Policy).

By 1982, business pressure had already pushed the Trudeauites off their nationalist agenda. By 1984, it had successfully helped replace them with the more pliable Conservatives. By 1985, it had managed to get its free trade program for downsizing the Canadian state legitimized by royal commission and adopted by government. As the rationale for this continentalist accumulation strategy and a market-driven mode of regulation had been inspired by neoclassical economics, the success of business meant that economics, too, had triumphed. The neoclassical paradigm had moved from the blackboard to the boardroom and from business to politics.

ECONOMICS AS THE NEW FUNDAMENTALISM

As the United States has become conscious of its global decline, it has taken steps to reinforce its power base within the western hemisphere. A measure of this supremacy is the extent to which its own ideology of neoconservatism has taken hold as the belief system among the power elite of its neighbors throughout North, Central and South America. Neoclassical economics has become their secular religion: the Invisible Hand has the aura formerly enjoyed by the Holy Spirit in the popular mind; the Market has acquired the quality of Providence; and achieving secure access to the U.S. market is the baptism through which a state can gain entry into the heavenly kingdom. The neoclassical school now legitimizes the attempts being made by the ruling parties of the United States's hemispheric partners to secure better access to its market. In making these attempts, they prove that hegemony — the internalized acceptance of the leader's policies and values by the other members of an international regime — still accrues to the United States within the sphere of influence first claimed for it in 1823 by President James Monroe.

Observers can only hope that the social and political polarization caused by the implementation of trade liberalization without adequate democratic controls (Polanyi, 1957) will not turn to dross the golden lure of unending economic growth and disempowered states described by the new ideologues and detailed in their writings.

REFERENCES

Canada, Department of External Affairs. (1987). *Canada-United States Free Trade Agreement.* Ottawa: Department of External Affairs.

Canadian-American Committee. (1963). *Preserving the Canadian-U.S. Common Market for Capital.* Washington, D.C.: Canadian-American Committee.

Canadian-American Committee. (1964). *Recent Canadian and U.S. Government Actions Affecting U.S. Investment in Canada.* Washington, D.C.: Canadian-American Committee.

Canadian-American Committee. (1970). *Toward a More Realistic Appraisal of the Automotive Agreement.* Washington, D.C.: Canadian-American Committee.

Clarkson, S. (Spring 1978). "Anti-Nationalism in Canada: The Ideology of Mainstream Economics." *Canadian Review of Studies in Nationalism* (5).

Crispo, J. (ed.). (1988). *Free Trade: The Real Story.* Toronto: Gage.

Dales, J. (1966). "Protection, Immigration and Canadian Nationalists." In P. Russell (ed.), *Nationalism in Canada.* Toronto: McGraw-Hill.

Davis, J. (1959). *Natural Gas and Canada-United States Relations.* Washington, D.C.: Canadian-American Committee.

Doern, G. B., & Tomlin, B. W. (1991). *Faith and Fear: The Free Trade Story.* Toronto: Stoddart.

Economic Council of Canada. (1975). *Looking Outward: A New Trade Strategy for Canada.* Ottawa.

Grinspun, R. (December 1991). "Are Economic Models Reliable Policy Tools? Forecasting Canadian Gains From Free Trade." Paper presented at conference titled "Critical Perspectives on North American Integration," York University, Toronto.

Johnson, H. G. (1966). "Possibilities and Limitations of Joint Planning." In *Canadian-American Planning. The Seventh Annual Conference on Canadian-American Relations, 1965.* Toronto.

Langille, D. (1987). "The Business Council on National Issues and the Canadian State." *Studies in Political Economy* (24).

Lipsey, R. (1988). "The Free Trade Agreement in Context." In M. Gold and D. Leyton-Brown (eds.), *Trade-offs on Free Trade.* Toronto: Carswell.

Macdonald, D. (1985). *Canada, Royal Commission on the Economic Union and Development Prospects for Canada* (Report, Vol. 1). Ottawa: Supply and Services Canada.

Masson, F., and Whitely, J. B. (1960). *Barriers to Trade Between Canada and the United States.* Montreal: Canadian-American Committee.

Polanyi, K. (1957). *The Great Transformation.* Boston: Beacon Press.

Simeon, R. (Spring 1987). "Inside the Macdonald Commission." *Studies in Political Economy* (22).

Watkins, M. (November 1978). "The Economics of Nationalism and the Nationality of Economics: A Critique of Neoclassical Theorizing." *Canadian Journal of Economics,* 11.

II

THE POLITICAL ECONOMY OF CANADIAN INTEGRATION

Chapter 5

Assessing the Benefits of Free Trade

Daniel Drache

Trade-centered strategies have become the preferred option for governments in the nineties. These policy initiatives need to be assessed to determine whether they are delivering their promise of economic renewal and a higher standard of living. There are two aspects to consider. First, because international markets are highly complex entities with many unintended consequences, a policy of free trade also has many unanticipated effects on state policy (Krugman, 1987). Second, the relocation of domestic and international resources poses major problems of adjustment and income distribution for workers and employers who have to bear the brunt of economic restructuring (Holland, 1980). With governments now constrained to use tariffs and subsidies to restructure and reorganize industry, this trend also raises unsettling questions about the benefits from increased capital mobility and investment flows that have occurred as a result of forming free trade areas. If enhanced access resulting from dismantling trade barriers fails to materialize, the issue of abrogation also has to be squarely addressed.

This paper argues that, in an era of global markets, trade-led adjustment cannot be separated from other factors that have depressed the economy. Bilateral trade agreements are not effective instruments for countries to achieve broader market access and increased competitiveness. The paper begins with an examination of the factors and forces that have transformed the Canada-United States trade deal into a high-risk activity for the weaker partner. The second part of the paper examines the quandary of trying to guarantee access by this policy instrument. The concluding section proposes an alternative concept of trade and competitiveness for countries with open economies.

TRADE AGREEMENTS: MORE THAN EXPORTS ARE AT STAKE

In the 1990s, trade negotiations are no longer principally about reducing barriers to trade or gaining access to export markets. They are mainly about building competitive industries and forming vast trading blocks for private sector actors (Drache and Gertler, 1991). Thus it makes little sense to identify the formation of trading blocks with the principal goal of increasing exports through longer production runs and achieving industry-centered economies of scale. Trade now provokes many other far-reaching and irreversible changes to an economy.

With the reorganization of markets worldwide, the pursuit of external markets has become a means to an end. And that end is to accelerate systemic change throughout the economy (Albert, 1991). The external market is being used to create a paradigm shift between domestic markets, regional economies, and states (Steelworkers, 1991).

The old model of state-market relations depended on a public system of regulated capitalism. In the new model, society is to be organized around private sector investment needs, an expanded market economy, a larger and more privileged role for private property, a transnational accumulation process, and massive state support for free enterprise.[1] The old Fordist methods of production are being abandoned as countries seek to dramatically alter production costs. The Japanese have pioneered a "lean" production model of high productivity growth that has widened their advantage over competitors who continue to rely on traditional Fordist production methods. The Japanese method of workplace control is associated with lower unit costs and higher productivity control (Drache, 1992). To keep in the running, all industrial countries are attempting to reorganize their industries on much the same footing (see chapter by Kreklewich in this volume). Thus, in the new global economy, states are struggling to find new ways to enhance their external performance.

Seen from this perspective, the decision of governments everywhere to look to export-led growth as a way to reactivate their economies poses many problems. Governments are being pushed down the path of trade liberalization by a complex set of forces. Some of these forces are tied to the current round of trade negotiations. Others stem from the introduction of new technologies, while still others are the result of increased capital mobility and capital movements, which bilateral trading agreements are designed to encourage. Regardless of the reason, it is clear that in the process of forming a trading block, major areas of state policy such as regional programs, health, environmental, and consumer protection—once thought to be off limits—are now subject to international market discipline (Cameron, 1989).

One of the most important changes occurring is that investment rules are being rewritten to facilitate increased capital mobility. Throughout Western Europe and North America, labor markets are becoming more competitive and state aid to troubled industries is coming under close scrutiny (Commission of the European Communities [CEC], 1990a, 1990b). The result is that state power to make policy independent of a country's major trading partner is being progressively eroded. Countries now find themselves trapped in an apparently seamless web of interdependency.

Two broad tendencies can thus be identified. First, in the drive to be competitive, modern consumers are being forced to choose between wanting cheaper goods and retaining their work and social identity as jobholders. The dilemma is that the pressures that lead to open borders also threaten to eliminate jobs for those whose employment future is increasingly uncertain. The second tendency is that national and international companies are required to reorient their activities. They have to decide what part of their "home base" should remain in their country of origin; where they prefer to locate their research and development; and where their strategic interests ultimately lie (Porter, 1991). Trade-driven competitiveness poses larger-than-life challenges for both private sector firms and public policy makers. Governments have to decide which sectors and firms are incapable of upgrading themselves and which stand a chance of carving out a niche in export markets.

Since CUFTA was negotiated, the linked issues of access, adjustment and competitiveness have worked at cross-purposes (see chapter by Campbell in this volume). With the Canadian economy less competitive than ever and experiencing more adjustment difficulties than previously, the question is, could the FTA have produced quite different outcomes? Answering this key concern requires looking at the final text that was negotiated and at Washington's and Ottawa's sharply divergent interpretations of CUFTA.

DIVERGENT PERSPECTIVES ON FREE TRADE

Without a well-defined concept of the state, conventional trade theory has no adequate conceptual framework to explain the causal links connecting a set of strategic negotiations, the resulting legal text, and the way governments read and interpret that text. In the absence of any precise methodology, governments are forced to wrestle with the many unintended consequences of trade adjustment. Thus, policymakers in Canada and the United States had differing expectations about the kind of market access, adjustment, and effects on competitiveness that a CUFTA would have.

U.S. PERSPECTIVES

Washington reads CUFTA as a straightforward trade deal having minimum impact on U.S. domestic policy. Neither the president nor the U.S. Congress believes that CUFTA reduces their authority to impose restrictions on foreign investment despite the clear intent of the agreement in this area. The U.S. Congress, for instance, may introduce legislation to restrict foreign investment as well as to assist hard-hit American industries suffering from market loss due to a tide of rising imports. This trend of disregarding the provisions of the CUFTA is also evident at the state level.

Recently, energy regulators in California have also chosen to disregard the intent, if not the letter, of this international agreement. The Public Utilities Commission of California ruled that natural gas buyers there can cancel their long-term contracts with 125 Alberta-based producers in order to take advantage of low prices for natural gas in short-term supply markets.

Washington's apparent indifference to the spirit and letter of the energy chapters of the final agreement raises many important questions about its understanding of its obligations. Canadian authorities may believe that state regulators are acting in bad faith. However, Washington has never made a secret of the fact that in its view CUFTA carries very little weight in affecting the U.S. domestic decision-making political process. For instance, the Reagan administration, early on, affirmed this belief in its legislative statement of intent when the House and Senate formally adopted CUFTA. The California decision unquestionably shocked Canada's Western energy producers, who mistakenly believed that CUFTA rendered energy contracts entered into with U.S. companies tamper-proof. But U.S. energy regulators have made many similar decisions in the past. Clearly, these kinds of regulatory agencies believe that their powers are little affected by CUFTA because there is no override provision in the agreement per se to limit the exercise of their statutory rights and rule making. Given this fact, they can be expected to continue to use their powers to protect the interests of U.S. consumers and the general public when they deem necessary.

Both examples drive home the point that legal texts are not neutral or definitive. A trade agreement must be interpreted and, therefore, while binding, is not the last word in a legal or, for that matter, in a political sense. Any trade agreement is itself subject to review, interpretation, and dispute. CUFTA is no exception. So long as a legal text like this one is so open to interpretation, the stronger partner can manipulate it for its own domestic ends. It can do this without any apparent violation of its obligations or rules as set out in the final agreement. This is why legal texts are not what they seem: they are objects for increased litigation rather than instruments to forge a new Canada-United States relationship.

CANADIAN PERSPECTIVES

Ottawa regards the final text as being much more than a trade deal; Ottawa feels that much was demanded of it by the agreement. It believes that the legal text imposes real limitations on the legislative powers of government to restrict foreign investment and to set energy prices. Ottawa further believes that it was obliged by CUFTA to open Canada's service sector to U.S. investors. Other, provincial governments subscribe to this view even when they are not of the same political persuasion as Mulroney. For instance, the social democratic Ontario New Democratic Party (NDP) government cited CUFTA as one of the principal reasons for not introducing a public auto insurance scheme, one of its key electoral planks (see chapter by Campbell in this volume). While any government may choose to hide behind an international agreement for its own political reasons, the substantive problem is that since coming into effect, CUFTA has had a chilling affect on Canadian government behavior and decision making (Cameron, 1988; Lipsey and York, 1988). It has created major problems for Canadian authorities who wish to restructure regional industries with subsidies or who believe that the public sector should be given greater importance if U.S. influence in the Canadian economy is to be reduced.

The wide discrepancy between the U.S. reading of CUFTA and the Canadian understanding of it raises many public policy issues. The foremost is that Canadian legislative sovereignty over a range of domestic issues is being challenged and reduced. These worries do not stem from an interpretative misunderstanding of the CUFTA text, but are substantive in nature and arise because of the asymmetrical power relationship between the trading partners. CUFTA has exacerbated this inequality. In addition, the final text is deficient on another count. There is no provision to ensure an equitable sharing of benefits. This dimension is entirely absent from the architecture of the legal text.

CAN ACCESS BE GUARANTEED?

Trade economists argue that when countries enter into bilateral or multi-lateral trading arrangements for traditional policy goals, the primary attraction is to better balance bilateral trade flows (Schott, 1989). But unless there is a redistributive mechanism of adjustment explicitly negotiated as part of a bilateral trade arrangement, bilateral relations are more likely to deteriorate than improve. The result is that trade imbalances become more, not less, pronounced.

The European Community (EC) has devised a number of policy instruments to ensure that trade-driven integration is not a one-sided process. Since 1989, it has had a proactive competition policy which empowers the European Commission to stop takeovers or mergers that do not, in their words, promote "effective competition." This was the reason invoked to stop the recent takeover attempt of DeHavilland by a French-Italian consortium. The Community is also committed to the need for economic restructuring as well as an industrial policy that takes full account of the magnitude of the adjustment process. For instance, it is a long established EC principle that economic integration requires the Community to provide social and economic assistance for workers in troubled industries. It has guidelines and rules for restructuring which attempt to address both the economic and social consequences that arise when industries need to be restructured. Finally, the EC has a strong regional program to build a level playing field between the developed North of the Community and the disfavored regions in the South (CEC, 1990a, 1990b).

The experience of CUFTA demonstrates that Canadian policymakers were mistaken in thinking that bilateral trade negotiations are an adequate framework to address the whole gamut of economic problems that arise from trying to guarantee market access. Trade specialists are in agreement that even in the sophisticated environment of the General Agreement on Tariffs and Trade (GATT), access can never be guaranteed in any definitive sense by legal means. The laws establishing and enforcing trade norms are reactive measures, which states rely on at their peril. In the case of the GATT, its "record of enforcement of [its] rules has been mixed. The dispute settlement process is prone to delaying tactics; indeed, decisions can be blocked outright by the disputing parties. . . ." (Schott, 1989, p. 8). Even with the best intent in the world, trade liberalization obligations remain vague and procedural delays interminable as countries invoke escape clauses to protect their industries from real and imagined difficulties. Most countries have long understood that the question of access is fundamentally an economic issue that can best be addressed through an industrial strategy that coordinates state policy with business and labor needs.

The kind of access provided in CUFTA highlights all of these concerns. Before CUFTA came into effect, 95 percent of Canada-United States trade was virtually tariff-free or subject to tariffs of 5 percent or less. With more than C$250 billion in total commercial trade, Canada and the United States had more access to each other's market than any other two countries. The failure to provide substantially new access for Canadian exporters raises the critical question of whether the agreement should be abrogated.

As it stands, the legal status of giving Canada enhanced access to U.S. markets remains highly imprecise, subject largely to U.S. judicial interpretation and mainly dependent on U.S. goodwill. CUFTA is deficient as a market-enhancing device because it has not delivered on its main promise— that a bilateral deal would deflate U.S. protectionist pressures (Schott, 1989). For this to happen would have required a fundamental change in U.S. trade laws with respect to antidumping, countervail, and safeguard trade legislation.[2] As well, the United States has an arsenal of other measures the administration deploys to negotiate "voluntary export restraint." What makes the system impossible to control is that it is industry-driven. Third parties can demand that Congress's trade police, the International Trade Commission, undertake an investigation for alleged trade injury. With a system so susceptible to U.S. industry pressure, the number of countervailing duty (CVD) investigations has grown as U.S. industry's power has declined. There was one CVD investigation in 1973, compared with 43 in 1985.

U.S. administrations rely on these powerful trade laws and trade institutions to support their industries. These measures are ad hoc, temporary, and adapted to the needs of the moment. It is this institutional flexibility that makes U.S. trade law easy to trigger. U.S. trade remedy legislation has very low thresholds to establish trade injury. This not only encourages firms and industries to use countervail and antidumping legislation to harass their competitors, but it also gives wide discretion to U.S. trade officials to find in favor of U.S. producers (Drache, 1988).

The Mulroney government's decision to place Canada's hopes on enhanced access was the wrong strategy to create "a stable North American trading system with competitive industries at home, an increased incentive for investments, and market niches for Canadian specialty products" (Canada, External Affairs, 1986, p.75). Canada's basic mistake was to try to guarantee enhanced legal access by artificial means rather than by being truly competitive and earning its way into U.S. markets by having superior products and innovative marketing strategies.

In retrospect, there are two principal reasons that explain the failure of Mulroney's "leap of faith." Canada lacked the leverage to negotiate a special bilateral relationship with Washington. The negotiations did not reduce the asymmetry of power between the parties. Canada made most of the concessions at the bargaining table. It wanted a blanket exemption from U.S. trade law to protect Canadian exporters from antidumping, countervail, and safeguards legislation. It failed to get it. Article 1902 of the CUFTA states unequivocally that Canada is subject to U.S. trade laws. In addition, Canada put great emphasis on getting a binding disputes-resolution mechanism. It believed that this remedy would provide for a more efficient, less costly, and more predictable system for solving trade disputes.

In the end, Canada got few of these objectives. Even Simon Reisman, Canada's chief negotiator, had to admit that exemption from U.S. trade laws was the "silliest proposition that I ever heard" (Drache, 1988, p. 252). At best, Canada got some language that only marginally improves the resolution of trade disputes. There is no binding trade-dispute procedure. Appeals can go to U.S. courts when they raise constitutional questions or, as the 1992 pork decision demonstrated, when U.S. authorities wish to challenge an unfavorable decision.[3]

Finally, Canadian negotiators set their sights on negotiating a definition of a trade subsidy. This would protect Canada's regional, social, and other programs from U.S. trade law. Here, too, Canadian negotiators drew a blank. There was no definition of a trade subsidy in the final text.

But even to negotiate a badly flawed legal text, the Canadian government had to give up something more. Prior to the signing of CUFTA, Canada had rung up a huge trade surplus with the United States. Canadian export success in U.S. markets was largely due to having a 78-cent dollar. The undervalued Canadian dollar had served an important purpose. Currency devaluation creates a huge price advantage for any country. Its goods are cheaper not because they are produced more efficiently or because their firms adopt aggressive and innovative marketing strategies. It is the cheaper currency, and that alone, that allows the country a leg up on its competitors. This was the strategy that Canadian governments had used effectively. While exchange-rate concessions were not formally part of CUFTA, there would be no trade deal without an informal understanding between Washington and Ottawa on this critical issue.

Since the signing of the trade deal, the Bank of Canada has informally followed a fixed exchange rate policy. The Canadian dollar jumped from its pre-CUFTA low of $0.78 to the U.S. dollar to almost $0.85 by 1990. The Mulroney government has categorically denied that any deal was made. But the facts are not mere circumstantial evidence. The signatories to the European Community also discovered that they were required to formally agree to align their currencies. Free trade areas work only if currency fluctuations are controlled and exchange rate movements reduced.

In a union of two, this means, of course, that the Canadian dollar would be pegged to its U.S. counterpart. In effect, Canada has given up the real economic access it had for something much more ambiguous. The higher Canadian dollar has, in fact, cost Canadian exporters important market share and undercut any of the gains from dismantling already low tariffs. This, in combination with high real interest rates, runs counter to the entire logic of a free trade deal. What the deal demanded was that interest rates be kept low to encourage Canadian manufacturers to restructure and invest in new plants and equipment. Clearly, Ottawa's monetarist policies make no sense from a trade point of view. The Bank of Canada, in targeting inflation as its number one priority, has kept interest rates high and the dollar overvalued. High interest rates have boosted Canada's international indebtedness to record levels. By the end of 1990 Canada was a net debtor to the rest of the world to the tune of C$259 billion, or about C$10,000 for every Canadian (Donner and Lazar, 1991).

TRADE DOMINANCE

For the United States, CUFTA has to be considered as a kind of prototype deal in which Canada, the weaker partner, emerges more structurally dependent on the United States than previously. What a cursory examination of Washington's trade objectives reveals is that it had a commanding position going into the negotiations and that the bilateral talks reinforced this dominance.

In contrast to the Canadians' lofty talk about access, Washington sought an agreement based on pragmatic strategic outcomes. It played hardball and won. It had five principal objectives, and all are part of the final text. A prime concern for Washington was access to Canada's banking and financial sector. Ottawa agreed to give U.S. interests access to this previously closed sector. Second, U.S. negotiators aimed for and got "secure and enhanced access" to Canada's resource sector. In the future, Canadian governments will not be allowed to have a two-price energy system (higher prices for U.S. customers and a lower price for the Canadian consumer—see chapter by Dillon in this volume). In the service sector, U.S. interests also prevailed. The United States was given the right of national presence and national treatment. Even in manufacturing, the Canadian government made an important concession in accepting an accelerated rate of tariff reduction for its manufacturing sector. The most controversial part of the trade deal is the provision that, in the future, no Canadian government can introduce legislation to screen foreign investment, restrict the flow-back of interest and dividend payments, or take other measures against U.S. companies in Canada's national interest (Doern and Tomlin, 1991; Hurtig, 1991; McQuaig, 1991).

What has been signed, then, is not a free trade agreement along European lines, with egalitarian national rights for the countries involved. Rather, by calling for the liberalization of all sectors of the economy, including agriculture, trade in services, business travel, and investment, the trade pact creates a de facto common market area but not a level playing field between the two countries. Its importance to U.S. hegemony, however, should not be underestimated.

Bilateral trading areas offer the United States a powerful alternative to promote its own version of trade liberalization with countries that have little bargaining leverage. The United States used the Canada-United States trade pact as a kind of side deal to spur the GATT to adopt its agenda with respect to investment rules, financial services, intellectual property, agriculture, and state subsidies.

At the geopolitical level, CUFTA has also proven to be indispensable. It now appears that U.S. authorities are ready to make use of its larger significance. Once a deal with Canada was signed, it gave a green light to Mexico to open bilateral negotiations with Washington. Without Canada on board, a deal with Mexico was less feasible. Washington could make the argument that if Canada, a supposedly tough negotiator, signed a deal, other countries could do the same without fear and in the expectation that there was something in it for them. They would benefit by negotiating with Washington new discipline codes to establish objective criteria that would take the politics out of trade. This is always the promise behind trade liberalization. The reality is that Washington is in the process of creating its own Fortress North America. If Mexico becomes part of this trade-centered system, it will give the United States secure access to two banking systems, the combined energy resources of Canada and Mexico, and a privileged place for U.S. consumer exports in the Canadian and Mexican markets.

TRADE COMPETITIVENESS: IS THERE AN ALTERNATIVE?

For countries with structural economic problems, there are two possible responses to globalization. The first is premised on a wholesale reorientation of state policy in order to maximize the search for export markets at all costs. This is likely to create more problems than solutions. A wholesale commitment by governments and the private sector to trade expansion is anything but benign. Countries both large and small are required to open their borders, regardless of the costs, in the hope that their industries will restructure and emerge stronger in response to new competitive pressures. The textbook view of trade-led growth promises a convergence of costs and benefits as well as a higher standard of living for all, even if some sectors are left worse off.

Trade theory holds that the dismantling of barriers creates growth that is automatic and self-sustaining and that, if the adjustment process is left to run its full course, the resulting conditions will create more efficient and productive industries in the long term. The operative elements are to specialize; to drive down costs; and to become efficient producers in a select number of industries. It is the latter assertion that supposedly ensures a higher standard of well-being. The unquestioned postulate of trade theory is that efficiency becomes "bred in the bone" when countries tap the competitive dynamic released from eliminating inefficient firms. This permits whole sectors and industries to restructure. What remains problematic is that a trade-driven model does not provide a way to manage the adjustment problem; nor does it offer a way to reconcile the conflicting needs unleashed by the drive for efficiency with the need for social stability. As for influencing state policy, it does not prove to be an effective way to deflate growing protectionist pressures, particularly with respect to the United States. Bilateral trade agreements are largely irrelevant to the scope and operation of U.S. trade laws and trade institutions. These kinds of agreements do not have the legal or political force to impose new standards or obligations on the U.S. Congress.

The other model to consider is one that is demand-driven. This response to globalization sees the reorganization of markets and the pursuit of higher levels of well-being in very different terms. Its principal aim is to create new wealth and generate productivity growth by striking a different balance between domestic and international forces. Under this choice, the first concern is that even if countries need to specialize, they also are required to diversify their industrial structure by broadening and deepening their industrial capacity across many sectors. This drive to deepen their industrial structure necessitates a fundamentally different view of the roles of industry, labor, and governments in shaping and organizing markets. Industries need to be reorganized and restructured rather than simply abandoned. Second, the central issue in this model is that countries avoid relying upon legal agreements to guarantee market access. Countries secure access to a competitor's market because they have distinct products to sell; because they are able to innovate and produce new goods and services; and because they have the technology to make their industries competitive.

In the 1990s, the concept of access has to be redefined as a strategic problem requiring a special kind of government involvement. Countries wishing to succeed have to have an institutional structure that can transform a static comparative advantage into a dynamic one. Many governments have accepted that they need to respond to the market imperfections that limit large economies of scale, discourage extensive research and development, or hinder training and skills creation (Yoffe and Milner, 1989). Thus, the key to having higher levels of economic and social well-being is to shape the traded-goods sectors and organize the internal market rather than drive a wedge between the two. This is an inherently different approach to trade than that espoused by trade liberalization.

At the heart of the alternative model is a single notion. Markets are social spaces that are not fully formed and need definition and direction. The most efficient way for national and international markets to work involves ensuring that markets do not become deterministic institutions. This requires building strategic relationships. One set must be between labor and business. Countries that want to have higher productivity levels must have a business strategy that is premised on a skilled work force that is paid fair wages. Its competitive edge has to come from tapping new sources of productivity growth rather than driving wages down. The high-skill option is compelling because it is based on maximizing the advantages derived from investing in the work force, realizing increased productivity gains, and maintaining high levels of domestic demand through an upward pressure on wages (Steelworkers, 1991).

A second set of strategic concerns has to address the way the private sector is organized. Strong industries capable of surviving competitive pressures have to be able to respond to increasing international competition. The speed and intensity with which they do so affects the structure of competition within an industry and among firms. Highly segmented industries where firms have no way to pool their expertise or knowledge produce a dispropor-tionate share of losers. These are usually small firms in the competitive side of the economy. Their economies of scale are small and they have no way to work together strategically to lower their cost structure—for example, by sharing cost-saving technologies. At the other end are industries that produce specialized, high-volume goods with substantial economies of scale. They understand that the "name of the game is to cooperate with one's competitors over common components, yet maintain keen competition at the final product stage." These firms are organized to make strategic moves and anticipate change (Buiges and Jacquemin, 1989, pp. 53-67).

The role of the state in this second model is to address the needs of the different, and often conflicting, industrial sectors. Some sectors have to be restructured, downsized, and radically reorganized. Others require a strategy of concentration along with a tough but flexible competition policy. In the latter case, this means creating mergers and takeovers aimed at exploiting returns to scale in the high-volume industries. At the same time, governments have to ensure that effective competition is promoted. Finally, attention has to be given to organizing business to facilitate cooperative arrangements and the strengthening of industrial districts. Ways have to be found to avoid costly duplication in investment activity and to promote the rapid dissemination of technological information between firms and among industries. In Europe, this latter strategy has been remarkably successful in a range of initiatives including the development of Airbus, high-definition television, and cellular radio broadcasting. These examples illustrate the many advantages that can result by moving away from reliance on hyperliberal trade ideologies and toward mobilizing strategies.

Finally, states have to rethink the strategic relationship between internal and external markets. The global reorganization of markets, as well as the emergence of a small number of multinational firms controlling much of the world's trading system, requires the state to have a more complex response to markets. Countries are unlikely to do well internationally if they do not exercise greater control over their basic internal market. Japan's strength comes, in part, from the fact that in critical areas of the economy, Japanese auto manufacturers control over 70 percent of their domestic market. This gives them leverage and power in international markets.

For other countries, these lessons should be patently clear. Building leverage requires them to find ways to protect themselves from the dangers of increased capital mobility and a volatile global business cycle. Trade has to be approached with a strategic assessment of what is in a country's interest and with the realization that imperfect markets demand innovative solutions and not ideological prescriptions. With tariffs at an all-time low, bilateral trade agreements offer little of lasting value. More importantly, they only proffer a semblance of access. In highly volatile global markets, real advantage depends on a country's strategic willingness to engage in long-term planning.

NOTES

1. It can be seen already that much that once was public—such as the delivery of health, education, public transport, and housing services—will eventually be provided to a greater degree by the market rather than the state.
2. The U.S. legal apparatus consists of the following instruments: safeguard legislation that protects U.S. industry if liberalization results in an unforeseen injury; Section 301, which authorizes the president to take retaliatory action if other countries restrict U.S. imports; countervailing duty that is imposed against a foreign competitor alleged to have caused trade injury; and finally, antidumping laws that result in fines against companies that sell goods for less that the cost of production.
3. Where one partly believes that there has been a serious breech of process, the agreement allows for a special panel to be struck to review a final decision for a second time. See Article 1904.13 of CUFTA.

REFERENCES

Albert, M. (1991). *Capitalisme Contre Capitalisme*. Paris: Seuil.

Buiges, P., and Jacquemin, A. (1989). "Strategies of Firms and Structural Environments in the Large Internal Market." *Journal of Common Market Studies,* 28 (1).

Cameron, D. (ed). (1988). *The Free Trade Deal*. Toronto: Lorimer.

Canada, External Affairs. (1986). *Canadian Trade Negotiations Selected Documents*. Ottawa: Minister of Supply and Services Canada.

Commission of the European Communities (CEC). (1991). *The Regions in the 1990s*. Brussels.

Commission of the European Communities (CEC). (1990a). *Employment in Europe 1990*. Brussels.

Commission of the European Communities (CEC). (1990b). *Industrial Policy in an Open and Competitive Environment Guidelines for a Community Approach*. Brussels.

Doern, B. G., and Tomlin, B. W. (1991). *Faith and Fear: The Free Trade Story*. Toronto: Stoddart.

Donner, A., and Lazar, F. (1991). "Deficits, Debts and the Economics of Mulroney." Unpublished manuscript.

Drache, D. (1988). "Canada-U.S. Free Trade: Not a Muddle, Not a Mess, but an Unparalleled Disaster." *The Round Table* (307), 251-266.

Drache, D. (ed). (1992). *Getting on Track: Social Democratic Strategies for Ontario.* Montreal: McGill-Queen's University Press.

Drache, D., and Gertler, M. S. (eds.). (1991). *The New Era of Global Competition: State Policy and Market Power.* Montreal: McGill-Queens University Press.

Holland, S. (1980). *Uncommon Market Capital, Class and Power in the European Community.* London: Macmillan.

Hurtig, M. (1991). *The Betrayal of Canada.* Toronto: Stoddard.

Krugman, P. R. (1987). "The Economic Integration in Europe: Some Conceptual Issues." In T. Padoa-Schioppa (ed.), *Efficiency, Stability and Equity: A Strategy for the Evolution of the Economic System of the European Community.* London: Oxford University Press.

Lipsey, R. G., and York, R. (1988). *Evaluating the Free Trade Deal.* Toronto: C. D. Howe Institute.

McQuaig, L. (1991). *The Quick and the Dead: Brian Mulroney, Big Business and the Seduction of Canada.* Toronto: Viking.

Porter, M. (1991). *Canada at the Crossroads. A Study Prepared for the Business Council on National Issues and the Government of Canada.* Ottawa: BCNI.

Schott, J. J. (1989). "More Free Trade Areas?" In J. J. Schott (ed.), *Free Trade Areas and U.S. Trade Policy.* Washington D.C.: Institute for International Economics.

Steelworkers, Canada. (1991). *Empowering Workers in the Global Economy: A Labour Agenda for the 1990s.* Toronto.

Yoffe, D. B., and Milner, H. V. (1989). "An Alternative to Free Trade or Protectionism: Why Corporations Seek Strategic Trade Policy." *California Management Review,* 31 (4), 111-131.

Chapter 6

Restructuring the Economy: Canada into the Free Trade Era

Bruce Campbell

Four years after the Canada-U.S. Free Trade Agreement (CUFTA) was implemented (on 1 January 1989), supporters and critics in Canada remained as divided in their assessments of its impact as they had been in their forecasts before the deal was signed. Critics saw the early years of implementation bearing out their predictions of severe adverse economic, social, and political consequences flowing directly and indirectly from the free trade agreement. Free trade defenders responded to the Canadian economic crisis in the early 1990s in a variety of ways. Some said it was still too early to judge CUFTA's impact and blamed worldwide recession, the overvalued dollar, and globalization. Others pointed to what they saw as positive signs regarding Canada's trade and foreign investment balances—signs that showed that free trade was working. Few acknowledged that the situation was the anticipated, if painful, consequence of a policy agenda (of which CUFTA was central) whose objective was to transform the Canadian economy.

The most remarkable of assessments came from those who argued that, as bad as it was, the situation would have been even worse without CUFTA in place (Ritchie, 1991). The logic of this assertion required the spectacular leap of faith that, years after the promise of an era of jobs and prosperity, Canadians should have been grateful that they were not even closer to the 1930s level of crisis. Those who arrived at this assessment did so by using the same computable general equilibrium models on which they relied so heavily in the original campaign to sell free trade—models that failed then to predict the effects of CUFTA.[1]

The free trade agreement's impact cannot be analyzed in isolation from the broader package of policies that constituted the neoconservative agenda. The agreement was an integral part of that package. It interacted with, reinforced, and was reinforced by other policies. It facilitated the introduction of policies with which it was compatible, and hindered those (existing or new) with which it was not. Moreover, the agreement acted upon a complex social reality, creating economic, political, psychological, and social effects. It had direct and indirect effects, some clear and some obscure, and produced effects that generated secondary effects that over time caused still further effects. The threads of causality were intricate and their effects have been cumulative.

THE MULTIPURPOSE CUFTA

Evaluations of CUFTA are self-evidently a function of the evaluation criteria utilized. CUFTA could be seen to be working quite well when viewed through the prism of the government's neoconservative agenda of deregulation, privatization, and liberalization.

Looking back over the first four years of its implementation, CUFTA, despite its major flaws in areas such as market access and dispute settlement, could be seen as an effective multipurpose device for securing and advancing a neoconservative restructuring of Canada. This chapter will examine five ways in which CUFTA has been utilized to this end: (1) the way it has acted as a wedge, providing impetus for two major policy initiatives to further entrench or "constitutionalize" the agenda; (2) the way it has acted as a ceiling, preventing intervention-minded governments from implementing their agendas and thwarting legislation that restricts corporate activity; (3) the way it has served as a vice within which the Conservative government continues to unilaterally deregulate, further compressing the policy space available to future governments; (4) the way it has been used by the United States in tandem with the General Agreement on Tariffs and Trade (GATT) as a whipsaw to further weaken or eliminate interventionist Canadian laws and regulations; and (5) the way it has served the Conservative government as a key lever to facilitate and hasten the implementation of its policy agenda: corporate restructuring and downward harmonization of standards, dismantling of the Canadian social contract, and implementation of "market friendly" policies.

A WEDGE

CUFTA gave impetus in the early 1990s to two major initiatives whose purposes were to further "lock in" the conservative agenda and put it beyond the reach of future governments.

In June 1990 consultations began to expand CUFTA and include Mexico in a North American Free Trade Agreement (NAFTA). NAFTA became a stepping-stone for the Bush administration's Enterprise for the Americas Initiative, which seeks to lay down new rules of economic order in the western hemisphere and thereby consolidate the U.S. sphere of dominance. John Negroponte, U.S. ambassador to Mexico, clearly articulated in a confidential April 1991 U.S. State Department memo a key purpose of a trilateral deal. "The NAFTA can be seen as an instrument to promote, consolidate, and guarantee continued policies of economic reform in Mexico beyond the Salinas administration."[2] Other Latin American countries were lining up to "dock in" even before a trilateral deal was concluded. By the end of 1991, U.S. officials had signed framework trade agreements (precursors to free trade agreements) with all Latin American and Caribbean countries except Cuba, Haiti, and Surinam.

With the negotiations now complete, the August 1992 document reveals that NAFTA is indeed a major renegotiation of the original bilateral trade deal. It extends the economic space within which large corporations can move freely in Canada and elsewhere on the continent, unrestrained by public accountability. It gives the corporations enormous new power and places further constraints on the ability of the Canadian governments to pursue industrial policy, to manage resources, and, therefore, to carry out social and environmental policies.

The second initiative occurred in September 1991, when the Mulroney government unveiled its proposal for entrenching a neoconservative agenda in the Canadian constitution. The proposal would extend the binational mobility rights and freedoms of capital entrenched in CUFTA to apply within Canada itself. It would also entrench economic union provisions, which would strengthen federal ability to enforce the provisions of the free trade agreement. The effect would be to remove important provincial government powers and reassign these powers to a body whose mandate would be to limit

provincial actions that might place "impediments . . . to the efficient functioning of the internal market" (Government of Canada, 1991a, 1991b). This
would be a recipe for paralysis and would, in effect, transfer this provincial
power to the market.

A CEILING

A clear example of CUFTA's success in protecting the "rights" of corporations
by frustrating or thwarting the actions of intervention-minded governments was
the case of public auto insurance in Ontario. One of the main promises of the
New Democratic Party (NDP) provincial government elected in September 1990
was to replace private auto insurance with a publicly administered system similar
to ones already in existence in three other provinces.

CUFTA, in theory, allows governments to do this, but in practice greatly
raises the price of implementation. Article 2010 of CUFTA requires prior
consultation with the U.S. government and leaves implementation subject to
the nullification and impairment clause (Article 2011), which says that, even
if an action is compatible with the agreement, if it reduces benefits otherwise
expected by U.S. corporations, then the United States is entitled to compensation. Moreover, Article 1605 requires "fair market compensation" to U.S.
firms for measures that are considered "tantamount to expropriation." Canadian law does not give this right to Canadian companies.

The U.S. auto insurance industry immediately began to prepare claims
for compensation under CUFTA. An industry-commissioned study by Coo-
per and Lyberand claimed that U.S. companies alone would be entitled under
CUFTA to $689 million in compensation if Ontario brought in its public auto
insurance scheme and that the total private sector compensation bill would
be $2 billion (Barlow, 1992). No such legal compensation would be required
for Canadian companies, but in practice, not extending compensation to them
would be politically unacceptable. Gordon Cloney, president of the International Insurance Council, wrote to U.S. Trade Representative Carla Hills,
saying Ontario's scheme "would compromise the most basic intention of the
Canada-U.S. Free Trade Agreement." He urged her to convey to the Canadians "the serious implications the Ontario action would have for future trade
relations" (*Insurance Week,* 1991, p. 6).

Hills agreed to this request. At an August 1991 trade ministers' meeting
in Seattle, she publicly warned Canadian Trade Minister Michael Wilson
that Ontario's proposed policy would violate CUFTA, and implied that the
United States would exact a very high price if Ontario were to proceed.

Consequently, a beleaguered Ontario government, weakened by a free trade-driven restructuring process that has seen the large-scale exodus of production facilities, the loss of hundreds of thousands of manufacturing jobs, the erosion of its revenue base, and the growth of its deficit, admitted defeat and reneged on its promise to Ontario voters to bring in public auto insurance.[3] The auto insurance example demonstrates concretely how CUFTA operates as a mechanism through which the United States can scrutinize, apply pressure, and retaliate against Canadian policies that threaten the interests of U.S. corporations.

CUFTA has frustrated democratic political choice by reducing the power of federal and provincial governments. But it has not transferred power, as the European Community has, to supranational institutions like the European Court or the European Commission. CUFTA has transferred power to the corporations and established the United States as the enforcer of the new order. Canada has surrendered sovereignty without having gained any voice in a supranational institution.

Ontario legislation pending in two other areas will also bump up against the constraints imposed by CUFTA: changes to labor legislation designed to modestly increase union bargaining power in negotiations with management, and legislation to facilitate ties between public capital funds and worker ownership schemes.

With respect to the first, the opposition has come from Ontario-based businesses that argue that the legislation will disadvantage them in competing with their U.S. counterparts. This pressure has already reached hysterical proportions, with media magnate Conrad Black warning that "capital and talented people will avoid or flee Ontario until a more favorable climate returns. . . . Ontario will pay dearly and long for its mindless adherence to the NDP" (Van Alphen, 1991).

As for joint government-worker buyouts, the first test may be that of ailing Algoma Steel in Sault Sainte Marie, whose exports could eventually be subject to countervailing action by U.S. producers alleging unfair government subsidies. More generally, to the extent that the United States views Ontario's interventions in capital markets as distortions that favor Canadian companies and hurt U.S. interests, it will demand compensation or retaliate.

One example of how the Conservative government used CUFTA to avoid bringing in new regulations that hinder corporate activity involved the advertising practices of transnationals that make baby formulas. Officials from Health and Welfare Canada and the Department of Consumer and Corporate Affairs advised the Infant Feeding Action Coalition in the fall of 1991 that the Canadian government could not bring in legislation to comply with the World Health Organization's (WHO) code protecting breast milk and breast feeding from the aggressive corporate advertising of infant formula. The reason was that the WHO code was "superseded by the free trade agreement" (Infant Feeding Action Coalition, 1991, pp. 1-2). The code was perceived to be a restriction of corporate rights under CUFTA.

A VICE

CUFTA has helped to advance the neoconservative agenda by operating as a vice. Many preexisting regulations and other practices that have been seen as barriers to (or derogations from) the basic principles of the deal—"the free and unimpeded functioning of the market"—were grandfathered. However, every subsequent action by the Mulroney government to unilaterally deregulate or privatize turns the vice and reduces the policy space available to a future government, preventing it from reimposing these regulations and other practices, should it so desire. Even if such a measure by a future government did not directly violate CUFTA, it would be very expensive to implement. Thus, it would be extremely difficult, if not impossible, to unscrew or reverse the direction of the vice.

Examples of this squeeze play included the privatization of Air Canada and Petro Canada; the deregulation of the trucking industry and financial institutions; the removal of transportation subsidies for moving grain through eastern ports; the withdrawal of legislation on film distribution; the deregulation of National Energy Board power to apply domestic supply tests as a condition of granting gas export licenses; the removal of foreign ownership restrictions in the book publishing and oil industries; and the deregulation of the telecommunications industry.

A WHIPSAW

The United States has used CUFTA in tandem with GATT as a whipsaw to further weaken or eliminate interventionist Canadian policies such as supply management and differential pricing of export or imports in relation to domestic goods. It is significant that, although the Conservative government has protested U.S actions, its complaints have been weak and ring hollow, reflecting its own ideological aversion to these policies.

Prominent examples of this whipsaw effect involved the United States getting GATT rulings declaring illegal (1) British Columbia's domestic fish processing laws; (2) federal import quotas on processed food products, ice cream, and yogurt; and (3) discriminatory sales and distribution practices against U.S. beer imports. With respect to the first, Canada could have, under GATT, brought in another measure, an export tax that would have achieved the same effect of safeguarding the B.C. processing industry. However, export taxes are illegal under CUFTA.

In the second case, CUFTA removed tariffs on all imports, including processed dairy products, ice cream, and yogurt. Tariffs were important tools, along with milk import quotas, for implementing supply management in the dairy sector. The government then transferred these products to its import control list, but GATT ruled, following a U.S. complaint, that the Canadian government could only put such quotas on basic milk and not on processed products.

Farmers, fishers, food processing workers, many small and medium-sized businesses, and communities were all hurt by this deregulation. Only corporations that have the resources to relocate production to "low-cost" areas and ship back into Canada will benefit.

In the third case, involving beer, discriminatory practices against U.S. beer imports were not subject to the terms of CUFTA (Article 1204). Presumably, the Canadian government paid a price in the negotiations to secure this exemption. Nevertheless, the United States ignored this commitment and brought a complaint to GATT on a variety of alleged discriminatory practices which, as expected, declared some to be illegal. The U.S. administration subsequently declared its intention to unilaterally retaliate if Canada did not quickly end these practices, despite Canada's having agreed with GATT on a timetable to comply with the ruling. GATT had ruled the same way in 1988 on a European complaint against Canadian wine and beer pricing and distribution regulations. Then, the federal government responded by undertaking to comply with the ruling once it had secured a deal with the provinces on international trade practices.

A final example involved Canada's intellectual property laws. In the GATT Uruguay Round negotiations, it was revealed that provisions extending the period of monopoly patent protection for transnational pharmaceutical corporations' new drugs by 10 to 20 years were on the table. This would further weaken the Canadian system of compulsory licensing, which has saved Canadian consumers hundreds of millions of dollars a year in drug costs.[4] Strengthening corporate monopoly rights was very much in line with the Mulroney government's own policy. Trade Minister Wilson announced in mid-January 1992 that his government would accept the GATT proposal for extending patent protection and, without waiting a final agreement, introduced amending legislation in Parliament. Few would disagree that a law previously passed in 1987 (Bill C-22) to extend the monopoly protection period from four to ten years was one of the side deals that accompanied the signing of CUFTA. What the government did not admit was that this issue was also on the NAFTA bargaining table. The NAFTA intellectual property chapter goes further than GATT in eliminating Canada's compulsory licensing system; and no future government will be able to reintroduce it.

A LEVER

Finally, CUFTA has served the Conservative government and its big-business allies well as an economic and psychological lever to facilitate and hasten the restructuring of the Canadian economy.

The logic of Canadian-based business arguing that it now has to compete on a level playing field has become very compelling. So, too, given the increased mobility of capital, have been the threats to leave. This remains a central aspect of CUFTA's importance as a lever advancing the neoconservative transformation of Canada.

To adjust to this new reality, governments have been under pressure to eliminate many features that make the Canadian economy distinctive. Aligning cost and regulatory structures has meant weakening unions and forcing down wages, social and labor standards, environmental standards, corporate taxes, and social program spending. The effect of this leveling on the political cohesion of Canada was foretold by political scientist Donald Smiley: "The bonds of Canadian nationhood are primarily in the sphere of government and in activities decisively shaped by government. Thus policy harmonization inherent in the FTA challenges Canadian distinctiveness in a very direct way" (Smiley, 1988, p. 445).

In its early years, the Mulroney government moved haltingly to implement its agenda and was forced under public pressure to back down on actions such as pension deindexation and unemployment insurance cuts. It was forced to move slowly and surreptitiously. The Tories had to go to great lengths during the 1988 election campaign to assure the population that social programs would not be weakened under free trade.

However, after the election, the Conservative government moved quickly and aggressively. Within months, old age security, family allowance, and unemployment insurance were all on the chopping block. The Conservative government broke its agreement on provincial cost-sharing for the Canada Assistance Program (welfare) by freezing transfer payments to Ontario,

British Columbia, and Alberta, where half of Canada's poor are located, even as it was forcing more people onto the welfare rolls through changes to unemployment insurance and through repressive monetary policy.

The cutbacks in federal transfers to the provinces for postsecondary education and health care begun in 1986 were greatly accelerated. The Canadian Labour Congress estimated that by 1994 they will have drained an estimated C$22 billion from the health care system and that by the year 2000 federal cash transfers to the provinces will have dropped to close to zero.[5]

Forcing up the Canadian dollar, beginning in 1988, through a high-interest rate policy was a central part of the government's drive to accelerate the harmonization and restructuring process CUFTA had cast in stone. There is a circumstantial case for arguing that a commitment by the Canadian government to raise the dollar exchange rate was likely a part of the free trade package (Barlow and Campbell, 1991). Whether this was imposed by the United States on the Conservative government or whether it was seen, with CUFTA in place, as a necessary companion measure to reinforce the integration of the two economies, the policy was deliberate. And since it was deliberate, its effects were anticipated in advance of the deal's implementation.

It is useful to recall that in 1986, when the Economic Council came out in favor of the government's free trade initiative, it presented a worst-case scenario in which, without a free trade deal, a protectionist U.S. Congress imposed a 20 percent surtax on imports from Canada, destroying 520,000 Canadian jobs over nine years (Economic Council of Canada, 1986). Between the time the Council made this prediction and June 1991, the dollar rose over 20 percent (the equivalent of not only a surtax on Canadian exporters but, in addition, a 20 percent subsidy for U.S. exporters), and there was a corresponding destruction of jobs.

It is also useful to recall that the rise in the exchange rate was completely the opposite of what free trade proponents said would happen to the dollar if wages and taxes got out of line as economic integration proceeded.

The high-interest, high exchange rate policy, which was sold to Canadians as being necessary to fight inflation, has been, more accurately, a policy of wage compression. High interest rates and consumer taxes such as the Goods and Services Tax were much more inflationary than was pressure from wages, which were constantly fighting a losing battle to catch up. But even though real wages of Canadian workers in the 1980s lost more ground to productivity, U.S. wages lost even more ground; and, therefore, Canadian wages had to be further disciplined and harmonized in the new free trade environment. The rise in the exchange rates greatly increased unit labor costs relative to those in the United

States, accentuating the "urgency" to cut Canadian wages, which as a result are now higher across the board than their U.S. counterparts.

The policy is having its intended effect on wages by producing one of the worst economic crises in the industrial world. As Wood Gundy economist Jeff Rubin put it: "The high dollar is a very powerful impetus for cost discipline . . . Without it, wage settlements wouldn't be slipping to 3% in 1991 from 6% last year" (Ip, 1991). The anxiety caused by the threat of job loss and exacerbated by a weakened social safety net has curbed wage demands. In the federal public sector, there was a blunter approach to wage compression: a legislated wage freeze.

Monetary policy has also been a key tool to create the sense of "urgency" to cut social and other government spending under the guise of reducing the deficit. A Statistics Canada (1991) study exposed the myth, assiduously cultivated by the federal government and big business, that "rampant social spending" was responsible for the federal debt and deficit crisis. In fact, for the last five years, the government has run operating budget *surpluses,* with revenue regularly exceeding federal program spending by C$10-12 billion to partially offset the roughly C$40 billion yearly outlay in interest payments on its more than C$400 billion debt.

All the while, the government maintained the fiction that it could not lower interest payments and cut billions from the deficit; that it could not eliminate the billions of dollars in corporate tax subsidies; and that it could not finance its deficit by returning to a policy of creating a greater proportion of new money itself through the Bank of Canada (rather than letting private financial institutions do it exclusively), thereby breaking the cycle of increasing government debt in order to pay interest on its old debt.[6]

PRODUCTION SHIFTS

A striking dimension of corporate restructuring in the new continental market has been the exodus of Canadian jobs and production, as companies, both Canadian-owned and U.S.-owned, have relocated to the United States, particularly to the southern states and the Mexican *maquiladora* strip, to take advantage of lower wages, lower taxes, weaker and unenforced labor and environmental laws, and so on.

One of the ways the U.S. Sunbelt states have kept wages and standards low was through "right to work" laws. These laws permit workers to opt out of certified unions and not pay dues, while requiring the unions to represent them at the bargaining table. This incentive to "free riding" has undermined the collective bargaining process to the extent that unionization rates have dropped below 5 percent in some states. Tennessee business recruiter Alf Barnette typified the "employer friendly" climate in large parts of the new free trade level playing field: "We don't care if you build bombs in our towns; just don't bring a union" (McNish, 1991).

Jim Stanford (1991) observed that right-to-work laws are deliberate arbitrary restrictions on labor practices that have had the effect of suppressing or subsidizing the wage costs of manufacturers (paid for involuntarily by the workers) by $1.45 per hour. Stanford calculated that, for a group of nine such states, this amounted to a subsidy to manufacturers of some $10 billion a year, or 15 percent of their total labor costs.

Further south is the *maquiladora* strip, the Mexican manufacturing export processing zone. Besides its location on the doorstep of the U.S. market, the most powerful magnet has been rock-bottom wages. Averaging between 60 and 70 cents an hour, these wages have been achieved and maintained in the last decade with the assistance of an imploding currency and an authoritarian government that smothered political opposition and suppressed independent labor movements.

The *maquiladora* zone remains populated almost entirely by transnational corporations (mainly U.S.-owned), many of whose export plants contain state-of-the-art equipment and processes allowing high levels of labor productivity. As business guru Peter Drucker said, "It takes three years at the most for a maquila to attain the labor productivity of a well-run U.S. or Japanese plant" (Drucker, 1987). The low-wage-high-productivity mix has given the corporations producing there an enormous windfall profit and an enormous incentive to relocate production. The Mexican-American Chamber of Commerce has estimated the average cost advantage of a *maquiladora* plant over its U.S. counterpart at $13 per worker per hour. This amounted to a collective windfall in 1990 of $15-20 billion for the 2,000 plants located in the *maquiladora* zone. Nothing remotely like this exists in the European Community, with which NAFTA proponents have constantly made comparisons. Differences in wages throughout the community are matched more or less evenly by differences in productivity that nullify the competitive advantage for corporations that might otherwise seek out cheaper labor.

EMPLOYMENT EFFECTS

In the early years after CUFTA was implemented, the destruction of jobs was the most visible manifestation of the restructuring of the Canadian economy. To find a period of greater collapse of manufacturing employment one has to go back to the Great Depression, where, beginning in 1929, employment fell 29.7 percent before bottoming out in 1933 (Statistics Canada, 1983). The net destruction of manufacturing jobs was at 26 percent of the manufacturing work force as of March 1992. A number of subsectors, including food and beverages, leather, textiles, clothing, printing and publishing, and chemicals, have already surpassed Depression levels of job loss.

According to Statistics Canada (1989, 1992), between June 1989 and March 1992 there was a net loss of 511,000 jobs (Table 6.1).[7] Manufacturing now employs only 15 percent of the total Canadian labor force, likely the lowest level in the industrial world.

For free trade observers, it was important to note that over 150,000 of these jobs disappeared before the formal onset of the so-called recession in April 1990. The connection between free trade and manufacturing job loss became apparent when it is considered that between 1981 and 1988 manufacturing employment overall remained constant, with some sectors declining and others growing. There was a drop of 270,000 jobs (17.5 percent) in the 1981-82 recession, but most of those jobs returned. From June 1989 to March 1992, all of the major manufacturing subsectors have experienced large declines in employment, with all but one shrinking by more than 15 percent.

Another clue that this employment crisis involved a free trade-driven restructuring superimposed on a business cycle downturn could be found in the Ontario government figures on plant closures. Although no other governments compiled such comprehensive statistics, Ontario has been the manufacturing heartland of Canada, and it can safely be assumed that processes similar to that occurring in Ontario were going on in other manufacturing centers. In 1981-82, 22 percent of workers who lost their jobs did so because of permanent plant closures. During the period 1989-92, 65 percent of lost jobs were due to permanent plant closures (Laughren, 1991, p. 3).

A third important way to indicate that the transformation of the Canadian economy cannot be dismissed as merely the result of "recession" is to compare manufacturing job losses in Canada with losses experienced in the U.S. economy. During roughly the same period, June 1989 to January 1992 (Table 6.1), the U.S. economy lost 1,096,000 manufacturing jobs net, or 5.7 percent of the manufacturing work force—only about one-fifth of the decline in the Canadian manufacturing sector. Major divergence is reflected in all the major manufacturing subsectors.

Other sectors of the Canadian economy have also experienced sharp declines. Goods-producing industries other than manufacturing (construction, mining, forestry) have lost 315,000 jobs (32 percent); and services, where most Canadians are employed, have lost 591,000 jobs (8 percent).

Table 6.1
**Changes in Manufacturing Employment:
Canada and United States[*] June 1989–March 1992**

	CANADA (%)		UNITED STATES (%)	
	change %	change in thousands	change %	change in thousands
Total Manufacturing	-26	-511	-5.7	-1,096
Food	-15	-65	+1.4	+23
Rubber & Plastics	-36	-31	-2.2	-19
Leather	-39	-7	-11.8	-16
Textiles	-32	-21	-6.9	-50
Apparel	-33	-30	-2.5	-27
Wood Products	-37	-45	-7.0	-56
Furniture & Fixtures	-39	-26	-8.3	-43
Paper & Allied	-19	-25	-1.0	-7
Printing & Publishing	-20	-30	-2.9	-46
Primary Metal	-24	-25	-8.0	-62
Fabricated Metal Products	-26	-43	-6.1	-88
Machinery & Equipment	-28	-30	-8.9	-189
Transportation Equipment	-18	-39	-10.6	-216
Electrical/Electronic	-24	-31	-10.0	-174
Petroleum & Coal Products	+1.7	+1	0.0	0
Chemicals	-11	-17	+1.8	+19

Source: Statistics Canada, *Employment Earnings and Hours;* U.S. Department of Labor, *Monthly Labor Review.*

[*]U.S. Figures as of January 1992.

CONCLUSION

If the free trade agreement is fulfilling its intended role in reshaping Canada in accordance with neoconservative ideology, then we have to ask: What kind of country are we left with in the wake of free trade and related policies?

Canada, at the end of 1992, has been deteriorating at a pace unforeseen even by the majority of critics. The national economy has broken down into regions increasingly disconnected from one another as they integrate along a north-south axis. The national transportation and communications infrastructure—the steel, asphalt, fiber optic, and aerial ribbons that tie us together—are weakening. The cultural pathways that link us are under threat. The system of East-West financial transfers that gives expression to our social values of community and sharing is shrinking. Income inequalities between regions and groups are widening at an accelerating pace.

The Canadian federation is moving in the direction of a major political fracture. And the alliance of big business and right-wing political forces that brought us free trade is now steering us toward a Canada where the overriding mandate of the federal government is to ensure competitiveness and where provinces vie with one another to offer corporations the most attractive conditions.

In a very short period of time, Canadians have sadly discovered a much different reality from the Mulroney government's promise of a new dawn of free trade–led prosperity, regional harmony, and national reconciliation.

NOTES

1. The most recent comes from Pauly (1991), who estimates that CUFTA has had a small but positive effect on a number of economic variables.
2. Reprinted in part in *Proceso* (758), (13 May 1991), p. 7.
3. It is important to note as well that if CUFTA had been in place in the 1960s, these same provisions and the same corporate pressure would probably have prevented Canada from bringing in its publicly funded and administered medical insurance.
4. See Lexchin (1992). Lexchin cites the figure of C$211 million of saving in 1983 calculated by the Eastman Commission. It has no doubt risen significantly since then. The Generic Drug Manufacturers claim that their products save the Canadian health care system C$1 billion per year. See editorial "Ottawa surrenders on drug patents." (1992, May 11). *Toronto Star.*
5. Canadian Labour Congress. (1991, Marc 18). Federal budget 1990-91. *Fact Sheets.* Ottawa. Estimates of federal transfer phase-out by groups like the Cana-

dian Association of University Teachers, the Canadian Health Coalition and the National Council on Welfare, while not identical, converge around this date.

6. The Bank of Canada currently creates about 2 percent of additions to the money supply; the rest is done by the private banks. When the Bank of Canada was created, it helped to stimulate recovery in 1935-39 by producing 46 percent of all new money and continued this trend throughout World War II. See Hotson (1991, pp. 8-10).

7. It is assumed that the effects of free trade-driven economic restructuring began to be reflected in the employment statistics after a six-month lag.

REFERENCES

Barlow, M. (1992). "The Road Back." In J. Sinclair (ed.), *Crossing the Line: Canada and Free Trade with Mexico.* Vancouver: New Star.

Barlow, M. and Campbell B. (1991). *Take Back the Nation.* Toronto: Key Porter.

Drucker, P. (22 April 1987). "The Rise and Fall of the Blue Collar Worker." *Wall Street Journal,* p. 32.

Economic Council of Canada. (1986). *Annual Report.* Ottawa: Ministry of Supply and Services, Canada.

Government of Canada. (September 1991a). *Shaping Canada's Future Together, Proposals.* Ottawa: Supply & Services, Canada.

Government of Canada. (September 1991b). *Economic Union, Partnership for Prosperity.* Ottawa: Supply & Services, Canada.

Hotson, J. (November 1991). "Big Lies from Big Brother." *Policy Options,* 12 (10), 8-10.

Infant Feeding Action Coalition. (Fall 1991). *Newsletter.* (Available from Infant Feeding Action Coalition, 10 Trinity Square, Toronto, Canada, M5G 181).

Insurance Week, 5 (32). (16 August 1991). (Available at P.O. Box 665Y, McLean, Virginia, 22106, U.S.A.).

Ip, G. (7 October 1991). "Wage Freeze in Competitive Big Chill." *Financial Post,* p. 3.

Laughren, F., Treasurer of Ontario. (3-5 May 1991). Speech to conference, *Solidarity Not Competition: Canada-U.S.-Mexico Free Trade.* Toronto: Metro Toronto Labour Council and Common Frontiers.

Lexchin, J. (January 1991). *Pharmaceuticals, Patents and Politics: Canada and Bill C-22.* Ottawa: Canadian Centre for Policy Alternatives.

McNish, J. (2 July 1991). "Throng of Firms Move to U.S. to Slash Costs." *Globe & Mail,* p. B1.

Pauly, P. (Fall 1991). "Macroeconomic Effects of the Canada-U.S. Free Trade Agreement: An Interim Assessment." Unpublished paper. University of Toronto: Institute for Quantitative Analysis.

Ritchie, G. (December 1991). *Free Trade: Year Three, Put to the Test.* (Available from Strategico Inc, Ottawa).

Smiley, D. (1988). "A Note on Canadian-American Free Trade and Canadian Policy Autonomy." In M. Gold and D. Leyton-Brown (eds.), *The Canada-U.S. Free Trade Agreement.* Toronto: Carswell.

Statistics Canada. (June 1991). The Growth of the Federal Debt 1975-90. *Canadian Economic Observer.* Ottawa: Supply & Services, Canada [Catalogue No. 11-010].

Statistics Canada. (1983). *Historical Statistics of Canada.* Ottawa: Supply & Services, Canada.

Statistics Canada. (1989 and 1992). *Survey of Establishments.* Ottawa: Supply & Services, Canada.

Van Alphen, T. (21 June 1991). "Conrad Black to Shun an NDP-led Ontario." *Toronto Star.*

Chapter 7

The Economics of Free Trade in Canada

Ricardo Grinspun

Proponents of a North American Free Trade Agreement (NAFTA) encompassing Canada, Mexico, and the United States forecast significant economic gains for each of the countries involved. This paper argues that, on the contrary, there is a strong economic case against NAFTA. There are significant weaknesses in the economic argument put forward by proponents of NAFTA. Aggregate economic gains are likely to be smaller than proclaimed, and various economic costs of the agreement are likely to be larger. The argument will be sketched mainly from the Canadian standpoint, but it also has important lessons for other small economies considering a free trade arrangement with the United States.

THE CANADIAN EXPERIENCE UNDER FREE TRADE

The Canada-U.S. Free Trade Agreement (CUFTA) was implemented beginning January 1989. A central Canadian objective in the CUFTA negotiations was to secure access to the U.S. market, thus promoting the development of Canada's natural resource industries, as well as a modern, technologically advanced, export-oriented manufacturing sector. CUFTA was to strengthen the incentives for outward-oriented growth by providing Canadian exporters with certain and stable access to their major export market, as well as with cheaper domestic and imported inputs. The economy would benefit from efficiency gains due to increased import competition and the spin-offs of a growing, dynamic export sector (Macdonald Report, 1985; Whalley, 1985).

Securing access to export markets, however, requires the elimination of both tariff and nontariff obstacles to trade. CUFTA provides for a gradual ten-year phaseout of bilateral tariffs. Although total elimination of tariffs between the two countries may seem an impressive outcome, the low level of tariffs before CUFTA diminishes the aggregate economic gains from their elimination. About 71 percent of Canadian exports to the United States entered duty free in 1986; the rest paid an average tariff of 3.3 percent (Bordé and Cross, 1989, p. 3.1). This implies that, except for a few protected sectors, the economic effects of tariff liberalization for Canadian exporters are likely to be minor.[1] Certainly, in some export sectors in Canada, like resource-based products that suffered from escalating U.S. tariffs, the effect may be beneficial—in this case, it may encourage domestic processing of raw materials. However, in those sectors where Canadian tariffs are highly protective, like textiles and furniture, the effects of tariff elimination are very costly in terms of Canadian employment.[2]

The reality of nontariff barriers is quite different. Before CUFTA, Canadian exporters to the United States faced ongoing harassment by border restrictions, bureaucratic red tape, technical and safety standards, "voluntary" restraint agreements and export surcharges, procurement restrictions, and increasingly active use of U.S. trade-remedy laws to impose countervailing and antidumping duties as well as safeguard measures (Lazar, 1981). The economic cost for Canada did not end with existing protective measures. In addition, the prospect of future protectionist measures in the United States—both in terms of new legislation and more intensive use of existing legislation—hampered investment, production, and employment in export-oriented industry (Macdonald Report, 1985).

CUFTA disappointed Canadians in terms of the limited liberalization obtained in the area of nontariff barriers. Certainly, "secure access to the U.S. market" was not obtained in this critical area.[3] Little was achieved in terms of access to U.S. government procurement—a key objective of the Canadian negotiators (Macdonald, 1987). Many protectionist practices by both sides were grandfathered. These seem to have greater negative effects on the Canadian economy than on the U.S. economy, because of the asymmetric relation between the two. Unable to agree on the contentious issues of countervailing and antidumping duties, the negotiators set up a new bilateral dispute-settlement mechanism, one that is still bound by the national laws of each country. This mechanism is considered by some as a gain for Canada, but it did not relieve Canada from ongoing application of U.S. trade-remedy laws. Many Canadians are disappointed by the small relief obtained from what is perceived to be a growing protectionist sentiment in the United

Table 7.1
Canada-U.S. Interest Rates and Exchange Rate, 1988-1991

| Year | Central Bank Discount Rate (Annual Average, %) | | | US$ per C$ |
	Canada	U.S.	Difference Canada-U.S.	
1988	9.69	6.21	3.48	0.81
1989	12.29	6.96	5.33	0.84
1990	13.04	6.96	6.08	0.86
1991	9.03	5.42	3.61	0.87

Source: Author, with data from Statistics Canada, *Canadian Economic Observer*, various issues.

States.[4] It is significant that Canada was not exempted from the provisions of the Omnibus Trade and Competitiveness Act, a protectionist bill that Congress passed in 1988—during the ratification of CUFTA.

The macroeconomic environment is an important determinant of the short-term effects of any new trading arrangement. In the late 1980s and early 1990s, macroeconomic policy in Canada promoted high real interest rates,[5] a large differential between Canadian and U.S. interest rates, and an appreciation of the Canadian dollar vis-à-vis the U.S. dollar (see table 7.1). Of particular significance were the tight monetary policies implemented by the Bank of Canada since 1986. These policies contributed to the increase in interest rates and the relative overvaluation of the Canadian dollar. As table 7.1 suggests, the cross-border differential in interest rates (much larger than the typical postwar differential of about two percent) encouraged capital inflows into Canada, creating demand for the Canadian dollar and propping up its value. Not surprisingly, the effect was a large and growing surplus in the capital account of the balance of payments. Monetary policies and nominal interest rates eased during 1991 and 1992, likely as a result of the deep and protracted recession, prompting a fall in nominal interest rates and in the value of the Canadian dollar to 80 cents (in U.S. currency) in October.

The anti-inflationary policy of the Bank of Canada, implemented concurrently with the introduction of the Goods and Services Tax (GST) in January 1991, made the recession in Canada deeper and longer than it was in the United States. Figure 7.1 shows the sharp downturn in manufacturing gross domestic product (GDP) and employment starting in 1989, at about the same

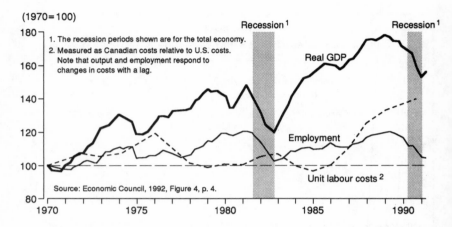

Figure 7.1 Manufacturing employment, real GDP, and relative unit labor costs, Canada, 1970-91.

time that CUFTA was implemented. In contrast to the 1982-83 recession, the manufacturing sector went into recession much earlier than the rest of the economy, and much deeper. During the years 1991 and 1992—not shown in Figure 7.1—the recession worsened: manufacturing production dropped another 6.7 percent in 1991 and stayed flat during early 1992. Capacity utilization in the manufacturing sector in early 1992—after three full years of recessionary conditions—was still a dismal 72.4 percent, hardly an incentive for new productive investment. Manufacturing employment during June 1992 was 1,632,251 persons, down from 2,048,990 during January 1989—a massive loss of 416,739 jobs.[6] These figures do not include the large shift from full-time to part-time employment during this period.

Recessionary conditions, together with the exchange rate imbalance, combined to lower the international competitiveness of Canadian industry, seriously hampering the investment in export-oriented sectors that was the cornerstone of CUFTA (Daly, 1990). Since labor costs are a main component of total costs of production, a key indicator of competitiveness is an index of domestic labor costs per unit of output relative to those of the competition in other countries. For export-oriented Canadian firms, this point of reference is unit labor costs of U.S. manufacturing. Figure 7.1 shows an index of unit labor costs in Canadian manufacturing relative to U.S. costs. This index depends on labor productivity and labor compensation—wages and sala- ries—in the two countries as well as on the exchange rate. The period since 1985 is characterized by a sharp rise in this index, indicating a loss of competitiveness by Canadian manufacturing and an exchange rate that is in disequilibrium. In simple terms, Canadian manufacturing is facing higher costs of production than U.S. manufacturing, placing Canadians at a competitive disadvantage.[7] Rao and Lemprière (1992, p. 5) show that the large appreciation of the Canadian dollar accounted for a significant part of the deterioration in relative costs between 1985 and 1990.

The appreciation of the Canadian dollar and trade liberalization intensified the Canadian propensity to spend money across the border, hurting the commercial and service sectors as well. Canadians—most of whom live a short distance from the border—flocked to the United States in ever larger numbers during the early 1990s to restock on everything from electronics to clothing and gasoline. These adverse conditions were seriously affecting the ability of Canadian firms to restructure in response to the demands from the new trading environment.

A major motivation for pursuing CUFTA was to reverse the productivity slowdown in Canadian manufacturing that occurred during the 1970s and 1980s. Canadian policymakers expected that the productivity gap with the United States would shrink significantly under the competitive pressures of a unified market (Baldwin and Gorecki, 1985). Productivity gains represent the basis for economic growth and higher standards of living for Canadians—one of the Canadian government's promises when it embarked on CUFTA (Government of Canada, 1988). Labor productivity has continued to increase during the years of CUFTA implementation, but only because of a drastic increase in the capital-labor ratio caused by shrinking employment. However, increased labor productivity has not translated into either a cost advantage or greater competitiveness:

> U.S. manufacturing unit labour costs in 1990 were about 26 per cent below Canadian costs, compared with a U.S. cost disadvantage of 3 per cent in 1985 . . . At no other time in the postwar period has the Canada-U.S. gap been so wide as in 1990. Moreover, the deterioration of Canada's cost position is pervasive across all . . . manufacturing industries (Rao and Lemprière, p. 4).[8]

Measures of total factor productivity (TFP) are more important since they indicate overall efficiency gains in production.[9] Indicators of TFP were heading *down* during 1989-91.[10] This indicates that, for the time being, the promised productivity gains were not being realized, in part due to the macroeconomic mishandling of the Canadian economy. The view that elimination of barriers to trade is enough to equalize productivity levels on both sides of the border is simplistic and fails to consider a host of other important factors that affect productivity (Lazar, 1981, chapter 4).

A key problem of free trade is that it restricts the ability of Canadian governments (at all levels) to carry out policies that make significant contributions to productivity gains and other legitimate goals—policies in areas like education, regional development, job training, research and development, technological deepening, and social and health programs. One must distinguish between the restrictive pressures applied on universal programs on the one side and targeted policies (i.e., policies targeted to a specific sector or region) on the other. The United States has challenged many of the *targeted* Canadian policies as "unfair" trade practices, since these policies may subsidize exports to the United States directly or indirectly. Canada is not protected adequately from these challenges—for example, on its regional development programs—since the question of subsidies and countervailing duties remained unresolved in both CUFTA and NAFTA (Sinclair, this volume).

Free trade also creates pressures that weaken Canadian *universal* policy programs, like unemployment insurance and social welfare. The mechanisms for these pressures are subtle and multiple; they derive not from liberalized trade per se but from liberalized capital flows and the institutional framework for free trade. The overall economic and political setting created by free trade favors neoconservative policies of deregulation and privatization and a stronger role for market forces. This setting promotes the erosion of universal welfare programs when the trading partners have lower tax rates and a less interventionist government, since capital will pressure for downward harmonization, threatening exit.[11] Also, the compensation clauses in CUFTA and NAFTA preclude the establishment of new universal programs—it is likely that Canada could not establish in the free trade era its exemplary socialized health care system, if it did not already exist (Cohen, 1988, pp. 146-7). The increased mobility of capital with the United States and Mexico, promoted by free trade, creates strong pressures for harmonization of public policies across the border (see chapters by Grinspun & Cameron and Campbell in this volume). In summary, neither CUFTA nor NAFTA recognizes that Canada needs to implement strong industrial and regional policies as well as social programs to achieve equitable and dynamic growth.

The restrictions on the Canadian government are stronger regarding export-enhancing policies. The free trade agreements make it practically impossible for the Canadian government to promote exports, either directly or indirectly. They also create pressures to redefine the role of government as noninterventionist. This is counterproductive to the stated goal of export-led growth, since countries that have achieved fast export-led growth usually have had a highly interventionist government that actively engages in export promotion (Gulati, 1992). The examples of Japan, the Asian newly industrializing countries (NICs), and Israel immediately come to mind.

Organized labor in Canada strongly opposes free trade. Labor spokespersons argue that CUFTA encourages the export of jobs to the United States and other countries—in particular from labor-intensive, low-skill Canadian industries. This prediction was being fulfilled during the early 1990s, encouraged by the overvalued dollar and the depressed state of the Canadian economy. Manufacturing was particularly hard-hit. The addition of a low-wage partner like Mexico to the free trade area would only worsen these concerns. Defenders of CUFTA argue that this restructuring of the Canadian economy would happen anyway, due to changes in the international economic scene. The truth probably lies somewhere in between: CUFTA has not caused, but it certainly has accelerated, the erosion of these labor-intensive industries. The economic and social cost is high, since many of the affected workers lack the skills to become integrated into more promising economic activities.

Free trade promoters envisioned a weakening of sectors that lack international competitiveness and a simultaneous growth of export-oriented sectors. Workers who lost their jobs in shrinking industries would shift, with adequate retraining, to newer ones. This vision has not materialized. In the manufacturing sector during the early 1990s, the first prediction (job losses) was being realized, but the second (job gains) was not, leading to a deep crisis in this sector. Free trade contributed to this crisis by liberalizing trade and capital flows without providing the perception of secure access to the U.S. market. The United States and Mexico continued to be preferred places for new investments in the North American market (except, perhaps, in resource-intensive investment). The lack of response of the Canadian government in terms of adjustment and retraining programs has worsened the situation.

A key aspect of free trade—its effects on capital flows—is often understated. The argument was made that as a trade liberalizing agreement, CUFTA had modest effects. The most significant effects of the agreement are the deregulation and liberalization of capital flows, foreign investment, and the activities of TNCs. From Canada's standpoint, NAFTA is another step in this wrong direction. The purpose of deregulating investment flows is to attract capital to dynamic export-oriented sectors, create jobs, and promote the import of technology as well as research and development operations.

The effects for now are quite different—perverse, even. Much foreign direct investment (FDI) seems to be going to the takeover of existing Canadian-owned firms, transforming them into subsidiaries of TNCs, rather than creating new productive capacity. Many of these subsidiaries are streamlining their operations—cutting costs, jobs, and production—and increasing their imports, as part of a continental rationalization of production in which Canada does not get the better part.[12] One cannot discern an upward trend in terms of the opening of new plants, implementation of new lines of production, investment projects, or technological innovation. One cannot point to newly emerging export-oriented industries.[13]

Supporters of CUFTA blame this negative situation on recessionary conditions; it should not be attributed, they say, to CUFTA.[14] Although this is partly true, it is wishful thinking to imagine that when macroeconomic conditions improve, all these worrying processes will reverse themselves. For example, if a new manufacturing plant is installed today in Tijuana or Buffalo instead of in Windsor, that decision will not be easily reversed in the future. In sharp contrast to the 1981-82 recession, most of the job losses in Canadian manufacturing in the 1990-92 recession were permanent, caused by plant closing.[15] The deep recession combined with the new trading and investment arrangements to cause a permanent structural change in Canadian manufacturing.[16] The change apparently included a permanent loss of jobs in the manufacturing sector, a restructuring of the economy toward part-time, low-paying service jobs and higher structural unemployment. The restructuring was driven by the lack of competitiveness of the manufacturing sector—in particular in import-competing and labor-intensive industries. Decisions on plant-closing and diversion of investment flows to other countries changed the shape of this sector. TNCs played a crucial role in this continental restructuring of manufacturing. Canada moved toward a new economic equilibrium characterized by a lower level of industrialization.

Proponents of CUFTA usually differentiated between the macroeconomic policies of the Canadian government and the trade policies involved in CUFTA. In their view, they expected to observe the benefits of CUFTA only in the longer term.[17] The short-term adjustment problems of the Canadian economy, they claim, were due to ill-advised macroeconomic policies that created unnecessarily high adjustment costs and worsened the recession (Doern and Tomlin, 1991, p. 292). The implicit—and likely misguided—belief underlying this view was that the economy had only one long-term equilibrium, which was independent of the macroeconomic policies applied in the short run. A more accurate view would have been that the macroeconomic imbalances, together with the dislocation caused by CUFTA and the TNC-led international restructuring of production, were likely to affect the economy adversely in the long run. The Canadian government, then, paid a large price to enter into CUFTA and, at the same time, applied macroeconomic policies that eroded the economic gains from the agreement.

Overall, Canada has not fared well during the first few years of free-trade implementation, and the prospects for the future are not much better. The large price Canada paid to enter into CUFTA included: accelerated dislocation of weak and protected sectors, with a powerful effect on employment and high social costs; likelihood of more concentration of industry in the hands of big, mainly U.S.-based TNCs; increased dependency on the United States, which restricts— sometimes in subtle ways—the Canadian government's ability to follow independent domestic policies; and downward pressures on social and environmental standards (see chapters by Campbell, Drache, Sinclair, and Shrybman in this volume). The free-trade gains are measured mainly in terms of improved—but not secure—access to the U.S. market. However, these gains were illusory during the first few years of implementation, since the appreciation of the Canadian dollar nullified the effect of lower tariffs. The hope for significant job creation through increased FDI is likely to be unfulfilled, due to diversion of physical investment to the United States, Mexico, and other lower cost countries, as well as the channeling of new capital to financial speculation. Canada has *not* become a more attractive place to develop new, strong, export-oriented industries. It is in this context that Canadian participation in NAFTA should be evaluated, since NAFTA, from the Canadian standpoint, constitutes an extension of CUFTA.

THE QUESTION OF LOW-WAGE MEXICAN LABOR

A key issue in NAFTA concerns the implications of joining low- and high-wage countries within one free trade area. Will the addition of a low-wage partner like Mexico to the free trade area hurt Canada and the United States? When presented with these arguments about low-wage labor, neoclassical economists often respond with classic tenets of international trade theory, which show how economies with different endowments and costs can benefit mutually from free trade (Krugman and Obstfeld, 1991, p. 22). The theory of comparative advantage, however, was developed in models with unrealistic assumptions (such as full employment and balanced trade). These propositions on the effects of free trade may fail in the presence of, say, large capital movements, exchange rate imbalances, market failure, unemployed resources, or significant intrafirm trade by TNCs.[18] Moreover, classical trade theory deals with patterns of trade, and has little to say regarding issues of economic growth.

The major economic effects of NAFTA will be on patterns of investment across sectors and between countries. Capital flows will determine these new patterns of investment, which in turn will affect the patterns of trade in goods and services. Will low-wage Mexican labor have a strong effect on capital flows? Organized labor in Canada and the United States has expressed this concern, fearing that capital moving south will not only shift jobs but also create pressures to lower wages and erode the labor contract in the larger economies. NAFTA is perceived as a frontal attack on unionized labor.

Some proponents of NAFTA have replied that capital will *not* move automatically toward places with low-wage labor (such as Mexico). Rather, production will be rationalized on a continental basis such that unit costs of production are minimized. Since low-wage labor has lower productivity, costs of production are not necessarily reduced when locating in an area of low-wage labor. This would mean that large losses of jobs in Canada and the United States are unlikely as a result of NAFTA (External Affairs and International Trade, 1990, p. 13).

This argument would be valid if the only reason for low wages in Mexico was lower labor productivity. However, other elements also contribute to low wages in Mexico: large labor surplus, historical cooptation of official workers' organizations by the state, and outright political repression of independent labor unions. The truth is, one can find world-class plants with high labor productivity in Mexican sectors such as the automotive sector (Shaiken, 1990). As an example, consider auto parts plants in the *maquiladora* sector and in Canada. One is likely to find plants in Canada where the productivity of labor is roughly the same as in Mexico, but where wages are five times higher than those in Mexico.[19] The conclusion is straightforward: Mexico has a large competitive advantage relative to Canada and the United States in production processes with a high unskilled labor content.[20] By definition, these are productive processes that involve many jobs, so we should therefore expect to see a significant number of unskilled jobs lost in Canada and the United States as economic integration proceeds.[21]

Certain nonwage costs in Mexico are also low—for example, occupational safety measures; improvement of working conditions; pollution control; and payroll taxes. The main problem seems to be the lack of enforcement of existing regulations. As long as this situation does not change, firms can expect to lower their costs significantly under these items if they move plants to Mexico. This asymmetry creates strong incentives for capital transfers when these costs are considerable (for highly polluting plants, for instance). The effects of these capital inflows are far from benign; for example, the Mexican environment—in particular in the northern border region—may become even more polluted.

The issue of low-wage labor is interesting in another respect: that of trade subsidies. Trade policy discussions in North America often focus on which economic policies constitute, or do not constitute, unfair subsidies to trade. The United States promotes a very broad definition of subsidies, which includes a series of government activities that at first glance are not even linked to trade. There is, however, a glaring exception: government policies that promote lower wages are not considered an unfair trade practice. Many Mexican policies, such as the violent repression of strikes and independent trade unions, fall under this category—and they are not challenged by the United States. If anything, NAFTA serves as a shield for the authoritarian character of the Salinas regime (Aguilar Zinser, this volume).

A similar argument holds for policies that promote environmental degradation or fast elimination of renewable or nonrenewable resources. After all, one can produce and export more cheaply than one's competitor if one can pay lower wages and does not need to spend as much on occupational safety, pollution control, or conservation of resources. The energy chapter in CUFTA is a relevant example. Canada is forced to sell oil to the United States from limited low-cost Canadian sources at a price lower than the real opportunity cost—the cost of extraction from higher-cost sources, such as the new Hibernia project (Dillon, this volume). This represents a subsidy to exports to the United States, but in this case the United States does not mind. It also goes against a reasonable conservation policy for a nonrenewable Canadian resource. It is very difficult to find a logic in this distinction between allowable and unallowable government policies, except the logic of adapting the definition of subsidies to the needs of the U.S. government and U.S.-based TNCs. This is a clear example of the trade agreement's reflecting the interests of those TNCs. One could ask, though, why the interests of trade unions, popular organizations, and environmental NGOs can not be represented as well in these agreements.

THE HUB-AND-SPOKE ARGUMENT

Various arguments were raised for and against Canadian participation in NAFTA negotiations. An often-quoted argument in favor of participating was the "hub-and-spoke" model.[22] Canada's absence from the negotiating table, according to this argument, would pave the way for a separate Mexican-U.S. bilateral free trade agreement and, later, for other bilateral agreements between the United States and other countries. This would place Mexico and Canada at a disadvantage in terms of new investment guided to the North American market. There would be significant investment diversion from the "spokes" (Canada and Mexico) to the "hub" (United States), since only plants established in the hub would have free access to all the markets in North America and beyond.

This argument is based on a distorted representation of firm decision making. Excessive weight is given to one aspect of the locational decision for a new manufacturing plant—market access to as many countries as possible. A host of other factors receive no consideration. Consider the decision to build a new export-oriented plant in Canada. Lack of tariff-free access to the Mexican market from Canada—which is the case when Canada and Mexico are spokes—may be a consideration for a particular plant that has strong sales potential in Mexico. However, given the relatively small size of the Mexican market, and the low tariffs in that country, in most cases this will not be a key consideration. Note that NAFTA would extend the tariff-free export markets for Canadian goods only marginally beyond what is defined by CUFTA, since the Mexican market is only about 3 percent as large as the U.S. market.

Other considerations are likely to play a stronger role in the investment decision in the Canadian export sector. A key one is the degree of access to the U.S. market—the main export market for Canada. The claim has been made that CUFTA and NAFTA eliminate tariffs but do not secure access due to nontariff barriers, legal harassment, and exchange rate imbalances. Another consideration in the investment decision is that of relative costs of production—which, as seen above, placed Canada at a large disadvantage during the relevant period, in part as a result of the dollar appreciation. Furthermore, there are other considerations, like availability of educated work force and adequate infrastructure; government assistance; and a favorable, growing domestic market. The ability of the Canadian government to affect the investment decision positively through all these other channels will likely be hampered by entrance into NAFTA, as argued in this and other chapters of this volume.

Eden and Molot (1992) have argued that a hub-and-spoke relationship already exists in terms of trade and investment patterns in North America even without the implementation of NAFTA. The bilateral trade and investment links between Canada and the United States, as well as between the latter and Mexico, are major, whereas those between Mexico and Canada are very small.

A trilateral agreement will not eliminate the hub-and-spoke phenomenon, as had been unrealistically suggested earlier by Wonnacott (1990) and Lipsey (1990). Although formally a trilateral agreement, the main substance of NAFTA is the restructuring of the bilateral relation between each of the spokes and the United States. This is clear in most NAFTA chapters. The chapter on intellectual property rights shapes the regulatory and legal framework in each spoke to increase the dominance of technologically advanced, U.S.-based TNCs. The provisions on petroleum open the Mexican market to U.S and Canadian investment. In practice, the vast majority of investment is likely to come from the United States (similarly, most of the Canadian oil industry is U.S.-owned). In the automobile sector, one is likely to witness increased Canada-Mexico trade, but only as part of a continentalized industry whose hub is made up of the Big Three U.S. auto corporations.

Lipsey (1992, p. 108) has suggested a system of *plurilateral regionalism* as a better alternative than the hub-and-spoke model. He believes that NAFTA will initiate the creation of such a system:

> What I call plurilateral regionalism refers to agreements . . . in which *each* member has the same privileges and obligations as all the other members. Whereas hub-and-spoke is a model of U.S. hegemony over the Americas, plurilateral regionalism is a model of equals. All members have the same access to each other's market, all bargain together, and all are free to make common cause with others of likemindedness in common trade negotiations.

It is true that one outcome of NAFTA implementation will be increased economic contact between Mexico and Canada. For example, in specific areas such as banking and telecommunications, where Canada has large corporations, one is likely to observe a significant flow of investment from Canada to Mexico. Certainly, there will be more shift of Canadian export platforms to Mexico attracted by the inexpensive labor force. Bilateral commodity trade will grow, although it is unlikely to become very important for either country.

So does NAFTA correspond to a system of plurilateral regionalism? Drache (this volume) argues that one must distinguish between the legal text of an agreement and its economic substance. Although the text of the NAFTA provides the same legal position to each of the three countries, even a superficial economic and political analysis shows the unequal status of the three partners. Plurilateral regionalism may be a nice idea, but it has little backing in the current hemispheric reality, and in particular in NAFTA. The trilateral agreement consolidates U.S. hegemony through a disguised hub-and-spoke model. As argued earlier, a key element in this new hegemonic model is the dominant role that TNCs play in shaping the new continental relations.

A key consideration involves the additional costs of NAFTA, beyond those of CUFTA, for Canada. It is clear that the United States intended to extract from Canada some of the concessions that it could not obtain in the CUFTA negotiations. An important one was an agreement on intellectual property rights (which will imply, among other effects, higher prices for pharmaceutical products in Canada). The NAFTA extends the rules of origin for duty-free trade to include a low-wage partner like Mexico, and this will hurt labor-intensive operations in Canada. At the same time, NAFTA moves one step further in restricting the ability of governments to implement economic, social, and environmental policies. These restrictions appear in multiple ways in the NAFTA, through measures such as liberalization of investment rules, national treatment clauses, and harmonization of phytosanitary and other standards. Similarly, it is likely that NAFTA will create further restrictions on Canadian macroeconomic policies.

Did Canada have the option of not participating in NAFTA? Supporters argued, following the logic of the hub-and-spoke model, that lack of participation would mean the signing of a bilateral free trade agreement between Mexico and the United States. This would have created significant diversion of investment to the United States. The cause would be the lack of tariff-free trade between Canada and Mexico, which would make the United States a preferable investment site. However, if this would ever become a serious problem—which is unlikely—Canada and Mexico could always sign a bilateral trade agreement to eliminate those tariffs. A series of bilateral arrangements may impose higher transaction costs than one multilateral arrangement, but it could avoid reopening CUFTA—which is, in fact, what Canada faced in the NAFTA negotiations—under very unfavorable conditions for Canada.

CONCLUSION

Whether motivated by naiveté or by political advocacy, the optimistic assessments regarding the impact of free trade on Canada find little support in recent economic trends. This chapter has analyzed the serious economic problems that Canada is facing under CUFTA and has argued that these are likely to worsen under NAFTA. The manufacturing sector in Canada is undergoing massive restructuring with a large economic and social cost. However, this restructuring is not, at this stage, following the beneficial pattern that some had expected. Manufacturing employment has fallen dramatically. The productivity gap with the United States has widened, while Canadian enterprises face a large cost disadvantage. Canada has *not* become a more attractive place to invest, and large inflows of capital were absorbed to a large degree in the financial sphere. The deficit in the current account of the balance of payments has significantly widened. Of particular concern is the movement toward a new economic equilibrium characterized by a lower level of industrialization, wages, and benefits.

Canada is facing a serious disadvantage in its ability to attract export-oriented investment, in particular in the manufacturing sector. This disadvantage has nothing to do with the hub-and-spoke effect, discussed earlier. Mistaken trade and macroeconomic policies have caused a serious loss of competitiveness in Canada's export sector. The wholesale relocation of plants to the south and southwest of the United States during 1991-92, as well as to Mexico, is a worrying symptom of this malaise. The decision by Canada to participate in NAFTA, supposedly in order to avoid the hub-and-spoke effect, seems to be doing nothing to stop the exit of firms.

There are policy actions that could reactivate the Canadian economy but are not being implemented. They are: macroeconomic policies that promote economic reactivation and an equilibrium exchange rate; a gradual liberalization of trade, in parallel to an aggressive program of promotion of new industry and creation of new skills and new jobs, based both on domestic and export markets; and restrictions on foreign investment in accordance with Canadian needs, including requirements in the areas of new productive capacity, domestic content, technology, and research and development. Moreover, the institutional framework of both CUFTA and NAFTA restricts the ability of the Canadian governments—at all levels—to implement such policies.

For Canada, the key issues under the new continental arrangement are a further loss of policy autonomy and a likely diversion of investment flows out of the country. Overall, Canada did not get a good deal with CUFTA and is likely to do worse with NAFTA.

NOTES

Parts of this chapter draw on an earlier paper entitled "NAFTA: A Critical Economic Perspective," presented at "Facing North/Facing South: A Multidisciplinary Conference on Contemporary United States-Canadian-Mexico Relations," The University of Calgary, 2-5 May 1991, and published as a discussion paper in August 1991 by the Canadian Centre for Policy Alternatives, in Ottawa. I am indebted to Michael Copeland and Fred Lazar for insightful observations, and to Lawrence Briskin, Peter Dorman, Teresa

Healy, Louis Lefeber, Kim Jarvi, Keith MacKinnon, and especially Robert Kreklewich for useful comments on an earlier draft. The views presented herein, as well as any remaining errors, are solely mine.

1. Note that the large appreciation of the Canadian dollar relative to the U.S. dollar during the first few years of CUFTA implementation nullified any beneficial effects of lower U.S. tariffs for Canadian exporters.

2. From January 1989 to July 1991, employment in the textile industry fell by 32 percent and in the furniture industry by 25 percent (Statistics Canada, *Employment, Earnings and Hours,* various issues). These losses are the result of a combination of trade liberalization and adverse macroeconomic environment.

3. This point is elaborated in Cameron, Clarkson and Watkins (1988). See also chapter by Sinclair in this volume.

4. This sentiment was fed during 1992 by a number of U.S. trade actions against Canadian exports. The events received wide coverage in the Canadian media (i.e., lumber, pork, Honda Civic cars).

5. Real interest rates represent the effective cost of borrowing: market interest rates minus expected inflation.

6. The preliminary data in this paragraph, except employment, are from *Bank of Canada Review,* July 1992. Employment figures are from *Employment, Earnings and Hours,* Statistics Canada, various issues.

7. A casual look at Figure 7.1 may seem to support the view that the early 1990s recession was not different from the one in 1982-83. The manufacturing sector recovered very energetically from the first one, so why will it not from the second? However, a careful analysis shows that the differences between these recessions are larger than the similarities. During the early 1990s, most of the job loss was related to permanent plant closings, in contrast to the cyclical element in the early 1980s. Second, unit labor costs were going down, relative to the United States, during 1983-86, and Canadian manufacturing was highly competitive. The contrast with the 1991 situation is stark, as the unit labor costs curve in Figure 7.1 shows.

8. It is interesting to analyze the causes of the growing gap between Canadian and U.S. costs. Business leaders have argued that stronger labor unionization in Canada promotes higher (real) wages and costs. Recent data does not support this thesis. Nominal hourly compensation in Canada (in C$) grew by 26.8 percent between 1985 and 1990. Of this growth, the largest part—24.5 percent—is explained by consumer price inflation, and a meager 1.5 percent by real wage growth (the rest, 0.8 percent, is due to higher payroll taxes) (Rao and Lemprière, 1992, p. 44).

9. In other words, an index of TFP indicates increases in production that are *not* due to increases in factors of production. For greater detail, see Statistics Canada (1992, part 2).

10. An index of TFP for the manufacturing sector went *down* 2.1 percent during 1989, 4.9 percent during 1990, and 3.8 percent during 1991. The index stood at 89.6 in 1991, down from 100 in 1986. (Statistics Canada, 1992, p. 8).

11. Interview with executives of auto parts plants reveals the following conclusion:

> All 13 of the Ontario-based respondents view Ontario's social programs as a disadvantage . . . (Booz et al., 1990, p. IV-14)

and a typical response was:

> "The cost of the social programs has become more than just an annoyance. During lean and difficult times the costs could lead to plant closures. At some stage it could become advantageous to discontinue operations in Ontario, sell the plants and use the real estate profits to relocate the profitable portion of the operations elsewhere" (ibid, p. IV-15).

12. These trends are discernible through careful reading of Canadian newspapers published during the 1989-1992 period. The author is not aware of formal studies that would prove or disprove these negative trends. There is aggregate statistical information that provides indirect support: the depressed levels of business investment, suggesting that incoming FDI is directed elsewhere; buoyant merger and acquisition operations, a likely target for incoming FDI; the low profitability of Canadian industrial operations; and the generally depressed manufacturing sector, where one has difficulty discerning—at this stage—"winning" sectors.

13. Out of 28 goods-producing industries, only 4 showed net gains in employment during the period January 1989-July 1991 (Statistics Canada, *Employment, Earnings, and Hours,* various issues). The three growing industries deal with natural resources or nontraded goods: forestry; nonferrous metals; petroleum and coal; and construction. This is *not* a picture of "losers" and "winners" in the manufacturing sector; only "losers" are discernible.

14. These supporters tend to assume that macroeconomic policies are independent of the free trade agreement. They refuse to recognize that both CUFTA and NAFTA place policy restrictions at both the micro and macro levels. In contrast, U.S., Mexican, and other Latin American policymakers are quite explicit about the links between trade agreements and the necessary macroeconomic environment needed for implementation—in particular, tight monetary and fiscal policies, low inflation, and a stable exchange rate (Meller, 1993, p. 14).

15. As noted by Campbell in this volume, in 1981-82, 22 percent of workers in Ontario who lost their jobs did so because of permanent plant closures. During the period 1989-92, 65 percent of lost jobs were due to permanent plant closures.

16. Economists have a new term for this kind of phenomenon: hysteresis. This term refers to a situation in which a transient event has long-term effects. One relevant example is when a temporary blow to a particular economic sector creates a permanent structural change. Another is when a temporary loss of jobs transforms into a permanent increase in unemployment. See Harris (1992, p. 36-38).

17. Michael Hart has argued, for example, that it will take "10 to 15 years" to observe the benefits of CUFTA in Canada (oral presentation at "Time for A North American Economic Community?: Exploring Economic and Cultural Alliances," Humphrey Institute, University of Minnesota, Minneapolis, February 25-26, 1991). Doern and Tomlin (1991, p. 291) state that "these [CUFTA] gains, by their nature, will only emerge over the medium to long term."

18. See, for example, Krugman (1987).

19. A study on the automotive parts industry finds that:

> Detailed cost comparisons performed in the 1986-1987 period indicated Mexico had a cost advantage compared to the U.S. in a number of [automotive parts] areas . . . (Booz et al., 1990, p. A-2) The primary reason for the cost advantage of Mexico and other developing countries is manufacturing labor costs. (ibid, p. II-11)

Restructuring and plant relocation since 1987 has increased even more the competitiveness of certain Mexican auto-parts plants.

20. Lester Thurow brings the example of

> a Toronto firm . . . [that has] a plant in Mexico where they pay $1.05 an hour and they get exactly the same productivity on this product as they do in their Toronto plant that pays $14 an hour.

Then he asks, "Now how long are you going to keep the Toronto plant open?" (Little, 1993)

21. The reader may get the impression that capital flight to Mexico should be highly beneficial for that country, creating jobs and industrial development. However, the growth of the *maquiladora* industry—which is attracting much of the capital—coincides with a massive loss of employment and production in the traditional industrial sector (see chapters by Velasco Arregui and Kopinak, this volume).

22. The hub and spoke argument is developed in Wonnacott (1990) and in Lipsey (1990).

REFERENCES

Baldwin, J., and Gorecki, P. K. (1985). "The Relationship Between Trade and Tariff Patterns and the Efficiency of the Canadian Manufacturing Sector in the 1970s: A Summary." In J. Whalley (1985). *Canada-United States Free Trade.* Toronto: University of Toronto Press.

Bank of Canada Review. (July 1992). Ottawa: Bank of Canada.

Booz, Allen, and Hamilton Inc. (March 1990). *A Comparative Study of the Cost Competitiveness of the Automotive Parts Manufacturing Industry in North America. Final Report.* Toronto.

Bordé, F. and Cross, P. (January 1989). "Tariffs in Canada-U.S. Trade." *Canadian Economic Observer.* Ottawa: Statistics Canada.

Cameron, D. (ed.). (1988). *The Free Trade Deal.* Toronto: Lorimer.

Cameron, D., Clarkson, S., and Watkins, M. (1988). "Market Access." In D. Cameron (ed.), *The Free Trade Deal.* Toronto: Lorimer.

Cohen, M. G. (1988). "Services: The Vanishing Opportunity." In D. Cameron (ed.), *The Free Trade Deal.* Toronto: Lorimer.

Daly, D. J. (1990). "The Canada-United States Free Trade Agreement: The Adjustment Process for Canadian-Owned Firms." *North American Review of Economics and Finance.* 1 (1): 105-115.

Doern, G. B., and Tomlin, B. W. (1991). *Faith and Fear: The Free Trade Story.* Toronto: Stoddart.

Economic Council. (1992). *Pulling Together: Productivity, Innovation, and Trade.* Ottawa: Minister of Supply and Services.

Eden, L., and Molot, M. A. (1992). "The View from the Spokes: Canada and Mexico Face the United States." In S. J. Randall with H. Konrad and S. Silverman (eds.). *North America without Borders? Integrating Canada, the United States and Mexico.* Calgary: University of Calgary.

External Affairs and International Trade. (1990). House of Commons. Minutes of Proceedings and Evidence of the Standing Committee on External Affairs and International Trade, Sixth Report, issue No. 76. Ottawa.

Government of Canada, Ministry of Finance. (1988). *The Canada-U.S. Free Trade Agreement: An Economic Assessment.* Ottawa: Minister of Supply and Services.

Gulati, U. C. (1992). "The Foundations of Rapid Economic Growth: The Case of the Four Tigers." *American Journal of Economics and Sociology.* 51 (2): 161-172.

Harris, R. (1992). *Exchange Rates and International Competitiveness of the Canadian Economy.* Economic Council of Canada. Ottawa: Minister of Supply and Services.

Krugman, P. R. (1987). "Is Free Trade Passé?" *Journal of Economic Perspectives,* 1 (2): 131-44.

Krugman, P. R., and Obstfeld, M. (1991). *International Economics: Theory and Policy* (2nd ed.). New York: HarperCollins.

Lazar, F. (1981). *The New Protectionism: Non-Tariff Barriers and Their Effects on Canada.* Toronto: Lorimer.

Lipsey, R. G. (August 1990). "Canada at the U.S.-Mexico Free Trade Dance: Wallflower or Partner?" *Commentary* (20). Toronto: C. D. Howe Institute.

————. (1992). "Getting There: The Path to a Western Hemisphere Free Trade Area and its Structure." In S. Saborio (ed.), *The Premise and the Promise: Free Trade in the Americas.* New Brunswick, New Jersey: Transaction Publishers.

Little, B. (January 15 1993). "Lester Thurow on Why Companies Move to Mexico." *The Globe and Mail,* p. B4.

Macdonald, D. (1987). "Overview of the Agreement." In M. G. Smith and F. Stone (eds.), *Assessing the Canada-U.S. Free Trade Agreement.* Halifax: Institute for Research on Public Policy.

Macdonald Report. (1985). *Report: Royal Commission on the Economic Union and Development Prospects for Canada.* Vol. I. Ottawa: Minister of Supply and Services.

Meller, P. (January-February 1993). "A Trade Strategy for Latin America." *Policy Options,* 13 (10): 12-16.

Rao, P. S., and Lemprière, T. (1992). "An Analysis of the Linkages Between Canadian Trade Flows, Productivity, and Costs." Working Paper No. 46, Ottawa: Economic Council of Canada.

Shaiken, H. (1990). *Mexico in the Global Economy: High Technology and Work Organization in Export Industries.* La Jolla, CA: Center for U.S.-Mexican Studies, University of California, San Diego.

Statistics Canada. (July 1992). *Aggregate Productivity Figures.* Ottawa: Minister of Supply and Services.

Whalley, J. (1985). *Canada-United States Free Trade.* Toronto: University of Toronto Press.

Wonnacott, R. (October 1990). "U.S. Hub-and-Spoke Bilaterals and the Multilateral Trading System." *Commentary* (23). Toronto: C. D. Howe Institute.

Chapter 8

An Alternative Trade and Development Model for Canada

Mel Watkins

The main purpose of this chapter is to attempt to outline an alternative trade and development model for Canada.[1] It is helpful, however, to pose some prior questions. Is Canada in need of an alternative? Is it possible that there is no feasible alternative? Unless the answer to the first question is in the affirmative and the second is in the negative, it will be pointless to proceed.

The anemic state of the Canadian economy in the early 1990s shows the need for an alternative. In spite of neoconservative allegations that there is no choice but to totally buy into globalization, alternatives are possible: there is limited room for maneuver in the global economy, but theory and practice suggest that there is some. With those answers, we must then face the fact that the Canada-U.S. Free Trade Agreement (CUFTA) is in place and has been extended to Mexico in the North American Free Trade Agreement (NAFTA). Would it have been a viable alternative to CUFTA to say no? Is it a viable alternative to NAFTA to say no? Then the most difficult practical question: if the Canadian government got the answer wrong the first time on CUFTA, should it, can it, now be abrogated? What is the prospect for an alternative model if CUFTA is not abrogated? Free trade has caused problems for Canada to the extent that one can reasonably infer that Canada would have been better off without it. Abrogation will admittedly risk costs, but they may well be less than the costs of not abrogating.

Another preliminary matter: if we are to formulate an alternative agenda, what exactly is it an alternative to? What has been and—with or without

CUFTA or NAFTA—what is the existing Canadian trade and development model? How viable is it? What are its weaknesses that must be overcome in developing an alternative? What are its strengths that can be built on? There is a large and compelling literature on Canadian political economy that demonstrates the resource or staples bias of the economy and, as the other side of that coin, a weak industrial structure, an industrially deficient business class, and an extraordinary integration of the Canadian economy into the U.S. economy.

Finally, what is the positive alternative? Public opinion polls show that opposition to CUFTA is at an all-time high in Canada—in mid-1992, only 4 percent of Canadians thought the deal was working to Canada's advantage; it is rejected in every region of Canada, including Quebec, which originally supported it. People believe it is not working and are apparently not in need of further critiques. The real issue is what can be put in its place. That very much includes the issue of whether the nature of the political economy of Canada, the constellation of social forces, creates any grounds for optimism that an alternative can actually be implemented. This chapter advances, cautiously, the possibility of a social democratic alternative—though it is easier to describe it than it is to see governments with the ability to stand up to business opposition long enough and firmly enough to implement it.

A free trade agreement constitutes an industrial policy—and, for Canada, a bad one. The issue of an appropriate trade and development model is linked to the question of whether Canada should have increased its economic integration with the United States through CUFTA and whether that process should continue through NAFTA. From a Canadian perspective, NAFTA is round two of CUFTA. The first round devastated Canada; there is very little public support for the second round, at least not at this time. It is an appropriate time to consider an alternative and to see what support exists in Mexico and the United States for rejecting NAFTA in its present form and working out an alternative trilateral arrangement.

THE NEED FOR AN ALTERNATIVE

Is Canada in need of an alternative? Most Canadians think so. Certainly the state of the economy during the early 1990s—in terms of unemployment, poverty (particularly of children in single-parent families), the homeless, food banks, real incomes that have not increased for a decade—leaves much to be desired.[2]

The corporate elite likewise believes that the Canadian economy is in an unsatisfactory state. It insists that the economy is uncompetitive and becoming increasingly so, though the concept of competitiveness is a slippery one and of uncertain scientific status.[3] When competitiveness is studied seriously, as by Michael Porter (1990, 1991), what is suggested, ironically, is that there may be a real problem with the nature and behavior of the Canadian corporate elite itself because of the extent of foreign, mostly U.S., control. The simplistic argument, much touted, is that to become competitive, economic policy must conform even more closely that it already does to the neoconservative business agenda: free trade, deregulation, privatization, regressive tax reform, and tough anti-inflation measures with no commitment to lessen unemployment.

Yet present policy, which is mostly of that neoconservative cast, seems not to be working; indeed, it can be argued that it is making things worse. Its promise—from the late seventies with Thatcher in Britain, to the early eighties with Reagan in the United States, to the mid-eighties with Mulroney in Canada—was to restore economic growth, but the nineties began with a serious recession and a faltering recovery. On the face of it, neoconservative policy has not gotten growth going, and it has worsened the distribution of wealth, income, and the amenities of life.

The fundamental fact is that the Canadian economy, like the economy of much of the world, is caught in a crisis that has lasted some two decades and has no end in sight. If the problems are cyclical, they result from a long cycle, long enough to be classified as structural. Not since the 1930s has there been such a compelling case for alternative policies. Under the circumstances, it seems reasonable to infer that any alternative will have to be concerted and comprehensive.

FEASIBILITY OF AN ALTERNATIVE

Is it possible, nevertheless, that there is no feasible alternative? The Soviet-type alternative has collapsed, at least in the First World. Swedish socialists—the architects of the famous middle way—have been defeated. In Ontario in 1990, a social democratic government was elected for the first time ever, but its program has been powerfully constrained by a recession and by the truculent opposition of business. Capitalism is hegemonic; globalization renders nation-states and their governments increasingly impotent.

The dominant neoconservative mind that so values choice for consumers and corporations insists that none exists at the societal level; there can be many kinds of light beer but only one way of life (but, of course, it is hard to tell the beers apart). The argument is admittedly self-serving; still, neoconservatives have the clout to push policies, like CUFTA, that explicitly constrain governments and hence limit choice.

It must be conceded that while there is not much political space in the world of transnational capitalism, there is some. Globalization, with its economic imperative, is a long-standing phenomenon, yet there remains some variety; for example, Canada and the United States, while similar in so many ways, have been distinctly different societies for as long as they have existed, and they will presumably remain different for as long as people so wish. Lester Thurow (1981) observed near the outset of the neoconservative era that a list of what was alleged to be wrong with the United States—too much big government, too many taxes, and so on—was in fact a fair description of its leading competitors, which were outperforming the United States. Economics teaches that what is scarce but in demand has a high value; the political space that remains should be treasured and used to the full.

There is agreement among commentators on contemporary Canadian politics that the elite to which deference has so long been paid, are presently discredited in the public mind in an unprecedented way. This would seem to create an unprecedented opportunity for alternative politics and alternative policies.

CUFTA: EXTENSION OR ABROGATION

Dissatisfaction with CUFTA is widespread in Canada; most Canadians wish it had never happened. The alternative to CUFTA was to reject it; the government could have done this by saying it was a bad deal and breaking off negotiations, or the public could have done it by defeating the Mulroney government in the election of 1988. Would the sky have fallen? Many Canadians would think it has fallen in because of CUFTA.

The multilateral trade system and the GATT (General Agreement on Tariffs and Trade) rules would still have been in place. That would hardly have meant the end of Canada's trading—indeed, trading very heavily—with the United States. Nor would it have stopped significant costs of adjustment, of restructuring, from having to be borne. The key difference would have lain in the fact that multilateral free trade is not likely to have the same political side effects as does bilateral free trade. It does not so clearly define Canada, to Canadians and to the world, as part of a U.S. block. While continental economic integration would still have proceeded incrementally, it would not have risked a quantum leap that political scientists such as Richard Simeon (1991) fear is feeding the forces of political disintegration.

As well, GATT rules and procedures do not so tightly tie the hands of federal and provincial governments in economic and social policy as does free trade with the United States. Indeed, the major risk of leaving CUFTA in place is that it rules out an alternative trade and development model that, in the nature of things, would require active government policy. A reading of the agreement reveals a considerable list of constraints; proponents and opponents have agreed on this point, dividing on whether that is a benefit or a cost. Notwithstanding the passage of almost four years, the question of what constraints exist for a government that might wish to be active remains mostly unanswered. The federal government has no inclination to test the matter. There are three NDP (New Democratic Party) governments in place at the provincial level, and Ontario's has been in power for two years, but none has yet done enough to constitute a relevant test of the limits of the possible.

CUFTA includes an abrogation clause that permits either Canada or the United States to terminate the agreement on six months' notice. There is no doubt, that a future Canadian government could legally abrogate the agreement. Furthermore, it lies within the competence of any government, including a provincial government, to pursue the policies it deems necessary and, if these risk violating CUFTA, to leave it to the United States to complain.

Still, no one should imagine that abrogation would be easy. It would, rather, be very difficult, both economically and politically. Restructuring by business under the terms of CUFTA would have to be readapted. A political party that advocates tough policies like abrogation while vying for power may change its mind, or have it changed, if elected. Business would do its best to discredit and destabilize any government that tried to abrogate. It would be helpful, if not essential, for that government to have a clear alternative set of policies in mind. Should abrogation never happen, it is important that there be a set of policies that could be implemented—to the extent possible—so as to permit the best outcome under constrained circumstances.[4]

What about extending free trade to Mexico, and beyond? The new dimension is that Mexico is a poor and developing country and that Canada is therefore making an important statement of its position on the North-South relationship. Canadian business that supports NAFTA says the deal will help Mexico develop, but critics within Mexico deny that (see chapter by Kopinak in this volume). There is a trinational corporate-state alliance pushing NAFTA; the Canadian members of that alliance see it as a necessary extension of CUFTA. But there is also a trinational alliance of labor and popular sector groups that is formulating an alternative continental development pact; it insists that no such pact is possible unless CUFTA is abrogated ("Working Propositions for Zacatecas," 1991).

THE STAPLE MODEL

What is the Canadian model of trade and development, past and present, and what is there about it that needs to be changed? Here we can draw on the rich writings of the Canadian political economy tradition (Clement and Williams, 1989; Drache and Clement, 1985; Neill, 1991). From the days of European contact with the aboriginal societies down to the present time, Canada has remained a substantially resource-based economy. The pace and character of development have been significantly determined throughout by staple exports. Development has tended to take place via the spread effects, or linkages, from the export base. Even the tariff as the centerpiece of Canada's historic National Policy should be understood not as an alternative to trade but as a means to increase domestic linkages in the context of export-led growth, to improve the terms under which Canada was integrated into the global economy. In the process, Canada has become one of the richest countries in the world, with membership in the exclusive G-7 club for developed industrial countries.

Yet the Canadian economy is characterized by serious flaws. It is unclear whether it is one economy or a collection of regional and disparate economies organized around different staples and with manufacturing overwhelmingly concentrated in central Canada. Even if it is thought of as one economy, perhaps it is really a northern extension, or region, of the U.S. economy. Certainly, the extent of economic integration through cross-border trade and investment is very high and, given the asymmetry, has rendered Canada highly dependent on the United States. The result has been a pattern of dependent branch-plant industrialization. Canada has a huge deficit in fully manufactured goods to match its huge surplus in staples. To a surprising degree, the resource exports are still in an unprocessed form. There is an evident failure to exploit the linkages between the resource sector and the manufacturing sector.

Historians properly point out that the Canadian state has been an economically active and interventionist state compared to the United States, but political economists insist that it can easily be judged as doing too little rather than too much. The Canadian business class, with its excessive commercial-staples cast, has never been up to the task of building a world-class industrial economy. The subordinate classes, the popular democratic forces, have been excessively subordinate and provided too little push from below; they have been deferential to the elite while themselves being fragmented and weakened by ethnic-linguistic splits (English vs. French), regional grievances, and metropolitan domination (international, or U.S.-based, unions).

In the post–World War II period, Canada moved to freer trade while keeping the door wide open for foreign capital. The staples model mostly continued to work, albeit in a truncated and limited way. Canada had continued success in finding new staples for export. It was able to work out special sectoral arrangements with the United States in autos and armaments that gave Canadian producers a fair share of the North American market. This managed trade policy increased the integration of the two economies while seemingly limiting political costs for Canada.

With the global economic crisis of the past two decades, however, have come harder economic times, and new and stringent policies. For a brief interlude in the seventies, the United States seemed willing to treat Canada with benign neglect, and, under Trudeau, Canada moved mildly toward economic nationalism. The basic thrust remained resource development but with more Canadian participation and Canadian content; it was dubbed the megaproject strategy. With Reagan and the new truculence of the 1980s, Trudeau retreated and Mulroney sought a bilateral free trade agreement with the United States to enshrine preferential status for the Canadian economy in the U.S. market.

The promise was held out that free trade would make inefficient Canadian industry efficient; mainstream Canadian economists concurred. For political economists, however, the fact that free trade meant more play for market forces and less scope for government policy meant that free trade might rather exacerbate the deep-seated staples bias of the Canadian economy and further weaken the manufacturing base.

There are further practical problems with this existing model of trade and development. Is Canada running out of resources? How much actual linkage is there from current staples such as minerals, and oil and gas (Phillips, 1991)? Is the megaproject mentality viable given the increasingly effective opposition of aboriginal people and mounting concerns about environmental degradation? It is noteworthy that the second stage of the massive James Bay hydroelectric project is presently on hold precisely because of these objections. An alternative may not be only desirable; it may be essential.

THE SOCIAL DEMOCRATIC ALTERNATIVE[5]

Honest scholars admit that description and diagnosis are fraught with value judgments (otherwise known as politics); prescription is, explicitly, a political exercise. The bias of this writer, at the margin of empire, is that of a political economist of a left nationalist persuasion. What, then, is my Canadian-style social democratic alternative?

Economies and societies ought not to be structured around trade; trade should be managed to suit the needs of economies and societies. This obvious rule is frequently ignored in these economistic and reductionist times. It is not surprising that Canada trades heavily with the United States, and not much can be done about that. The problem with free trade—indeed, with most of what is proposed in the name of competitiveness—is that it compels radical restructuring of the Canadian economy, even of the Canadian society, in the name of enhancing trade.

There can be too much emphasis on trade. There can likewise be too much made of the virtues of cross-border investment (see chapter by Wilkinson in this volume). They are hard to distinguish; most trade today is intrafirm. Agreements to trade more freely are simultaneously agreements to facilitate foreign direct investment, through rights of establishment and national treatment provisions. Capital, as institutionalized in the transnational corporation, finds its mobility facilitated, while labor—the general population— remains much less mobile. The balance of power swings further in favor of capital; this is not necessarily to the benefit of any particular populace.

Countries are entitled to control the entry of foreign capital and monitor its subsequent behavior. Protecting one's own firms from foreign takeover, particularly in key sectors—say, energy and culture for Canada—makes sense. So too does policy to correct apparent weaknesses of foreign capital in Canada, notably the tendency of subsidiaries to do less research than their parents and import parts and business services. It matters where head offices are located because of the inherent tendency of certain functions (research and development, finance) to be headquarters functions. Even Porter's report on Canada, done for a business organization with a significant presence of chief executive officers of foreign subsidiaries, talks of the need for more "home-based firms" (Porter, 1991). A reading of the Canadian financial press suggests that, because of free trade, U.S. firms with Canadian operations are buying out minority Canadian shareholdings and are collapsing the Canadian structure into a North American unit headquartered in the United States;[6] if so, Toronto, with its many head offices, is in trouble.

Countries are likewise entitled to control the exit of firms, to make it more difficult for them to walk away from their obligations to workers and communities, and to encourage them to restructure in such a way as to maintain the viability of their Canadian operations.

Given the size of the U.S. market, it has always been the case that Canadian firms that were successful in penetrating it might shift operations to the United States; the present leading case in point is Northern Telecom.

Smaller countries have little choice but to play the contemporary capitalist game by allowing themselves to be used as sites for multinational firms, but these countries need to be aware of the limitations of this strategy. Government assistance to build viable Canadian firms should be made conditional on their retaining a commitment to Canada.

For these and other reasons, there should be active encouragement of enterprises owned by workers and controlled by workers. Labor has a lesser interest in its capital being so mobile. Also, a worker-controlled firm might be expected to be more concerned about the environment (because workers live in the community), about their health and safety, and about training themselves. This is an important new direction in which to move, a long-standing idea whose time may finally have come; the Ontario NDP government in 1991 announced a proposed program to facilitate worker ownership—though it seems intended mostly to deal with firms in trouble (Ontario, Ministry of Treasury and Economics, 1991a).

Trade should be conducted under the rule of "trade smart" rather than "trade cheap." Do not try to trade on the basis of cheapening labor, pushing down wages, eroding the welfare state. Neither theory (notably the new trade theory) nor empirical evidence suggests that the advantage of industrial countries lies in the low-wage option. Trade should be conducted, rather, on the basis of being innovative, of being there first and staying ahead of the competition. The object is to move to higher-value-added activity that permits a high-wage economy. To do that, the public sector has to be used creatively to overcome structural weaknesses in the economy.[7]

There is a considerable consensus now in the scholarly literature about how growth, at its best, takes place around clusters of firms (preferably of the home-based variety), through strategic partnerships, and with an active government. There is certainly debate about how much government should do, but this typically entails a larger role for government than the rhetoric of neoconservatism admits.[8]

More value added in the resource sector means more processing and more manufacturing of inputs like machinery; these mean more benefit from any volume of trade. There should be more, and more efficient, spending in the public sector—on infrastructure, on training, on education. There should be new financial mechanisms for assisting small and medium-sized firms that are presently being victimized by gaps in the capital market. Governments must become more effective facilitators of structural change. If markets are to rule our lives—and for the moment, at least, there is apparently no alternative to that—then governments must mold and shape these markets more.

Here lies the means to revitalize a social democracy that otherwise risks falling prey to the corrosive ideology of neoconservatism. Social democrats are taunted with the charge that they only know how to redistribute wealth, not how to create it; their reply lies in making an activist job-creating trade and development policy the new and central thrust. It is the only hope of maintaining the commitment to full employment that was an integral part—and the most progressive part—of the now defunct Keynesian consensus.

But if such policies are to matter for most people, it is essential that they not be confined simply to high-tech, already highly unionized, sectors. They must be combined with labor legislation that strengthens unions, with employment equity, with stringent environmental regulations; only then will such legislation infuse the private sector generally and impact broadly on society.

Heed should be taken of the call, notably by Premier Bob Rae of Ontario, for new social partnership arrangements that would bring together government, business, labor, and popular sector groups; the inclusion of the latter seems essential if the new social forces of contemporary society are to be represented. For the labor movement and the other social movements, such arrangements, which are impossible with governments committed to a neoconservative agenda of competitiveness, become feasible. The labor movement will be understandably concerned about maintaining its independence and its capacity for militancy (Canadian Auto Workers, 1991). The earlier Keynesian compromise—jobs and rising wages in return for leaving the private sector private—did not, in fact, rule out adversarial relations between labor and capital in collective bargaining; nor should any new social contract.

The stumbling block becomes, rather, whether business is prepared to participate. Perhaps there is not even a Canadian business class—or a business class with a commitment to Canada—with which to strike a bargain. There is, in the case of Ontario, some evidence that public service has been unreceptive to the NDP's interventionist philosophy. Admittedly, the inability in the past to formulate an industrial policy shows the inherent difficulty in what is being proposed (Atkinson and Coleman, 1989), but the alternative to not trying is bleak indeed.[9]

The Ontario government calls for partnership, only to encounter business and bureaucratic opposition. What is needed is for the labor movement and the social movements "to take the lead in developing the ideas, structures, policies, and alliances that will make a progressive restructuring [of Canada] feasible" (Gindin, 1992). The bottom line on alternative policies is that they grow out of alternative politics.

CONCLUSION

In the early 1990s, with NDP governments in Ontario, British Columbia, and Saskatchewan, the majority of Canadians were being governed at the provincial level by social democratic administrations. The relative decentralization characteristic of Canadian federalism provided some scope for these governments to act and to experiment. Unlike its U.S. counterpart, the Canadian labor movement remained solidly entrenched. Coalitions with the social movements at the national and local levels, which emerged in the fight against free trade prior to the 1988 federal election, survived and altered the shape of left-wing politics. The public remained disgruntled and impatient. It would be wrong to imagine that there is vast room for maneuver, but some things are possible.

Having formal trilateral trade arrangements among the United States, Canada, and Mexico—and extending beyond them to the rest of the hemisphere—may well be what the future is about. But the Canadian experience with CUFTA argues against rushing into such deals. One need not be opposed to any NAFTA to be opposed to the one presently on offer. Let alternative politics flourish, in Canada and elsewhere, to supply the alternative policies that are increasingly and understandably in demand.

NOTES

1. In thinking about this topic, I have benefitted greatly from my involvement in Common Frontiers, and particularly from working with Ken Traynor. I have also found it difficult to add much to the splendid article by Marjorie Cohen (1991) other than by making more explicit the implications of its analysis for alternative policies. Of course, neither can be held responsible for what this chapter actually says. See too the chapter by Drache in this volume, which deals with many of the same issues that flow from the trade-centered model.
2. For an assessment of how much of Canadian economy's bad performance can be attributed to CUFTA, see Campbell (1992a).
3. The most frequently cited ranking of competitiveness is from the *World Competitiveness Report,* issued annually by the International Management Development Institute and the World Economic Forum, both of which are based in Switzerland. Canada was actually ranked a high fifth among 23 industrialized countries in 1990. While that was down from fourth in 1989, it was still up from seventh in 1986.
4. On the case for abrogation, see Campbell (1992b).

5. For a collection of stimulating and relevant essays on this alternative for Ontario, see Drache (1992).
6. I am indebted to David Crane, Economics Editor of the *Toronto Star,* for drawing this matter to my attention.
7. The best Canadian writer on this topic is David Wolfe; see, for example, Wolfe (1991, 1992); significantly, he has been a senior adviser on such matters to the Ontario government.
8. See in particular Science Council of Canada (1988), United Steelworkers of America (1991), Ontario, Ministry of Treasury and Economics (1991b), and Ontario, Ministry of Industry, Trade and Technology (1992).
9. As well, governments in Canada have been preoccupied with constitutional matters for much of 1992 and the economy has tended to get short shrift. In particular, the Ontario government in general and the premier in particular have been much more active on the Constitution than on the economy, though the priorities of the Ontario public are very much the reverse.

REFERENCES

Atkinson, M., and Coleman, W. (1989). *The State, Business and Industrial Change in Canada.* Toronto: University of Toronto Press.

Campbell, B. (1992a). *Canada Under Siege: Three Years into the Free Trade Era.* Ottawa: Canadian Centre for Policy Alternatives.

———. (1992b). *We Need Free Trade Abrogation to Rebuild the Nation.* Ottawa: Canadian Centre for Policy Alternatives, Popular Economics Series.

Canadian Auto Workers. (1991). *Economics, Politics, and the Union.* Statement for 3rd Constitutional Convention, Halifax N.S. [Mimeo available from CAW, Toronto].

Clement, W., and Williams, G. (eds.). (1989). *The New Canadian Political Economy.* Kingston: McGill-Queen's University Press.

Cohen, M. (1991). "Exports, Unemployment, and Regional Inequality: Economic Policy and Trade Theory." In D. Drache, and M. S. Gertler (eds.), *The New Era of Global Competition: State Policy and Market Power.* Montreal and Kingston: McGill-Queen's University Press.

Drache, D. and Clement, W. (eds.). (1985). *The New Practical Guide to Canadian Political Economy.* Toronto: Lorimer.

Drache, D. (ed.). (1992). *Getting on Track: Social Democratic Strategies for Ontario.* Ottawa: Canadian Centre for Policy Alternatives; Montreal and Kingston: McGill-Queen's University Press.

Gindin, S. (May 1992). "Putting the Con Back in the Economy." *This Magazine,* 25 (6).

Neill, R. (1991). *A History of Canadian Economic Thought.* London and New York: Routledge.

Ontario, Ministry of Industry, Trade and Technology. (1992). *An Industrial Policy Framework for Ontario.* Toronto: Queen's Printer for Ontario.

Ontario, Ministry of Treasury and Economics. (1991a). *Ontario Investment and Worker Ownership Program: A Proposal for Discussion.* Mimeo.

————. (1991b). "Budget Paper E: Ontario in the 1990s." In *1991 Ontario Budget.* Toronto: Queen's Printer for Ontario.

Phillips, P. (1991). "New Staples and Mega-Projects: Reaching the Limits to Sustainable Development." In D. Drache, and M. S. Gertler (eds.), *The New Era of Global Competition: State Policy and Market Power.* Montreal and Kingston: McGill-Queen's University Press.

Porter, M. E. (1990). *The Competitive Advantage of Nations.* New York: The Free Press.

————. (1991). *Canada at the Crossroads: The Reality of a New Competitive Environment.* Ottawa: Business Council of National Issues and Minister of Supply and Services, Canada.

Science Council of Canada. (1988). *Gearing up for Global Markets: From Industry Challenge to Industry Commitment.* Ottawa: Ministry of Supply and Services.

Simeon, R. (1991). "Globalization and the Canadian Nation-State." In G. B. Doern and B. B. Purchase (eds.), *Canada at Risk? Canadian Public Policy in the 1990s.* Toronto: C. D. Howe Institute.

Thurow, L. C. (1981). *The Zero-Sum Society: Distribution and the Possibilities for Economic Change.* New York: Penguin Books.

United Steelworkers of America. (1991). *Empowering Workers in the Global Economy: A Labor Agenda for the 1990s.* Toronto.

Wolfe, D. (1991). "Technology and Trade." In S. Rosenblum and P. Findlay (eds.), *Debating Canada's Future: Views from the Left.* Toronto: Lorimer.

————. (1992). "Technology and Trade: Finding the Right Mix." In Drache, D. (ed.), *Getting on Track: Social Democratic Strategies for Ontario.* Ottawa: Canadian Centre for Policy Alternatives; Montreal and Kingston: McGill-Queen's University Press.

"Working Propositions for Zacatecas: Elements of an Alternative Approach to North American Trade and Development." (23-25 October 1991). A Working Paper of the Canadian Delegation participating in the "Counter Conference to the Trilateral Talks for a North American Free Trade Agreement" held in Zacatecas, Mexico.

III

THE POLITICAL ECONOMY OF MEXICAN INTEGRATION

Chapter 9

The Maquiladorization
of the Mexican Economy

Kathryn Kopinak

While the significance of *maquiladoras* has changed over time, Angulo (1990, p. 139) says that "the modern meaning of the word evolved in practice from its use to designate any partial activity in an industrial process, such as assembly or packaging effected by a party other than the original manufacturer." Changes in U.S. and Mexican law that permitted the emergence of *maquiladoras* in 1965 allowed for machinery, vehicles, and parts to be imported into Mexico duty free, for assembly to take place there, and then for the product to be returned without duty to the United States. Mexico taxed only value added, which was almost all labor. The program was limited to northern border regions, where the Mexican government had experimented with free trade zones in the 1930s.

Mexico's intention with this legislation was to provide jobs lost through the U.S. cancelation of the *Bracero* Program, which since 1942 had permitted Mexican males to migrate to the U.S. for temporary agricultural work. For U.S. capital, the legislation was a way of using cheap Mexican labor without criticism from U.S. unions, the main group lobbying for an end to the *Bracero* Program. Its timing also dovetailed perfectly with restructuring efforts to cope with economic crisis. This unanticipated last factor has been responsible for the rapid growth of *maquiladora* industries in Mexico. By January 1992, there were 1,954 factories established as *maquiladoras* in Mexico, employing about 489,000 people.

Historically, *maquilas* have been used by capital as instruments to reduce costs—by using cheap labor, or through flexibility (deploying labor without regard to job categories, regulations on hours worked, rules specified in collective contracts, and so on). The vast majority of *maquilas* are owned by U.S. companies, although ownership by Japanese companies has grown recently. While Hart (1990, p. 73) has argued that only a few Canadian companies are likely to relocate to Mexico, interest on the part of the Canadian business community has grown. Even without further movement of Canadian capital to Mexico, *maquiladoras* continue to be significant for Canada because of their role in the current continental restructuring of transnational capital. Many companies with head offices in the United States produce in both Canada and in Mexican *maquiladoras*, so that the industrial structure of the three nations is tied through the transnational corporation (TNC).

This continental economic integration was stimulated by a debt-ridden Mexican government, which, in the early 1980s, attempted to transform *maquilas* into permanent industrial bases by encouraging more capital-intensive operations and devaluing the peso to cheapen labor. *Maquiladora* employment tripled in response to these policies. Much of the "new investment" during the mid-1980s was used to convert already existing non-*maquiladora* plants to *maquiladoras*. These changes did not necessarily represent net additions to the country's wealth but rather a qualitative change in the productive process—particularly in electronics, auto, and auto parts production (González Aréchiga and Ramírez, 1989, p. 876).

Some of the "new investment" was from transnational automotive companies that had set up operations in Mexico. They sent their products back to the United States to take advantage of greatly reduced tariffs under the Generalized System of Preferences (GSP). Such companies are referred to as "new" *maquilas* (see Gambrill, 1991, p. 37). Although they were not legally *maquiladoras*, the way in which they organized production was similar. From a social point of view, this represented "maquiladorization." In the automotive sector this entailed feminizing the labor force; highly segmenting skill categories (with a greater majority of personnel in unskilled jobs); relatively low salaries; and a non-union orientation (Carrillo, 1990a, p. 110).

The Mexican government decree of 1989 encouraged this informal maquiladorization. It recognized *maquiladora* investment as "the principal means of inserting the Mexican economy into the global world economy" (Angulo, 1990, p. 140). Formally, the 1989 decree blurred the legal distinctions between *maquilas* and non-*maquilas* and allowed for part-time *maquilas* (companies given rights to sell domestically and to export). Gambrill (1991) argues that the Mexican government used this decree to prepare for a free trade environment that it was to negotiate later. This decree created an economic enclave functioning under fully liberalized rules. Thus, the expectation of free trade had a maquiladorizing impact even before NAFTA was negotiated.

REVIEW OF DEBATES IN THE ANALYTICAL LITERATURE

From the *maquiladora* program's inception, there has been a clear conceptual and analytic division of commentators into "apologists" and "critics," summarized in Carrillo (1989b, pp. 13-14). "Critics" argue that the *maquiladora* program increases Mexico's economic dependence on the United States, and they note that its highly selective employment policy has not alleviated joblessness but has increased migration to the border. Moreover, its promotion of labor policies that prevent workers' autonomous organization subordinates them to unions and companies that roll back benefits and rights guaranteed in federal labor law. Critics have often pointed to the fact that the vast majority of workers are women to explain continued high unemployment and the lack of autonomous union organizations.[1] "Apologists" have argued that social costs are outweighed by the potential net benefits of regional development through employment generation, greater income available at the local level, and growth in industrial employment opportunities for women.

Negotiation of the North American Free Trade Agreement (NAFTA) occurred during a process of tremendous change in the *maquiladora* industries, which had reached a turning point, according to González and Ramírez (1989). The political agenda has moved ahead faster than the research agenda, and this has contributed to confusion about the exact nature of the changes undergone and the directions possible at any turning point. It is just such changes and future directions that NAFTA would institutionalize in a more permanent way.

Some researchers, most notably those supporting Mexican government policies, see the turning point arrived at after the economic integration of the 1980s as leading to two types of *maquiladoras*: the traditional, or old, and the new, which are sometimes said to form a second wave. Gereffi (1992, pp. 138-39) describes them this way:

> The old-style *maquiladoras* are characterized by the use of labor-intensive operations that combine minimum wages with piecework, and hire mostly women. This situation tends to prevail in garment production, basic semicon-

ductor assembly, and other types of light manufacturing. In recent years, though, the program has attracted more sophisticated forms of production in automobile-related manufactures and advanced electronics assembly. This second wave of *maquiladora* plants, some of which are Japanese-owned, has made substantial investments in complex technology. They are also hiring growing numbers of male workers.

Hector (1990, p. 164) further distinguishes the new wave of *maquilas* by pointing out that, in comparison to the traditional ones, they have a higher level of integration with regional Mexican economies that surround them, and that their male labor force is more likely to be unionized by the large centrals allied with the government and covered under social security legislation.

President Salinas responded to critics who charged that free trade would only bring Mexico low–paying, unskilled jobs like those of the traditional *maquiladoras* by arguing that his goal was an agreement that would promote *maquiladora* diversification on a sectoral and geographical level, integrate it into the Mexican economy, transfer more technology, and create skilled jobs. His underlying assumption was that of modernization theory, in that the traditional *maquiladoras* are portrayed as representing the necessary first step leading to industrialization that includes more value added, transfers more technology, and trains workers. High–tech auto production is usually given as an example of what the future can hold for Mexico under a free trade agreement with the United States.

Likewise, Gereffi (1992, pp. 136, 149-50) focuses on "the potential contributions of the *maquiladora* program to national development in Mexico." He suggests Mexico will follow the model of the East Asian newly industrializing countries in allowing many of the old *maquiladoras* to migrate to the Caribbean and Central America, which would not be covered by rules of origin in the NAFTA. While he admits that it is too early to tell if the new *maquiladoras* will bring Mexico to a higher stage of development, he argues that they do open up the possibility of helping it reach this goal by fostering greater technology transfer and the training of a skilled and well–educated work force.

The social costs and disadvantages of the traditional *maquiladoras* are legitimated in Mexican government policy as temporary evils in what is considered an inevitable process of development toward a modern future. Salinas's intellectual formation was heavily based in Almond and Verba's (1963) notion of the civic culture. This school, popular in the 1960s but later dismissed by numerous critics, idealizes Anglo–U.S. political culture and assumes that less–developed countries are moving along some uni-dimensional continuum that has the U.S. model as its end point (see Salinas, 1982). Mexican government authorities argue that they expect their policies to have the country jump directly from the Third World to the First World, despite the asymmetry between the Mexican and U.S. economies that makes this unlikely.

This focus on the second wave of new *maquiladoras* as leading to a higher stage of development that is above all *modern,* is, however, inaccurate and largely politically motivated. While there has been much discussion in the literature about the emergence of dual technology in the *maquiladoras,* there is certainly no agreement on this conceptualization. When the phenomenon is considered in scholarly research of both the supporters and critics, special-ized, automated technology is hardly presented as a factor that will inevitably lead toward modernization. Neither can it be seen as replacing the first type of *maquiladora,* which concentrated on simple assembly operations. The remainder of this section will present evidence from the literature that strongly supports this assertion.

A 1989 study (González, Barajas, Arón & Ramírez, p. 5), which examined the electronics and automotive sectors in Tijuana, proposes that there is an ongoing process of growing technological dualism. This involves an increase in technological sophistication and productivity on the part of some compa-nies, and simultaneously an expansion in the number of new plants that carry out simple assembly at the low end of the technological scale. González & Ramírez (1989, p. 882) predict that in the nineties there will be growth in both these currents of the *maquiladora* industry: traditional simple assembly will be maintained and grow, while more capital–intensive processing of finished products will also be strengthened. Both these models will persist, they argue, although they hope that the traditional *maquiladora* will lose ground with an increase in the number of manufacturing plants doing more than assembly. Contrary to Gereffi, they conclude:

> The evidence demonstrates that while the recently industrialized Asian countries are headed for postmaquiladorization, in Mexico the industry is in a phase of rapid growth that is reorganizing and redefining it, but still maintaining the profoundly rooted model of the traditional maquiladora (González & Ramírez, 1989, p. 886. Trans. by K. Kopinak).

Carrillo (1990, p. 84) thinks that the concept of dual technology in the *maquiladoras* is oversimplified, preferring the term technological heteroge-neity, which he argues is extensive in both the machine technology and organization of the labor process of the automotive sector. His work also reinforces the position of González-Aréchiga and Ramírez quoted above when he says:

> It is important to point out that the process of automation in the electronic and automotive *maquiladora* industry and the new forms of organization do not follow an evolutionary and linear process, but that on the contrary . . . we are witnessing technological heterogeneity (Carrillo, 1989a, p. 47).

Numerous other researchers strongly agree with Carrillo and González-Aréchiga and Ramírez on this point. Brown and Domínguez (1989), for example, also consider *maquiladoras* to be technologically heterogeneous, with labor–intensive companies using rudimentary equipment coexisting with others that are more technologically advanced. They observe heterogeneity within the same companies, which combine capital– and labor–intensive processes. While new microelectronic technologies are quickly diffusing, many firms remain that are not interested in their adoption. Brown and Domínguez include many industries in the automotive sector among the firms uninterested in the adoption of microelectronic technologies: those assembling batteries, vacuum pumps, harnesses, coils, switches, and power sources. These components are produced on long manual assembly lines with a minimum of equipment, and they are closest to the traditional type of export *maquila.*

It is important to avoid conflating the concepts of technological dualism and heterogeneity, and to be accurate about the fact that technological dualism is not what has happened in Mexican *maquiladoras,* and that it is not likely to happen under NAFTA. The level of technology associated with new *maquiladoras* in the future cannot be anticipated (see González-Aréchiga & Ramírez, 1989, p. 876). Technological heterogeneity is also distinct from the concept of "heterogeneity of growth," which started appearing frequently in official Mexican discourse and the press in 1990. "Heterogeneity of growth" has usually been used to refer to the fact that while economic activity associated with exports was dynamized briefly as a result of the economic opening, activity associated with imports stagnated (see Alcocer, 1992). The National Manufacturing Industries Chamber (CANACINTRA) reported that while many Mexican–owned industries had closed or declined, others, particularly those geared to export, were thriving.[2] It criticized the government's policy of opening borders to foreign products while unsuccessfully promoting better ties between Mexican industries and the world market. Thus, the goal of the 1989 government decree of merging Mexican and foreign industry in a system of shared production appears to be failing to date.

Technological dualism has been used as an ideological tool to construct a bifurcated understanding of reality (see Smith, 1987), in order to dismiss one of its dimensions: the labor–intensive assembly *maquiladoras*. What is connoted by labeling some industries old is that these *maquilas* are part of an era that is over, that they are an outdated example that is no longer relevant to industrial policy or politics.

Analysts dismissing the traditional *maquiladoras* are also less likely to address the importance of the gender composition of the labor force. Unlike "critics" who argued that foreign capital took advantage of Mexican patriarchy to exploit women, or "apologists" who argued that women's employment provided opportunities for improving their situation, those promoting the policies of the present Mexican government tend to exhibit gender blindness. They assume that if the new *maquiladoras* are going to hire more men, gender no longer needs to be addressed as an explanatory variable. When they are mentioned, women workers are sometimes said to be absent *because* of the increase in high–tech production, thus reinforcing the stereotype that women do not have the aptitude for technologically sophisticated work. In any case, the technological determinism of this literature has been accompanied by a misrepresentation of the gender composition of the labor force.

In fact, data collected for automotive *maquiladoras* show the proportion of women in the direct labor force to have increased in the process of their conversion into *maquiladoras*. This is why feminization of the labor force is a central part of the definition of maquiladorization, as noted above. Carrillo (1990, p. 94) shows that while the previous Mexican auto industry for finished products employed only men, 52.1 percent of the total labor force in auto parts *maquiladoras* in the late 1980s were women.

Carrillo (1992, forthcoming) studied nine Ford automotive plants and showed how, for the first time in the history of the automotive industry in that country, women played a significant role in production. He calculated that approximately 20 percent of the total foreign currency generated by this firm came from women's work. While women were mostly employed in labor–intensive jobs, some of them have retained jobs that have been automated. He argued that women have been increasingly employed in the auto sector because of their flexibility; that is, quality production requires not only a consensual attitude on the part of workers, but also the ability to regulate working conditions, both of which are facilitated by women workers.

Simultaneously, several researchers observe a process of masculiniza-tion ongoing in the labor force of the entire *maquiladora* sector, of which auto production is only one part. This is due to the fact that while the proportion of women direct workers has increased in auto *maquilas,* it has decreased in other *maquiladora* industries. In a case study of Juárez, Brannon and Lucker argue (1989, p. 48) that the rate of male employment increased after the crisis in 1982 because the preferred labor force, young women, was not large enough to meet the needs of industries' rapid explosion. Instead of raising wages to compete for them, management decided to hire groups like men, women over twenty–five, migrants, and so on more often than previously. Most researchers hypothesize that *if* the number of *maquiladoras* continues to increase at the high rate it has in the 1980s, the proportion of males in the *maquiladora* labor force will also increase. This will be especially true if labor markets are consolidated by industries' need for overtime, for which women are often not available because of their work in the home.

It is clear from recent research findings that this new segmentation of the *maquiladora* labor force has disadvantaged women workers. Like Carrillo, Barajas and Rodríguez (1989) find women electronics workers in the least skilled and automated jobs. In his study of *maquiladoras* that use only high–tech processes, Shaiken (1990) shows that women still work in less–skilled electronics jobs and are managed with patriarchal management ideologies (focusing workers' attention on the improvement of personal hygiene, and housekeeping, for example) as opposed to empowered work teams and quality circles. Solís (1991, p. 5) has shown how the deregula-tion of federal labor law has had salary flexibility as its goal and has resulted in different salary levels between men and women and among sectors of production and companies.

Some authors have avoided the conceptual trap set up by the notion of old and new *maquilas* by using the Fordism/post-Fordism framework. Wilson (1990, p. 136) describes the *maquiladora* industry as being at a historic crossroads.

> Will it continue to provide mainly a cost-saving respite for U.S. manufacturers faced with stiff international competition? Or will it find a role in the new corporate strategies of flexible production that permit a longer-term competitive advantage in the global economy?

Post-Fordist industries, Wilson asserts, incorporate more fixed capital by employing computerized technology that allows the production process to be more flexible. They also restructure the labor process by practicing multiskilling, job rotation, decision making by workers in teams, quality circles, and cooperative relations between management and labor. This is in comparison to the Taylorist scientific management techniques applied in Fordism, in which workers are less skilled, managed through a hierarchy of supervision, and organized into unions that can represent them on the shop floor. Post-Fordism also subcontracts more and has a closer relationship between firms and their suppliers.

Wilson's survey of managers in 71 *maquiladoras* on the border and in the interior finds (weighted nationally) that 21 percent of plants fall into the post-Fordist category, even though the one post-Fordist characteristic that was not present was flexible production through subcontracting. On this basis, she concludes that post-Fordist production is not incompatible with being located in Mexico (either at the border or in the interior). She also notes that none of these post-Fordist plants was fully automated, and many have maintained traditional assembly lines, where most of the production may still be carried out. She bridges these contradictory findings by saying that

> post-Fordist plants have adapted to their cheap labor content with low wages, short job ladders, a largely female labor force, little or no research and development, and no fully integrated flexible manufacturing. The result is a caricature of the post-Fordism being experienced in the advanced countries (Wilson, 1990, p. 149).

On a national level, she finds that the largest category (44 percent) of *maquiladoras* is still the labor-intensive assembly plant and says, "The plants in this group are not aging leftovers of a bygone era, either, as 75 percent of them were established after 1982 and nearly half of them since 1986" (Wilson, 1990, p. 150).

The most rapidly growing segment of the *maquiladora* industry, according to her study, is Fordist manufacturers, that is, those who manufacture but do not use post-Fordist technology. These plants hired the largest proportion of male workers, gave the most training to their workers, were the youngest plants, and were rapidly proliferating. She concludes that U.S. producers are using *maquiladoras* primarily for Fordist manufacturing and labor-intensive assembly in order to reduce costs without fundamental restructuring, and that Mexico may suffer in the future if real post-Fordist production techniques are adopted on a world scale throughout industry, since their caricatured post-Fordist and Fordist industry will not be able to compete.

POTENTIAL IMPACT OF NAFTA ON MAQUILADORAS

Economic integration has led to growth of the number of *maquiladoras* and an internal differentiation of their kind. As Carrillo (1989a, p. 38) indicates, the program has changed from being perceived as a palliative for unemployment to being seen as an unstable industry of capital in flight to being considered a permanent industrial base. There is no longer any question of whether Mexican industry will be maquiladorized, since this has already taken place. Maquiladorization, as a form of industrial organization, has spread to industries not legally considered *maquiladoras*. A more relevant question is what the mix will be between the different types of *maquiladoras*. Available research findings still do not allow an answer to this question, previously raised by Shaiken (1990, p. 122):

> One critical question from the perspective of national development is whether successful high-tech manufacturing precipitates significant backward and forward linkages, or whether high-tech plants become "islands of automation" surrounded by "footloose" production that is likely to relocate quickly based on fluctuations in wages, exchange rates, and political stability.

The neomodernization thesis of the "apologists" has been explored above; the "critics" are reconsidered in this final section of the chapter for an exploration of the null hypothesis. While there is an amazing degree of conformity within the Mexican professorate to the hegemonic paradigm promoted by the government, some critical voices can still be found (albeit more often outside than inside Mexico) with alternative explanations. Jorge Calderón, for example, argues that the policies of economic liberalization that have included maquiladorization and free trade (as well as opening to foreign imports, privatization of state industries, withdrawing support from peasants, and so on) have resulted in a process of deindustrialization. This is the opposite of the reindustrialization suggested by the movement of industries from Canada and the United States to Mexico (CBC, 1991, p. 15).

Calderón suggests that there are two processes occurring simultaneously in Mexico. On the one hand, the opening of the Mexican market to foreign imports, which began in 1982, is wiping out domestic Mexican industries, which have historically been located in the geographic triangle formed by Mexico City, Monterrey, and Guadalajara and once employed two and a half million workers. These industries were geared to the internal market and provided a range of jobs and salary levels. On the other hand, the new industries established in the *maquiladoras*, still located mostly at the northern border, provide fewer jobs than the number lost from Mexican–owned industry and agriculture. The jobs *maquiladoras* provide are comparatively unskilled and poorly paid, so that workers have less buying power and the internal domestic market has shrunk with the focus on export production. Calderón argues that while exports have doubled in the last ten years, imports have at least tripled, and this is leading to a new debt crisis and problems with current accounts, since Mexico is now using borrowed funds to pay for the imports (CBC, 1991, p. 16). As a result of this deindustrialization, economic inequalities in Mexico are increasing.

It is not difficult to find empirical evidence that the deindustrialization thesis is currently becoming a reality if one follows emerging trends in the pages of Mexico's most prominent business daily, *El Financiero*. Migueles (1992) showed how Mexico's trade deficit with Canada and the United States had substantially increased during 1991 due to a standstill in exports and an increase in imports. Observing that the principal beneficiary of the commercial opening had been the United States, he concluded that Mexico should put more energy into getting its products into other international markets besides those of Canada and the United States, even though he acknowledged that the signing of NAFTA and the formation of economic blocks on a world level might make this difficult in the next few years. Barragán (1992), in a later article, explained that the demand in 1991 for intermediate and capital goods needed for the creation of competitive industry has been responsible for this trade deficit, which is the greatest in the economic history of Mexico. He argued that since almost all these imports have had to be paid for with U.S. dollars at a constantly slipping exchange rate of Mexican pesos, this has contributed to inflation.

There is also no dearth of evidence about the decline of Mexican domestic industry. Gutiérrez (1992) reported a decrease in the rate of manufacturing growth in 1991, which was attributed to Mexico's technological backwardness, the influx of imports due to the government's trade–opening policy, and protectionism in international markets. The most dynamic performance in manufacturing was recorded by exporters in 1991, with the top exporters in the manufacturing sector being food processing, equipment, chemicals, *maquiladoras*, agroindustry, nonmetallic minerals, lumber, and paper. Meanwhile, the president of the CANACINTRA announced on 23 January 1992 that the previous year had seen small–scale manufacturers struggling to stay afloat because of restricted access to credit, high taxes and operating costs, and depressed prices for manufactures. These factors, as well as displacement by foreign companies and large industrial consortiums, had caused nearly 600 small–scale enterprises to close down in 1991, and many more were predicted to disappear in the following year (SourceMex, 15 January 1992).

Parra (1992) reports that a study by economists at the National Autonomous University of Mexico, titled "Industrial Modernization and Workers," showed how the development of productivity in Mexico has caused both the accumulation of wealth and unemployment. They found that while the purchasing power of the minimum wage went down 16 percent in the last two years, prices increased 57 percent. In the last 14 years, the purchasing power accumulated over the previous 55 years has been wiped out and is now half of what it was between 1936 and 1938. The economists explained the low wages in terms of high levels of unemployment (particularly among the unskilled), government policies regarding minimum salaries, and the weakening of the power of trade unions.

Similarly, Provencio (1992) reported on a study carried out by National Informatics and Statistics Institute (INEGI) that showed that between 1984 and 1989, the top 10 percent of Mexican families had increased their share of national income, while all other deciles—especially the lowest 10 percent, but also middle income groups—decreased their proportion of the national income. This increased inequality was attributed to the economic crisis and the failure of government policies to improve the situation. Even the patriarch of Mexican labor, Fidel Velázquez, railed against the unemployment of 5.5 million people, a fifth of the country's labor force, caused by the commercial opening, and warned that social peace was threatened by the fact that workers have had to absorb the effects of the economic crisis (Herrera, 1992b).

While information about these trends supporting the deindustrialization hypothesis has been available only in the press and from critics who are largely ignored in powerful circles, President Salinas himself declared at the end of May 1992 that the economy was slowing down and that it would not reach the previously set targets for growth. According to Alcocer (1992), this was tantamount to a lightning bolt in an otherwise calm sky, and the president recanted within a few hours because of the unexpected drop in confidence from the business community that resulted. Alcocer suggests that what is happening is not an economic slowdown, but growth under conditions of structural disequilibrium, which government policy exacerbates rather than corrects. The conditions leading to structural disequilibrium are exactly those observed in the press, and Salinas is responding by trying to restrain the Mexican economy and cut back spending, in order to counter exaggerated expectations of the effects of NAFTA, which he created.

It is against this backdrop of events that NAFTA negotiations have taken place. Gambrill (1991) notes that while the United States did not include *maquiladoras* on the agenda of the negotiations, despite their strategic value in relations between the two countries, Mexico tried to introduce them in order to get concessions. Mexico's goal was to get the U.S. tariffs on the value added to *maquiladora* products dissolved, so that companies in Mexico can supply more than the 1.5 percent of the inputs to *maquiladora* production that they now supply. Similarly, in April 1992, Mexican automotive industrialists demanded that their government refuse to sign a NAFTA that failed to consolidate the tariffs on goods protected under the GSP at zero. Both of these demands are consistent with the goal of shared production, which would allow the *maquiladoras* to contribute substantially to Mexico's gross domestic product and manufacture more finished products.

While it is difficult to know the exact impact of NAFTA on *maquiladoras*, some possibilities can be sketched. Some analysts have argued that NAFTA will remove the special privileges of existing *maquiladoras*, because all industries will be regulated under a system that is as open or more open than the one they have enjoyed. While this might disadvantage already established *maquiladoras* and Mexican domestic industries by giving them more competition, it would advantage capital that still wishes to relocate to Mexico.

Herrera (1992a) reported on a study carried out by *El Financiero* with data from Banco de México and INEGI. The study warned that in the first two years of NAFTA's operation, Mexico could lose 23 percent of its manufacturing industry and 14 percent of its jobs. It predicted the greatest job losses in the metal, food, textile, and wood sectors, because those domestic industries have the most obsolete technology and have had the least access to credit since the beginning of the 1970s.

With the de facto maquiladorization of the Mexican economy even without NAFTA, some have predicted that under NAFTA *maquiladoras* would not only be maintained, but that their numbers would increase even more rapidly than they have been doing. Székely and Vera (1990, p. 54), for example, argued in the early stages of the NAFTA debate that it would be in the interest of Mexico to maintain the *maquiladoras* in order to continue to attract certain kinds of investment. They suggested that the Mexican government try to negotiate differential tariffs in order to help Mexican industries that have arisen as important suppliers of *maquiladoras* (that is, higher tariffs for some time on auto parts, textiles, and furniture). In its 1992 annual *maquiladora* report, Ciemex-Wharton predicted that the implementation of NAFTA would increase foreign investment in *maquilas*. However, because this increased investment under NAFTA will be attracted by cheap labor, wages are expected to increase by only $0.47 per hour by 1995, bringing the average wage (including benefits) to $2.64 per hour. The report also predicted that the Mexican content of *maquila* products would stay the same and not rise above 2 percent (see Cárdenas, 1992). It is noteworthy that their prediction of the maintenance of low wages and negligible Mexican inputs implies that *maquiladoras* will remain a separate enclave.

Inadequacy of Mexican infrastructure for industrial development will continue to be relevant even if NAFTA is postponed or canceled. Gambrill (1991, p. 39) argues that deficient infrastructure for industrial production in Mexico is a structural obstacle to the participation of domestic Mexican industry as suppliers in coproduction. Thus, it could be thought of as a nontariff barrier to the economic integration of Mexico into a continental economy. However, as González-Aréchiga and Ramírez (1989, p. 879) indicate, if there is going to be greater investment in *maquiladoras*, it must take place outside the border region, where the infrastructure and labor force are already severely overtaxed. The problem will be that infrastructure is even worse in the interior. As Sinkin, a prominent business consultant assisting industries moving to Mexico, has indicated, "the drive by the Mexican government to get more plants to locate in the interior is not going to be wildly successful," since companies do not want to move out of reach of U.S. executive expertise (cited in Ferguson, 1991). As long as *maquiladoras* operate as centers for cost reduction, it would be contradictory for them to pay for infrastructure. This is a longstanding problem of coordination between the *maquilas* and other sectors of the economy and society, since they have not contributed much to the financing of infrastructure in the past, but have received government support far greater than their real importance in the generation of industrial jobs (González-Aréchiga & Barajas, 1989, p. 332). It is difficult to see how development under NAFTA could do anything but exacerbate this problem, when it has not been improved by the commercial opening of the 1980s.

While *maquiladora* managers have always complained about the inadequacy of transportation and communication facilities, the awareness of environmental risks and dangers to public and workers' health has emerged more recently in Mexico. Sánchez (1989) argues that environmental issues were unheard of in Mexico until 1985 because of the priority given to *maquilas* by the state and federal governments, and the lack of coordination and resources among Mexican government agencies responsible.

As a result, *maquiladoras* have had enormous freedom to leave toxic residues in the country, and many located there for exactly this reason. It is especially the *maquilas* at the northern border, where most large plants are located, that are responsible. Belated recognition of the problem means that solutions cannot be forthcoming quickly. On 3 October 1991, Reyes, deputy environment and urban development minister, said that the Mexican government's environmental agency had acknowledged that 50 percent of the *maquiladora* plants near the U.S. border were producing toxic waste (Ballinas, 1991). The deputy minister admitted that the Mexican government had failed to adequately enforce regulations specifying that toxic wastes produced by such plants must be returned to the country supplying the inputs responsible for the toxicity. He also said that many *maquilas* currently lack necessary equipment to safely dispose of the toxic wastes they generate. Waste material is often dumped in vacant lots, resulting in soil and water table contamination.

It is generally recognized that Mexico does not have the resources to independently implement good environmental legislation, although many consider that this is already on the books. The United States and Mexico have agreed on an eight–year plan to treat sewage, improve roads, and study environmental impacts at the border, for which the Mexican government has earmarked $460 million over three years, while the U.S. government has committed $379 million over two years (Marquis, 1992, p. 8a). Jan Gilbreath, project coordinator for the U.S.–Mexican Policy Studies Program at the University of Texas, criticized the amount committed by the United States as inadequate, saying, "It's insulting. This is almost a way of saying pollution is a Mexican problem."

Employers are worried about free trade because an increase in *maquiladoras* will mean more competition for the resource that companies go to Mexico to get: cheap labor. This will be especially salient in border cities, where rotation rates are already high. Many of the most talented Mexican employees may quit to start their own businesses. An increase in rotation is expected. Elias (1991, p. 23) suggests that ultimately, employers may have to pay higher wages.

The question of wages brings sensitive labor issues to the fore. Since the beginning of the 1980s, given the absence of strong unions, *maquiladoras* have acted as a laboratory in the north of Mexico to test flexible labor policies. Much of the deregulation heretofore prevalent only in the *maquiladoras* (like the linking of salary to productivity and piecework, individualized relations of work, and withholding of permanent contracts and severance pay) may very well be extended to the entire Mexican labor force. Constitutional reform of federal labor legislation became a subject of debate among Mexican political parties early in 1992 due to NAFTA negotiations, and will undoubtedly be carried out within the term of President Salinas. Also proposed as part of the revision are other basic aspects of flexibility such as job rotation, modification of the working day and its categories, legal regulation of unions, and reform of the social security and subsidized housing programs.

As noted earlier in this section, wages have plummeted in the last 14 years in Mexico, and subsistence has become more difficult for those who earn the least, especially in the recent past. Carrillo (1991) argues that while no one questions that salaries are relatively low among *maquila* workers, his research in Monterrey, Juárez, and Tijuana found direct *maquila* workers on the average to be earning almost three times the legal minimum wage. This is hardly a recommendation for the evolution of *maquiladora* employment, however, since, as De Los Angeles (1991) has indicated, workers she studied in Monterrey needed to have two or three minimum wages earned in their households just to survive. She reported that the cost of living for the average worker's family of five was two times the current minimum wage, even when considering only indispensable consumer goods and not counting costs for education, clothing, entertainment, and so on. Given these circumstances, it is not surprising that *maquiladora* workers often prefer to earn their living in the informal economy if they can.

What will happen to Mexican wages in the future will depend very much on how federal labor law reforms deal with unions. Unlike unions in Canada and the United States, officially recognized unions in Mexico have always been part of the highly centralized state and are instruments of managerial domination and self–aggrandizement. Given that the party in power—the Institutional Revolutionary Party (PRI)—has reduced the power of unions in its legislation during the first half of its current term, this can be expected to be the direction taken by future reforms. A new form of union has developed in *maquiladoras* since 1976, which Carrillo and Ramírez (1990) call regressive and functional. It is functional in that like traditional unions, it supports state and local governments, but regressive in that it has little presence in the workplace, and tends to negotiate clauses into collective contracts below the minimum standards set by federal labor law.

These organizations leave *maquiladora* workers with no capacity to negotiate, which is why they often quit their jobs in response to dissatisfaction, pushing up rotation rates. Ramírez (1988, p. 113) drew the link quite clearly between the failure of unions to defend workers' rights and rotation, arguing that high rates of rotation of workers between factories would not be reduced until free and open unionism prevailed. Recent government actions, however, indicate that this is not likely. The January 1992 arrest of Gonzáles, one of the few relatively effective union leaders, on two–year-old tax–evasion charges—an event that occurred in the middle of strikes by eight of the *maquiladora* unions he led in Matamoros—is generally recognized as state intervention on behalf of management. Victories Gonzáles had helped win for workers in his leadership career included a 40–hour week with pay for 56 hours, and the payment by the companies of social security fees and taxes on workers' salaries (Corro and Garza, 1992).

Mexican academic critics of the government's debilitating control of union activities have generally adopted the language of the hegemonic paradigm. Arteaga (1990), for example, in his reaction to the well–known assassination of an independent union leader at Ford Cuautitlán, referred to the process as one of "savage flexibility." Micheli (1990) expresses his disagreement in the language of official orthodoxy, arguing that historically developed forms of union control demonstrate that official unions in Mexico lack the ability to adapt themselves to the era of industrial modernization now emerging. He says that what is called for in such situations is not the reproduction of the conspicuous monopoly of power that arose in the decades of corporatism within the Mexican state, but instead a recognition of heterogeneity among unions, and new criteria for organization, representation, and participation through which labor can shape itself as a social force. De Los Angeles (1991) has suggested that the Authentic Labor Front (FAT) represents such a new union movement, but so far it has been active mostly in Mexico City and is only beginning to have a presence in the northern *maquiladoras*.

CONCLUSION

A general criticism of the strategy of continental economic integration has been that it will turn Mexico into a giant *maquiladora* of the traditional variety. It is the conclusion of this chapter that Mexico does indeed seem to be moving in this direction, rather than being able to modernize. As noted above, in the section considering the modernization thesis, labor–intensive assembly plants still constitute the largest category of *maquiladoras* and are not expected to disappear. As Gambrill (1991, p. 59) notes,

> the fear that the country will be converted into a great *maquiladora* is dispelled only in part with the discussion over the speed with which the *maquiladora* industry can evolve toward coproduction. It depends how many national companies are not going to be able to compete head–on in the world market with the same products coming from other countries (Trans. by K. Kopinak).

The preceding section demonstrated that between 1989—at the start of the government decree written to strengthen national production by joining it to foreign production—and mid-1992, there was evidence pointing to the fact that with some exceptions, national industry in Mexico has not been able to compete very well on an international level.

The economic opening of Mexico has not been accompanied by real material redistribution or democratization. This makes political participation that would address the problems of deindustrialization and increased inequality difficult. Critics like Aguilar Zinser (CBC, 1991, p. 19) have predicted that eventually there will be a "strong political reaction" in Mexico, but he does not believe the United States will allow the Mexican state to change its course, especially if it has already signed away its right to do so through NAFTA.

NOTES

I would like to thank Ken Traynor and Stephen Herzenberg for comments on earlier drafts of this paper, and Hugo Ciceri S. for help with sources.

1. See for example Fernandez-Kelly (1983; 1987); Ruiz and Tiano (1987).
2. "Totalmente heterogéneo, el desarrollo de la planta productiva nacional." (29 January 1992). *El Financiero.*
3. The Instituto Nacional de Estadística e Informática defines direct workers as men and women whose work is related directly to the productive process of the *maquila* in assembly, inspection, maintenance, repair, and so on.
4. Her finding that some of these labor-intensive plants used technology associated with post-Fordism raises questions for this author about the usefulness of the Fordist/post-Fordist categories, although this cannot be fully elaborated within the space of this chapter.

REFERENCES

Alcocer, J. (1992). "Señales de alarma oficiales." *Proceso* (813), 32-34.

Almond, G., and Verba, S. (1963). *The Civic Culture.* Princeton: Princeton University Press.

Angulo, C. (1990). "Foreign Investment and the *Maquiladora* Export Industry." *Inversión Extranjera Directa-Direct Foreign Investment.* Mexico, D.F.: Banamex, 139-143.

Arteaga, A. (1990). "Nacido Ford, Crecido Flexible." *Trabajo* 2, 64-74.

Ballinas, V. (4 October 1991). "Producen Las Maquiladoras Residuos Peligrosos: SEDUE." *La Jornada.*

Barragán, A. (4 February 1992). "Persiste el Dinamismo en Importaciones, Crecieron 23.2% en 1991." *El Financiero.*

Barajas, R., and Rodríguez, C. (1989). *Mujer y Trabajo en la Industria Maquiladora de Exportación en Tijuana, Baja California.* (Mimeograph, Tijuana).

Brannon, J. and Lucker, G. (1989). "The Impact of Mexico's Economic Crisis on the Demographic Composition of the *Maquiladora* Labor Force." *Journal of Borderlands Studies.* 4 (1), 39-70.

Brown, F., and Domíngez, L. (1989). "Nuevas Tecnologías en la Industria Maquiladora de Exportación." *Comercio Exterior,* 39 (3), 215-223.

CBC (1991). "Inside Mexico." *Ideas.* Toronto: Canadian Broadcasting Corporation.

Cárdenas, L. (9 January 1992). "En 92 Llegarán a Mexico Más de 200 Maquiladoras." *La Jornada.*

Carrillo, J. (1992, forthcoming). *Mujeres en la Industria Automotriz en Mexico.* (Por publicarse en Cuadernos de Trabajo, El Colegio de la Frontera Norte).

———. (1991). "Las Maquiladoras en el TLC: Integración Complementaria o Competencia Desigual." *Trabajo.* (5-6), 52-61.

———. (1990). "Maquilización de la Industria Automotriz en México. De la Industria Terminal a la Industria de Ensamble." In J. Carrillo V. (ed.), *La Nueva Era de la Industria Automotriz en México.* Tijuana, B.C.: El Colegio de la Frontera Norte, 67-114.

———. (1989a). "Transformaciones en la Industria Maquiladora de Exportación." In B. González-Aréchiga and R. Barajas Escamilla (eds.), *Las Maquiladoras: Ajuste Estructural y Desarrollo Regional.* Tijuana: Fundación Friedrich Ebert, 37-54.

———. (1989b). "Introducción." In J. Carrillo (ed.), *Reestructuración Industrial: Maquiladoras en la Frontera Mexico-Estados Unidos.* Tijuana: Colegio de la Frontera Norte, 13-25.

Carrillo, J. and Ramírez, M. (1990). "Maquiladoras en la Frontera Norte: Opinión sobre los Sindicatos." *Frontera Norte,* 2 (4), 121-152.

Corro, S. and Garza, J. A. (1992). "Los Maquiladores se Quejaron con Salinas y Agapito González fue Detenido." *Proceso* (797), 32-33.

De Los Angeles, M. (1991). "Modernización de las Relaciones en las Empresas Regiomontanas." Paper presented in the seminar "Mercados de Trabajo: Una Perspectiva Comparativa, Tendencias Generales y Cambios Recientes."

Elias, L. (October 1991). "Preparations for Free trade: Preparing Your Work Force." *Twin Plant News,* 22-24.

Ferguson, T. W. (21 May 1991). "Mr. Chips Says Goodbye U.S. Plants, Hello Mexico." *Wall Street Journal,* A23.

Fernández-Kelly, M. P. (1987). "Technology and Employment along the U.S.-Mexican Border." In C. L. Thorup et al. (eds.), *The United States and Mexico: Face to Face with New Technology.* Washington, D.C.: Overseas Development Council, 149-167.

———. (1983). *For We Are Sold, I and My People: Women and Industry in Mexico's Frontier.* Albany, N.Y.: State University of New York Press.

Gambrill, M. C. (1991). "El Impacto del Tratado de Libre Comercio sobre la Industria Maquiladora." In B. Driscoll de Alvarado and M. Gambrill (eds.), *El Tratado de Libre Comercio, entre el Viejo y el Nuevo Orden.* Mexico: Universidad Nacional Autónoma de México, 35-59.

Gereffi, G. (1992). "Mexico's *Maquiladora* Industries and North American Integration." In S. J. Randall, with H. Konrad and S. Silverman (eds.), *North America without Borders? Integrating Canada, the United States and Mexico.* Calgary: University of Calgary.

González-Aréchiga, B., Barajas, R., Arón, N., and Ramírez, J. (1989). *La Industria Maquiladora Mexicana en los Sectores Electrónico y de Autopartes.* Mexico: Fundación Friedrich Ebert.

——— and Ramírez, J. (1989). "Perspectivas Estructurales de la Industria Maquiladora." *Comercio Exterior,* 39 (10), 874-886.

——— and Barajas, R. (1989). "Retos para el Aprovechamiento y la Coordinación de la Industria Maquiladora." In B. González-Aréchiga and R. Barajas Escamilla (eds.), *Las Maquiladoras: Ajuste Estructural y Desarrollo Regional.* Tijuana: Fundación Friedrich Ebert, 323-339.

Gutiérrez, E. (16 March 1992). "Desaceleración del Crecimiento en la Industria Manufacturera Durante 1991." *El Financiero.*

Hart, M. (1990). *A North American Free Trade Agreement: The Strategic Implications for Canada.* Ottawa: Centre for Trade Policy and Law.

Hector, C. (1990). "Las Maquiladoras Mexicanas y el Libro Intercambio Canadiense-Americano: ¿Un Caballo de Troya Insospechado?" *Problemas del Desarrollo,* 21, 157-180.

Herrera, E. (7 May 1992a). "En Riesgo de Perderse, el 23% de la Industria Manufacturera." *El Financiero,* 18.

———. (8 May 1992b). "5.5 Millones de Desempleados, Fruto de la Apertura: Fidel." *El Financiero.*

Marquis, C. (1 June 1992). "The Free Trade Trade-off." *Miami Herald,* 1a,8a.

Migueles, R. (9 January 1992). "Déficit Comercial de México con Norteamérica de 3 mil mdd en 91." *El Financiero,* 5a.

Micheli, J. (1990). "Los Límites de la Intoleracia." *Trabajo* (2), 2-3.

Parra, F. (17 March 1992). "Bajó 16% el Poder de Compra de los Salarios Mínimos; Los Precios Subieron en 2 Años." *El Financiero,* 27.

Provencio E. (8 May 1992). "Una Nación Mas Desigual. *La Jornada.*

Ramírez, J. C. (1988). "La Nueva Industria Sonorense: el Caso de las Maquilas de Exportación." In J. C. Ramírez (ed.), *La Nueva Industrialización en Sonora: el Caso de los Sectores de Alta Tecnología.* Hermosillo: El Colegio de Sonora, 17-132.

Ruiz, V., and Tiano, S. (eds.). (1987). *Women on the U.S.-Mexican Border: Responses to Change.* Boston: Allen and Unwin.

Sánchez, R. (1989). "Contaminación de la Industria Fronteriza: Riesgos para la Salud y el Medio Ambiente." In B. González-Aréchiga and R. Barajas Escamilla (eds.), *Las Maquiladoras: Ajuste Estructural y Desarrollo Regional.* Tijuana: Fundación Friedrich Ebert, 155-184.

Salinas, C. (1982). *Political Participation, Public Investment, and Support for the System.* University of California at San Diego: Center for U.S.-Mexican Studies.

Shaiken, H. (1990). *Mexico in the Global Economy: High Technology and Work Organization in Export Industries* (Monograph Series, 33). University of California, San Diego: Center for U.S.-Mexican Studies.

Smith, D. (1987). *The Everyday World as Problematic: A Feminist Sociology.* Toronto: University of Toronto Press.

Solís, A.A. (1991). "Política Laboral, Productividad y Mujeres Trabajadores." *Fem* (15), 4-8.

SourceMex. (1992, January 15), 3 (1).

Székely, G., and Vera, O. (1990). "Integración: La Hora de los Sectores." *Nexos,* 49-60.

Wilson, P. A. (1990). "The New *Maquiladoras*: Flexible Production in Low-Wage Regions." In K. Fatemi (ed.), *The Maquiladora Industry: Economic Solution or Problem?* New York: Praeger, 135-158.

Chapter 10

Industrial Restructuring in Mexico During the 1980s

Edur Velasco Arregui

The Mexican industrialization project undertaken during the decade following the end of the petroleum boom in 1981 is characterized as one of fragmentary export industrialization (FEI), a phrase used to describe industrial growth oriented toward the export of semifinished products with low value added. Such industrial growth captures only a fragment of the productive process, and does not develop new, technologically advanced products. The precursor of FEI was the import-substitution industrialization (ISI) model, which, after three decades of a protected domestic market and state control of the labor movement, failed to develop an industrial structure capable of meeting the needs of a growing population.

This chapter argues that FEI has not resolved the problems that led to the crisis of ISI during the 1970s. This new industrial project is as exclusionary as the former one, despite changes that cause it to revolve not around the state, but rather around external markets. The problems of unemployment, marginalized sectors, and extremely unequal distribution of wealth and income, worsened during the 1980s. The restructuring of manufacturing in Mexico has been significant, particularly in terms of the sectoral composition of industry and its geographic location. Manufacturing has spread into sectors and regions capable of providing the productive services required by world markets. More importantly, the fragmentary export project has caused a deterioration in the terms of trade between Mexico and other countries. Furthermore, after ten years, FEI has reached its growth limits; the exhaustion of industrial expansion, an inundation of imports, and the stagnation of labor productivity provide dramatic evidence of this.

THE CRISIS OF IMPORT-SUBSTITUTION INDUSTRIALIZATION

The essential stimulus for the restructuring of Mexican industry in the 1980s was a crisis of ISI. In the period following the end of World War II, Mexican industrialization relied not only on a protected domestic market, but also on the state's tendency to co-opt or repress social and labor union dissidence.[1]

The state, in alliance with transnational capital, promoted the rise of a domestic industrial oligarchy. This oligarchy developed an unbalanced and inefficient manufacturing sector. In spite of the intense capitalization of Mexican factories during the period 1960-85, productivity advanced at a low rate. Total factor productivity[2] (TFP) in the industrial sector grew at a rate of only 0.9 percent per year during this period, while the corresponding rate for the United States was 1.8 percent. By 1960, TFP in Mexican manufacturing was only 70 percent of that in the United States; by 1985, Mexico's TFP was down to 53 percent. The productivity gap between Mexico and the United States had widened (Hernandez Laos & Velasco, 1990).

Post–World War II industrial development supported a dismal distribution of income in the country. The so-called Mexican Miracle (i.e., rapid growth from the 1940s to the mid-1970s) was incapable of absorbing the large numbers of rural-urban migrants into the labor force. Thanks to a combination of the flooding of the labor market caused by thousands of job-seekers from the countryside on the one hand, and the blocking of trade unions' capacity for resistance on the other hand, the share of wages in national income dropped dramatically from a high in the 1970s of about 35 percent to 25 percent in the late 1980s (Velasco, 1990).

During the period of ISI, Mexican manufacturing failed to branch out from consumer goods production into production of machinery and equipment. As a result, industrial expansion depended on imported machinery and equipment. In 1981, the trade imbalance was such that for every dollar's worth of manufactured goods that Mexico exported, it imported six of intermediate and capital goods (Banco de México, 1989).

The end of the petroleum boom in 1982 revealed the weakness and vulnerability of the Mexican industrial structure. In the two years that followed, industrial production contracted by 12 percent. Nonetheless, the profound devaluation of the peso—600 percent in less than ten months

(March-December 1982)—created a barrier that protected the damaged Mexican manufacturing sector from total collapse. A real undervaluation of the peso, which reached a peak of 34 percent in 1986, complemented a web of tariff and nontariff barriers (Banco de México, 1992b). Thus, Mexican industry ended the phase of ISI neither triumphantly nor in utter defeat, but rather with a long period of stagnation. It was only in 1988 that the volume of industrial production recovered its 1981 level. In 1992, per capita industrial production was still less than it had been 12 years earlier (Instituto Nacional de Estadistica, Geografía e Informática [INEGI], 1992b). The continuing massive emigration of workers to the United States was the clearest indicator that the Mexican industrial oligarchy had failed to organize a viable economic system.

THE PROJECT OF FRAGMENTARY
EXPORT INDUSTRIALIZATION

Beginning in 1983, a new Mexican industrial project was initiated. Some authors have termed this a secondary export project.[3] This term is generally used to refer to industrialization processes based on long-term strategies for raising the competitiveness of the manufacturing sector. Secondary export involves industrialization aimed at export markets through a complex development of products, something Michael Porter (1990) terms a *value chain.* This chain includes research and development, as well as the upgrading of human resources and the engineering and design of new products and processes.

What Mexico is doing in its new export operations, particularly those of the *maquiladora* type, is so different from the above description that it ought not to be called *secondary export* at all. Mexico's new industries do not produce export goods; rather, they provide productive services that represent a fragment of the value chain of other nations. *Maquiladora* plants perform low-value-added industrial operations but have no influence in how these operations fit into the industrial process as a whole. To describe Mexico's industrial project, therefore, as *secondary* is less accurate a term than *fragmentary,* since the latter conveys a sense both of an isolated segment and of an unfinished product.

ISI policies attempted to raise the national content of the final product through backward linkages with national suppliers. Although it had serious shortcomings, ISI contributed to the creation of an integrated, endogenous industrial nucleus; unlike ISI, FEI does not contribute to such industrial

Table 10.1
Mexico: Terms of Trade in International Trade (1981-1991)

Year	Terms of trade (1971 = 100)
1981	123.5
1982	107.5
1983	98.2
1984	96.3
1985	91.1
1986	65.6
1987	72.5
1988	65.5
1989	68.9
1990	74.3
1991	61.8

Source: Banco de México, *Informe Anual 1991*.

integration. The goal of FEI is to create flexible and dynamic industrial enclaves, with as little articulation between different companies as possible. The strategic objective of developing an "endogenous nucleus" is abandoned and replaced by the goal of inserting the export sector into the global economy. Under the new regime, Mexico does not export any one product in particular. Rather, it exports its industrial flexibility—mainly based on ample supply of cheap labor—which allows it to accomplish certain tasks at a lower cost.

The new export orientation has deepened the asymmetrical integration of Mexico to the United States. The relationship is based on Mexico exporting an ever-growing volume of cheap labor services and, in return, receiving industrial products and financial resources that, in relative terms, are falling in value. The reason is that Mexico's FEI gambit has been characterized by worsening terms of trade. In 1991, Mexico's terms of trade were only half what they had been in 1981 (see Table 10.1). In 1991, a given amount of imports cost Mexico twice the volume of exports it had to pay in 1981.

At one point, it was believed that the decline in the terms of trade was a consequence of the fall in the price of petroleum. But by 1992, when petroleum exports represented a mere fifth of Mexico's total exports, it was safe to conclude that the decline in the terms of trade was intrinsic to the fragmentary export project. The reason for this is that under FEI, in order for Mexico to compete in the world market, it must undervalue the labor performed by the national work force. It is no coincidence that the implementation of FEI was accompanied by a drastic fall in real wages.

The production of a growing volume of exports with continually declining value added does not compare to the secondary export project of the "Four Tigers" in Southeast Asia, which have advanced in precisely the opposite direction. Hong Kong, South Korea, Singapore, and Taiwan, while pursuing a steady increase in value added in their exports, have at the same time systematically increased the technological sophistication of their products. In the case of FEI, falling terms of trade implies investing more and more labor in the export sector to pay for a given stream of imports and interest payments on the external debt. Such a waste of resources just to obtain the foreign currency needed to maintain macroeconomic and external stability does not constitute a real development project. Rather, it is a mercantilist project, in the classic sense of the term, but with one difference: while mercantilism was originally oriented toward the accumulation of precious metals in the coffers of the nation, the fragmentary export project serves instead to maintain the profits of foreign bankers.

STRUCTURAL CHANGE IN MEXICAN INDUSTRY

The composition of the Mexican industrial sector has changed in the last decade. There has been a significant reduction in the relative size of some nondurable consumer goods industries, such as textiles, clothing, and leather; lumber products; and paper products. The combined weight of these industries, as a proportion of total manufacturing production, has gone down from 22.3 percent in 1980 to 17.7 percent in 1991.[4] This change is the result of two forces: first, the stagnant purchasing power of Mexican consumers; and second, the massive presence of imported goods. Import liberalization has eroded the Mexican base of production in sectors like clothing and footwear, and even of certain branches of food production such as beverages, beer, and dairy products.

At the opposite extreme are industries such as chemical and petrochemicals; and metal, machinery, and transportation equipment. Their relative weight in total manufacturing production grew from 39.1 percent in 1980 to about 44.6 percent in 1991.[5] Contrary to the theory of comparative advantage, this area of activities is highly capital intensive.[6] These are areas of production dominated by transnational corporations (TNCs), and FEI is adapted to their competitive strategy. Mexico offers these TNCs optimal conditions in terms of location (close to the huge U.S. market), ample energy resources, cheap labor, and lack of (enforceable) environmental regulations. These two industrial divisions exported a total of $11,789 million in 1991, whereas the imported inputs they required totaled $11,722 million for the same year. The magnitude of the latter figure as compared to the former is solid evidence that these industries are textbook examples of FEI (INEGI, 1980-1992).

Another dimension of the restructuring of Mexican industry is the relocation of the industrial core. As can be appreciated from Table 10.2, between 1981 and 1991 there was a significant displacement of manufacturing production from the center of the country to the Northern Industrial Belt (NIB), which consists of Aguascalientes plus the six states that border the United States.[7] Between 1981 and 1991, industrial employment in the NIB doubled, accounting for 30.9 percent of the national total in 1991, almost ten points more than in 1981. Even within the NIB there are noticeable differences in industrial concentration. The favored locations for new industrial plants are Baja California, Chihuahua, and Tamaulipas, where large industrial clusters have emerged quite suddenly in the last few years. In the Valley of Mexico, the number of industrial laborers grew by barely 5 percent between 1981 and 1991. In that period, this zone's share of national industrial employment fell from 45 percent to 34 percent.

These changes in the location of industry have weakened the capacity of workers' organizations to resist abuses. During the years preceding the spread of the new FEI, a key nucleus of workers became increasingly involved in independent labor union activity in the Valley of Mexico (Alvárez, 1987, p. 134). This growth in independent union organizing, although it did not last long, did manage to push up wages in the region. In the early 1990s, wages in the new industrial districts in the North were 20 percent lower than those paid in the Valley of Mexico (INEGI, 1991). Lower wages are not the only indication that the movement of industry to the NIB represents a setback for workers. The new industrial cities in the North spend barely a third of what the older urban areas do on social infrastructure— health, education, housing, and transportation (INFONAVIT, 1985-1990). This implies a worsening of living standards, beyond the effect of lower wages, for workers who migrate to the new industrial cities.

Table 10.2
Regional Relocation of Industrial Employment in Mexico
(1981-1991)

(Number of industrial workers insured by IMSS—
Mexican Institute for Social Insurance)

States and Regions	1981	Percent	1991	Percent
Northern Industrial Belt (NIB)				
Baja California	16,598	0.7	102,805	3.3
Sonora	39,863	1.8	78,181	2.5
Chihuahua	71,573	3.2	223,463	7.3
Coahuila	76,269	3.4	134,816	4.4
Nuevo León	201,687	9.0	244,085	7.9
Tamaulipas	49,680	2.2	131,122	4.3
Aguascalientes	18,500	0.8	35,705	1.2
Subtotal, NIB	**474,170 2**	**1.3**	**950,177**	**30.9**
Center Industrial Belt (CIB)				
Metropolitan area, Valley of Mexico	1,006,877	45.2	1,052,676	34.2
Jalisco	157,601	7.1	209,304	6.8
Veracruz	71,345	3.2	123,120	4.0
Puebla	85,198	3.8	120,042	3.9
Subtotal	**1,321,021**	**59.3**	**1,505,142**	**48.9**
Total Mexico	**2,228,879**	**100.0**	**3,078,000**	**100.0**

Source: INEGI, *Estadística Económica y Social por Entidad Federativa,* 1981-1991.

Note: Sum of Subtotals does not add up to Total. The difference indicates the number of industrial workers in regions other than NIB and CIB.

EXHAUSTION OF THE FRAGMENTARY EXPORT PROJECT

The growth in Mexican manufacturing exports during the decade 1981-1991 rested on a conjunctural outward reorientation of certain lines of production and industrial districts. There was no fundamental change in the country's industrial base that would establish conditions for stable, long-term growth. The hypothesis of this work is that FEI was already pushing its built-in limits during the early 1990s. From 1982 to 1988, Mexican manufacturing exports grew at an average annual rate of 25 percent. In the following four years (from 1988 to 1991), that rate was only 7 percent—less than the rate of growth of world trade. By 1991, the U.S. recession, combined with the paralysis of Mexico's internal market, had reduced Mexico's industrial growth to half its 1988 level (Banco de México, 1992a). The fragmentary export project had seemingly exhausted its potential for growth.

Optimists can always point to a measure of ephemeral industrial success during the first years of the Salinas's administration. These years coincided with a recession in the United States, recessions which always have a paradoxical impact on the Mexican economy. In effect, the Mexican expansion of 1989 to 1991, far from being a symptom of strength, trapped Mexico once again in a wave of financial speculation. As with U.S. recessions in 1973-75 and 1980-83, low returns from investments in the United States prompted speculative capital from Wall Street to recycle, for a short while, through the financial markets of Mexico. In a market as small as Mexico's, its presence naturally generated a frightening rise in asset values, which inevitably ends in financial collapse when a new growth cycle begins in the United States.

The *maquiladora* industry, whose development in 15 cities of northern Mexico is the clearest expression of FEI growth, is experiencing a disturbing slowdown in its previously dizzying expansion (see chapter by Kopinak in this volume). For the first time in a decade, in 1990-91, the number of new *maquiladora* plants established was smaller than the number in the previous year. This decline is particularly impressive if one considers that there were years in the 1980s in which a new *maquiladora* was established every 24 hours (INEGI, 1992a). From 1985 to 1989, the number of assembly plant workers in the NIB grew at the extraordinary rate of 20 percent annually. It now appears that those golden years of boom are gone: between October 1991 and May 1992, the growth in *maquiladora* employment slowed down considerably, to reach a yearly rate of only 6 percent (Banco de México, 1989-1990; INEGI, 1992b).

Another worrying aspect of *maquiladora* growth is that the supporting urban infrastructure has reached its saturation point. The population of the cities in the

NIB tripled in one decade. Not surprisingly, the region suffers some of the severest housing problems in the country, and is among the nation's weakest in delivery of services. The improvised network of public services is unraveling. As a result of these difficulties, it appears that the *maquiladoras* will not be able to advance beyond their current fragile and rudimentary competitiveness. A tax hike on their activities by the municipalities, to help pay for improved services, is not viable. It could provoke closures and capital displacement to other Third World cities, where the TNCs would repeat their parasitic cycle of depredation of fragile infrastructures.

To appreciate the implications of the slowdown in *maquiladora* growth, it is necessary to recall that between 1985 and 1990 this sector generated 40 percent of the new industrial jobs in Mexico. During the second half of the 1980s, total employment in the manufacturing sector grew by a rate of 4.8 percent annually. In the 18-month period following October 1990, though, the rate of growth of total industrial employment, paralleling the decline of the *maquiladora* industry, slowed to a modest 1.5 percent annually (INEGI, 1992b).

There are further disquieting signs in Mexican industry. Although the economy experienced a substantial capital inflow during 1990 and 1991— estimated by the Bank of Mexico at $21 billion—a huge proportion of this has gone towards the acquisition of stock shares and other financial investments, rather than to the development of new productive capacity. Fixed gross investment continues to be limited, and barely reached 20 percent of GNP during 1991, far below the 1981 rate of 27 percent. The increase in business inventories was also worrisome, achieving a level in 1991 three times that of 1989—an indicator of incipient recession.

FEI has created an increasingly polarized industrial structure. At one extreme, there is a nucleus of 2,000 companies, where export production is concentrated. Labor productivity in this nucleus is only 40 percent of that in U.S. manufacturing and unit labor costs are much lower, since wages are so low (INEGI, 1991). This export sector has gradually increased its ability to absorb new technologies. In the process, it has destroyed many collective agreements established with unions; significantly increased the amount of work each worker must do; and diminished its own capacity to create new jobs. The other sector comprises about 135,000 companies, with an average productivity of $8,000 dollars per worker per year (INEGI, 1991). The survival of these companies is due more to protected markets and the absence of strong competition than to their capacity for innovation. This rudimentary sector of Mexican industry employs a third of the industrial work force. The restructuring process has modified neither the technology of the work process nor the design of its products.

The technological gap between large and small enterprises is one of the key strategic weaknesses in FEI. The absence of interindustry links has led to a slowdown in productivity, demonstrating the superficiality of the restructuring process that took place in the 1980s. Between 1981 and 1991, for the manufacturing industry as a whole, labor productivity increased by an average of only one percent annually; TFP grew at only half that annual rate for the same period (Hernández Laos & Velasco, 1990). Under these circumstances, the continued expansion of manufacturing exports is possible only if the unequal exchange with Mexico's principal commercial partners is further accentuated.

FEI has heightened the traditional Mexican dichotomy between high-technology enclaves and the primitive state of the industrial structure as a whole. During part of the 1980s, this duality allowed for simultaneous advances in manufacturing exports and the servicing of the foreign debt. However, by 1992, it appeared that only the massive incorporation of new technologies in small and medium-size industry would allow even mild advances in productivity in the manufacturing sector to continue steadily. Technological innovation in this sector would have to be geared toward increasing the quality of production, rather than substituting machinery for labor. Such technological intensification would require directing massive resources toward training, education, and the acquisition of technology. However, this approach would conflict with Mexico's agreements with international banking (which require the channeling of resources to pay the external debt) and with the concentration of savings (and investment funds) in the hands of the new financial oligarchy.[8] Consequently, once the potential of its high-technology enclaves has been fulfilled, the fragmentary export project faces a basic structural incapacity to increase, in any significant way, the competitiveness of Mexican manufacturing.

The incongruities of FEI have contributed to a growing deficit in Mexican manufacturing trade, which has worsened due to macroeconomic factors and the advances toward a North American Free Trade Agreement (NAFTA). During the period immediately following Mexico's 1986 entrance into the General Agreement on Tariffs and Trade (GATT), the devaluation of the peso protected Mexico's manufacturing industry. The tendency toward overvaluation of the peso in the period from 1989 to 1992 had the opposite effect. This overvaluation contributed to macroeconomic stability—in particular, by eliminating inflationary pressures—which is required to guarantee the inflow of capital and the advancement of NAFTA. It is in this context that the implementation of NAFTA, even beyond the tariff concessions that it requires, implies a qualitative jump in the unequal integration of the economies of Mexico and the United States. NAFTA has snatched away from

Mexican industry the exchange rate protection that characterized the first phase of Mexico's commercial liberalization, from 1986 to 1988.[9]

From 1988 to 1992, the country was shaken by an avalanche of industrial imports. In 1987, manufacturing imports totalled almost $11 billion. In 1991, the total was $28.5 billion, almost three times that of 1987, and the equivalent of about 40 percent of the total domestic demand for manufactured goods (Banco de México, 1992a). In 1992, Mexico was experiencing the most intense process of industrial dismantling in its recent history. Diverse industrial sectors were reaching the breaking point.

CONCLUSION

The fragmentary export project, launched in 1983, is not a viable strategy for the long-term competitiveness of the Mexican industrial sector. It has reorganized Mexico's industries as low-value-added productive segments in other nation's value chains. This segmented industrialization, driven by TNCs, does not promote an integrated industrial network and does not promote sustainable and stable growth. One important indicator is that productive investment has not significantly increased.

TNCs have once again established disarticulated export-oriented enclaves within what is, overall, a highly polarized industrialized structure. The Mexican economy remains incapable of serving growing needs—in particular, integrating huge numbers of rural-urban migrants into the labor force. Public infrastructures have been stretched beyond their limits, especially in the *maquiladora* border zone, where municipalities lack the ability to raise taxes for fear of losing foreign investment. Equally troubling is that this phase of export industrialization has been as exclusionary as ISI was before it. For the broad masses of Mexican peoples, who must seek the basic comforts of life within a primitive domestic industrial structure and deteriorating public infrastructure, this is simply not good enough.

NOTES

This chapter was translated from Spanish by Patricia Landolt.

1. The first stage of import-substitution industrialization was initiated after real wages had fallen by 50 percent during the 1940s and after the repression of the

petroleum strike of 1947. The last phase of ISI, fueled by the petroleum boom of 1978 to 1981, was accompanied by the dismantling of the electrical workers' democratic resistance (1977-78), the police occupation of the National Autonomous University of Mexico (1977), and the military occupation of dissident neighborhoods, such as Juchitan, in the state of Oaxaca, in southern Mexico (Bortz, 1986; Velasco, 1987).

2. Total factor productivity is a measure of the overall effectiveness with which the economy uses factors of production (labor and capital). An increase in TFP means that there has been an increase in output that is *not* explained by increased quantities of labor and/or capital. Such an increase can be explained by improvements in technology, better management techniques, or other changes that allow more effective utilization of capital and labor (Abel and Bernanke, 1992, p. 68).

3. "Overall, the country has begun to advance towards a new pattern of accumulation, and it is none other than that of *secondary-exportation,* which already reigns in the Southern Cone" (Valenzuela Feijo, 1986, p. 166; Spanish in the original). The term "secondary" contrasts with the traditional pattern of exports from Latin America, particularly of primary products.

4. Data from INEGI, *Sistema de Cuentas Nacionales* (1980-1992) and Banco de México, *Informe Anual* (various issues). Data for 1991 is preliminary.

5. See source for data in note 4.

6. Given that Mexico has an abundance of labor and a scarcity of capital, the theory of comparative advantage would predict that Mexico will export labor-intensive goods.

7. The data on industrial employment are based on the number of industrial workers insured by the Social Security Institute of Mexico (IMSS).

8. A relevant aspect of Salinas's economic policies has been the reprivatization of the banking system, which has benefitted mainly the oligarchy. This oligarchy has increased its capacity for speculation, which shifts resources away from long term investment in small- and medium-size industry.

9. Compare to the overvaluation of the Canadian dollar during the implementation of the Canada-U.S. Free Trade Agreement and its injurious effect on Canadian industry (Grinspun, this volume).

REFERENCES

Abel, A. and Bernanke, B. (1992). *Macroeconomics.* Reading, MA.: Addison-Wesley.

Alvárez, A. (1987). *La Crisis Global del Capitalismo Méxicano.* México, D.F.: Editorial ERA.

Banco de México. (1992a). *Informe Anual 1991.*

————. (November 1989). *Indicadores Económicos*. Table IV-H-5.

————. (1989-90). *Indicadores Económicos*.

————. (January 1992b). *Indicadores Económicos*. Table IV-22.

Bortz, J. (1986). *El Salario en México*. México, D.F.: Ediciones El Caballito.

Hernández Laos, E., and Velasco Arregui, E. (1990). "Competitividad y Productividad de la Industria Manufacturera Méxicana." *Comercio Exterior,* 40 (7).

Instituto Nacional de Estadística, Geográfica e Informática [INEGI]. (1980-1992). *Sistema de Cuentas Nacionales*. Annual.

————. (1991). *1989 Mexico Industrial Census*.

————. (1992a). *Avances de Información Oportuna: Industria Maquiladora de Exportación*. Monthly.

————. (1992b). *Cuadernos de Información Oportuna*. Monthly.

INFONAVIT. (1985-1990). *Informe Anual*. Annual.

Porter, M. (1990). *The Competitive Advantage of Nations*. New York: Free Press.

Valenzuela Feijo, J. (1986). *El Capitalismo Méxicano de los Ochentas*. México, D.F.: Editorial ERA.

Velasco Arregui, E. (1981). *Raíces Históricas de la Industrialización Subordinada de América Latina*. México, D.F.: UNAM.

————. (1987). "El Ciclo del Salario en México 1940-1988." in J. Lechuga (ed.), *El Dilema de la Economía Méxicana*. México, D.F.: Universidad Autónoma Metropolitana.

————. (1990). "El Resurgimiento del Cuarto Estado en México; Los Asalariados y su Ciclo." In A. Alvárez (ed.), *La Clase Obrera y el Sindicalismo en México*. México, D.F.: UNAM.

Chapter 11

Dismantling the Mexican State and the Role of the Private Sector

Judith Teichman

Mexico's 1982 economic crisis was the catalyst for a neoconservative-inspired economic liberalization program. The major objective of this program has been to overcome Mexico's economic crisis through the establishment of an export platform in manufactured goods. The success of the strategy, however, is contingent upon the acquisition of stable and secure markets for these goods and investment capital. Hence, Mexico's pursuit of the North American Free Trade Agreement (NAFTA) is the logical and inevitable extension of the restructuring program introduced by President de la Madrid in 1983 and further deepened by the current president, Carlos Salinas de Gortari.

This article examines the implications of that economic restructuring program for the respective economic roles of the state and the private sector. The international economic context in which this policy change occurred—specifically, pressures exerted by the International Monetary Fund, the World Bank, and private creditors—is of paramount importance in explaining the neoconservative direction of economic policy.[1]

The argument made here is that the new policy involves the withdrawal of the state from a variety of areas where it has traditionally played a highly interventionist role, particularly from activities of direct production, and allocates an increased role for Mexico's most powerful industrial/financial groups and their transnational allies. This new model is reflected at the political level in a new understanding between Mexico's political elite and big business. While the process by which the new economic program was formulated is not our concern here,[2] suffice it to say that the process of policy reorientation has been a state-led affair, largely excluding consultation with business, even big business.

THE TRANSITION FROM STATISM
AND THE PROTECTED ECONOMY

Mexico's economic restructuring program represents a dramatic departure from its previous economic model, which was highly protective of national industry. After 1940, the Mexican state assumed leadership in industrial growth. It provided essential infrastructure, cheap industrial inputs, protection through high tariffs and import license requirements, and stimulus to fledgling industries through low taxes and easy credit. Most of this support was provided through state-owned companies, known as parastatals. Hence, whereas in 1940 there were only 57 parastatals, there were 845 by 1975, and by 1982, there were 1,150. In 1975, the parastatal sector represented 6.6 percent of gross domestic product (GDP). By 1982, this figure was 14 percent (Secretaría de la Contraloría General de la Federación, 1988, p. 16).

By 1973, government protection of domestic industry was further extended through legislation that sought to control foreign investment. Legislation passed in that year reserved certain activities entirely for the state (petroleum, basic petrochemicals, radioactive minerals, nuclear and electrical energy, and certain mining activities) and established the proportion of foreign investment allowable in other areas.[3] In early 1983, the administration of President de la Madrid enshrined the state's role in the economy in his constitutional reform package. Article 25 established the state's leadership role in national development, and Article 28 stipulated the "strategic" areas that were reserved exclusively for the state.[4] In addition, the state retained its exclusive responsibility for public banking and credit.

Economic liberalization was the centerpiece of Mexico's new economic strategy. Trade liberalization would both reduce inflation and force domestic firms to become more efficient and export competitive. Restructuring (the streamlining and trimming of operations) of the mammoth parastatal sector would facilitate export competitiveness for those parastatals with export markets (such as steel and petroleum) while enabling others to provide industrial inputs more cheaply and efficiently. The National Development Plan (1983) called for the strengthening of the state's role in "strategic" and "priority" areas and its elimination from areas that were neither. Increased foreign capital investment was an important aspect of the strategy, although it would become much more important in the following administration.[5] In short, while the state's direct economic role was to be diminished, economic recovery was to be carried forward by an internationally competitive private sector of national and foreign capital.

While economic liberalization proceeded slowly in 1983-84, renewed economic shocks in 1985—the deterioration of petroleum prices and increased interest rates—followed by an earthquake, propelled the economic liberalization program forward. The package of emergency measures, announced that year, included the replacement of import licenses by tariffs for over 3,000 product categories. With Mexico's entry into the General Agreement on Tariffs and Trade (GATT) in 1986, an even more concerted effort was made to bring about export competitiveness. "Industrial reconversion," mandatory for the public sector and optional for the private sector, focused upon the modernization of the productive plant and labor relations.[6]

The divestiture program was also accelerated. As shown in Table 11.1, after 1985, divestiture began to affect large state enterprises having symbolic if not strategic importance (airlines, steel, copper). The year 1988, the last year of the de la Madrid administration, witnessed a flurry of divestiture announcements: the government declared its intention of divesting itself of most of its enterprises in the capital goods sector, the majority of its holdings in the fishing sector, and most of its sugar refineries. In addition, the sale of the state's silver and gold companies was announced, as was the sale of Cananea, an enterprise possessing one of the ten largest copper mines in the world.

The administration also began to privatize certain activities within the petroleum sector—which the constitution reserves exclusively to the state. In 1986, 36 basic petrochemicals were declared secondary, thereby opening them to private, including foreign, capital investment.[7] Responsibility for the international marketing of petroleum crude was taken away from PEMEX's Office for International Trade and PEMEX representatives in London, Madrid, New York, and Houston, and handed over to a new holding company, Mexican International Petroleum composed of six foreign subsidiaries.[8] Another company, Mexpetrol, a joint venture between the state (35 percent) and national capital (65 percent) replaced PEMEX's Projects and Capital Works Division in the marketing abroad of petroleum technology, goods, and services (Zúniga and Cárdenas, 1989).

Concurrently with the withdrawal from direct production in a variety of areas, the government was taking an activist role in the promotion of manufactured exports from the private sector. In addition to new legislation

Table 11.1
Major Divestitures

Dates of Announcement & Divestments	Company	Purchaser
1983/83	Renault	Renault France
1983/83	Renault/VAM	Renault France
1986/89	Mexicana de Aviación	Grupo Xabre (Mexican) & Am. & Brit. investors
1986/86	Fundidora Monterrey (steel)	closed down
1986/86	Somex: to sell 40 companies	electro-domestic grp. to Grupo Vitro (Mexican)
1988/87-90	64 state sugar refineries	soft drink companies: most impt.: Grupo Escorpión & FOMEX (Grupo Visa, Eugenio Garza Lagüera*)
1988/88	Aeroméxico	Pilots Assoc. Mexican consortium of M. Alemán Velasco* & Bancomer
1988/89	DINA (buses, motores)	4 affiliates to Consorcio G. de CV (Mexican)
1988/90	Cananea (copper)	Mexican (Jorge Larrea* & Belgian mining groups)
1988	Mexicana de Cobre	Minera Mexico (Larrea)
1989	Bank Reprivatization	
/92	Banca Serfin	Gp. Operadora de Bolsa (B.Graza Sada*)
/92	Comermex	Grp. Inverlat (A.Legorreta*)
/91	Banca Cremi	Multivalores
/91	Banca Confía	Abaco (Monterrey)
/91	Banamex	Grp. Acciones y Valores (Roberto Hernández & Harp Helú*)
/91	Bancreser	Roberto Alcantara
/91	Banco de Oriente	Margen

Dates of Announcement & Divestments	Company	Purchaser
/91	Banco B.G.H.	Cabral& Bracho
/91	Bancomer	Valores Monterrey (Lagüera)
1990/90	Telmex	Grupo Carso (C. Slim*) Mexican & U.S. & French capital
1990/92	AHMSA (steel)	Acero Norte
1990/92	Sicartsa	Villacero
1990	Fertimex (fertilizer)	
1991	Concarril (railway cars)	Bombardier (Canadian)
1992	Railways declared open to foreign investment	

Sources: *Latin America Weekly Report, La Jornada, Proceso,* 1983-1992.

*Members of the Consejo Mexicano de Hombres de Negocios, an elite group of 37 Mexican businessmen who control the principle industrial, financial, and commercial groups in Mexico.

to further promote the *maquiladora* (assembly plant) industry (see the chapter by Kopinak in this volume), and the establishment of a commission to provide technical and financial support for enterprises wishing to export, the 1986 Program for Advanced Exporters (ALTEX) established preferential treatment in the areas of credit, tax relief, and preferential access to import permits for those enterprises exporting an important proportion of their production.

Most private sector firms, however, were unwilling or unable to step quickly into the enlarged economic space created by a state wishing to retreat from its extensive activities. Lacking state resources for plant modernization, government officials were seeking to privatize viable entities that could be modernized by the private sector, and to liquidate those that were not viable so that the state could focus its resources on the modernization of entities remaining under its control. This strategy, however, was soon to falter in the face of continuing economic crisis and diminishing investment capital. Through 1987 and 1988, a further decline in the price and demand for hydrocarbons, a burgeoning public deficit (due in large part to the increase in interest rates), and inflation of over 150 percent continued to plague the economy and to discourage private investors. Another difficulty was the delay in obtaining new loans from the private banking sector.

Indeed, the 1982 economic crisis had left Mexico's biggest national industrial conglomerates—which, like the government, had borrowed heavily on the international market—in a precarious economic situation.[9] Through FICORCA, a government trust company set up to protect highly indebted private sector enterprises against fluctuations in the exchange rate, bankruptcies of Mexico's major conglomerates were avoided. However, business confidence remained low, particularly with the renewed shocks of 1985, and was shaken further by the continuation of price controls and severe credit restriction, measures implemented in response to the 1985 shocks. Between 1982 and 1986, gross fixed investment of the private sector declined 15.4 percent (Huerta, 1987, p. 298); it declined 11.0 percent in 1986, and stagnated in 1987 (Brailovsky, Clarke and Warman, 1989, p. 394). Gross investment between 1983 and 1990 was not able to cover the cost of the replacement of equipment (Brailovsky et al., 1989, p. 351). The situation became so severe that the big industrialists of Monterrey threatened a moratorium on the payment of their debt if more credit was not made available (*Quarterly Economic Review*, 1, 1986, p. 16). Particularly for small and medium firms, the severity of the credit restriction made it impossible to carry out industrial reconversion. Even business organizations such as CONCAMIN (Mexican Confederation of Industrial Chambers) and COPERMEX (Mexican Confederation of Employers), representing Mexico's biggest industrialists, feared international competition and opposed the government's trade liberalization program (Pizarro, 12 October 1987).

Not surprisingly, in these circumstances, the government had difficulty finding national buyers for the many state enterprises it was attempting to privatize—despite the fact that the private sector had lobbied long and hard for an acceleration of the government's privatization program. Recourse to foreign capital was increasingly perceived as the way out of these financial difficulties. In 1986, in an attempt to facilitate industrial reconversion, the government adopted a debt-for-equity swap program for heavily indebted private and public sector firms, which was offered to foreign creditors and investors.[10] It tried to interest foreign investors, especially Japanese capital, in its steel industry (Gardner, 1986). With the election of Carlos Salinas in 1988, economic policy moved even more firmly in the direction of increasing the opening to foreign capital, while the divestiture of state enterprises was accelerated.

ECONOMIC RESTRUCTURING UNDER PRESIDENT CARLOS SALINAS: THE DISMANTLING OF THE STATE AND THE OPENING TO FOREIGN CAPITAL

By 1989, it was clear that the new administration of Carlos Salinas envisioned an even smaller state than that contemplated by his predecessor. The major divestitures announced and carried out during the Salinas years are shown in Table 11.1. In addition to the privatization of fertilizer, steel, and the telephone company, which the previous administration had pledged would not occur, the reprivatization of the banks was announced—a sacred area of exclusive government control incorporated into the 1983 constitutional reforms. The number of firms in the public sector had been reduced from 1,155 in 1982 to 420 in 1988 to 285 by 1990 (Table 11.2). Other figures included in Table 11.2 underestimate the impact of the privatization program, as they do not include the recent very large privatizations of TELMEX (the telephone company), the banks, or the steel industry. By 1989, parastatal GDP as a proportion of total GDP had declined, as had employment in the sector, with the decline being particularly marked in parastatal manufacturing (Table 11.2).

Basic petrochemicals have been further opened up to private capital under President Carlos Salinas with the reclassification of an additional 15 basic petrochemicals to secondary status in 1989 and 20 more in 1990. Moreover, new regulations opened the doors for the private sector in those basic petrochemicals that had not yet been opened up to them through reclassification. Through financial lease arrangements, private investors could construct processing plants in basic petrochemicals, which the government would then rent from the owners (Rodríguez Reyna, 1989, p. 16).

With the objective of raising foreign investment, the 1989 regulations of the Foreign Investment Law removed the 49 percent restriction on foreign ownership for all industries reserved neither exclusively for the state nor for Mexican nationals under certain specified conditions.[11] No longer was permission required for foreign investors to take over Mexican firms, and neither *maquiladoras* nor export companies would require official authorization for their establishment. The new regulations also effectively gave foreign capital access to areas from which it had been, according to old regulations, completely excluded or restricted. Foreign capital could participate up to 100 percent in the shares of companies through temporary trust companies (established for a maximum of 20 years and non-renewable) in activities exclusively reserved for Mexicans (domestic air and maritime transportation, and forestry) and in sectors where foreign investment was

Table 11.2
Parastatal Sector
Basic Indicators

	# Companies	Employment (1000s)	Employment Manufact. (1000s)	Parast. Expend. % Total Public Expenditure
1983	1050	1000.2	226.9	45.2
1984	1025	1042.0	237.1	47.9
1985	920	1057.1	232.5	42.7
1986	710	1028.0	212.6	38.5
1987	605	1031.8	184.5	33.9
1988	420	1017.0	159.5	34.0
1989	390	950.3	126.4	35.0
1990	285	n.a.	n.a.	n.a.

Source: Hacienda (1991), p. 15; Salinas de Gortari (1990), pp. 138, 144-146, 155, 157, 166.

	Parastatal Invest. % Public Exp.	% Total GDP		
		Total Para-statal Sec.	Manuf. Parast.	Parastatal Investment
1983	14.7	15.3	4.8	6.0
1984	15.1	15.3	4.9	5.9
1985	13.0	14.7	4.7	4.9
1986	11.5	14.5	4.8	4.8
1987	10.2	14.8	4.5	4.5
1988	10.1	14.3	3.2	4.0
1989	10.6	13.5	2.0	3.6
1990	n.a.	n.a.	n.a.	n.a.

otherwise restricted to 40 percent—such as mining, petrochemicals, and automotive components (Ministry of Commerce and Industrial Promotion [SECOFI], 1990, p. 46). Moreover, while investors were required to sell 51 percent of their shares to Mexicans within 20 years, they could do so on the Mexican stock exchange, scattering shares among small investors and thereby retaining control (*Los Angeles Times*, 1990). The new regulations also established a Committee for the Promotion of Foreign Investment to encourage foreign and national investment. And resolutions passed the same year sought to reduce the red tape and simplify bureaucratic procedures for foreign investors.

The scope of private sector activity was further expanded in areas constitutionally reserved exclusively for the state. In 1989, the government gave the go-ahead to joint ventures on the part of PEMEX (the government's petroleum corporation) and the CFE (its electricity company), and the private sector; this move had been made necessary, according to senior officials, by the severe financial restrictions these two parastatals faced. Such projects would include the construction of industrial and electrical generating plants, the construction of gas ducts, and drilling for oil and gas (Serrano, 1989).

A government program that enlarged the scope of the private sector and encouraged manufactured exports, combined with the decline in the prices and demand for petroleum, resulted in a marked increase in manufacturing exports, which rose from 14 percent of the value of total exports in 1982 to 49 percent by 1989 (Table 11.3). Moreover, the private sector increased its share of total exports from 43.0 percent in 1982 to 63.3 percent by 1988 (Table 11.3). At the same time, foreign investment has also risen (Table 11.3). Between May 1989 and December 1990, new direct foreign investment amounted to $6.45 billion, representing 20.9 percent of the total stock of foreign direct investment (Hacienda, 1991, p. 27).

PRIVATIZATION, EXPORT PROMOTION, AND ECONOMIC CONCENTRATION

Hence, it is Mexico's largest industrial conglomerates and transnational corporations (TNCs) that are rapidly replacing the state's leadership role in the economy. Only TNCs and big national capital have the resources to institute industrial reconversion and become export competitive. Indeed, industrial reconversion, initiated halfway through the last decade, had already been accomplished in most TNCs in Mexico, in such industries as electronics, automobiles, chemicals, and *maquiladoras*. A minority of big

Table 11.3
Basic Trade and Investment Indicators

Year	Petroleum % Total Exports	Manufactures % Total Exports	Private Sector % Total Exports	Public Sector % Total Exports	Foreign Direct Investment (Million US$)
1982	74.6	13.7	43.0	57.0	1658
1983	69.3	19.8	50.3	49.5	461
1984	65.5	22.1	53.4	46.6	391
1985	64.3	21.7	55.1	44.9	491
1986	36.4	41.1	65.3	34.4	1522
1987	36.5	44.5	69.9	30.1	3248
1988	29.3	50.3	63.3	36.2	2595
1989	30.5	48.5	n.a.	n.a.	2500

Source: Salinas de Gortari (1990), p. 292; Brailovsky et al. (1988), p. 399; Hacienda (1988), p. 27.

national enterprises were also able to undergo reconversion: the synthetic fibers industry, for example, was able to modernize and to enter the international market in 1982, as was the cement industry. Small and medium enterprises, on the other hand, were not able to modernize, due to the absence of adequate financing programs, and were therefore not in a position to benefit from export incentive policies, which benefitted those big firms (like ALTEX) already exporting an important proportion of their production. Modernization and the creation of competitive export capacity in many of the parastatals was blocked not only by insufficient resources but also by corrupt and clientelistic labor relations (de la Garza, 1988, pp. 5-7).

The government's argument—that through reducing the size of the state sector, the state's economic leadership role will be strengthened—appears problematic. The state's ability to pattern the direction of economic events through its role in direct production has been reduced, as has its ability to regulate through such measures as the loosening up of foreign investment regulations. While major privatizations, such as that of TELMEX, have entailed the imposition of investment and other conditions upon purchasers, it remains to be seen whether the state will be able to ensure the fulfillment of such conditions. State intervention has not, however, disappeared: it is now geared toward policies stimulative to big business.

The big national and foreign private sector companies are the major beneficiaries of the government's export incentives and lead in the export of manufactured goods. In 1987, five products accounted for 60 percent of the total value of nontraditional exports, while 25 products accounted for 75 percent (Banamex, 1987, December, p. 482). Most of the enterprises that export are large, manufacturing motors and auto parts (Banamex, 1987, November, p. 446). The top three exporting companies, after PEMEX, are transnational auto manufacturers: Chrysler of Mexico, Ford, and GM of Mexico.[12] Of the 317 top exporting enterprises, accounting for 73.3 percent of all Mexican exports (including petroleum), 216 are predominantly national capital (*La Jornada,* 1988).

At the same time, big national and transnational firms have benefited from the government's privatization program. The reclassification of a large number of basic petrochemicals, and their consequent opening to private capital investment, is such a case. A large number of the companies that manufacture secondary petrochemicals are subsidiaries of Mexico's eight major industrial groups: Alfa, Celanese, Cydsa, Idesa, Irsa, Penwalt, Oxy, and Primex (Rodríguez Reyna, 1989: 21-22). Moreover, it was those national companies with foreign associates, controlling 40 percent of the Mexican secondary petrochemical market, that were in a position to move into the production of the new petrochemical products reclassified by the government (Reyna, 1989).

The closure of state enterprises benefited big domestic and foreign capital by leaving it with a larger share of the market. The closure of the state firm Monterrey Steel Foundry, for example, gave a greater market share to the steel producer Hylsa, of the Alfa group, leaving as it did a production gap of some one million tons a year (Gardner, 14 May 1986), while U.S. airlines took over Aeroméxico's international routes following its restructuring and sale (*Proceso,* 8 April 1988).

Mexico's most important public enterprises have been sold to the biggest national industrial conglomerates and to transnational corporations. As shown in Table 11.1, the purchasers of Mexico's most important parastatals have been Mexico's most powerful economic groups in association with foreign consortia, in the cases of the biggest purchases, such as TELMEX. In some cases the degree of economic concentration is startling: Jorge Larrea, a principal shareholder in nine of Mexico's industrial conglomerates, including two major banks, now controls over 90 percent of Mexico's copper production through his company, Minera México.

While there was business opposition to trade liberalization, particularly during the early years, the Salinas administration has succeeded in restoring much of the business confidence (at least on the part of Mexico's most powerful business interests) that had been lost as a consequence of the 1982 bank nationalization and subsequent economic difficulties during the de la Madrid years. President Salinas has had close links to big business. Its representatives were found on the Committee for the Financing and Consolidation of Resources of the Institutional Revolutionary Party (PRI), responsible for raising funds for Salinas's campaign (Fernández-Vega, 1 April 1991). The Mexican Council of Businessmen, grouping together Mexico's most powerful business interests, was believed to have the closest and most readily available access to public authorities (Pizarro, 27 November 1989). Moreover, businessman Claudio X. González (president of Kimberly-Clark Mexico and former leader of the peak business association, the Business Coordinating Council) is one of Carlos Salinas's principal advisers on foreign investment (Robles and Yera, 1990). While formal consultation with the business sector in general appears not to have been a feature of either the de la Madrid years or the early Salinas years, close personal contacts between the SECOFI and powerful individuals in the private sector characterize recent years.[13]

CONCLUSIONS

Mexico's new economic strategy, the principal objective of which is the expansion of manufactured exports, has entailed a package of policies that has transferred the engine of economic expansion from the state to big national capital and TNCs. Privatization was pursued to reduce the public deficit because it was seen as necessary to the strategy, given the presumed greater efficiency of the private sector and the impact that such a program would have on raising business confidence. Particularly with the administration of President Carlos Salinas, as a consequence of various administrative manipulations, even those areas exclusively reserved for the state are being opened up to private capital, including foreign capital. The inadequacy of national resources for plant modernization—which is needed for industrial competitiveness—has meant that TNCs and a few large industrial conglomerates dominate Mexican manufactured exports. Meanwhile, small and medium firms, largely left out of the process of reconversion, have become strong opponents of a number of aspects of the government's restructuring program, particularly trade liberalization (Teichman, 1992a).

State intervention, however, has remained in a number of spheres critical to the success of the new economic model: state policy provides incentives for export promotion to the private sector (the major beneficiaries being big conglomerates), and it has ensured a dramatic reduction in the cost of labor and in benefits.[14] NAFTA, in providing Mexican exporters better access to U.S. and Canadian markets, will, in the absence of specific policies to counteract growing economic concentration, reinforce and deepen the model.

While there is no question that Mexico's earlier economic model benefited the private sector more than any other social group, this new model has provided even greater benefits to the most powerful fractions within that sector and their transnational allies. At the same time, the dismantling of the state has weakened support for the regime from the state bureaucracy and from the powerful trade unions of the parastatals—the virtual core of the Mexican corporatist structure.[15] The success of the opposition National Democratic Front (FDN) in the 1988 election (it won, according to official figures, 31 percent of the popular vote) is attributable to FDN's stiff opposition to the government's restructuring program and its ability to tap into labor discontent (Teichman, 1992b). The FDN called for a return to populist redistributive policies, a suspension of payments on the foreign debt, and a reversal of privatization. Although the PRI continues to win elections, charges of electoral fraud are undermining the regime's legitimacy. It is of critical importance that the current economic model bring about rapid economic growth along with a significant improvement in general living standards. Unless this happens soon, the inordinate benefits provided to big capital can be expected to have important implications for the continued erosion of the PRI's capacity to incorporate support from a broad spectrum of social groups.

NOTES

A research grant from the Social Sciences and Humanities Research Council of Canada supported a portion of the research upon which this article is based.

1. For a discussion of the role of these pressures in the formulation of Mexico's economic restructuring program, see Teichman (1992a).
2. The process by which Mexico's restructuring program was formulated and implemented will not be discussed here. A full discussion occurs in Teichman, "Privatization and Political Transition in Mexico" (manuscript in preparation).
3. In the exploitation of mineral reserves, and in the petrochemical industry, foreign ownership was restricted to 34 percent; in the manufacture of auto components,

it was restricted to 40 percent. In all other activities, foreign investment was restricted to 49 percent, although the National Foreign Investment Commission could make exceptions (Carrión, 1977, p. 80). Although this legislation could be circumvented through such maneuvers as the use of *prestanombres* (the purchase by foreign investors of the use of the names of Mexican citizens to front companies where foreign ownership surpassed allowable limits), conventional wisdom maintains that it discouraged the inflow of foreign capital.

4. The strategic areas are: the printing of money, mail, telegraph, radio-telegraph, satellite communication, petroleum, basic petrochemicals, radioactive minerals, nuclear energy, electricity, railways, and "activities expressly indicated through acts of Congress" (*Nafinsa,* No. 7, 14 February 1983, p. 165).

5. In 1983, the new administration announced that the 1973 Foreign Investment Law would be interpreted "more flexibly." Specifically, majority foreign participation would be allowed for firms with substantial exports of manufactured goods (*Quarterly Economic Review* (3), 1983, p. 8).

6. "Industrial reconversion" was introduced in 1986 by the then secretary of mines and parastatals, Alfredo del Mazo, as the means by which Mexico's industry was to become export competitive. Modernization of labor relations meant the "flexibilization" of labor contracts, a process involving fundamental changes in collective contracts with labor, with the objectives of reducing union power and increasing investment and international competitiveness. Such changes include the removal of restrictions on management's rights to replace union workers by non-union personnel, the removal of restrictions on management's ability to move labor between departments and regions, and the removal of requirements for union consultation or approval for technological innovations.

7. The constitutional restrictions on private and foreign ownership hold only for "basic" petrochemicals, not for "secondary" ones. The Constitution, of course, does not specify what is basic and what is secondary. The criteria for deciding exactly what was to be declared secondary remains something of a mystery. While the standard official response is that these were technical decisions, intense pressure from the private sector to open up basic petrochemicals to private investment, the pressing need for investment capital in sectors of high domestic demand, and tough resistance from the PEMEX bureaucracy to the opening up of basic petrochemicals were all ingredients in the highly politicized decisions.

8. Leftist opponents argued that this and other measures to open up areas hitherto reserved for the state to private domestic and foreign capital contravened Article 27 of the Constitution, which gives the state direct dominion over subsoil resources. See: N. A. (10 July 1989). "El Status Jurídico del Holding PMI Viola el Artículo 27 Constitucional." *La Jornada,* p. 29).

9. Alfa's debt, for example, was reported to be equivalent to 88 percent of its assets. In 1986, it ceded 45 percent of its stock to its creditors as payment for part of its $920 million debt. See C. Acosta. (15 October 1984). "Ni el Apuntalamiento del Gobierno las Salvó y las Empresas se Desnacionalizan." *Proceso,* p. 29.

10. The program was suspended between 1987 and 1990 due to its inflationary effects.

11. Foreign investment continued to be limited to minority ownership (34-40 percent) in mining (except oil, gas, and uranium, which continued to be reserved for the state), secondary petrochemicals, auto parts, and telecommunications (except telegraph). The specified conditions under which foreign investment could reach 100 percent were: the project was less than $100 million; it was financed from foreign sources; it would generate permanent employment; the firm would be set up outside of Mexico's major industrial centers, use adequate technology, and observe environmental regulations (*Nafinsa,* No. 10, October 1989, pp. 22-24).

12. The most important exporting companies after PEMEX, which is responsible for 55.9 percent of the value of total exports, are Chrysler of Mexico (6.4 percent), Ford Motor Company (4.7 percent), GM of Mexico (4.6 percent); Mexican Aviation Company (2.5 percent); Telmex (2.3 percent), Penoles (2.2 percent), Volkswagen (1.4 percent); IBM of Mexico (1.4 percent), and Celanese Mexicana (.9 percent) (*La Jornada,* 22 October 1988, p. 13).

13. A number of business leaders interviewed in the course of this research reported fairly frequent direct communication with top officials of SECOFI.

14. For a full discussion of the labor policies of both the de la Madrid and Salinas administrations, and their political implications, see Teichman (1992b).

15. For further elaboration, see Teichman (1992b).

REFERENCES

Brailovsky, V., Clarke, R., & Warman, N. (1989). *La Política Económica del Desperdicio.* México DF: UNAM.

Carrión, J. (1977). "La Inversión Extranjera y el Desarrollo del Imperialismo." In A. Aguilar M. et al. (eds.), *Política Mexicana Sobre Inversiones Extranjeras.* México DF: UNAM.

de la Garza, E. (1988). "Desindustrialización y Reconversión en México." *El Cotidiano,* 21, 2-7.

Fernández-Vega, C. (1 April 1991). "La Elite del Empresariado Mexicano." *La Jornada,* p. 11.

Gardner. D. (13 May 1986). "Mexico Closes State Owned Steel Plant." *Financial Times,* p. 41.

———. (14 May 1986). "Protest by Steel Workers in Mexico. *Financial Times,* p. 6.

Hacienda, Ministry of Finance and Public Credit. (January 1991). *Mexico: A New Economic Profile*. México, D.F.

Huerta, A. (1987). "El Estancamiento del Sector Industrial." *El Cotidiano,* 19, 290-299.

La Jornada. (22 October 1988), p. 13.

Los Angeles Times. (28 September 1990), p. 12.

Ministry of Commerce and Industrial Promotion (SECOFI). (1990). *Legal Framework for Foreign Investment in Mexico.* México DF.

Pizarro, F. Ortega. (12 October 1987). "La Concamin Falló, Pero Pedirá a Salinas los Cambios que Solicitaría a Bartlett." *Proceso* (571), p. 23.

————. (27 November 1989). "Los 37 Más Ricos del País Descartan la Democracia y se Adueñan del Trato con el Gobierno." *Proceso,* (682), p. 20.

Proceso (598). (8 April 1988), p. 30.

Reyna, J. Ignacio Rodríguez. (23 August 1989). "Beneficiará a Grandes Consorcios la Reclasificacíon de Petroquímicas." *El Financiero,* p. 23.

————. (1989). "La Privatización de la Petroquímica Basica." *El Cotidiano,* 29, 16-22.

Robles, M. and R. Yera. (1 January 1990). "Los Asesores del Gobierno Anónimos, sin Responsabilidad, pero con Información y Poder." *Proceso* (687), p. 22.

Salinas de Gortari, C. (1990). *Segundo Informe de Gobierno 1990.* Mexico, D.F.: Anexo.

Secretaría de la Contraloría General de la Federación. (1988). *Restructuración del Sector Parastatal.* México, D.F.

Serrano, N. Cruz. (13 December 1989). "'Luz Verde' al Capital Extranjero en Energéticos; Coinvertirán Pemex, CFE y Empresas Foráneas." *El Financiero,* p. 25.

Teichman, J. (1992a). "The Mexican State and the Political Implications of Economic Restructuring." *Latin American Perspectives,* 19 (73).

Teichman, J. (1992b, forthcoming). "Economic Restructuring and the Breakdown of Mexican Corporatism." In G. Otero (ed.), *Latin America's Future.* Penn State University Press.

Zúniga J. Antonio and L. Cárdenas. (18 December 1989). "Se Concreta Mex-Petrol, con 65% de Capital Privado." *El Universal,* p. 1.

Chapter 12

Mexican Perceptions of Free Trade: Support and Opposition to NAFTA

Judith Adler Hellman

Much of the debate around free trade and, in particular, much of the North American opposition to the North American Free Trade Agreement (NAFTA) has been framed in terms that would suggest that Canadian and U.S. losses will be Mexico's gain. Even before an agreement was worked out, it appeared that, in aggregate economic terms, Mexico could be the partner that might benefit most from a free trade treaty. But while Mexico may improve its economic situation, undoubtedly many Mexicans will not. However, precisely *which* Mexicans—that is, which sectors of the economy and which social classes—will gain or lose ground was difficult to predict before the details of the bilateral negotiations with the United States were known.

It is also difficult to establish who will benefit because the closed, authoritarian nature of the Mexican system has produced silence in precisely those places—the legislature and the press—where a vigorous national debate should be unfolding. As Adolfo Aguilar Zinser argues in his contribution to this book, the Mexican regime's intolerance of dissent has largely stifled those dissident voices that, under other circumstances, would offer critical analysis and alternative proposals to the neoconservative project that underpins the official Mexican position on NAFTA.

In the absence of critical public debate, it is not possible to predict who the Mexican beneficiaries will be. Indeed, the winners will not be known until the treaty is not only ratified but also implemented. Rather, I will focus on what Mexicans know about free trade, their perceptions of their prospects under such an agreement, and how those perceptions have led them to positions of support or opposition to the process of economic integration.

SUPPORT FOR AND OPPOSITION TO NAFTA

In both the United States and Canada, support and opposition to NAFTA is easy to pinpoint. The loose coalition of interests that oppose economic integration includes, first and foremost, organized labor.[1] The trade unions are joined in their opposition by an assortment of human rights advocates and environmentalists, as well as small manufacturers and growers who fear they will lose out to cheaper Mexican imports. To be sure, in the Canadian case, the cultural community and the nationalists weigh in with a particular set of concerns that do not much worry U.S. opponents of NAFTA. And the criticism offered by U.S. environmentalists is, if anything, more intense than that of their Canadian counterparts because of the immediacy of the environmental threat to the U.S. border states. But notwithstanding these specific differences, the alignment of supporters and opponents in both countries is quite clear and logically predictable.

When we attempt to estimate public opinion on North American integration in either Canada or the United States, we find some reasonably clear clues that we can decipher. In Canada, the November 1988 election was explicitly fought on the issue of free trade. In the United States, it was possible to predict positions on free trade with a high degree of accuracy; the 1991 congressional vote on fast-track could be broken down and analyzed according to the economic profile of the district from which each representative was sent to Congress.

The measurement of Mexican support for NAFTA is an altogether different problem. In the Mexican case, we have no reliable electoral results from which a broader popular will might be deduced. What we have, instead, is falsified vote counts produced in a series of fraudulent electoral contests that the Salinas regime insists represent effective referenda on the president's neoconservative economic program. In Mexico, elections are fixed and freedom of expression is limited by a variety of devices that range from state control of the press (through its monopoly on newsprint and the "subsidies" it pays to registered journalists) to direct harassment of vocal critics (Hellman, 1988, pp. 127-128). Thus, it is impossible to use the same indicators of support and opposition that serve us in our analysis of the U.S. or Canadian cases, where, however limited the range of choice offered in political contests, the final vote tabulations at least provide some reliable data.

How, then, can we know what Mexicans of various social classes and sectors of the economy make of their prospects under free trade? In November 1990, *El Día* published the results of a poll showing that 61 percent of Mexicans favor the negotiation of a free trade agreement with the United States, while an even larger majority, 73 percent, would be eager to pursue free trade with the rest of Latin America.[2] Possibly the only hard data comparing Mexican public opinion with the views of Canadian and U.S. citizens come from a survey carried out by the Centro de Estudios de Opinión Pública for the *Encuesta Mundial de Valores 1990*.[3] The study found that, compared with the far more sober assessments of the public in the U.S. and Canada, Mexicans are enthusiastic about economic integration. Moreover, Mexicans' acceptance of economic integration was virtually "unconditional" insofar as their positive responses varied only slightly when they were asked if they favored foreign trade "without restrictions" (71 percent), "as long as no jobs were lost" (81 percent) or "only when there is full reciprocity" (78 percent). In contrast, a minority in the United States and only a bare majority of Canadians favor trade without restrictions, although their approval rate rises to 64 percent (in the United States) and 83 percent (Canadians) when they believe no jobs will be lost, and approaches Mexican levels of support when full reciprocity is guaranteed (Basañez, 1991, pp. 3-4).

Why do Mexicans of various social classes seem more sanguine about greater economic integration? The difference between the relatively optimistic Mexican responses and the cautious or pessimistic Canadian and U.S. responses is probably best explained by the fact that Mexicans had almost no information on which to base their calculations of how their lives and fortunes may be transformed by a free trade agreement. Indeed, the explanation offered by Basañez (1991, p. 3) for the data cited above is, very simply, that "the figures show high expectations but little knowledge."

When organized labor in Canada or the United States opposes free trade on the grounds that "jobs will move South," they know of what they speak. The development of rust belts in central Canada and in the northeastern and midwestern United States is a process that has been observed and measured by factory closings over the last decade as industrial jobs have migrated first to the U.S. sunbelt and later to the Mexican border and overseas to Asia and the Caribbean basin. Mexicans, however, do not have as clear a picture of their future. It is difficult for them to make projections based on the expansion of the existing *maquila* sector because, depending on the provisions of NAFTA, the border-based *maquila* program as presently constituted may well disappear, leaving an altogether new form of assembly production in its place. In general, confusion prevails because the regime tells the public—

including the economic elites—only what it wants them to know. A textile manufacturer confided to me that, depending on the "rules of origin" clauses that could be won in the agreement by the Mexican negotiators (over whom neither he nor his manufacturing association had the least influence), he would either "make out like a bandit" or face immediate financial ruin. Indeed, for many Mexican industries (textiles, apparel, glass, electronics, and cement, among others), there are best and worst case scenarios which, when sketched out, are diametrically opposed and miles apart.

Mexicans not only lack experience and hard data on which to base their opinions about free trade. They are unable to make knowledgeable judgements because information has been willfully distorted by the Salinas regime. For example, in an April 1990 speech, President Salinas reported that free trade had created more than 250,000 jobs in Canada. In fact, Statistics Canada's *Labor Force Survey* indicates that 180,000 Canadian manufacturing jobs were lost just in the first year after the free trade agreement came into effect. For Salinas's statement to be true, 430,000 new jobs would have to have been created in that first year! (Campbell, 1991).

Remarkably, in five months of fieldwork I carried out in Mexico in 1990 and 1991, apart from the Mexicans I met through contacts with groups like Common Frontiers and other anti-free trade activists, I met no Mexican of any social class who was aware that the free trade agreement was widely regarded in Canada as anything from damaging to an all-out economic disaster. Wherever I went, I carried with me a short article from the Mexico City English-language daily, *The News* (14 December 1990), that reported that a majority of Canadians polled by Gallup in late 1990 favored abrogation of the treaty.[4] This news was greeted with astonishment (and general dismay) by everyone to whom I showed the clipping, including heads of various chambers of industry, government planners, and professors of economics.

MEXICAN OPINION

With this general lack of information in mind, I set out in May of 1991 to learn more about Mexicans' perception of free trade. The people I interviewed did not comprise a broad, random sample. Rather, I gathered opinions on NAFTA in the context of lengthy, in-depth interviews that I was conducting with a group of Mexicans whom I had selected as key informants.

These interviews did not focus on the question of economic integration. Rather, they were wide-ranging discussions (each lasting several hours) in which I sought to gain a comprehensive picture of the individual's overall assessment of his or her present condition, interpretation of the past, and hopes for the future. In these sessions, I gathered personal histories and data on political attitudes and behavior, religious beliefs, economic survival strategies, work and consumption patterns, personal and family income, and the overall improvement or decline of each person's fortunes in the period of economic restructuring in the 1980s.

During the open-ended interviews I conducted in 1990, the issue of free trade often came up in the course of conversation. When I returned to complete the cycle of interviews in 1991, I decided to include questions on NAFTA in each session, even if the issue did not arise spontaneously. When talking with middle-class people and the elite, I simply asked, "What do you think about the free trade agreement? What will it mean for you?" When interviewing poor people (peasants, industrial workers, transport workers, street vendors, waitresses, and domestic servants) I preceded those two questions with the query, "Have you heard any talk about something called a 'free trade treaty'?"

No one I spoke to in Mexico in 1991, no matter how poor, how marginalized, or, indeed, illiterate, had not heard of the treaty (*tratado*) which was, to be sure, front page news every day in the summer of 1991. Some people responded to my first question by saying, "Yes, but I don't know what it is." However, even those who answered in this way revealed, after some prodding, that they had at least a notion that the *tratado* was an agreement that their government was trying to strike with the *norteamericanos* (North Americans). They knew that it involved some kind of bilateral arrangement with the United States, but most had no idea that Canadians might become involved at some future stage. Indeed, the very term *norteamericano,* for Mexicans as for other Latin Americans, denotes U.S. citizens, not Canadians (*canadienses*).

What was the range of knowledge and opinion about the *tratado*? The responses I gathered in 1990 and 1991 fall into four rough categories which I will describe in turn.

The first group includes those people who are confused about what the agreement will bring because they lack either information or the analytical tools to process whatever information they do have. Typical of this group is the reply to my question that I received from a man selling children's apparel in a street market:

> Yes, I have heard of it, but the truth is, I don't really know what it is, whether it will be positive or negative. I haven't found anyone who could explain it to me in a clear way.

A rural school teacher told me:

> Free trade? It is possible that it will benefit us. We really don't know the road
> that we are going down but we hope that the results will be beneficial because
> we are surely going to have free trade but we don't know what this is going to
> mean in the future. What we produce is very cheap but everything we need to
> buy is expensive. I don't know what the repercussions of free trade will be.

One of the teacher's neighbors, a peasant, was more hopeful: "I don't
know what it will mean," he replied, "but maybe it will serve to get the money
lenders off our backs."

The second category is formed by those respondents who can work out
complex projections for the future, including alternative scenarios for their
business affairs, but lack the specific data to feed into their models. These
people, like the textile entrepreneur quoted above, know that things could
go very badly or very well, but that their fortunes depend on a set of
negotiations over which they have little if any influence and absolutely no
control.

Among the people I spoke to who fit this description was a producer of
consumer electronics who viewed the disappearance of the domestic consumer electronics industry as a direct consequence of the opening of the
Mexican economy in 1986. This was a sudden move in which tariff barriers
were lifted from one day to the next. Sixteen Mexican TV manufacturers and
30 audio manufacturers were driven out of business, leaving only a Japanese
firm in the field. This man's assessment of the free trade deal came down to
whether the Mexican team would bargain away all protective clauses or
would retain some protection for the industry.

> The way I see it is that the parts industry will grow again if we protect certain
> areas a little bit, just like the United States protects its areas, just like Canada
> protects its own. It's just a temporary thing that will end, but it has to be a process
> . . . or else the entire industry is wiped out.

A textile manufacturer told me,

> The economic opening was badly managed by the Mexican government because
> it permitted the entry of cheap goods from Asia. We Mexican manufacturers
> have to meet certain standards of quality and labeling, but the goods that our
> government has let in meet none of these standards. The future of this firm and
> of the industry depends on what the treaty stipulates in this regard. If apparel

that has a high proportion of Asian-made fabric is regarded as "Mexican made" I will be out of business. There is no way I can complete with the Asian textile prices offered to Mexican garment makers. My quality is better, but it is not that much better, and I am not going to invest to bring my standard up in a situation that is so uncertain.

Finally, a sometime market woman/sometime laundress shared with both the first and second group of interviewees the feeling that she lacked the basic information she needed. "Oh yes," she exclaimed on hearing my question. "I would really like to know more about free trade, because I don't have information, and I would like to know more in order to do something."

After listening to my explanation with keen interest, she revealed that she had already formulated an economic strategy based on guesswork about what *libre comercio* (free trade) might bring. She had entered a raffle (*tanda*) in order to raise the cash to pay a sister-in-law to bring a sewing machine back from Texas. They intended to set up a workshop to produce sweaters and dresses, so, as she put it, "we will be able to enter into free trade and send stuff to the places where people have money to buy."

The next category is comprised of people whose view of what to anticipate under a free trade agreement is shaped not so much by the specific information they receive, but rather by ideological commitment to a particular vision of reality. This group includes an agribusiness tycoon and a number of industrialists who were confident that NAFTA would work well for them in the end because it is the perfect expression of the neoconservative, market-oriented capitalism in which they profoundly believe.

One industrialist had no illusions whatsoever regarding Mexico's relative influence in the bargaining process, but he was sanguine all the same:

The United States is going to construct the treaty. We will be invited to the bargaining table but, as was the case for you in Canada, the U.S. will call the shots . . . But we cannot be worse off than we were before [with state intervention and protectionism] because we couldn't be worse off. Consumption will grow and this demand will stimulate Mexican industries. . . . My conclusion is that we Mexicans are going to end up with two choices: either go to work for the transnational corporations that will move in, or work as busboys and waiters in services. But the important thing is that we Mexicans should have work. I believe that the word "sovereignty" is one we will all come to forget. Sovereignty is going to reside in the notion that every Mexican every day is going to be a little better off.

The agribusinessman I interviewed was less cynical in his enthusiasm. Although normally a supporter of the conservative National Action Party (PAN), he was unqualified in his admiration for Salinas and the "team of economists who are running the country."

> Free trade is going to be very positive for the country. At first it will be difficult for Mexico to adapt, because we have had an economy that was too protected. The quality of our goods was low because we had a captive market. Likewise, productivity was unimportant, especially in agriculture, because the government set prices and subsidized inputs. Suddenly we found ourselves in a new reality that made us wake up. Now we know that Mexico has great opportunities with free trade because we have many advantages in climate, manpower, raw materials and enjoy complementarity with the markets of Canada and the U.S. At first we will face problems and some industries will disappear definitively while others flourish . . . but in the end it will be a very positive change.

Also guided by ideology, but holding a very different view of free trade, is the final category of interviewees. These are the people who believe that anything that arouses the enthusiasm of the ruling party (PRI), the PAN, and most of the economic elite will, by definition, turn out to be very rough on popular and middle-class Mexicans. As in the third category of respondents, the views of people in this group are not based on specific details of NAFTA, but on their broader perceptions and analysis of reality. Their experience suggests to them that they are no more likely to reap benefits from a free trade agreement, economic integration, or a "neoconservative package" than from any of the development programs instituted in the past. In general, we can say that these people do not know what, specifically, is going to happen to them under NAFTA because they, too, lack information. But they know it is not going to be good.

Some, like a street vendor who sells cheap Asian imports (watches, radios, electric fans, cassette players) on the sidewalk near the Basilica de Guadalupe, express an elegantly simple view:

> I don't understand much about this treaty. But only yesterday I was commenting to a friend that the ones who will benefit are the large enterprises. The small merchant like me, no. The big fish are going to eat the little fish.

Or the banana vendor in a squatter community on the western periphery of Mexico City who did not need to think more than a second before he replied:

Free trade? It's going to be bad for the small merchants. The government is doing it for the big entrepreneurs and the rich. The government always defends the rich, not the poor.

Or the waitress who said:

Yes, I've heard of free trade but I think that, in the end, it will not benefit us poor people in any way because the poor are not going to be part of it. The treaty is only going to be for the big businessmen, for the rich. Their money is going to grow. But as for us— I hope you will excuse my language—we will get screwed. We will be the same or even worse off than before.

One of the most interesting and insightful responses I received came in an interview with a woman who sold used clothing, a contraband item, in a public market in the northern part of Mexico City. Her major overhead expense consisted of the bribes or *mordidas* she was obliged to pay to the border police. (Her arrangements in the market were looked after by a local political boss). Once a week she would travel to Laredo, Texas, sleeping two nights in a bus during the 36-hour, round-trip journey. There she purchased 500 pounds of used clothing for $150. The *mordidas* she was forced to pay at the border cost her another $300.

I asked her if free trade would not improve her situation because her activities would no longer be illegal and she would no longer be a target for extortion. She replied,

Don't worry, the police will find a way. Thousands of people at the border live from extortion. It is a way of life. They are not going to stand with their arms folded while their main source of income disappears. They will find another way to shake us down, or maybe they won't let us cross at all. The treaty isn't meant to help us out, it is meant for the rich.

Others with whom I spoke gave more complex analyses of free trade. But they, too, were guided by a world view similar to the people cited above. For example, when I questioned her about NAFTA, a teacher told me:

It worries me a great deal that the trade unions here are not discussing the matter and they have not been brought into the negotiations. You might imagine that the unions would be involved in the matter because the workers are the principal ones who will be affected. But this discussion is not taking place, not even in the more democratic unions. We totally lack information and I, for one, am very worried about the treaty. Essentially, anything that the government is pushing automatically inspires distrust in me.

Finally, another teacher who was moved by the same instinctive distrust of Salinas's initiatives expressed his concerns in these terms:

There are sectors here that think that there will be a favorable standardization of salaries, levels of well being and so on. This is the expectation that the Mexican government is trying to encourage, in order to promote the idea that we are going to benefit from all that is better or more advanced in American and Canadian society. But to me it looks like the standardization is downward because under the logic of comparative advantage, what Mexico has to bring to the arrangement is cheap labor, and the wages of Canadians and Americans unquestionably will be undercut. It seems clear to me that the agreement will promote the hegemony of the United States over Canada and Mexico, not only with respect to production and commerce, but culture and every aspect of life. For the Mexicans, national identity, cultural heritage, language, indeed everything is at stake.

CONCLUSIONS

Until the details are worked out, most Mexicans will not know if they will benefit or be hurt by NAFTA. In the absence of a free press and open debate, it is virtually impossible for Mexicans to make informed assessments about their future prospects under the *tratado*. Thus, lacking concrete information, many Mexicans' support for NAFTA is based only on vague, ill-informed hopes that "better must come," that nothing could be worse than the economic situation presently facing them. But at the extreme ends of the social spectrum, people are presently making realistic projections. The strongest entrepreneurs, for example, hold the reasonable expectation that theirs are the enterprises that will survive, that they are the ones who will attract the foreign partners, that they will be successful in coming up with the investment funds to modernize, expand, and integrate their operations and to move into new markets. In short, they are the Mexicans who will manage to take full advantage of the new opportunities offered by economic integration. They are, as the street vendor put it, the "big fish."

At the other extreme are the Mexicans who correctly perceive themselves as outside of history, as insignificant at best in the greater scheme of neoconservative transformation. They clearly see that the free trade agreement is a deal that is being worked out over their heads and promises little good, and much that is threatening, to the "little fish" like themselves. Their attitudes toward free trade are based on quite realistic projections. They understand that the benefits of development that have eluded them in the previous decades will continue to pass them by in a redesigned, "continental" Mexico, while the burden of the changes will continue to be borne by them in higher costs of living.

NOTES

The research on which this paper is based was supported by a grant from the Social Science and Humanities Research Council of Canada.

1. As William Orme (1991) has pointed out, steel and auto workers oppose NAFTA, while the transnationals that employ them are pushing hard for its passage. Textile and garment workers and employers have joined hands in opposition. In one of labor history's sad ironies, U.S. fruit and sugar growers oppose NAFTA, but have crushed the organizational efforts of their workers that would have produced unions capable of supporting the growers in their fight against free trade.
2. Investigación Pública SC poll, (26 November 1990, pp. 6-8). The 61 percent favoring free trade with the United States represents a 6 point gain over results recorded by the same pollsters in October 1989.
3. See Centro de Estudios de Opinión Pública, *Encuesta Mundial de Valores 1990.* Results from this comparison of values held by Mexicans, Canadians and people in the United States were presented by Basañez (1991, pp. 3-9).
4. According to Gallup's figures, only 31 percent of Canadians supported the deal, while 17 percent expressed no opinion and 52 percent were opposed. In the province of Ontario, the industrial heartland of Canada, 62 percent were against the agreement, and only 26 percent supported the deal. Only in Quebec, where the free trade agreement enjoys support among those who hope to secede from Canada, did more people (40 percent) favor the agreement than oppose it.

REFERENCES

Basañez, M. (April 1991). "Integración Económica y Nacionalismo: Canadá, Estados Unidos y México." *Este País* (1), 3-9.

Campbell, B. (May 1991). "Beggar Thy Neighbor." NACLA, *Report on the Americas,* 24 (6).

Centro de Estudios de Opinión Pública. (n.d.). *Encuesta Mundial de Valores* 1990.

Hellman, J. A. (1988). *Mexico in Crisis* (2nd ed.). New York: Holmes & Meier.

Investigación Pública SC poll. (26 November 1990). *El Día.* Mexico City.

Orme, Jr., W. A. (May 1991). "The Sunbelt Moves South." NACLA, *Report on the Americas,* 24 (6).

Rivera Godínez, C. (ed.). (1991). *Siete Puntos sobre el Padrón Electoral de San Luís Postosí, 1991.* México, D.F.: Editorial Nueva Sociología.

United States Department of State. (February 1991). *Country Reports on Human Rights Practices for 1991.* Washington, D.C.: U.S. Government Printing Office.

UPI. (14 December 1990). "Most Canadians Reject Trade Pact According to Poll." *The News.* Mexico City.

Chapter 13

Authoritarianism and North American Free Trade: The Debate in Mexico

Adolfo Aguilar Zinser

How do political and economic factors interact in the process of North American economic integration, and how will Mexico's authoritarian political system affect the outcome of the agreement? This chapter examines how free trade and open markets function in a highly centralized, presidentialist, authoritarian regime. Optimists think that the opening of the Mexican economy, by itself, will create an environment conducive also to political liberalization, freedom of expression, and clean elections, and to a parallel economic and political decentralization. Free trade, it is often said, will create adequate social and economic pressures, as well as incentives, to clean up and strengthen the corrupt and unreliable Mexican legal system, and it may force Mexico to adopt, and actually enforce, international environmental standards to protect its own habitat and to preserve its natural resources.

This optimistic assessment is questionable for a number of reasons. The purpose of this paper is to explore some preliminary ideas about this issue. This chapter is not concerned with whether Mexico's authoritarian regime has the moral or political right to negotiate a free trade deal with two democracies. Rather, it addresses whether the authoritarian character of Mexico's political system makes a difference to how North American economic integration will unfold.

AUTHORITARIANISM, THE PARTNER OF FREE TRADE

In today's political discourse, democracy is often identified with capitalism. There is seen to be an inseparable and linear relationship between capitalist modernization and democratization. However, it is also evident that free market economies can function very well outside of democratic processes. In fact, there is ample evidence from recent Latin American history that the ideal environment for business is not always democracy (Collier, 1979).

In the United States, Canada, and Western Europe, democracy, representative institutions, and public accountability have resulted in a fairly sophisticated and complex regulatory structure that restricts at least some of the inherent tendencies of capitalist economies to form monopolies, exploit workers, and abuse the environment. Without such regulations, free markets lead to mean, unequal, and unsustainable economic structures. But capitalism does not behave identically or even predictably everywhere. Different combinations of factors can give quite contrasting results. For instance, Asian countries such as Japan or South Korea, which have relatively large populations in small national territories, are bound together by strong traditional cultures but have mercantilist inclinations, and are governed by authoritarian regimes, have experienced a remarkably cruel, efficient, competitive, and aggressive capitalism, characterized by a multitude of small-scale businesses and a few very large corporations. In contrast, Latin American authoritarian regimes have generated an extremely wealthy class but have not formed very competitive capitalist economies. In Latin America, culture, economics, and authoritarian politics result in a fairly unproductive and economically unsound combination.

Given Mexico's political culture, income distribution, social values, and organizations, free trade combined with authoritarian rule will create new sources of wealth but will result in a further concentration of income and in the reinforcement of authoritarian features of Mexico's political system. It is unlikely to significantly promote economic efficiency and competitiveness. In other words, in the absence of a profound political opening, current Mexican liberalization policies and the free trade initiative will only help to reinforce the authoritarian regime and to favor the interests of a small industrial and commercial oligarchy.

We can identify two concrete indications that free trade is actually undermining the prospects for a democratic change in Mexico: the absence of an open national debate and the international "immunization" of the authoritarian Mexican regime.

ABSENCE OF A NATIONAL DEBATE

Negotiations toward a North American Free Trade Agreement (NAFTA) have sparked a heated debate. In the United States and Canada, the benefits of freer trade have been strongly questioned by labor unions, environmental groups, human rights organizations, some producers, and other dissident voices. The free trade agreement that Canada has already signed with the United States (CUFTA) has been opposed by an array of forces including opposition political parties, unions, environmentalists, community organizers, church groups, and countless individuals. In contrast, and contradicting Mexico's long-standing suspicion and hostility toward the United States, Mexicans seem either silent or complacent; only isolated voices have articulated opposition or alternatives to current NAFTA negotiations (see the chapter by Hellman in this volume). Are Mexicans more convinced of the virtues of free trade than the citizens of Canada or the United States are? Or are Mexicans not really free to learn about the possible implications of free trade and to raise their concerns?

The answer lies in the stark contrasts among the three countries: whereas the United States and Canada are open societies where dissent can be articulately expressed and tolerated, Mexico is an authoritarian regime plagued with abuses and inequalities (Aguilar Zinser, 1987-88). Mexicans have little access to the information they would need to form their own opinion; official propaganda is overwhelming; the few free unions are constantly being crushed; and Congress is totally subordinated to the executive.

The Mexican government has given NAFTA negotiations the equivalent status of a national security affair, keeping information almost a state secret, preventing any meaningful public debate, maintaining a close vigilance on its opponents, and transmitting only general propaganda messages to the public. After months of being told their government had no intention of negotiating a free trade agreement with the United States, the Mexican public learned from a leaked story printed in the *Wall Street Journal* on 27 March 1990 that arrangements for such negotiations had already been made. The financial newspaper said that government officials from the two countries had agreed at a private meeting in New York in late February 1990 to negotiate a trade accord.[1]

There have been numerous attempts to open up a real debate in Mexico and to initiate a substantive legislative discussion that could influence the outcome of the agreement. Government officials, though, have dedicated considerable time and effort to derailing, neutralizing, discrediting, or even boycotting these initiatives. The most significant government move has been to prevent the Mexican Chamber of Deputies from having any input in the agreement. The president, his aides, and the ruling Institutional Revolutionary Party (PRI) have claimed that, according to the Constitution, only the Senate may ratify international treaties, and that, therefore, the 500-member Chamber of Deputies could not discuss the negotiations towards a free trade deal.[2] Informally, and outside congressional offices, trade officials have met with individual deputies, but no formal hearings or consultations have been held. The government's refusal to allow the Chamber of Deputies to discuss the trade negotiations is simply explained. As a result of the 1988 election, opposition deputies held an unprecedented 45 percent of the seats in the lower house of the Mexican Congress. An open debate in Congress would have given the opposition opportunities to confront government officials, demand information, and show the public aspects of the negotiations the government wanted to hide.

In contrast to the situation in the Chamber of Deputies, the official party has an all but unanimous majority in the Senate. With 60 of the 64 seats controlled by the ruling party, the Senate offers a safe environment to "debate" NAFTA. In fact, in April 1990, President Salinas asked the Senate to convoke a national dialogue to advise the government on Mexico's future international trade policy. In a tightly controlled environment, the Senate held several forums in various cities. As anticipated, the Senate virtually unconditionally recommended that "in virtue of Mexico's geographic location, of the history of its trade relations and the potential for complementing its economy in relation to the United States, [Mexico] negotiate with that country a free trade agreement" (Foro Nacional de Consulta, 1990, p. 293). Salinas did not even wait to hear the Senate recommendation; in mid-May he publicly announced his intention to go ahead with the negotiation of the agreement.

In November 1990, when the lack of debate in Mexico was already evident, a group of six Mexican intellectuals, writers, experts, and opinion leaders—Jorge G. Castañeda, Carlos Fuentes, Lorenzo Meyer, Carlos Monsiváis, Jesús Silva-Herzog, and Adolfo Aguilar Zinser—wrote an open letter to the head of the Mexican Congress suggesting that social security standards for labor as well as consumer and environmental protection should be discussed as crucial matters to be included in the free trade initiative. This document was inspired by a similar letter written by Congressmen Don Pease (a Democrat from Ohio) and Terry Bruce (a Democrat from Illinois), signed by several other members of Congress, and sent to President Bush on 31 October 1990. The letter by Peace and Bruce sparked a serious congressional debate in the United States. The letter from the Mexican intellectuals was ignored by its addressee. Salinas's officials tried to intimidate some of its signatories and few Mexican newspapers acknowledged its existence.

On 15 January 1991, critics of NAFTA in the United States and Canada organized an informal congressional conference on Capitol Hill to inform others of their concerns. Two of the cosigners of the Mexican letter (Jorge G. Castañeda and Adolfo Aguilar Zinser) were invited to speak. Their views were distorted, or simply not reported, by the Mexican press. However, on 27 January on the front page of *Excélsior,* Mexico's most prominent daily, a top PRI official (later named head of Channel 13, the government television station), in an ominous and threatening statement, accused the two of betraying the Mexican nation and becoming enemies of the country by criticizing the government while in Washington. This response served as an effective deterrent to other Mexican critics of Salinas's free trade initiative.

In February 1990, Cuauhtémoc Cárdenas—presidential candidate in 1988, leader of the Mexican Party of the Democratic Revolution (PRD), and the strongest contender ever to face the PRI in an election—outlined a proposal for a Continental Development and Trade Pact as an alternative to the narrow free trade agreement proposed by presidents Salinas and Bush and Prime Minister Mulroney. Cárdenas first presented the idea of a continental pact in November 1990, at the annual convention of the British Columbia Federation of Labour in Vancouver. Later, in a widely read statement, he said:

> We cannot be satisfied with the kind of future that would emerge from a simple economic liberalization. This would only extrapolate present trends and exacerbate present vices . . . not any kind of trade is a mutually advantageous exchange; not just any type of investment is going to transform our productive foundations and create the jobs and incomes we want for our people; not just any kind of industry is going to optimize the use of our resources and protect our habitat; not any profitable business is a responsible enterprise. Economic liberalization is not our objective; it is one of our tools. Development, social justice, and a clean environment are our objectives (Cárdenas, 1991, pp. 1-2).

Cárdenas's proposal was intended not to open up a debate on free trade from a purely negative perspective, but rather to offer a series of alternative concepts that could be introduced into the discussion. In Canada and the United States, the idea of a Continental Development Pact was received with interest and sympathy by political parties, unions, and academics; in

Mexico, the government managed to keep Cárdenas's proposal out of sight. Only vague references to the proposal were made in the Mexican press. Far from succeeding in opening up debate, the opposition leader was accused of opposing change and "modernization" and of promoting foreign intervention in Mexico.

In another attempt to open up the debate in Mexico, nongovernmental organizations from Mexico and the United States (Equipo Pueblo and Development Gap) agreed to help Democratic congressmen to hold, in Mexico, a congressional forum on the NAFTA. On 25 March, two U.S. congressmen sent letters to the leaders of Mexico's Chamber of Deputies, proposing a joint sponsorship of the conference. The forum was planned for June 1991, right after the U.S. congressional vote on President Bush's request for "fast-track" authority to negotiate NAFTA, and two months before mid-term elections for Mexico's Congress.

A combined effort of the Mexican government and the U.S. embassy in Mexico persuaded the congressmen to change the list of participants and postpone the forum until after 18 August, the date of Mexico's congressional elections. Later, during the fall—allegedly at the request of top Mexican leaders—President Bush intervened with one of the conference's sponsors in the U.S. Congress to cancel the forum. An authoritative account of the incident reads as follows:

> One of the members of Congress who considered sponsoring the forum was told by another member that he had received a call from the President (Bush) saying this forum will not be helpful to US-Mexican relations and could well complicate FTA negotiations (Counger, 1991).

Despite all efforts to prevent a public debate, a pluralist forum, entitled "Public Opinion and Free Trade: Citizens, Views and Alternatives," was eventually held in Zacatecas—coinciding with a round of official negotiations—on 23-25 October 1991. This forum of prominent Mexican scholars, journalists, politicians, businessmen, and opinion-makers was convened by a number of nongovernmental organizations linked together under the Mexican Action Network on Free Trade, the U.S. Mobilization for Development, Trade, and the Environment (MODTLE), and, from Canada, the Action Canada Network and Common Frontiers. The forum was sponsored by the U.S. group Development Gap and by Mexico's Equipo Pueblo and Lázaro Cárdenas Foundation.

A citizens' consensus was expressed in more than 50 presentations, including the keynote participation of Cárdenas and Salvador Nava, leader of the civic movement of the State of San Luis Potosí. Agreement was reached around the need to bring Mexican free trade negotiators to a democratic process of public accountability. On the eve of the forum's inauguration, the governor of Zacatecas, hoping to thwart the organizers, blocked the use of the local theater in which the meeting was to be held.

The impediments to debate about free trade in Mexico illustrate not only the lack of tolerance of Mexico's officials to any kind of public scrutiny and the intense security overtones they attach to NAFTA negotiations, but also how Mexico's authoritarian practices can be endorsed and even emulated by the U. S. administration—suggesting that economic liberalization is not, in fact, an opportunity for the United States to support the process of political liberalization in Mexico.

INTERNATIONAL "IMMUNIZATION" OF THE AUTHORITARIAN MEXICAN REGIME

Mexico today enjoys a unique international status. It is the only remaining single-party authoritarian system that can practice massive electoral fraud and violate human rights without confronting serious recrimination by the international community. Any other Latin America country with such persistent misconduct would cause an international outcry; Mexico not only escapes the censorship of Western democracies, its leaders are often praised and warmly welcomed in virtually all capitals of the world. Such good standing is possible thanks to a combination of two very powerful circumstances: first, the sweeping economic policies implemented by the Mexican government, which follow current world trends—including negotiations toward NAFTA; and second, and more important, President Salinas, the first authentically pro-United States politician ever to rule Mexico, has (at the time of this writing) the unequivocal support of President Bush and the Washington establishment.

The international "immunization" of the Mexican regime is also helped by the peculiar ability of Mexican authorities to deny, hide, or disguise serious violations of the human, civil, and political rights of its citizens. In June 1990, 19 months after President Salinas took office, Americas Watch published its first overall report on human rights violations in Mexico. In the opening paragraph, Americas Watch explains clearly why Mexico's immunity to international scrutiny persists.

> More often than not, Mexico is overlooked when lists of countries that violate internationally recognized human rights are compiled. That this is so is more a

testament to the Mexican government's careful cultivation of its pro-human rights image than its care to ensure that individual human rights are respected (Americas Watch 1990).

Such elusiveness has earned the Mexican regime the distinction of being named "the perfect dictatorship" by Mario Vargas Llosa, Peru's leading literary figure and former presidential candidate. One of the most eloquent manifestations of that "perfection" is the fact that despite opposition leaders' frequent denunciations of electoral fraud, political persecution, corruption, and repression, and regardless of the very critical reports prepared by Americas Watch (1990) and Amnesty International, the United States government does not seem a bit embarrassed to negotiate NAFTA with the Salinas government. The U. S. Congress has expressed reservations about the virtues of the proposed deal because labor exploitation in Mexico would undermine wages and take jobs away from American workers, but most members of Congress have essentially ignored the issue of the suppression of political rights in Mexico.

Support for Mexico's regime reflected in the process of NAFTA negotiations might be justified by Washington as only a circumstantial and temporary step to assure the economic transition. Certain features of Mexico's authoritarianism, however, have proven useful to consolidate and expand U.S. economic and political interests in Mexico.

Contradicting Washington's enthusiasm for events in Eastern Europe and for the process of democratization under way in Latin America, the United States does not seem opposed to the authoritarian character of the Mexican regime. On the contrary, there are indications that Mexico's peculiar kind of repressive controls are seen favorably in Washington as a guarantee of political stability as well as a framework within which to rapidly and effectively implement the economic reforms demanded by the IMF and the World Bank.

APPARENT ADVANTAGES OF AUTHORITARIANISM

Corporatism

Under the liberalization program, Mexico's corporatism has been refurbished. Corporatism has taken the new form of a solidarity program designed to assist the poor with their most basic needs in exchange for electoral loyalty. This instrument has given the Salinas administration enough political control to maintain the appearance of consensus and order.

On the other hand, corporatism in its more traditional forms of labor controls has given Salinas a number of advantages, including the capability to implement a sharp reduction of wages—a more than 50 percent cut in real terms has been experienced in a decade. Such artificially depressed wage levels represent a crucial comparative advantage to attract foreign investment to Mexico. As long as Mexican wages can be largely determined by presidential fiat, not by the collective bargaining power of trade unions or by the forces of supply and demand, free trade and other economic advantages offered by Mexico will give foreign investors a combination of incentives difficult to find elsewhere. It is true that cheap labor is not by itself sufficient to attract foreign investors and is often not the most important factor determining the investment decisions of multi-national corporations. However, under free trade, Mexico could have the opportunity to expand its infrastructure and organize its production capacity around a "package" of incentives within which cheap labor is an essential component. Thus, an opportunity exists for Mexico to "specialize," at least over a considerable period of time, in cheap labor as its "niche" in the international economy.

Political Centralization

In its 22 June 1991 issue, *Business Week* published a cover article on Mexico's new business elite. It described the means by which Salinas sold the most profitable public enterprises to a handful of tycoons bound to him by strong personal loyalties and political relationships. With few exceptions, this new corporate class is not composed of the type of entrepreneurs that could compete on an equal footing with world-class corporations. However, its members are the beneficiaries of Salinas's economic liberalization, and are likely to be shielded and protected as a privileged elite closely associated with the regime.

Inefficient economic concentration is possible thanks to the presidential powers enjoyed by Salinas above and beyond any formal legal structure. Public enterprises are sold without any accountability or surveillance by Congress, the judiciary, or even the press or public opinion. Decisions are made in the presidential palace and are based mostly on political calculations.

The same political calculus is manifested in the allocation of federal resources for investments in infrastructure throughout the country. States are favored or punished according to the president's personal sympathies and political objectives. Under the centralized system of decisionmaking, the opportunities flowing from free trade are likely to be channeled toward certain regions of the country, particularly the relatively more industrialized and developed northern states where Salinas built his political stronghold. Uneven regional development will take place at the expense of southern rural states, which are rich in energy and natural resources but largely abandoned and abused by the federal government.

Impunity

The arbitrary, casuistic, and unpredictable way in which laws are applied and enforced in Mexico creates a system of widespread impunity at all levels of government. The most visible manifestations of this impunity are police abuses and persistent human rights violations. However, the absence of the rule of law also permeates the economy and the management of the environment. If, in the past, arbitrary extralegal power was used to expropriate, today the same illegal and unaccountable methods are used to sell government property.

The Mexican government has the ability to adjust to foreign demands without significantly altering its policies. A good example is in the area of environmental protection. As a response to concerns raised in the United States, the Mexican government took highly visible steps to institute a series of ecological policies and programs. While the fast-track process was being discussed in the U.S. Congress, President Salinas ordered the closure of the Azcapotzalco oil refinery, a significant source of air pollution in Mexico City. To appease U.S. environmentalists, the president also instituted a border environmental plan and a program for the protection of dolphins (but did not ban the dolphin-killing methods used by the Mexican tuna fishing industry). These moves were accompanied by a multimillion-dollar public relations campaign in the U.S. media aimed at reinforcing Salinas's image as an environmentally conscious president. These actions were intended for external consumption, though, and contrasted sharply with the indifference of Mexican authorities toward domestic pollution concerns. For instance, just 50 miles outside Mexico City, in the Tula River valley of the State of Hidalgo, little attention was given to the serious and life-threatening contamination of the agricultural valleys irrigated by that river, which carries the virtually untreated sewage of Mexico City and the industrial waste of the Tula oil refinery and other Tula oil-related plants. Neglected by the authorities despite constant warnings by local residents and environmental groups, the pestilent Tula valley suffers steady environmental deterioration. In the summer of 1991, an outbreak of cholera spread from there to the Huasteca highlands of the State of Hidalgo, causing a serious health crisis in the region.

CONCLUSIONS

Without democratic reform, liberal economic policies in Mexico will only strengthen the power of the elite, deepen inequalities, broaden social problems, and reinvigorate the authoritarian features of the Mexican political system. When President Salinas cautioned against the dangers of implementing radical political reforms while economic reforms were in process, he was not really suggesting that once economic transition is consolidated he will proceed with a political opening. In fact, his economic liberalization is consistent with, and dependent on, the preservation of authoritarianism.

There is a trade-off between cutting the state budget, selling public enterprises, and opening the economy to the United States, on the one hand, and, on the other, democratizing the Mexican political system. Indeed, all the achievements for which Salinas has been praised and respected in U.S. political, financial, corporate, and academic circles have been possible only because Salinas has preserved and enhanced the authoritarian features of the one-party presidential system. In any open political system, the liberalization program would not have gone so far as it has in Mexico: voters would have attenuated or even rejected it; the media and the press would have discussed and conditioned it; the Congress would have screened, slowed, and regulated it; and unions would have cut slices off of it. Because none of these checks and balances exist in Mexico, Salinas has appeared as a reformer and free trade hero to many people in the United States and Canada.

President Salinas's supporters in Western democracies think that when the expansion and consolidation of private enterprise are at stake, democracy can wait. In fact, the combination of free trade with thinly disguised authoritarian controls might be an acceptable type of regime in the "new world order" emerging from the post–Cold War era. Mexico may be inaugurating a new breed of "legitimate" authoritarianism.

NOTES

1. On the Mexican side, Commerce Secretary Jaime Serra Puche, and President Salinas's economic advisor, José Cordoba, were present. U.S. Secretary of State James Baker III, National Security Adviser Brent Scowcroft, U.S. Trade Representative Carla Hills, Commerce Secretary Robert Mosbacher, and Michael Boskin, chairman of the Council of Economic Advisers, were also present.

2. For an analysis of the PRI, see Meyer (1989).

REFERENCES

Aguilar Zinser, A. (1987-88). "Mexico: The Presidential Problem." *Foreign Policy,* 69, 40-60.

Americas Watch. (June 1990). "Human Rights in Mexico: A Policy of Impunity." New York.

Cárdenas, C. (8 February 1991). "The Continental Development and Trade Initiative: A Statement." New York.

Collier, D. (ed.). (1979). *The New Authoritarianism in Latin America.* Princeton: Princeton University Press.

Counger, L. (24 September 1991). "FTA Political Perspectives: The Bilateral Free Trade Forum That Never Happened." *Free Trade Advisory,* 1 (2).

Foro Nacional de Consulta. (1990). *Las Relaciones Comerciales de México con el Mundo* (Memoria, Tomo II). Senado de la República, México D.F.

IV

**NAFTA, THE UNITED STATES, AND
NEW CONTINENTAL RELATIONS**

Chapter 14

NAFTA and U.S. Trade Policy: Implications for Canada and Mexico

Scott Sinclair

The treatment of U.S. trade-remedy laws is a major issue in the drive for a North American Free Trade Agreement (NAFTA). On the one hand, the continued use of U.S. trade remedies against Canada and Mexico could erode any increased access to the U.S. domestic market gained through trilateral negotiations. On the other hand, the assertion of U.S. power through its trade-remedy laws has resulted in significant pressures for domestic economic and political adjustment in Canada and Mexico. Hence, the continued application of U.S. trade-remedy laws raises important considerations for both Canadian and Mexican trade and sovereignty.

U.S. trade legislation will continue to be a contentious issue in continental trade relations, even under a free trade regime. The new salience of these trade laws results from basic changes in the U.S. position in the international political economy. Strengthened U.S. trade-remedy legislation is a reaction to U.S. hegemonic decline. It reflects a determination to use U.S. structural power in the international trading system, based on control over its large internal market, to bolster U.S. dominance. These trade remedies are also a means to manage domestic political pressures resulting from U.S. economic decline.

This essay will examine U.S.-Canadian and U.S.-Mexican trade disputes in the decade leading up to the free trade negotiations. It will consider which Canadian and Mexican exports were most at risk from U.S. trade remedies and which Canadian and Mexican policies and programs were targeted by

U.S. trade legislation. Next, it will assess, based on the experience of the Canada-U.S. Free Trade Agreement (CUFTA), the adequacy of new bilateral or trilateral dispute-settlement arrangements to withstand these pressures emanating from U.S. trade legislation. Finally, it will survey the options open to Canada and Mexico in adapting to U.S. trade legislation.

THE SHIFT TO POWER BARGAINING

The decline of U.S. hegemony in the international political economy conditions U.S. trade-remedy laws. The continued preeminence of its large domestic market, and the ability of the state to deny access to that market, is a structural source of U.S. power in international trade politics. Through strengthened trade legislation, the United States has signaled its determination to wield this power.

The U.S. internal market is the world's largest. In fact, while the U.S. share of world exports declined steadily from 1960 to 1987, its share of world imports increased steadily, especially after 1983. The structural power afforded by controlling access to the U.S. domestic market has actually increased as U.S. industrial competitiveness has diminished. Moreover, trade still represents a smaller proportion of GNP in the United States than in any other developed country, lessening the impact of counter-retaliation.[1] Power in the international trading system is asymmetrical. U.S. power is far greater than that of nations with smaller domestic markets.

The increasingly frequent U.S. practice of resorting to trade remedies has also undermined the multilateral trade institutions formed under U.S. hegemony, particularly the General Agreement on Tariffs and Trade (GATT). U.S. trade remedies are unilateral. The laws and standards applied against foreign practices are those of the United States. They are also nonreciprocal. The quasi-judicial trade-remedy procedures do not formally consider whether U.S. businesses or governments adhere to the standards applied against nonresidents. Finally, the approach is coercive and discriminatory. Trade remedies single out successful foreign competitors or recalcitrant national governments, threatening their access to the large U.S. domestic market.[2]

U.S. unilateralism is part of a movement "into an aggressively competitive trading pattern in which negotiating power, rather than the impersonal rules of liberal economic behavior, determine outcomes in a zero-sum game" (Cox, 1987, p. 299). In this competitive struggle for global market shares, the United States will wield the threat of restricted access—if only to enhance the bargaining power of U.S. transnational corporations (TNCs), rather than to actually close its internal market.[3]

THE OFFENSIVE AND DEFENSIVE
AGENDAS OF U.S. TRADE LEGISLATION

Economic decline has created strong domestic political pressures to restrict import competition—the defensive agenda of U.S. trade legislation. Concurrently, U.S.-based transnational capital and the U.S. state aggressively assert free trade policies in globally competitive or strategic sectors—the offensive agenda of U.S. trade legislation.

As tariffs have declined in the postwar era, most nations have turned to nontariff measures to cushion domestic industries from import competition. The U.S. pioneered many of these flexible instruments of protection including countervail, antidumping, and punitive provisions (see glossary for definitions) against "unfair trade practices." With the United States insistence some of these provisions have been incorporated into multilateral GATT codes.[4]

Trade remedies play an indispensable role in the U.S. political system. Both the growing competitiveness of Europe and Japan and the globalization of U.S.-based multinationals are fundamentally altering the U.S. economy. Trade-remedy laws are a way to channel and control the resulting protectionism. By blaming adjustment problems on unfair foreign competition, trade-remedy laws preserve the ideology of free trade and the prerogatives of U.S. investment capital. These laws also give U.S. workers and domestic businesses a small, if indirect, measure of control over the economic upheaval that is steadily eroding their employment and earnings.

The agenda of U.S. trade-remedy legislation, however, is not solely import restrictive. It has an important expansionist aspect. The offensive agenda of U.S. trade policy, of which the punitive provisions of Section 301 of the U.S. Trade Act (see glossary) are the purest expression, is designed to attack perceived foreign barriers to U.S. trade and investment. This agenda is sectoral and highly selective. It focuses on areas of U.S. competitive advantage or vital interest, including investment rights, trade in services, intellectual property rights, access to strategic resources, and globalization of agricultural markets.

Trade-remedy laws are instruments for exercising U.S. structural power. They can be turned to both defensive and offensive ends. They reconcile the need for defensive measures to curb foreign import competition with the search for new offensive instruments to assert U.S. power in the international political economy. Where the United States is strong enough, as with dependent trading partners like Canada and Mexico, it can pursue both agendas simultaneously.

U.S. MARKET ACCESS

The shift to power bargaining is evident in the pattern of North American trade disputes during the 1980s. U.S. interests employed trade remedies for defensive and offensive purposes—that is, to provide import relief for U.S. industries threatened by imports from Mexico or Canada, and to pressure Canada and/or Mexico to alter or abandon policies judged inimical to U.S. interests.[5]

Certain Canadian and Mexican exports are at greater risk from trade-remedy actions than others. The relationship between trade and foreign direct investment (FDI) is the key to understanding which exports are most vulnerable. U.S. defensive protectionism is directed almost exclusively at foreign-controlled imports, while the intrafirm trade of U.S.-based TNCs is facilitated by trade, tariff, investment, and taxation policy.[6]

Finger and Murray (1990, p. 43) have compared the number of U.S. countervailing duty and antidumping cases against various countries with those countries' shares of U.S. merchandise imports from 1980 to 1988. Canada provided 18 percent of U.S. merchandise imports between 1980 and 1988, yet accounted for only 5 percent of total cases. Mexico, which provided 4.9 percent of U.S. merchandise imports, accounted for 4.5 percent of total cases. Given the alarmism of the Canadian corporate sector and the Conservative government, the relatively low incidence of cases against Canada is surprising.

An important factor insulating Canadian exports against U.S. trade actions was the high level of affiliated trade between the two countries. In analyzing U.S. trade politics, it is crucial to distinguish between foreign-controlled imports (that portion of U.S. trade controlled by foreign-owned enterprises) and affiliated imports (the intrafirm trade of U.S.-based TNCs). Over one-third of total U.S. merchandise imports from Canada are affiliated, the largest proportion for any major U.S. trade partner (U.S. Dept. of Commerce, 1988, p. 33). For obvious reasons, U.S. TNCs are unlikely to challenge these imports through trade actions.

In highly integrated industries like the auto industry, the only challenge is likely to come from subordinate social forces such as trade unions or state governments in auto-producing regions. In these instances, however, intrafirm trade enjoys the support of U.S. TNCs, which are among the most powerful of U.S. domestic social forces. Consequently, this portion of bilateral trade is at low risk from import-restrictive measures.

Since 1980, U.S. defensive trade actions against Canadian exporters have been concentrated against Canadian-controlled agricultural, fish, forestry, and resource-related products or largely Canadian-owned manufacturing industries such as steel.[7]

The same pattern holds for trade actions against Mexican products. Most of the trade actions against Mexican exports, especially the numerous countervailing duty cases, were concentrated between 1982 and 1986.[8] At the beginning of the decade, Mexico closely regulated FDI in domestic industries. Furthermore, the initial response of the de la Madrid administration to the debt and balance-of-payments crisis in 1982 included emergency import restrictions.[9] The U.S. reaction to these investment and trade restrictions combined with the recession in the U.S. economy to produce a rash of countervailing duty cases against Mexican products. By 31 December 1984, 11 countervailing duty orders were in effect against Mexican products, including steel, bricks, cement, ceramic tile, chemicals, clothing, and lime (USITC, 1985, p. 96).

Under pressure from the United States and its foreign creditors, the Mexican government eventually eased import restraints and relaxed its restrictions on FDI, especially in the export-oriented *maquiladoras*. Bilateral negotiations also led to an agreement, signed 23 April 1985, in which Mexico phased out certain subsidies in return for an entitlement to an injury test under U.S. countervailing duty law. Investment liberalization contributed to a sharp increase in affiliated trade between Mexico and the United States.[10] As the share of affiliated imports from Mexico increased, U.S. countervailing duty cases against Mexico diminished (in relation to its share of total exports). Continuing trade actions were, as in the Canadian case, concentrated against Mexican-controlled imports such as cement, textiles, steel products, agricultural produce, and fish (USITC, 1985, pp. 91-97).[11]

By the end of the decade, two-way trade in similar manufactured goods dominated U.S. bilateral merchandise trade with Canada and Mexico (Council of Economic Advisors, [CEA], 1991, p. 254). Where U.S.-based TNCs dominate these highly integrated sectors, continental trade is insulated from U.S. protectionism. Trade frictions will be concentrated in that portion of continental trade accounted for by Canadian and Mexican indigenous exports.

SOVEREIGNTY AND POWER BARGAINING

The impact of U.S. trade actions and asymmetrical power bargaining on Canadian and Mexican sovereignty is arguably as serious as the problem of secure U.S. market access. Many distinctive Canadian and Mexican policies—including regional development programs, investment screening and performance requirements, energy pricing, resource conservation, cultural policies, certain social programs (such as unemployment insurance), patent regulations, and agricultural marketing arrangements—have been challenged as unfair trade practices.

There was a strong affinity between Canadian and Mexican policy efforts at the beginning of the 1980s; both nations sought to develop natural resources to meet national development priorities, to strengthen public enterprise, to promote regional development, and to regulate foreign investment. In each of these areas, the underlying philosophies of state intervention and mixed economy clashed with the prevailing U.S. market ideology. This clash was clear in continental trade disputes.

The United States used its trade laws to challenge interventionist and nationalist policies in both Canada and Mexico. Because public ownership and state involvement in trade and investment was greater in Mexico, that country often bore the brunt of U.S. offensives. A number of precedents established against Mexican practices were subsequently applied against similar Canadian programs.

One of the most important of these interactions stemmed from a 1986 countervailing duty case against carbon black from Mexico. At issue was the claim by U.S. producers that Mexican inputs of natural gas, heavy fuel oil, and petroleum feedstock are much cheaper than in the U.S., amounting to subsidies on downstream products such as ammonia, cement, and carbon black. What particularly galled U.S. producers and many U.S. politicians was that "the two-tier pricing system was combined with restrictions on foreign ownership in the energy sector" (Percy and Yoder, 1987, p. 48).

In several earlier countervailing duty cases against Mexican energy-intensive industries, the U.S. Department of Commerce (DOC) had upheld a concept known as "general availability," which held that if subsidies were available on a general basis to all users, they did not distort trade and therefore were not countervailable. In the 1986 carbon black case, under pressure from U.S. legislators and the U.S. Court of International Trade, DOC modified its position. It ruled that the benefits from Mexico's two-tier pricing of energy and hydrocarbons, while "generally available," were concentrated in a few "specific" industries. A countervailing duty was placed on the Mexican product (*Federal Register,* 1983, p. 29,564).

Using the Carbon Black ruling as their basis, U.S. forest companies renewed their attempt to countervail softwood lumber from Canada. Although a virtually identical case had been dismissed in 1983, in 1986 the U.S. industry won an affirmative preliminary ruling against the Canadian industry. The Mulroney government subsequently settled the case "out of court," agreeing to collect a 15 percent export tax on softwood lumber exports to the United States. The terms of this settlement gave the U.S. government and private U.S. industry unprecedented influence, extending to the minutia of Canadian forest management policy.

There are more examples of this type of connection between Mexican and Canadian cases. In countervailing duty cases against energy-intensive Mexican industries in the early 1980s, U.S. administrators established the rule that subsidies available in a specific region were not "generally available" and hence were subject to countervail. Ever since a successful countervailing duty case against Michelin in the early 1970s, Canadian governments had defended Canadian regional development programs against the U.S. charge that they were trade-distorting subsidies. The rulings against Mexican regional development incentives sealed the fate of these Canadian diplomatic efforts and paved the way for a series of U.S. trade actions in which expenditures under every major Canadian regional development program were countervailed.[12]

The process worked both ways. Section 409 of the U.S. legislation implementing the CUFTA (the so-called Baucus-Danforth amendment) specifically targets alleged Canadian subsidy practices. It instructs the United States trade representative (USTR) to consider requests from any U.S. industry that has reason to believe it will suffer from subsidized competition from Canada before new bilateral rules and disciplines are developed. The USTR will investigate on the industry's behalf and then consider action under Section 301. Several Canadian industries have been investigated under this clause, which perversely makes it easier for a U.S. industry to initiate a trade action against Canada than against other GATT signatories.

Despite high-level entreaties, Canadian objections were dismissed. The Mulroney government managed only to get a clause added to the U.S. legislation that extends Section 409 provisions to any country concluding a trade agreement with the United States. As a result, Mexican subsidy practices will be subject to investigation under Baucus-Danforth when Mexico concludes a free trade agreement with the United States.

The power bargaining tactics of the United States, honed in the trade disputes of the 1980s, will intensify in a continental free trade regime. Once either Canada or Mexico bows to U.S. pressure, it then joins forces with the U.S. to impose the new precedent on the third party. Instead of combining to check U.S. preponderance, Mexico and Canada become collaborators in U.S. efforts to enforce a "level playing field."

Moreover, the United States will retain full recourse to its trade-remedy laws. Since the provisions of the CUFTA form the basis of NAFTA, the curbs on continuing U.S. trade actions within a continental free trade regime are liable to be ineffectual.

DISPUTE SETTLEMENT UNDER CUFTA

Canada's key objective in bilateral free trade talks was to get exempted from U.S. trade-remedy laws, or, at least, to negotiate binding bilateral rules to curb them. In 1987, Prime Minister Mulroney declared, "Our biggest priority is to have an agreement that ends the threat to Canadian industry from U.S. protectionists who harass and restrict exports through the misuse of trade laws."[13]

Keenly aware that the U.S. Congress would not accept constraints on U.S. trade-remedy laws, U.S. negotiators never seriously responded to Canada's insistent proposals for new rules. Despite an 11th-hour walkout of the Canadian negotiating team, the temporary breakdown of the talks, and a hasty face-saving compromise, U.S. trade-remedy laws remained largely untouched.

Of the trade laws of most concern to Canada, only safeguard rules were modified marginally in Canada's favor. Under the terms of CUFTA, U.S. trade laws, "including relevant statutes, legislative history, regulations, administrative practices, and judicial precedents," continue to apply to Canadian exports (Minister for International Trade, Canada, 1988, p. 172; House of Representatives, 1988). The United States can amend its trade-remedy laws without Canada's consent. If a new trade law or amendment specifies Canada, then it will apply (Article 1903). Moreover, Section 102 of the U.S. implementing act states that the laws of the United States are to prevail if they conflict with CUFTA.[14]

At the request of either government, a binational panel may be set up to consider any dispute arising from "any actual or proposed measure or any other matter that it considers affects the operation of this Agreement" (Articles 1804-1807). In addition, binational review panels can now replace domestic judicial review when a countervailing duty or antidumping ruling is appealed (Article 1904). Chapter 18 panels are not binding. Chapter 19 panels merely rule on whether the domestic laws of the investigating country have been applied properly, not on the merits of the case or the fairness of the laws themselves.

As the Government of Ontario concluded in 1988,

> as to the principal goal of secure U.S. market access, there appears to be little change from the status quo. Neither the present rules governing antidumping and subsidy/countervail investigations nor the administering bodies are affected in any way by the Agreement. The new binational dispute settlement panel . . . does not possess any increased power or differing review mandate than the present system. . . . Overall, the inability of the Agreement to secure meaningfully [*sic*] U.S. market access in effect maintains the vulnerability of Canadian exports to U.S. trade remedy laws and would not appear to reduce it in future (Government of Ontario, 1988, p. ii).

A review of the caseload and decisions of the dispute-settlement panels to date shows that rather than transcending the dynamics of unequal power bargaining, the dispute-settlement process has reproduced them.

As expected, most Chapter 19 panels (on countervail and antidumping) have been initiated by Canadian exporters. As of 5 November 1991, there were 19 cases against U.S. agencies, involving nine Canadian products. There were just four cases against Canadian agencies, involving two U.S. products. Two of the cases against Canada were brought by a U.S. subsidiary of a Japanese transnational corporation (Binational Secretariat, 1991).

This disparity underscores the missing impetus from the U.S. side for a strong bilateral regime governing trade remedies and disputes. Indeed, in the only case involving a bona fide U.S. complaint, a dispute over beer, the United States circumvented the dispute-settlement process. Before the CUFTA panel reported, U.S. Trade Representative Carla Hills presented Canada with an ultimatum: to open its market to U.S. beer, or face retaliation under Section 301.

Under the terms of CUFTA, all the Chapter 19 cases against U.S. agencies have been reviewed under U.S. law. It is important to recall that the binational panels perform a judicial review function. The panel cannot hear evidence or conduct a new, independent trial. It must either uphold a final determination or refer it to the administering authority for further consideration.

Given these strict constraints, the binational panels have been fairly assertive. Cases involving Canadian raspberries and pork have been remanded, resulting in the U.S. agency dropping punitive duties. On the other hand, U.S. duties against Canadian steel rails and paving equipment have been upheld. A number of other cases have been terminated, some as the result of negotiated "out-of-court" settlements.

Before celebrating these modest successes, however, the process deserves a closer look. First, similar remands were not uncommon before the U.S. Court of International Trade, the previous avenue for judicial review. Second, in the case involving steel rails, the panel upheld prohibitive punitive duties of 94.57 percent. Third, in the pork case, a rather small, regional U.S. industry was able to command sufficient political support in the U.S. Congress to force an "extraordinary challenge" of the panel decision. Although the challenge committee upheld the panel's remand, this was a clear warning to Canadian pork producers that increased exports into the U.S. would be met by further trade actions, under one or more trade laws. U.S. negotiators successfully strengthened this "extraordinary challenge" provision in NAFTA.

Finally, the body of rulings and precedents being built up by the panels is based on U.S. trade law. The United States can change these laws unilaterally to negate the effect of an unfavorable panel ruling. Perhaps more importantly, prior to participating in these binational panels, Canada had never accepted the U.S. contention that its agricultural support, regional development, or transportation programs were trade-distorting or illegitimate subsidies. In each of these instances, and several more, binational panels have upheld U.S. rulings against such programs. This marks an important shift in Canada's trade diplomacy. The risk is that Canadian participation in the panel process has sanctioned these adverse decisions, weakening the country's position in subsequent international subsidy negotiations.

NAFTA's dispute-settlement procedures are no stronger than those in CUFTA. They will prove as ineffectual for Mexican exporters as they have for Canadian. The notion that the fundamental forces restructuring U.S. trade politics or the underlying power disparities between the United States and its closest neighbors can be finessed through dispute-settlement mechanisms is quixotic.

CONCLUSION: CANADA, MEXICO, AND THE POLITICIZATION OF U.S. TRADE LAW

To return to the two basic issues of secure U.S. market access and free trade's impact on Canadian and Mexican sovereignty, the NAFTA trade-off is likely to be unsatisfactory for Canada and Mexico. NAFTA will leave potent U.S.

trade-remedy laws intact, while significantly restricting Canadian and Mexican policy options.

What, then, are the lessons for Canada and Mexico in the face of this growing politicization of trade and investment relations and increasing pressure from the United States?

First, a portion of continental trade, the intrafirm transfers of U.S.-based TNCs, is insulated from U.S. defensive protectionism. As U.S. FDI in Canada and Mexico increases under the investment provisions of CUFTA and NAFTA, this portion will increase. The costs and benefits of increased U.S. corporate domination of the Canadian and Mexican economies should, of course, be weighed according to its impact on national welfare, independence, and economic development strategy, rather than with respect to its secondary effect on U.S. trade actions. After all, political absorption would be the securest form of U.S. market access.

Second, even under a free trade regime, Canadian- and Mexican-controlled exporters to the United States (or third-country investors in Canada and Mexico) have little choice but to accept U.S. protectionism as a cost of doing business in the U.S. market. Provision must be made for legal costs and possible market disruption. The Canadian and Mexican governments could take a more active role in supporting their exporters by helping to build political alliances with U.S. consumers, monitoring trade frictions, subsidizing the legal costs of firms embroiled in trade disputes, and supporting market diversification.

Third, little faith should be placed in the prospect of common subsidy rules or dispute-settlement mechanisms. The ineffectual mechanisms established under CUFTA are not commensurate with the sweeping concessions made in other sectors and policy areas. At best, early dispute-settlement experience indicates that the data used by U.S. agencies in prosecuting Canadian exporters may become more accurate. The substance of trade-remedy laws will not, however, be challenged. They apply, and the United States can change them as it pleases. At worst, CUFTA has generated ever more intense scrutiny of Canadian programs in Washington. The Baucus-Danforth amendment has even created a new weapon to deploy against successful Canadian exporters. Canadian and Mexican governments ought to be wary of dispute settlement based on the shifting sands of U.S. trade law.

Fourth, stronger bilateral or multilateral trade-enforcement mechanisms and binding supranational trade and investment dispute-settlement agencies would further erode sovereignty. Even if U.S. agreement could be attained, the integrity of a range of Canadian, Mexican, and U.S. domestic programs to protect the environment, labor rights, cultural independence, and social equity would still be threatened. The economic impact of U.S. trade laws on Canada, although significant, has been greatly exaggerated. The transfer of democratic regulatory authority to a secretive, unaccountable, corporate-dominated, supranational dispute-settlement process is a high price to pay for access to an already largely open continental market.

Finally, Canadians and Mexicans should recognize the internal differences of opinion and interest shaping continental trade politics. Dominant, and increasingly transnational, social forces in Mexico and Canada welcome the constraints placed on the state and subordinate social forces by free trade agreements. The threat of U.S. protectionism legitimates unpopular internal reforms.[15]

From the outset, diplomatic efforts to convince the United States to curb its protectionist trade laws were destined to fail. Instead, Canadians and Mexicans should face pragmatically, as sovereign nations, the pressures stemming from U.S. trade-remedy laws. Sometimes, where the vulnerability is great, this will mean yielding to U.S. pressure to modify domestic policies. But, too often, the impact of U.S. protectionism is exaggerated to justify a regressive, neoconservative reordering of Canadian and Mexican domestic priorities.

NOTES

I would like to thank Thea Lee for helpful comments on an earlier draft of this paper. Only the author, however, is responsible for the content of this chapter.

1. "Trade represents a smaller portion of the economy in the United States (merchandise exports at 5.6% of GNP, imports at 9.1% in 1987) than any other developed country. . . ." (President's Export Council, 1988, p. 9).
2. Nondiscrimination is a basic principle of the GATT. Under the most-favored-nation rule, benefits granted to any trading partner are to be extended to all signatories.
3. The new world trade order is characterized by a high degree of capital mobility among blocks. Aggressive bargaining creates a "web of contracts" linking competing states and TNCs of different nationalities (Strange, 1985). Increased competitive pressures in the world system may encourage uniformity rather than diversity among the regional blocks. "The competitive pressures present in the world system . . . are likely . . . to encourage the adoption of similar forms of state-capitalist development geared

to an offensive strategy in world markets and sustained by corporatist organization of society and economy" (Cox, 1987, p. 299).

4. Rodney Grey, Canada's chief negotiator during the Tokyo Round, coined the term *contingency protection* to describe this shift "away from reliance on fixed measures or techniques of intervention to regulate competition between imports and domestic competition and towards much greater reliance on flexible methods of protecting the domestic producer" (Grey, 1982, quoted in Cameron, 1986, p. 74).

5. The U.S. trade laws of most importance to Canada and Mexico are safeguards (Section 201), antidumping (Section 731), countervail (Section 701), the special provisions of Section 337 on "unfair practices in import trade," and Section 301 on "removing foreign barriers." See the glossary for a brief description of these five U.S. trade remedies.

6. Strategic or scarce natural resources are also less vulnerable to defensive protectionism. Here, U.S. policy, driven by domestic industrial consumers and the military-industrial complex, is to secure long-term access to foreign resources at stable prices.

7. Between 1980 and 1988 there were 21 antidumping cases against Canadian products. Of these cases, seven were negative, dismissed, or discontinued. The other 14 resulted in trade restrictions (including "voluntary" export restraints). During the same period there were 14 countervailing duty cases against Canadian exports, five of which ended in trade restrictions (Finger & Murray, 1990). Given the priority attached to curbing countervail by Canadian free trade negotiators, the number of successful cases is surprisingly small.

8. From 1980 to 1988 there were six antidumping cases against Mexican products, five of which ended in trade restrictions. Over the same period there were 29 countervailing duty cases against Mexican products, 27 of which ended in trade restrictions (Finger & Murray, 1990). In contrast to Canada, the large number and high rate of success of countervailing duty cases against Mexican exporters is striking.

9. In 1982 the Mexican government set itself the target of reducing imports by $6 billion. To attain this objective, it reestablished or extended import licensing requirements slated to expire, increased import duty rates on hundreds of items, and imposed embargoes on the import of luxury items. At this time, Mexico remained outside the GATT and had no international obligations that interfered with these measures.

10. The percentage share of affiliated imports from Mexico increased from 9.9 percent in 1982 to 17.2 percent in 1985 (U.S. Dept. of Commerce, 1988, p. 32).

11. Steel is a good example of how U.S. countervail was used as leverage to selectively limit Mexican imports. Mexico was one of seven countries with which the United States negotiated a "voluntary restraint agreement" in December 1984. It agreed to limit its exports of finished steel to the United States. In return, the United States

made a commitment to seek termination of unfair trade investigations. However, the largely non-arm's-length steel imports from the *maquiladoras* were unaffected by the restraint agreement (USITC, 1985, p. 96).

12. In the cases of Fresh Atlantic Groundfish (1986), the preliminary Softwood Lumber ruling (1986), and Fresh, Chilled and Frozen Pork (1989), Canadian expenditures under Canada's Regional Development Incentive Programs, Agricultural and Regional Development Agreements, General Development Agreements, and Industrial and Regional Development Program were judged actionable under U.S. trade law. Expenditures under dozens of other federal and provincial programs were also affected, including more than 50 programs in the Atlantic groundfish case alone.

13. Brian Mulroney, quoted in Clark (1990, p. 10).

14. House of Representatives, 1988, pp. 43, 47. The most contentious issues were postponed. CUFTA set up a working party to negotiate a substitute system of rules for countervailing duties and subsidies. The United States showed little interest in this process. NAFTA replaces the CUFTA deadlines with agreement merely to consult on these issues (Article 1907).

15. The same divisions are present in the United States. Progressive social forces in Canada and Mexico should welcome and support, if possible, attempts by their U.S. counterparts to assert national and community control over economic restructuring through U.S. trade legislation. In particular, they should make common cause with U.S. labor and environmental movements trying to introduce workers' rights and environmental standards into the international trade arena.

REFERENCES

Binational Secretariat, FTA, Canadian Section. (5 November 1991). *Status Report of Cases.* [Mimeo].

Cameron, D. (ed.). (1986). *The Free Trade Papers.* Toronto: Lorimer.

Clark, M. (June 1990). "Why Renegotiating Free Trade Won't Work." *Canadian Forum.*

Council of Economic Advisers, (CEA). (February 1991). *Economic Report of the President.* Washington: U.S. Government Printing Office.

Cox, R. (1987). *Production, Power, and World Order: Social Forces in the Making of History.* New York: Columbia University Press.

Federal Register. (27 June 1983). "Final Affirmative Countervailing Duty Determination and Countervailing Duty Order; Carbon Black from Mexico," 48 (4), 29564-70.

Finger, J. M., & Murray, T. (1990). "Policing Unfair Imports: The United States Example." *Journal of World Trade,* 24 (4), 39-53.

Government of Ontario. (1988). *The Question of Secure U.S. Market Access in the Canada-U.S. Free Trade Agreement.* [Mimeo].

Grey, R. (1982). *United States Trade Policy Legislation: A Canadian View.* Montreal: Institute for Research on Public Policy.

House of Representatives. (1988). Doc. No. 216. 100th Congress, 2nd session 208.

Ministry for International Trade, Canada. (1988). *An Act to Implement the Free Trade Agreement between Canada and the United States of America* (Vol. II). Ottawa: Minister for International Trade.

Percy, M. B., & Yoder, C. (1987). *The Softwood Lumber Dispute and Canada-U.S. Trade in Natural Resources.* Halifax: Institute for Research on Public Policy.

President's Export Council. (1988). *U.S. Trade in Transition: Maintaining the Gains* (Vol 1). Washington: U.S. Government Printing Office.

Strange, S. (1985). "Protectionism and World Politics." *International Organization,* 39 (2).

United States Department of Commerce, International Trade Administration. (1988). *International Direct Investment: Global Trends and the U.S. Role.* Washington: U.S. Government Printing Office.

United States International Trade Commission, (USITC). (1985). *Operation of the Trade Agreements Program* (36th Report, 1984). Washington: USITC.

Chapter 15

Implications of NAFTA for the United States: Investment, Jobs, and Productivity

Jeff Faux and *Thea Lee*

The ultimate goal in formulating and negotiating a North American Free Trade Agreement (NAFTA) should not be the abstract or ideological one of free trade. It should be the improvement of living standards for the 360 million people in the United States, Canada, and Mexico. If it is clear that the agreement produced by the trilateral negotiations will achieve this result, it should be accepted. If not, it should be rejected.

The issue now is not *whether* the United States should trade with Mexico and Canada or *whether* investment should be allowed to move freely within North America. Canada and Mexico are already among the most important trading partners of the United States, and—as is evident in all three countries—investment is already quite mobile. The question is *how* such increased trade and investment should take place.

How the North American countries choose to integrate their economies will in some measure define their course of economic development during the next several decades. Two strategies suggest themselves. One is modeled on the European path to integration, which was slow and gradual, sensitive to the disparities of income and social institutions between countries, and committed to achieving integration without penalizing workers. The other is the neoconservative model implicit in the agreement proposed by the Bush, Salinas, and Mulroney administrations—to rapidly remove all remaining barriers to the flow of capital, goods, and services across borders within the North American continent, while labor's mobility is left unchanged.

This paper will explore the probable outcomes for the U.S. labor force if NAFTA is implemented in its current form. We will then outline the additional policies necessary in order for there to be any chance of achieving the ultimate goal of higher living standards for the majority of the population in the United States. To some degree, what is true for the U.S. work force will be true for the Canadian work force. It is also likely that an integration strategy that maintains wages and living standards in the high-wage nations is the optimal path for the long-term prospects of the Mexican work force as well.

NAFTA'S IMPACT ON THE UNITED STATES

As presently contemplated by the U.S., Canadian, and Mexican governments, the proposed free trade agreement will harm long-term U.S. economic competitiveness and put in jeopardy the jobs of hundreds of thousands of U.S. workers. It will also put downward pressure on the wages of millions more U.S. citizens working in sectors not directly affected by the agreement.

Two qualitative arguments have been put forth in support of NAFTA: first, that NAFTA will generate more jobs for the United States, as U.S. exports to Mexico continue to expand; second, to the extent that dislocation occurs in the wake of NAFTA, U.S. workers will ultimately benefit as they take better and higher-paying jobs.

Rudiger Dornbusch (1991, p. 2) claims, for example, that the free trade agreement with Mexico will focus trade policy on "creating *more* and *better* jobs." The bad (low-wage) jobs will move to Mexico, he argues, while U.S. workers will move up the ladder to the high-paying, high-tech jobs that the agreement will create.

U.S. Trade Representative Carla Hills, among others, has argued that the free trade agreement will greatly increase U.S. exports to Mexico, and that these increased exports will generate hundreds of thousands of new jobs for U.S. workers. The U.S. Commerce Department (1991) released a study that detailed state-by-state increases in U.S. exports to Mexico. While it is true that U.S. exports to Mexico have risen rapidly since 1986, it is also the case that U.S. imports from Mexico have been rising almost as fast (International Monetary Fund, 1992). This occurs because the vast majority of U.S. exports to Mexico are capital goods and components, not consumer goods. These goods are used mainly to produce goods for export back to the United States, not for consumption by Mexican consumers. Jobs are generated by increases in net exports (the excess of exports over imports), not by exports that turn around and come back as manufactured goods a few weeks or months later. It is inconsistent to argue, as Trade Representative Hills did, that exports create jobs, without also recognizing that imports can thus cost jobs.

Beyond the question of whether NAFTA will create or destroy jobs in the United States is the question of what kind of jobs will remain here after NAFTA is implemented. Dornbusch's optimism that NAFTA will create better jobs is belied by all our past experience and all available data. These indicate that U.S. workers displaced by trade end up moving *down* the job ladder to lower-paying jobs, or off the ladder to permanent unemployment, not up to better jobs than those with which they started.

The Bureau of Labor Statistics surveys of displaced workers follow workers for several years following their layoff from a long-term job. The results vary somewhat, depending on the time period and the industry involved: the workers surveyed took bigger pay cuts and experienced much longer periods of unemployment during recessions than otherwise, and workers in relatively high-paying industries (such as steel or autos) took bigger percentage pay cuts than those whose wages were low to begin with. But even during the more prosperous period covering the late 1980s, the average loss in real weekly earnings was 10 percent for all displaced manufacturing workers (Podgursky, 1991, p. 4).

And that loss covers only workers lucky enough to have gotten a new job at all. A large number of displaced workers *had not succeeded in finding a new job by the survey cut-off date—sometimes as much as five years after they were first laid off*. About half of these drop out of the labor force altogether, while the others are officially unemployed. In apparel, for example, which tends to suffer disproportionately due to the geographic immobility and demographic makeup of its workers, 48 percent of the workers laid off between 1981 and 1986 had not found new jobs by January 1986. Of those who had not found a new job, 62 percent were no longer in the labor force.[1]

Nothing in the Bush administration's NAFTA strategy suggests that workers dislocated as a result of this new trade agreement will fare any better than dislocated workers have fared in the past. Moreover, the consensus of long-range public and private forecasters is that growth in the U.S. economy will be considerably slower over the next decade than in the last, suggesting that trade-dislocated workers in the United States will suffer more.

UNDERSTANDING INVESTMENT FLOWS

One of the pivotal issues in the NAFTA debate concerns the location of investment before and after the implementation of the agreement. To the extent that the agreement encourages or facilitates the closing of factories in the high-wage countries in favor of production in Mexico, it will tend to displace workers in the United States and Canada. Looking more closely at past investment shifts and the motivations behind them will allow us to understand better the nature and magnitude of investment shifts likely to occur after a NAFTA.

On a purely theoretical level, it makes sense that corporations seeking to maximize profits will locate production where overall costs—including unit labor costs (wages per unit of output), corporate taxes, and the costs incurred in complying with environmental or workplace safety regulations—are lowest. Of course, firms base production decisions on many less easily quantifiable factors as well: worker skills and reliability, quality of physical infrastructure, communications networks, and political stability, among others. And the likelihood of transplanting production depends also on the nature of the good produced. Even so, the vast disparity between U.S. and Mexican wages and the inconsistent enforcement of labor standards and workplace regulations in Mexico will combine to provide a powerful pull for transnational corporations currently producing (or contemplating production) in the United States.

That this pull has been enough to lure many firms south is evidenced by past experience, both Canada's with the Canada-United States Free Trade Agreement (CUFTA) implemented in 1989, and that of the United States with the Mexican *maquiladora* sector. In the case of Canada, a relatively small wage differential (about 1.17 to 1 as of early 1991) was sufficient to induce hundreds of firms—both U.S. subsidiaries and Canadian companies—to relocate production from Canada to the United States (Farnsworth, 1991). Eighty-seven Canadian firms had moved to Buffalo, New York, *alone* as of the summer of 1991. Lower wages, lower taxes, and cheaper real estate in the United States, combined with "practically unrestricted access" to the Canadian market, apparently offered firms an irresistible temptation to relocate (Farnsworth, 1991). According to Statistics Canada, 461,000 manufacturing jobs were lost between June 1989 and October 1991—almost a quarter of the manufacturing work force.[2]

The Mulroney government and other CUFTA proponents claim that the severe job loss can be attributed entirely to the overvalued Canadian dollar and the recession. They argue that without CUFTA, even more jobs would have been lost. While the recession and overall "restructuring" of the Canadian economy certainly contributed to the problem, the magnitude and nature of the Canadian job loss undermines the credibility of this line of argument. During the same period, the United States lost only about 6 percent of its manufacturing jobs, although it was also in a recession. In Ontario, the proportion of jobs lost due to plant closings (as opposed to temporary layoffs) was more than twice as high from 1990 to 1992 as it was during the 1982 recession (Ontario Ministry of Labour, 1992).

Many critics of CUFTA also argue convincingly that the appreciation of the Canadian dollar was negotiated secretly as a precondition to the signing of the agreement (see Campbell, 1991, p. 18). If this is the case, then a larger portion of the job loss can be attributed indirectly to CUFTA. (The 20 percent appreciation in the Canadian dollar put Canadian products at a significant cost disadvantage relative to imports, similar to the U.S. experience in the mid-1980s.) But wherever the truth lies on that question, it is indisputable that an enormous number of jobs have been lost and that the confident predictions of job gains for Canadian workers have not been borne out.

Beyond the immediate job losses, CUFTA raises other, broader economic issues. Canada's well-developed social insurance, safety net, and public investment policies are already being eroded by its trade agreement with the United States. As Ricardo Grinspun (1991, p. 3) puts it:

> A key problem of [CUFTA] is that it restricts the ability to carry out policies that make significant contributions to productivity gains and other legitimate policy goals. These policies are in areas like education, regional development, job training, research and development, technology, social programs and health. The United States challenges many of these targeted Canadian policies as 'unfair' trade practices.

Extending the free trade agreement to include Mexico puts the Canadian public sector in even more jeopardy. "Whether all or part of our troubles come from free trade, I don't know," said Bev Taylor, a motel owner and member of the executive board of the Chamber of Commerce of Collingwood, Ontario (Claiborne, 1992). "All I know is that they're happening at the same time, and if free trade with the United States is contributing to the recession, then free trade with Mexico would devastate this city."

U.S. experience with Mexico's *maquiladora* export zone also reinforces the idea that investment decisions are quite sensitive to changes in trade policy. The rapid expansion of *maquiladora* production—in which goods are assembled in Mexico from imported parts and reexported to the United States, with tariffs paid only on the value added in Mexico—has shifted hundreds of thousands of jobs from the United States to Mexico (Beckman, 1991). Currently, about half a million Mexican workers are employed in *maquiladoras,* at an average wage approximately half that prevailing in the rest of Mexico's manufacturing sector.[3]

A popular conception about *maquiladoras* is that they produce only those goods not requiring high skills. While this may have been true when the *maquiladora* zone was set up twenty years ago and the main activity was sewing garments, it is no longer the case. Apparel now accounts for fewer than 10 percent of *maquiladora* workers; more than 40 percent work in electronics and 20 percent in transportation equipment (Schoepfle, 1990). One-third of non-oil U.S. imports from Mexico come from the *maquiladora* sector. Auto and electronics companies in particular have been increasingly willing to put sophisticated, state-of-the-art plants in Mexico, as skills, infrastructure, and corporate experience there have increased.[4] In the future, it can be expected that Mexico's productive capabilities will continue to evolve and grow as they have done in the past.

The real advantage of producing in the *maquiladora* sector does not lie in avoiding tariffs, however, but rather in taking advantage of ultracheap wages and lax labor and environmental standards. Wages in the *maquiladora* sector are approximately one-tenth to one-fourteenth as high as U.S. manufacturing wages, and the Mexican government has lacked both the resources and the will to enforce even basic worker safety provisions or environmental regulations.

Although the Mexican government has proclaimed its commitment to strengthening environmental and worker protection, it seems unlikely, under current political circumstances, that changes will go deep enough to close the gap between the two countries in these arenas. Indeed, whatever progress has been made so far—such as the highly publicized closing of the port of Veracruz—is a result of personal pressure from Salinas. He is engaged in a transparent campaign to win ratification for the trade agreement from the U.S. Congress. There is no serious, independent political force in Mexico to maintain such pressure once the treaty is ratified. In fact, Mexican political scientist Adolfo Aguilar Zinser (see chapter 13 in this volume) has argued that NAFTA will exacerbate Mexico's tendency toward centralized political and economic power. Thus, it is likely that the factors that have attracted U.S. investment to the *maquiladoras* during the last 10 or 20 years will continue to play a role—and perhaps an increasingly important one—in the post-NAFTA business climate.

NAFTA AND INCENTIVES FOR
FUTURE INVESTMENT IN MEXICO

NAFTA is likely to make Mexico a *more* attractive prospect for foreign investment—both from the United States and elsewhere—for several reasons. First, it will improve access to the U.S. and Canadian markets for companies producing anywhere in the continent. Even though most of the tariffs between the United States and Mexico have been removed or reduced since Mexico joined the General Agreement on Tariffs and Trade (GATT) in 1986, many nontariff barriers remain. NAFTA would likely eliminate most of these, including the Multi-Fiber Arrangement, which limits U.S. imports of textiles and apparel.

Second, in the past, because of concern over the political climate, transnational corporations have been reluctant to make the massive long-term investment in plant and equipment needed to take full advantage of cheaper costs in Mexico. Specifically, they fear a return of popular hostility to foreign investment and the threat of nationalization. NAFTA would put the rights of foreign investors into an international agreement that future Mexican governments would find difficult or impossible to change (see Faux and Rothstein, 1991). An International Trade Commission report notes that, "By codifying liberal trade and investment policies in an international agreement, . . . a United States-Mexico FTA would increase the confidence of investors in Mexico's economy" (ITC, 1991, p. viii).

In addition to enhancing access to U.S. and Canadian markets, NAFTA will encourage investment by removing or weakening Mexico's remaining investment regulations. In particular, Mexico's negotiators made critical concessions late in the talks in the politically sensitive areas of oil and agriculture. Without going so far as to amend the Constitution, Mexico has changed its laws to allow foreign investment in petroleum exploration and refining. Salinas has also agreed to redefine "basic petrochemicals"— which are completely off-limits to foreign investment—more narrowly, reducing the number of basic petrochemicals from 19 to 5 (see chapter by Dillon in this volume).

NAFTA will also regularize Mexico's intellectual property laws, bringing them up to First World standards. U.S. firms had complained that Mexico's past failure to protect patents and copyrights had deterred investment there, especially by pharmaceutical and computer software companies who feared piracy by Mexican firms. After fast-track legislation passed in the United States in the spring of 1991, Mexican lawmakers did in fact enact more stringent patent and copyright laws—unparalleled elsewhere in the developing countries. The opposition Party of the Democratic Revolution (PRD) criticized the reform of the patent/trademark and copyright laws because it would raise prices, especially for the poor, who had benefited in the past from the relatively low price of medicine (*U.S.-Mexico Free Trade Reporter,* 1991).

While some protection of intellectual property rights is a legitimate and necessary means of ensuring that researchers receive a fair return on their efforts and artists are able to profit from their talents, some intellectual property restrictions simply serve to raise corporate profits and consumer prices long after the original research or artistic effort has been paid for. The final NAFTA text provides extensive protection for the holders of intellectual property rights, including the right to sue for damages and legal costs. The judicial authorities of each country may order the destruction or disposal of the offending goods or the materials used to produce them "*without compensation of any sort.*" In the case of copyrighted works and sound recordings, the authorities may order the repayment of profits or damages even if the infringer did not know, or have reasonable grounds to know, that he or she was "engaged in an infringing activity." The contrast between these protections and those afforded to environmental or labor considerations is striking. Not only are standards laid out in detail for intellectual property violations, but the enforcement mechanisms and penalties are clearly delineated. On the other hand, for a country that relaxes environmental standards in order to attract investment, the penalty is that its trading partner may "request consultations."

The pressure that the U.S. business community puts on Mexico to further strengthen its intellectual property laws highlights the hypocrisy underlying the debate over NAFTA. Ron Wyden, a Democratic congressman from Oregon, wrote to Kay Whitmore, of the Business Roundtable, a U.S. business organization that has lobbied in favor of the free trade agreement:

> The contradiction I see that greatly concerns me is that, while the Roundtable believes that the United States should require Mexico to raise its standards on intellectual property and investment to our level, I have been told that it does not believe that Mexico and the United States should raise their standards on environmental and labor safety to the higher level in either country. I do not understand the rationale for that distinction.[5]

Unfortunately, the rationale is fairly simple: as it stands, the agreement's purpose is to facilitate the mobility of capital while deliberately preserving the relative immobility of labor. While aggressively imposing strict investment standards that will have the effect of preserving or even raising corporate profits, the negotiators have modestly shied away from encroaching on Mexico's sovereignty in the areas of environmental and labor standards.

The result of this agreement will be to throw U.S., Mexican, and Canadian workers into competition with each other to attract investment by offering the lowest wages and the least restrictive regulations. The threat of moving production abroad is already a weapon many businesses use to oppose wage demands, environmental restrictions, higher corporate taxes, or stricter health and safety regulations (see chapter by Kreklewich in this volume).

MEASURING THE EFFECT OF CAPITAL FLOWS ON JOB LOSS

Most of the conventional studies that have attempted to quantify NAFTA's impact on the U.S. economy have either ignored the shift of investment from the United States to Mexico or have examined only the Mexican side of the equation.[6] Yet, the extent to which investment in Mexico replaces investment in U.S. plants will clearly determine NAFTA's overall impact on U.S. jobs.

Estimating the magnitude of capital flows is no more inherently problematic than estimating migration flows or sectoral shifts. Employing different methodologies, two recent studies have estimated the impact that a shift of investment from the United States to Mexico will have on the domestic labor market. Their results give a range of estimates that expands the limits of the debate.

An Economic Policy Institute briefing paper (Faux and Spriggs, 1991) reported the dramatic results of modifying one standard computable general equilibrium model of United States-Mexico relations to allow for a modest shift of capital between the two countries. The analysis, by economists Raul Hinojosa-Ojeda and Robert McCleery, involved reducing the risk premium for U.S. firms investing in Mexico. Free trade was modeled as an elimination of tariffs between the two countries over ten years beginning in 1992. The differential in returns to capital between the United States and Mexico was allowed to fall by 2 percent the first year of the agreement, and 1 percent each additional year until the year 2000, for a 10 percent overall decline in the risk premium. This scenario results in a movement of $44 billion in capital from the United States to Mexico over the decade. As a consequence, during the first ten years of the agreement, 550,000 fewer high-wage jobs are created in the United States than would have been the case in the absence of the agreement, and the U.S. gross domestic product falls by $36 billion relative to the no-NAFTA scenario. Because the model assumes full employment, these workers do get jobs, but they take a 50 percent wage cut. Some of this employment-shifting effect is due to the repercussions of reduced immigration from Mexico, since the model finds that real wages in Mexico rise as a result of the increased investment.

Economists Timothy Koechlin and Mehrene Larudee (1992) have also developed an estimate of job displacement. They find that 290,000 to 490,000 U.S. jobs will be lost over the next ten years, as U.S. and foreign investors build new capacity in Mexico, rather than in the United States, attracted by improved access to the U.S. market and a more stable invest-ment climate in Mexico. They base their estimate on historical examples of the increases in U.S. foreign direct investment that took place when Ireland and Spain joined the European Community (in 1974 and 1986, respectively). Since both Ireland and Mexico are relatively low-wage areas and both joined markets many times their size, Koechlin and Larudee argue that there is good reason to think that U.S. investment in Mexico will also take off as a result of NAFTA.

Some analysts have pointed out that the predicted changes in aggregate U.S. employment—in either direction—are tiny relative to the U.S. labor force. Estimates range from a net gain of 130,000 jobs (Hufbauer and Schott, 1992) to a loss of about half a million jobs (Cohen and Tonelson, 1991; Faux and Spriggs, 1991; Koechlin and Larudee, 1992). While these figures do appear small relative to the entire U.S. labor force of 126 million, we will argue here that they are nonetheless significant.

First, to the extent that job losses will be concentrated in certain industries and regions, their impact will be greater. Second, the distributional conse-quences of NAFTA—that is, its impact on wages and income distribution— may be at least as important as aggregate job loss. Edward Leamer (1992, p. 46) has argued, on the basis of a theoretical trade model, that NAFTA is likely to further polarize the U.S. earnings distribution:

> Indeed, if the reason for the expansion of international commerce is increased access to low-wage unskilled foreign labor it is virtually certain that our low-skilled workers will have their earnings reduced. Earning reductions on the order of $1000 per year . . . seem very plausible.

NAFTA AND ECONOMIC DEVELOPMENT GOALS

The central economic objection to a NAFTA is that it provides an incentive for U.S. producers to respond to market competition with a low-wage strategy, which will lower incomes and productivity over the long run, rather than the more difficult path of producing quality products more efficiently. With NAFTA in place, business will be able to relocate to Mexico, pay dollar-an-hour wages, hire a young, eager work force, and have few pollution or environmental standards to worry about. Businesses remaining in the United States will have a difficult time competing on these terms.

One way in which several of the European governments have attempted to guide their economies onto a high-wage, high-value-added growth path has been to shut off the low-wage option—by setting a relatively high minimum wage, regulating plant closings, and legislating livable welfare, pension, and unemployment compensation benefits. This has forced companies to seek productivity improvements via investments in modern equipment and new technology and more interactive labor-management relations. A NAFTA takes the United States in exactly the opposite direction—opening the door wide for U.S. corporations to seek the low-wage solution, obviating the need for investment in the labor force of either Mexico or the United States. While this may add to corporate profits in the short run, in the long run it will undermine the productivity and thus the competitiveness of the entire continent.

LABOR-MARKET POLICIES FOR THE NEW WORLD ORDER

Unprecedented and rapid moves toward global integration of the U.S. economy call for unprecedented changes in our labor-market and industrial policies. To meet the challenge of increasing global economic integration— of which NAFTA is only one element—the United States must embark on a permanent and continuous upgrading of its labor force in conjunction with trade and industrial policies that provide support for high-wage job creation. Only if such policies become conscious national goals is there any realistic chance for displaced U.S. workers to avoid higher unemployment and lower-paying jobs and climb up to the next rung.

Without a skilled, well-paid, and adaptable labor force, the United States will find it virtually impossible to compete in global markets for anything but standardized, mass-produced goods. One example of the broader vision necessary for the United States to absorb the shock of the free trade agreement can be found in the proposals outlined in *America's Choice: High Skills or Low Wages,* the 1990 report of the Commission on the Skills of the American Workforce. The Commission recommends giving all employers "incentives and assistance to invest in the further education and training of their workers and to pursue high productivity forms of work organization" (Commission, 1990, p. 7).

Yet far from rising to meet the challenge of global competition, federal spending on education and training as a percentage of gross national product (GNP) has fallen in the last 15 years. In 1976, the federal government spent 0.8 percent of GNP on education and training; by 1990, this figure was only 0.5 percent. This decrease in spending has real consequences for workers whose skills need upgrading: the primary federally supported training program, the Jobs Training and Partnership Act, currently serves only 6 percent of a narrowly defined eligible population (Faux and Schafer, 1991). During a period when the U.S. trade deficit increased nearly fivefold (from the late 1970s to the late 1980s), the Trade Adjustment Assistance Program *reduced* the number of applicants it served from 199,000 to 37,000. It now serves only one out of four eligible workers (Friedman, 1991).

A trade agreement should not be signed until the administration and Congress have agreed to a credible and comprehensive strategy for worker training and job creation—*and* committed themselves to fully funding such a strategy. The major provisions of a free trade agreement should not be implemented until such a system is in place. The onus is on those who advocate NAFTA to develop a plan for providing U.S. workers with a ladder of upward mobility. They need to convince their fellow citizens why the pattern that has been seen so often and so clearly in the past—that of workers displaced by trade bearing most of the burden of adjustment—will not repeat itself in the future. Otherwise, there is reason to believe that those individuals who actually lose their jobs as a result of trade and investment will not suffer alone. Every worker whose wage is bid down by the threat of corporate mobility, every community whose environmental standards are weakened, and everyone whose community is disrupted by the large-scale loss of jobs will pay part of the price.

THE BOTTOM LINE

If the NAFTA cheerleaders are right, and incomes and employment levels rise in all three countries as a result of the agreement, then the stringent standards and adjustment programs we advocate here will be, at worst, an inconvenience. They also will not impede positive change. For example, if income growth in Mexico actually does lead firms to act more environmentally responsibly, then they will not mind having to abide by stricter standards. And if few workers are displaced by the free trade agreement, then the training and adjustment programs will not cost very much to run.

But if the cheerleaders are wrong, then their policy prescription—to barrel ahead with an "unencumbered" agreement and desultory adjustment assistance—could have disastrous short-term consequences for hundreds of thousands of U.S. working people and negative long-term effects on the living standards and competitiveness of the entire continent.

NOTES

1. U.S. Department of Labor, Bureau of Labor Statistics (1987), p. 3). The sample includes only those workers who had worked at their jobs for three or more years before being laid off due to plant closings or moves, slack work, or the abolishment of their positions or shifts.
2. See chapter by Campbell in this volume for a more thorough discussion of this point.
3. The wage figure refers to 1989, while the number of *maquiladora* workers is for 1991. The source for the *maquiladora* and average manufacturing wage figures is the U.S. Department of Labor, Bureau of Labor Statistics (1991). There are some indications that the *maquiladora* wage has risen relative to the average manufacturing wage since 1989, but no official estimates are available at this time.
4. Note, however, that these modern plants coexist with old-fashioned labor-intensive sweatshops. For a different perspective, see the chapter by Kopinak in this volume.
5. Unpublished letter to Mr. Kay Whitmore of the Business Roundtable (19 August 1991), p. 1.
6. See Faux and Spriggs (1991) for a critique of the computable general equilibrium models and their overly optimistic predictions of NAFTA's impact. See Faux and Lee (1992) for further discussion.

REFERENCES

Beckman, S., UAW economist. Testimony before the Trade Policy Staff, 9 April 1991.

Campbell, B. (January-February 1991). "Goin' South—Two Years Under Free Trade." *Canadian Dimension.*

Claiborne, W. (18 May 1992). "Does Free Trade Cut Jobs or Boost Sales?" *Washington Post*, p. A17.

Cohen, R., and Tonelson, A. (1991). *Doing it Right: A Winning Strategy for U.S.-Mexico Trade.* Washington, D.C.: Economic Strategy Institute.

Commission on the Skills of the American Workforce. (1990). *America's Choice: High Skills or Low Wages.* Rochester, N.Y.: National Center on Education and the Economy.

Dornbusch, R. (1991). "U.S.-Mexico Free Trade: Good Jobs at Good Wages." Testimony before the Subcommittee on Labor-Management Relations and Employment Opportunities, Committee on Education and Labor, U.S. House of Representatives, 30 April.

Farnsworth, C. H. (9 August 1991). "Free Trade Accord is Enticing Canadian Companies to U.S." *The New York Times,* p. A1.

Faux, J., and Lee, T. (July 1992). *The Effect of George Bush's NAFTA on American Workers: Ladder Up or Ladder Down?* Washington, D.C.: Economic Policy Institute.

Faux, J., and Rothstein, R. (1991). *Fast Track-Fast Shuffle: The Economic Consequences of the Administration's Proposed Trade Agreement with Mexico.* Washington, D.C.: Economic Policy Institute.

Faux, J., and Schafer, T. (1991). *Increasing Public Investment: New Budget Priorities for Economic Growth in the Post-Cold War World.* Washington, D.C.: Economic Policy Institute.

Faux, J., and Spriggs, W. (1991). *U.S. Jobs and the Mexico Trade Proposal.* Washington, D.C.: Economic Policy Institute.

Friedman, S. (September 1991). "Trade Adjustment Assistance: Time for Action, not False Promises." *AFL-CIO Reviews the Issues* (Report No. 53).

Gereffi, G. (1992). "Mexico's *Maquiladora* Industries and North American Integration." In S. J. Randall with H. Konrad and S. Silverman (eds.), *North America Without Borders? Integrating Canada, the United States and Mexico.* Calgary: University of Calgary Press.

Grinspun, R. (May 1991). "North American Free Trade Area: A Critical Perspective." Paper presented at conference titled, "Facing North/Facing South," University of Calgary, Calgary, Alberta.

Hufbauer, G. C., and Schott, J. J. (1992). *North American Free Trade: Issues and Recommendations.* Washington, D.C.: Institute for International Economics.

International Monetary Fund. (June 1992). *Direction of Trade Statistics.*

Koechlin, T., and Larudee, M. (September-October 1992). "The High Cost of NAFTA." *Challenge.*

Leamer, E. E. (February 1991). *Wage Effects of a U.S.-Mexican Free Trade Agreement* (NBER Working Paper No. 3991). Cambridge, Mass.: National Bureau of Economic Research.

Ontario Ministry of Labour, Office of Labour Adjustment. (June 1992). *Monthly Report on Permanent and Indefinite Layoffs in Ontario.* Toronto: Ontario Ministry of Labour.

Podgursky, M. (April 1991). *Estimated Losses Due to Job Displacement: Evidence from the Displaced Worker Surveys.* Paper prepared for the Economic Policy Institute.

Schoepfle, G. K. (April 1990). *U.S.-Mexico Free Trade Agreement: The Maquilazation of Mexico?* Bureau of International Labor Affairs, U.S. Department of Labor.

U.S. Department of Commerce, International Trade Administration. (August 1991). *U.S. Exports to Mexico: A State-by-State Overview, 1987-90.* Washington, D.C.

U.S. Department of Labor, Bureau of Labor Statistics. (September 1987). *Displaced Workers, 1981-85* (Bulletin No. 2289). Washington, D.C.

U.S. Department of Labor, Bureau of Labor Statistics, Office of Productivity and Technology. (March 1991). *Mexico: Hourly Compensation Costs for Production Workers in Manufacturing.* (Mimeo).

U.S. International Trade Commission. (February 1991). *The Likely Impact on the United States of a Free Trade Agreement with Mexico* (USITC Publication 2353). Washington, D.C.

U.S.-Mexico Free Trade Reporter. (12 July 1991), 1 (2).

Chapter 16

U.S. Labor and North American Economic Integration: Toward a Constructive Critique

Stephen Fielding Diamond

In the spring of 1991, the U.S. labor movement suffered one of its most important recent political defeats: congressional approval of the Bush administration's request for "fast-track" negotiating authority for a free trade agreement between the United States and Mexico. Labor was unable to hold on to some of its staunchest congressional allies. Democratic Congressman Richard Gephardt, for example, backed fast-track despite the protectionist industrial policy that lay at the heart of his presidential campaign in 1988. Thus, what AFL-CIO Secretary Treasurer Tom Donahue declared would be labor's "top priority" for the 1991 legislative calendar signaled, instead, the very low priority that trade unionism holds in U.S. political life. A fresh perspective is desperately needed by labor if it is to understand this defeat and move beyond it.

LABOR'S RESPONSE

In response to the trade pact negotiations, U.S. labor has begun a battle to hold tenaciously to what little they have left (AFL-CIO, 1990; Anderson, 1990). Though there is little serious discussion of this topic within trade unions, every member knows the telling impact economic globalization is having on life in the United States. It is not just a matter of protecting a textile plant here or an auto parts assembly plant there. The globalization of the economy has begun to break down the general fabric of U.S. society. Fewer and fewer people in the United States are able to be productively integrated into the economy. Visible signs of this situation are seen in the decline of productivity in the service sector, in long-term unemployment, in a steelworkers' union trying to steal members from a union representing supermarket employees, in the number of street people living off the recycling of aluminum cans.

The less visible reality is also coming to light. A recent Census Bureau study found that the median income of the most affluent fifth of all U.S. households rose 14 percent from 1984 to 1988, after adjusting for inflation. But income remained unchanged for the remaining four-fifths. The statistics comparing white and non-white U.S. citizens are equally disturbing. The median income of all households in 1988 was $35,750, but the median for whites was $43,280, while that for blacks was $4,170, and that for Hispanics was $5,520 (Pear, 1991). Robert Reich (1991) has pointed to the increasing isolation of that top fifth from the rest of U.S. society. He notes that we now live in a country where there are more private security guards than publicly financed police officers. More and more, the top fifth live in areas of the country insulated from the world around them; they belong to private health clubs and send their children to private schools. How far away is the United States from the brick walls embedded with glass shards so common in the developing world?

In this setting, the so-called protectionism of the working class is no more surprising than the constant attempt of the middle class to live upstream from the foul air and decaying streets of our inner cities. Given the historic goal of the trade union movement to defend and improve the wages, hours, and working conditions of its dues-paying members, their opposition to so-called free trade is understandable. Unfortunately, it is also destined to be ineffective.

The protectionist response of labor is, in essence, as narrowly drawn as the drive by management for cheaper labor across the border. It pits union-ized workers in one sector of the economy against fellow unionized workers who may indeed gain jobs and income by greater trade (Lustig, 1991; Reynolds, 1990). It can cause a rise in the price of those goods that might improve in quality and decline in price when made with new technology or new material resources, or when affected by new competition. The result is a divide between organized labor and consumers. The union movement, in turn, is viewed as a drag on productivity rather than as a spur to new innovation in technology and economic organization. Finally, protectionism divides this nation's union movement from that of other nations, where different levels of development naturally give rise to different perspectives for trade unionism. Hence, the Mexican labor movement, while apparently cautious about Salinas's imperial approach to negotiating a free trade agreement, looks forward to future job gains from increased trade with the United States and to less pressure on its members to migrate northward (see Aguilar Zinser, 1990; Cárdenas, 1991; Castañeda, 1990).

This is not to underestimate the potential damage a "pure" free trade agreement could do to workers in all three countries. As Robert Dunn (1990) points out, in the United States and Canada, low-skilled workers will lose jobs unless trade policy is broadly developed to include compensatory financing for genuine retraining and job placement. Also, the horrific conditions under which many Mexicans labor will not be altered simply by the lowering of tariff barriers. In fact, these conditions are part of the attraction of Mexican workers. Their low pay, relative to the north, and unregulated social and workplace conditions mean greater profits to investors (Anderson, 1990; Kochan, n.d.; Peters, 1990). To date, however, organized labor has been willing to discuss only this tragic side of the debate. Their unwillingness to counter the free market position with more viable, positive-sum policy alternatives increases labor's political isolation. United States labor's anti–free trade position is, in fact, relatively new. Its trajectory has followed the structural shifts in the U.S. economy (see Mitchell, 1978).

The anti–free trade view is disturbing from another angle as well. While having a historic tradition of defending the wages and working hours of its current membership, trade unionism has also often taken advantage of an expanding and changing economic structure to recruit new members. International trade and financial integration would appear to offer labor a new vista for organizational expansion, transnational bargaining, and a place at the table of new international institutions. All this will be made difficult by labor's protectionist stance.

AN ALTERNATIVE STRATEGY FOR LABOR

Managed Versus Free Trade

How can labor respond adequately to the challenges of the free trade debate? A starting point would be to note that there is no such thing as "free" trade any more than there is a free lunch. In fact, there is now a very intense debate within the business community about how U.S.–Canadian–Mexican economic integration must be "managed" to achieve its full potential. "Free trade" is little more than a label aimed at limiting the participants in the debate to business representatives. This "management" debate takes for granted the need to form elaborate legal and institutional structures to put the agreement into place and to regulate its impact once it has taken effect. Many different subject areas are dealt with in the agreement, including intellectual property rules, changes in Mexico's rules on foreign investment, the cross-border harmonization of product standards and certification, the establishment of a dispute-resolution mechanism, and rules of origin that are intended to ensure that the benefits of cross-border trade are limited to substantial investors in the region.

This "managed trade" position represents what might be called the neutron bomb approach to economic integration. It secures a safe and level playing field for capital, but it ignores the general human and social cost of the agreement. It pays no attention to the unemployed stagnating in the Rust Belt, it ignores cross-border pollution, and it fails to examine the implications of integrating societies with vastly different standards of living. As an alternative, labor should argue for an agreement that reckons with the total social cost of the integration process.

Such costs are often labeled externalities or political factors precisely because of the inability of mainstream economic theory to deal with the full impact of economic change and development (see the chapter by Helleiner in this volume). But the existence of this wider reality is, in fact, the reason for the establishment in every advanced economy of institutions such as collective bargaining, environmental regulation, and minimum standards for labor and products. Only democratic institutions can adequately examine, debate, and regulate this integration process. The rules and standards of such institutions must encompass more than the agenda of the corporate community.

The corporate agenda, with its trickle-down approach to economic development, has failed in the post–Cold War era to avoid crises of the economy and labor force in the United States and Canada. A decade of speculation in real estate and junk bonds has pushed us into a deep recession. Have we reached such a stage in human development that, to rescue our economy, we must pay another nation's productive adult population $0.60 an hour to assemble advanced computers and $20,000 automobiles while denying them basic social services and human rights? Can we claim, with any sincerity, that this will be the basis upon which to build a reasonable future for their community and nation?

REGULATING THE SOCIAL COST OF INTEGRATION

The market alone cannot be relied upon to take account of social and human resources—the horizon of any individual business is inherently narrowed by competitive pressures. Contrary to the neutron bomb approach of the so-called free market, the social costs of economic growth and integration should be made central to the debate. Job creation, health care, labor standards, water and air pollution control, migration issues, wages, housing, education, progressive taxation systems, and debt relief—these should form the basis of a new regional economy. If Mexico and the United States can cooperate to expand bilateral trade, why can they not cooperate to create employment opportunities, protect the environment, and enforce occupational health and safety standards?

Some partial efforts in this direction have been made. The AFL-CIO has backed labor and human rights provisions in U.S. trade legislation (International Labor Rights, 1988). Such efforts are limited in their impact by broader political conflict and the development needs of the targeted countries. In essence, they raise the cost of development while not necessarily reorganizing economic structures. Another approach is being tried in the Mexican context. The Coalition for Justice in the Maquiladoras, with the backing of the AFL-CIO's Industrial Union Department and church groups, has proposed a code of conduct aimed at U.S. firms operating in the already existing, export-based free trade zone of northern Mexico (Coalition for Justice, n.d.). In addition, an attempt to expand the very limited nature of bilateral trade unionism between U.S. and Mexican labor has been made. But only a few meetings have been held at the highest levels of the Confederation of Mexican Workers and the AFL-CIO, with little or no impact on union activity (*California AFL-CIO News,* 1988).

Efforts in all three areas—labor rights tied to trade, expanding labor law to cover international investment, and transnational trade unionism—must continue. One of the likely by-products of any trade negotiation process, even one limited to a Bush-type agenda, is that these efforts will be stepped up. International attention to human and labor rights in Mexico can greatly aid the efforts of Mexican workers and their unions. Such pressures will raise the social standards of living in Mexico while resisting a decline in the living conditions of U.S. and Canadian citizens. But these efforts will remain partial and ameliorative and the process they stimulate in Mexico will take many years.

Labor must now attempt to institutionalize these efforts within the framework of the emerging economic structures. One concrete possibility would be to include labor issues as constituent parts of the dispute-resolution mechanisms that are integral to trade agreements. U.S. workers, for example, should be able to monitor any plant closings or new investments by U.S. firms. If there is a factual basis for a claim that such investments are aimed not at new markets in Mexico but at taking advantage of cheaper labor costs to reexport to old markets here, then the affected U.S. (and Canadian) workers should be able to bring a charge to a new trinational social rights agency. Compensation or adjustment spending could be ordered. Or, at the minimum, the agency could order the company to undertake "mandatory" bargaining with the union. This would mean a commitment to negotiate over alternatives to plant closure until a compromise is reached.

Similarly, Mexican workers should have access to this agency. They should be able to bring claims that foreign investors are refusing to recognize their collective bargaining rights or are not acting as good corporate citizens. The latter concept could cover environmental concerns, plant health and safety issues, and taxation. The internal political problems in Mexico point to the need for such an autonomous agency concerned with the social impact of economic integration. This agency could be investor-financed. Those companies that win new markets or higher profits because of integration would be taxed to fund the agency and its essential investigative units.

The advantages of a such an agency are many. To private investment capital, it would provide a policing effort to keep out sweatshop competition. It would mean the establishment of some basic sense of due process and fairness in investment decision-making. It would provide a public forum for argument over the investment process. This would be essential to encouraging Mexican workers to come forward. It would provide an organizing tool for labor movements in all three countries. To bring successful charges forward on behalf of U.S. workers, for example, would require an investigation of investment patterns in Mexico by U.S. corporations. This could force U.S. and Mexican workers into greater contact and, eventually, cooperation. It would, at the same time, require a constant assessment of the genuine benefits of the integration process.

SHAPING ECONOMIC GROWTH

A second leg on which labor's response must stand should be a positive alternative strategy for economic growth and job creation on an international basis. Austerity, rationalization, and retrenchment are the bywords of today's global economy. In the process, millions are being denied productive work. Labor should begin an internal and then public discussion about how the global economy can be restructured in a progressive and positive-sum fashion. Dramatic debt reduction for the Third World, and a shift of workers in the advanced economies out of unproductive labor (such as military production), would be important starting points to a fundamental reorganization of the economy.

In a partial way, labor, environmental, and human rights groups have raised some of these issues. In pointing to the emergence of a "social charter" in the European Community and suggesting that a similar effort be made in North America, these groups aim to shape the process of economic and social progress (Aguilar Zinser et al., 1990; Donahue, 1991). But the fundamental goal of many of these arguments during the NAFTA negotiations was to weigh down the discussion in order to stop the agreement from going forward—not to recognize the global and strategic context in which the free trade debate has inevitably emerged. The social charter perspective ignores the serious limitations of the charter process in Europe itself, where a much larger agenda is controlled by business interests (Dewetring, 1990; Schmitter and Streeck, 1990). In Europe, the charter appears as an addendum to the debate about integration rather than as a basis for arguing that social costs are inherent in economic expansion and can only be dealt with by an alternative strategic view of economic institutions.

This type of defensive response is, to an extent, inherent within trade unionism. It is indicative of the strength and importance of trade unionism within a classical capitalist world. But we no longer live, if we ever did, in an era of individual business people who trust social and economic well-being to the invisible hand of Adam Smith. Instead, we live in a world of global markets made up of large and small competing corporations, backed by and sometimes competing with huge state powers, locked in a battle to integrate new technologies using large populations of unorganized, often cheap, human labor. These corporations are engaged in this battle largely over the heads of the majority of the world's population—in boardrooms and conferences closed to the everyday working (and out-of-work) population. Corporate managers have difficulty understanding why such a system cannot resolve the problems it encounters. Their social perspective is narrowed by the very competitive battle in which they are mired.

CONCLUSION

The process of North American integration can and should be shaped differently. For this, critics of NAFTA must recognize that if the process of economic integration is regulated, consciously and openly, through democratic institutions, it can be shaped in a progressive direction with benefits to all three societies. In a number of discussions with Canadian and U.S. labor and business groups, Mexico's Cuauhtémoc Cárdenas (1991, pp. 1-2) has begun to discuss this perspective. His arguments go beyond labor rights and social standards to the very nature of economic progress itself:

> We cannot be satisfied with the kind of future that would emerge from a simple economic liberalization. This would only extrapolate present trends and exacerbate present vices. . . . Economic liberalization is not our objective, it is one of our tools. Development, social justice and a clean environment are our objectives. We are in favor of a broad Continental Trade and Development Pact that primarily includes free trade between Mexico, the United States and Canada and that is, at the same time, in the interest of Mexico's development and not at the expense of U.S. or Canadian welfare standards.

If U.S. labor begins to engage in this kind of debate, the establishment of a transnational trading area could represent an opportunity for labor to strengthen its place in social and economic affairs and emerge with a new paradigm based on the democratic and socially just development of the world economy.

REFERENCES

AFL-CIO. (24 May 1990). Statement by the AFL-CIO Executive Council on U.S.-Mexican Free Trade Agreement. Washington, D.C.

Aguilar Zinser, A. (5 October 1990). "Open to Business, Sí; to Dissent, No." *Los Angeles Times.*

———, et al. (28 November 1990). Letter to Gonzalo Martinez Corbala. Mexico City.

Anderson, M. (28 June 1990). Statement before the Subcommittee on Trade, Committee on Ways and Means, U.S. House of Representatives.

California AFL-CIO News. (1988). Also interviews by author of various regional and national AFL-CIO officials, 1990-1991.

California AFL-CIO. (18 November 1988). "*Maquiladora* Dialogue OK'd at Labor Summit." *California AFL-CIO News.*

Cárdenas, C. (8 February 1991). *The Continental Development and Trade Initiative: A Statement.* New York.

Castañeda, J. (22 July 1990). "Mexico's Human-Rights Image Takes a Beating." *Los Angeles Times.*

Coalition for Justice in the Maquiladoras. (n.d.). *Maquiladora Standards of Conduct.* Available from Industrial Union Department, AFL-CIO, Washington, D.C.

Dewetring, J. (6 February 1990). *Europe 1992: The Social Dimension.* Ottawa: Library of Parliament, Economics Division.

Donahue, T. R. (Summer 1991). "The Case Against a North American Free Trade Agreement." *Columbia Journal of World Business,* pp. 92-96.

Dunn, R. M., Jr. (1 August 1990). "Low-paid Workers Would Lose Even More in Free-Trade Pact with Mexico. *The Washington Post.*

Financial Times. (3 June 1989). "A benign scenario."

International Labor Rights Education and Research Fund. (1988). *Worker Rights in a Changing International Economy.* Washington, D.C.

Kochan, L. (n.d.). *The Hidden Costs of Production South of the Border.* Pamphlet available from AFL-CIO, Washington, D.C..

Kochan, T. A., Katz, H. C., and McKersie, R. B. (1986). *The Transformation of American Industrial Relations.* New York: Basic Books.

Lustig, N. (25 February 1991). *Bordering on Partnership: The U.S.-Mexico Free Trade Agreement.* Washington, D.C.: The Brookings Institution.

Mitchell, D. J. (1978). "The Impact of International Trade on U.S. Employment." In W. Morehouse (ed.), *American Labor in a Changing World Economy.* New York: Praeger Publishers.

Pear, R. (11 January 1991). "Rich got Richer in 80's; Others Held Even." *The New York Times.*

Peters, S. (1990). "Labor Law for the *Maquiladoras*: Choosing Between Workers' Rights and Foreign Investment." *Comparative Labor Law Journal,* 11, 226-248.

Reich, R. (20 January 1991). "Secession of the Successful." *The New York Times Magazine.*

Reynolds, C. (December 1990). "Integrating the U.S. and Mexican Economies." *Business Mexico.*

Schmitter, P. C. and Streeck, W. (1990). "Organized interests and the Europe of 1992." Paper prepared for conference titled "The United States and Europe in the 1990's." American Enterprise Institute, Washington, D.C.

Ulman, L. (1961). "American Trade Unionism: Past and Present." Reprinted from *American Economic History.* Berkeley: Institute of Industrial Relations, University of California. Reprint Series #157.

Chapter 17

North American Integration and Industrial Relations: Neoconservatism and Neo-Fordism?

Robert Kreklewich

Since the early 1970s, a massive restructuring of production has emerged globally, notably in mature consumer durable goods sectors. This restructuring followed upon an erosion of Fordism. The Fordist model and its decline have been researched extensively.[1] More attention needs to be given to specific neo-Fordist alternatives experimented with by manufacturers. These have social and labor implications. The historical-institutional context and sociopolitical environment in which these processes are evolving also bear on their long-term success on an industry, as well as national, basis. These critically affect the complex transitions from Fordist to post-Fordist production processes under way across advanced industrial countries.

In North America, these transitions began well before the implementation of the Canada-U.S. Free Trade Agreement (CUFTA) in January 1989 and the reaching of a North American Free Trade Agreement (NAFTA) in August 1992. They will undoubtedly continue as North American integration proceeds further. More importantly, they bear the imprint of a right-of-center political shift toward neoconservatism,[2] which emerged in Canada and the United States in the early 1980s and has since underlain the specific nature of North American economic integration. Canada and the United States have embarked upon a unique, market-pushed trajectory toward neo-Fordism; more specifically, they are implementing flexible manufacturing systems (FMS) to replace Fordism.[3] This particular course of North American

integration will exacerbate already existing tendencies for FMS to be implemented across North America with insensitivity to regional and community concerns—resulting in a disturbing degree of social tension, political
polarization, and some regressive working conditions. These pose serious
obstacles to FMS's long-term success.

One must be aware that a transition to FMS can proceed in either a progressive
or regressive manner. The transition can be progressive to the extent that it builds
up human capital in the labor force; to the extent that labor democratically
participates in shop floor decisions; to the extent that it builds trust between labor
and management; to the extent labor has reasonable safeguards to ensure that
collective bargaining will not lead simply to concessions demanded by management. FMS can evolve in a regressive manner to the extent that management seeks
to exploit labor's increased vulnerability as traditional mechanisms of union
protection are removed. This involves management shortsightedly seeking
quicker, easier routes to competitive advantage by coercively "sweating" labor.
Work teams can as easily facilitate worker autonomy as provide means for
increased managerial control. Rigorous cost-cutting can be demanded of smaller
suppliers by more powerful manufacturers, forcing suppliers to come down hard
on their employees for concessions. This leads to regressive wage competition,
concessionary bargaining, and increased intra-industry labor segmentation. Industrial relations can degenerate into a whipsawing of supplier against supplier or plant
against plant as all attempt to bid competitively for short-term production contracts.

For a transition to FMS to be progressive, it must emerge in an institutional
context and policy matrix that respects a sense of community, social purpose,
and solidarity. Flexible manufacturing must be "embedded" within society.[4]
Limits must be placed on forms of competition that aim simply to "drive down
factor costs." Community norms that regulate entry and exit from a regional
economy of producers must exist to deter "whipsawing." There must be safeguards to labor (wage stabilization and job guarantees, for example) that prevent
producers from placing the burden of adjustment on the weakest groups. These
"secure labor's place in the community" and "stabilize relations among federated
firms" (Piore and Sabel, 1985, p. 272).

THE NORTH AMERICAN TRANSITION TO FMS

By the early 1980s, U.S. and Canadian transnationals predominantly concentrated their efforts to begin a massive transition to FMS. This is certainly
the case in the North American automotive industry.[5] A similar major
restructuring of production toward flexible manufacturing has also been

under way across the European continent (Boyer, 1988, 1989). Nevertheless, Canada and the United States are special in one major respect: they are the *only* advanced industrial countries that are relying primarily on the private sector, particularly transnational capital, in alliance with conservative state administrations to push this transition to FMS.[6] Three successive Reagan/Bush administrations in the United States since 1980, two successive Mulroney governments in Canada since 1984, and the Salinas administration in Mexico since 1988 have ensured that North American integration will proceed in a significantly different manner than if it were pursued following social democratic principles.

The CUFTA of January 1989 is a logical culmination of this turn to neoconservatism. Granted, CUFTA was sought by both the Canadian and U.S. governments for many reasons, some political, others economic; but whether realized or not by all major parties to the negotiations, it is apparent that CUFTA formally institutionalizes neoconservatism within the macroeconomy of North America.[7] It enlarges the boundaries of market freedom for transnational capital in two principal ways: by completely liberalizing most Canadian-U.S. trade in goods and services and, more importantly, by virtually ending any bilateral regulation of foreign direct investment. When fully implemented, CUFTA will ensure Canadian and U.S. corporations virtual freedom to trade and invest in each other's markets without government interference. In effect, CUFTA, as Watkins (1988, p. 84) notes, "gives both American and Canadian companies *North American* citizenship. It is *their* Charter of Rights." Equally important is what is *not* included in CUFTA, namely any provisions to guarantee corporate behavior that is fully respectful of community and social goals as investment liberal-ization proceeds. These provisions would include the community's right to participate in decisions regarding plant closures, or new technology intro-duction; local employment and production content levels;[8] minimum levels of research and development; environmental standards; and mobility rights for labor. They would also encompass safeguards for labor within a social charter that defines minimum labor standards, industrial practices, and employment guarantees across North America and provides for adjustment assistance. Contrary to all this, the NAFTA of August 1992 will simply extend the same neoconservative principles across North America.

If the comparative studies of Piore and Sabel, as well as Boyer, are indeed correct, a neoconservative, market-pushed strategy toward neo-Fordism will be more coercive and politically polarizing than a social democratic transition. It is less likely to encourage a climate of trust, cooperation and consensus among labor, management, and government, which is essential for FMS's long-term success. Though one cannot yet reach any final conclusions, much evidence does suggest that the ongoing transition to neo-Fordism in North America shows regressive tendencies similar to those earlier outlined. The persistence of these tendencies should concern business and government as much as it has distressed labor, social, and community-based organizations across North America.

REGRESSIVE TENDENCIES PRIOR TO CUFTA

The implementing of quality of control work teams in Canada and the United States has encountered difficulties. By 1981, such work teams were put into place at approximately one-half of all General Motors assembly plants in Canada and the United States. Rinehart (1984) studied work teams in a GM diesel plant in London, Ontario and found workers ambivalent, distrustful of management, and increasingly uninterested in participating in such programs. Management was using work teams to intensify work and subtly inculcate managerial norms and values into the labor force. Little effort was made to increase worker autonomy or promote worker-management collaboration. By December 1983, the United Auto Workers Local 27 shop committee withdrew its support for the team program.

Shaiken, Herzenberg, and Kuhn (1986) studied ten different firms at 13 work sites, representing a broad cross-section of U.S. manufacturing, and found much the same. Introducing numerically controlled, reprogrammable technology increased managerial control over the shop floor, further deskilled the work force, and promoted work intensification. During the 1982 collective bargaining round, notably in the U.S. automotive industry, workers and unions reacted by agreeing to further wage, benefit, and work rule concessions. The threat of plant closures, global surplus capacities of production, and a weak recovery from recession weakened the workers' and their unions' bargaining positions. But the disturbing conclusion remains that U.S. manufacturers, on balance, were taking advantage of labor's vulnerability to introduce a more vulgarized cost-reduction version of FMS. As Shaiken et al. (1986, p. 181) conclude:

> The cases we examined have disturbing implications for the quality of work life in U.S. manufacturing. Managers in the plants we studied introduced new technology guided by a vision of the automatic factory, or continuous process plant, not nineteenth century craft production. They attempted to remove planning responsibility and autonomy from the shop floor more often than they tried to combine flexible technology with broadly skilled workers.

Middlebrook (1991) found similar tendencies in the Mexican automotive industry during the 1980s. For instance, transnational corporations (mostly U.S.) shifted production from Mexico City and constructed export-oriented, FMS assembly and component facilities in central and northern Mexico during the 1980s. These new facilities emphasize an increase of managerial control and lower production costs. These have negatively affected the quality of work life. One objective of the transnationals is to circumvent and thereby undercut the strength of democratic, independent trade unions, which emerged in traditional assembly production areas of Mexico City during the 1970s and which had begun to make substantial progress in negotiating for better wages and working conditions. Most of these new plants in central and northern Mexico were chosen in areas with little or no labor organizing experience; the only unions, if any, tolerated are those set up by the official Confederation of Mexican Workers, long known for its corruption and dependent relationship with the Mexican state. Middlebrook's broad analysis of 1988 contract agreements reveals that working conditions, benefits, and wages in these plants are noticeably worse than those in the traditional assembly plants of Mexico City. Among the new plants themselves, wage disparities and quality of work life vary greatly. Transnationals have exploited these disparities and established regressive competition among auto workers within the new plants and those in Mexico City (Middlebrook, 1991, p. 284).

THE AFTERMATH OF CUFTA

These disturbing tendencies were apparent in North America prior to CUFTA and ongoing negotiations toward NAFTA. There is much evidence to suggest that CUFTA has worsened this situation. The 1988 federal election in Canada, in which CUFTA was a major issue, was very bitter and divisive. This bitter polarization between Canadian business and labor, social, and community-based groups continued into the NAFTA negotiations, which formally began in February 1991. The onset of negotiations drew immediate support from Canada's two most powerful business organizations, the Business Council on National Issues and the Canadian Chamber of Commerce, as well as the Canadian Export Association, on grounds of opening markets to Canadian companies, providing opportunities for further economies of scale, and luring more international investment to the North American continent. Sharp opposition was leveled in return by the Canadian Labour Congress, which represents an affiliated union membership of approximately two million; the 170,000-member Canadian Auto Workers union; the grassroots Pro-Canada Network and 15,000-member Council of Canadians; the 225,000-member Canadian Federation of Labour; the federal opposition Liberal and New Democratic parties; and the governing provincial New Democratic Party in Ontario, Canada's most economically powerful and most populous province. Labor organizations across Canada called immediately for a social charter to protect collective bargaining rights and establish minimum occupational, health, and safety standards. Canadian labor unions have also avoided any participation in Federal Industry Minister Michael Wilson's national consultation initiative to stimulate prosperity and competitive restructuring, announced in October 1991 (McCarthy, 1991).

Organized labor in Canada has been more vulnerable to business demands in light of greater market pressures stimulated by CUFTA. Evidence shows that Canada's most powerful unions, hitherto more able than their U.S. and Mexican counterparts to fend off concessionary bargaining, are becoming more susceptible to such demands in the post-CUFTA era. One such area is that of work intensification. The Canadian Auto Workers (CAW) have agreed to Chrysler's demands to add a third shift in assembly plants in Bramalea (near Toronto) and Windsor, Ontario.[9] Another area is that of plant "whipsawing." General Motors has aggressively embarked on a strategy "pitting plant against plant in a fierce battle for survival" (Heinzl, 1991). Workers at a highly modern GM Autoplex plant in Oshawa, Ontario were told by company officials that the most inefficient of the four plants currently producing mid-size cars (Autoplex and three U.S. plants) will be scrapped in the near future. Each plant's survival is dependent upon submitting bids to GM to produce the highest-quality vehicle at the lowest possible cost. GM officials are exploiting this Darwinian competitive process to pressure the Oshawa CAW local to change work-place practices—in particular, to make concessions the United Auto Workers' union has already made in the United States, such as granting management the right to enforce mandatory overtime. GM's intent is quite clear: to exploit the stick of "global competitiveness" and its surplus capacity of production in North America in order to bargain working standards to as low a denominator as is possible. As Dennis DesRosiers, an automotive consultant, commented:

> You get into more of a ruthless type of game, and everybody plays it. . . . You have to push plants against each other. It's worker against worker, dog-eat-dog (Heinzl, 1991).

GM has since continued this strategy on a larger scale with a major announcement in December 1991 that it planned to close 21 assembly and components plants and eliminate 70,000 jobs through attrition or lay-offs by 1995. GM chairman Robert Stempel provided no details as to which plants might be closed and vigorously denied that "whipsawing" was the prime motive for not being more forthcoming. Until such time as formal plant closings are announced, their widespread threat puts every GM worker in every plant across North America in a vulnerable position. In the interim, GM places itself in a favorable position to demand concessions from local unions and subsidies from municipal, subnational, and national governments to keep particular plants in operation.

If such pressures continue and are exacerbated by NAFTA, the 1980s trend toward a more segmented and peripheralized labor force in the automotive industry will continue. At the core of the industry will remain a shrinking proportion of relatively stable, higher-wage assembly jobs. As the higher-wage assembly "core" shrinks, the proportion of the lower-wage periphery will continue to expand. Three-quarters of all employment in the U.S. automotive industry was in the independent supplier firm sector by 1990. More than two-thirds of these laborers in the first and second tiers of the auto parts industry do not enjoy any union protection. Their wages declined by over 10 percent in real terms from 1983 to 1989. They fell to an average of $9.00 an hour in 1990, less than 60 percent of assembly company wages (Herzenberg, 1989, pp. 25-26). A progressive transition to FMS envisions the creation of high-wage, highly skilled, artisanal industrial districts. These should bring together close, collaborative networks of final manufacturers and tiers of sophisticated supplier firms, the weakest of which would be protected by community norms and values. The regressive alternative would continue to build upon trends already apparent in the North American automotive industry. This alternative, as one labor economist sums up, is nothing more than "high tech 'islands of automation' in the industry core," outside of which "supplier firms would compete based more on low wages and high work effort than skill development and labor-management cooperation" (Herzenberg, 1989, p. 29).

CONCLUSION

Neoconservatism as an ideology, and the powerful social forces behind it, made an imprint on restructuring and rationalizing production across North America. CUFTA and NAFTA represent a logical culmination of the right-of-center political shift that has occurred since the early 1980s. The scope of market freedom for corporate capital has been enlarged; a rather transparent alliance of big business and the state continues to drive a transition from Fordism in North America. Although this process is ongoing, some consequences of a market-pushed strategy toward neo-Fordism are already apparent. Manufacturers' efforts to introduce FMS display some disturbing regressive tendencies. On the whole, the transition thus far has been adversarial, leading to distrust between labor and management. The North American corporate community has focused too narrowly on easy, quick routes to restructuring—one of which is exploiting labor's relative vulnerability—to restore profitability. Insecure, stressed work forces do little to enhance long-term productivity and innovation. If these are the "fruits" of this massive restructuring effort, they are worrisome from a social and labor perspective. The degree of political polarization and labor segmentation such restructuring has already wrought in North America should concern government and business alike. These conditions remain obstacles to a more progressive transition to flexible manufacturing.

NOTES

1. Fordism is generally characterized as standardized mass production using assembly-line techniques, single-purpose machinery, and semiskilled and unskilled labor. Large inventories of parts are used as buffer stocks to ensure continuous high-volume production runs. Labor is integrated into the machinery of production with minimal discretionary control over assembly pace or volume. For a more detailed discussion see Boyer (1988, 1989); Cox (1987). Kreklewich (1991), following Cox (1987), attributes Fordism's decline to a complex interaction of change in the world economy, nation-state, and production.

2. I broadly define neoconservative as an ideology rationalizing: a corporate agenda of deregulation, privatization and investment liberalization; fiscal austerity; and a commitment to erode the Keynesian-welfare state and the postwar social contract between capital and labor. This includes the state's retreat from Keynesian demand management and funding of social programs.

3. Flexible manufacturing is defined by a number of interrelated elements, many pioneered by the Japanese. One is a heavy reliance on technical innovations, such as information technology, computer-aided design and manufacturing technology, and numerically controlled machine tools and robots. These facilitate quick reprogramming of assembly line equipment and smaller batch production without sacrificing efficiency. Two, assembler-supplier relations become close, collabo-

rative networks, instead of arm's-length, competitive links. This facilitates greater trust, a prerequisite for just-in-time delivery of parts and supplies to manufacturers. Three, industrial relations are qualitatively restructured. Multipurpose machinery requires more multiskilled, highly trained workers, usually organized in work teams. Workers gain responsibility for total quality control and practice a highly sophisticated learning by doing on the job. For a more detailed discussion see Boyer (1989); Piore and Sabel (1985).

4. I use the term *embedded* in the same sense as Polanyi (1957, pp. 56-57).

5. See in particular Holmes (1987, 1991); Tolliday and Zeitlin (1986). In general, the transition to FMS in the automotive sector has occurred in an uneven manner and has varied greatly from plant to plant and enterprise by enterprise.

6. Germany, Austria, and Sweden are following a much different, social democratic strategy, one that is more sensitive to the "strength and solidarity of the worker's movement, and its close ties to the social democratic party" (Boyer, 1989, p. 54). Mechanisms are in place to ensure worker mobility and adjustment to technology changes. Other European countries have pursued what Boyer calls a "hybrid model," incorporating elements from both social democratic and market-pushed strategies, in varying degrees, to effect this transition. Britain, for example, has emphasized more of the latter; France, the former.

7. For more discussion of this issue, see Kreklewich (1991, pp. 6-9); Warnock (1988, pp. 60-80).

8. The one exception here is the preserving of production-to-sales ratios and Canadian content levels that were originally part of the Auto Pact. But the reduction of bilateral tariffs with CUFTA makes these Auto Pact safeguards much less punitive. See MacDonald (1989).

9. These respective plants will produce mid-size cars beginning June 1992 and Chrysler minivans. See J. Heinzl (28 May 1991). "Chrysler plans third shift at Windsor, Bramalea." *Globe & Mail,* p. B4. The CAW did negotiate provisions for workers to receive eight hours pay for a seven-hour workday to offset this concession. See L. Papp (29 May 1991). "Union leaders praising pact with Chrysler." *Toronto Star,* p. B3.

REFERENCES

Boyer, R. (March 1989). "Capital-Labor Relations in OECD Countries: From the Fordist 'Golden-Age' to Contrasted National Trajectories." Paper presented at the WIDER Project on Capital-Labor Relations, Harvard University.

Boyer, R. (ed.). (1988). *The Search for Labor Market Flexibility.* Oxford: Clarendon Press.

Cox, R. (1987). *Production, Power, and World Order: Social Forces in the Making of History.* New York: Columbia University Press.

Heinzl, J. (6 August 1991). "GM Canada Workers Facing a Fight Within the Family." *Globe & Mail,* p. B1.

Herzenberg, S. (February 1989). "Whither Social Unionism? Labor and Restructuring in the U.S. Auto Industry." Revised version of a paper prepared for the Conference on North American Labor Movements: Similarities and Differences, Center for International Affairs, Harvard University.

Holmes, J. (1987). "The Crisis of Fordism and the Restructuring of the Canadian Auto Industry." In J. Holmes and C. Leys (eds.), *Frontyard/Backyard: The Americas in the Global Crisis.* Toronto: Between the Lines.

Holmes, J. (1991). "The Globalization of Production and the Future of Canada's Mature Industries." In D. Drache and M. S. Gertler (eds.), *The New Era of Global Competition: State Policy and Market Power.* Montreal and Kingston: McGill-Queen's University Press.

Kreklewich, R. (April 1991). *North American Integration: Interplay of World Order, State & Production* (CERLAC Occasional Papers in Latin American and Caribbean Studies, No. 2). Toronto: York University, Centre for Research on Latin America and the Caribbean.

MacDonald, N. B. (1989). "Will the Free Trade Deal Drive a Gaping Hole Through the Auto Pact?" *Policy Options,* 10 (1).

McCarthy. S. (17 October 1991). "Labour Rejects Tory Invitation to Join Task Force." *Toronto Star,* p. D1.

Middlebrook, K. J. (1991). "The Politics of Industrial Restructuring: Transnational Firms' Search for Flexible Production in the Mexican Automobile Industry." *Comparative Politics,* 23 (3).

Piore, M. J., and C. Sabel. (1985). *The Second Industrial Divide: Possibilities for Prosperity.* New York: Basic Books.

Polanyi, K. (1957). *The Great Transformation.* Boston: Beacon Press.

Rinehart, J. (1984). "Appropriating Workers' Knowledge: Quality Control Circles at a General Motors Plant." *Studies in Political Economy* (13).

Shaiken, H., Herzenberg, S., and Kuhn, S. (1986). "The Work Process Under More Flexible Production." *Industrial Relations,* 25 (2).

Tolliday, S., and Zeitlin, J., (eds.). (1986). *The Automobile Industry and its Workers: Between Fordism and Flexibility.* Cambridge: Basil Blackwell.

Warnock, J. (1988). *Free Trade and the New Right Agenda.* Vancouver: New Star Books.

Watkins, M. (1988). "Investment." In D. Cameron (ed.), *The Free Trade Deal.* Toronto: Lorimer.

Chapter 18

Trading Away the Environment

Steven Shrybman

The environment has recently emerged as an important dimension of the public debate over international trade. For the first time in the history of trade negotiations, governments must respond to concerns about the environmental consequences of trade policy. These concerns reflect a growing recognition that current attempts to revise the rules governing regional and global trade threaten environmental protection efforts worldwide.

The Canada-U.S. Free Trade Agreement (CUFTA), implemented in 1989, has been invoked on several occasions by governments and business interests on both sides of the border to assail environmental and resource-conservation initiatives. Canadian acid rain reduction programs, fish-conservation policies, and the regulation of energy exports have all come under fire by U.S. parties claiming that these measures are at odds with Canada's obligations under CUFTA. Similarly, U.S. asbestos regulations and paper-recycling laws have been challenged by Canadian corporations and governments as inconsistent with the rules of free trade established by CUFTA.

CUFTA is one of several important trade accords that, taken together, are changing the shape of the global trading order. Two major international trade initiatives will have a major impact if implemented. These are the Uruguay Round of the General Agreement on Tariffs and Trade (GATT), which is seeking to lower barriers to trade among its 101 participant nations; and the North American Free Trade Agreement (NAFTA), which will unite Mexico, Canada, and the United States in a vast free trade zone. A third accord has recently concluded the economic and trade integration of the European

Community (EC). While each of these initiatives is distinct, they are all intended to achieve the same overall policy objective—trade liberalization—by reducing or eliminating tariffs and other regulations that may interfere with the free flow of goods and resources between nations.

Should NAFTA and GATT proceed, the resulting trade regimes will largely determine the character of international economic activity for the rest of this decade and the beginning of the next century. Yet these new global economic arrangements are being crafted with little regard for the environmental consequences that may flow from them. The stakes are enormous. By failing to adequately comprehend and satisfactorily address the environmental implications of present trade negotiations, our national governments are undermining the prospects of meeting pressing ecological challenges.

THE ENVIRONMENT, THE ECONOMY, AND TRADE

In 1987, the report of the World Commission on Environment and Development—also known as the Brundtland Commission—offered a chilling assessment of the ecological problems that confront us and presented various proposals for responding to them. Central to the commission's recommendations was integration of environmental and economic planning:

> It is impossible to separate economic development issues from environmental issues; many forms of development erode the environmental resources upon which they must be based, and environmental degradation can undermine economic development (Brundtland, 1987, p. 3).

The Brundtland Report, and other warnings that have echoed it, cannot be easily ignored. The importance of integrating environmental and economic planning has clearly gained wide acceptance—rhetorically, at least. But there have been only tentative efforts to actually put this principle into practice. Certainly many nations have begun to take collective action in response to the growing number of ecological crises assuming increasingly global dimensions. This is reflected in the various multilateral agreements that have been negotiated in recent years, including the Convention on Long-Range Transboundary Air Pollution, the Convention on the Law of the Sea, and the Convention for the Protection of the Ozone Layer. But these initiatives have been limited to resource- and environment-specific issues; to this day, national and international economic institutions remain largely indifferent to the importance of incorporating environmental considerations into economic planning.

The danger of proceeding with economic and environmental policy objectives on entirely separate tracks is evident from recent U.S.-Canadian experience. In 1988, while the two countries were negotiating the deregulation of energy trade as part of their free trade agreement, they were at the same time participants in an international conference convened by Canada to address the problem of global warming. At the conference, representatives of both the Canadian and U.S. governments endorsed recommendations to reduce carbon emissions by 20 percent over the next two decades and to devise energy policies in support of that objective, including the adoption of conservation measures (Environment Canada, 1988, p. 5). Yet as part of the free trade agreement signed the following year, the two countries also committed themselves to encouraging greater energy development through the relaxation of regulatory controls. The positions adopted in the two forums could not be more at odds with each other. Enhanced exploitation of Canada's energy resources will only prolong the inefficient use of carbon-based fuels—the single largest contributor to global warming.

When confronted with the obvious contradictions between its commitments to integrating economic and environmental planning, on the one hand, and its apparent indifference to the potentially harmful environmental consequences of the free trade agreement, on the other, the Canadian government claimed that the trade deal would have no significant environmental effects. "The free trade agreement is a commercial accord between the world's two largest trading partners. It is not an environmental agreement," the government insisted. "The environment was not, therefore, a subject for negotiations; nor are environmental matters included in the text of the agreement."[1] This was an astonishing assertion indeed, given that the agreement explicitly addresses energy, agricultural policies, forest management practices, food safety, and pesticide regulation—matters that could not bear more directly on the environment.

Free trade agreements are intended to accelerate the expansion of global trade. International trade is already perhaps the most dynamic component of global economic activity. The value of world trade in 1990 was in excess of $3 trillion, and it is growing. Dependence on foreign trade is also growing, and for many developing countries, trade represents more than 50 percent of gross domestic product.

In the language of multilateral trade, the NAFTA, GATT, and EC agreements aim to "liberalize" and thus facilitate international trade, reducing export and import controls and eliminating nontariff trade barriers. Yet a closer look at those objectives reveals serious and often unconsidered consequences for the environment. Recent GATT and CUFTA rulings suggest, further, that aspects of the emerging trading order may be fundamentally at odds with the goals of international environmental accords. In the confrontations between trade and environmental objectives that will increasingly arise, there is thus little reason to be optimistic that environmental considerations will prevail. And yet, by ignoring the imperative to sustain our environment, trade agreements may well undermine the very economic activity they are meant to promote.

REDUCING EXPORT CONTROLS

The ability to control the export of resources is arguably vital to any country seeking to establish conservation policies to protect indigenous and nonrenewable resources. One need only consider logging practices in Malaysia, which have greatly depleted timber stock, or overgrazing in Costa Rica, which has severely degraded rangeland—activities pursued in the interest of producing goods for overseas markets—to appreciate the need for adequate export controls. Yet GATT's Article 11, which is mirrored in many other trade initiatives, virtually eliminates the right to limit exports. "No prohibitions or restrictions other than duties, taxes, or other charges," it states, "shall be instituted . . . on the exportation or sale for export of any product destined for the territory of any other contracting party." Furthermore, it is the intent of the Uruguay Round negotiations to reduce and ultimately eliminate even the limited safeguards that currently allow nations some control over the flow of resources from their respective territories.

Limiting the right of nation-states to restrict the export of resources is, not surprisingly, of considerable interest to developed countries that have co-opted the largest share of those resources and would like to ensure that these remain freely and cheaply available. Indeed, one of the principal objectives of U.S. policy in negotiating CUFTA, according to the U.S. trade representative (USTR), was to secure supplies of energy at stable and reasonable prices by proscribing future government interference in energy trade (Dillon, 1988). This explains why the central and perhaps most important provisions of CUFTA relate to export controls and fundamentally diminish Canada's sovereign right to restrict the export flow of its resources. CUFTA's restrictions on export controls go far beyond those set out in GATT and oblige Canada to share its resources with the United States even if it has to ration them domestically.[2]

An entire chapter of CUFTA is devoted to deregulating Canadian and U.S. energy development and trade. Under Chapter 9 of the deal, both countries agree to forgo the use of regulatory controls that could be used to inhibit the development of energy resources for export markets. In addition, subsidies for oil and gas exploration and development are given special status and are insulated from the trade protection laws of either country.[3] It is instructive to compare this special status for subsidies to the oil and gas industry with the treatment accorded subsidies and other programs intended to encourage energy efficiency and conservation measures. The latter are left entirely vulnerable to countervailing measures and other trade sanctions. By limiting the right of the two governments to regulate the development of natural resources or to control that development, CUFTA thus undermines critical opportunities to achieve vitally important environmental objectives. The NAFTA agreement would have a similar effect on Mexico. The United States is using NAFTA to open and further develop the Mexican energy sector, which will create one large continental market (see chapter by Dillon in this volume). In light of the urgent need to reverse global warming trends, along with other environmental problems to which our energy consumption habits contribute, this policy is at best reckless and at worst suicidal.

Among the first and most visible effects of CUFTA has been a new round of energy megaprojects designed to serve U.S. markets. These include two of the largest energy projects in Canadian history. Both are to be established in the Canadian north and will, if implemented, have far-reaching and profound effects on indigenous peoples and regional ecosystems. One is the *Arctic Gas Project,* which is being promoted by the Canadian subsidiaries of Exxon, Gulf, and Shell. These companies—which have vigorously supported both CUFTA and NAFTA—would invest some $10 billion to exploit natural gas reserves in the Mackenzie Delta on the shore of the Beaufort Sea. The project will undercut conservation efforts. It is impossible to reconcile a proposal that seeks to export 87 percent of the delta's gas reserves over a 20-year period with any reasonable notion of resource conservation. In the past, Canada's National Energy Board (NEB) might have challenged a project of such dubious value to the country's long-term interests. But the regulatory mandate of the agency has been all but abrogated by Article 904 of CUFTA.

The other energy megaproject, the second stage of the James Bay Hydro-electric Project in northern Quebec, can also be viewed as a direct consequence of the economic and resource policies favored by CUFTA. Together with the first stage, begun nearly two decades ago, James Bay II will reshape a territory the size of France and flood an area the size of Vermont to generate a staggering 26,000 megawatts of electricity annually, making it the largest hydroelectric power project in North American history. While some of the power produced will serve Canada, most of it will be exported to utilities along the eastern seaboard of the United States. If completed, the James Bay project will effect a radical transformation of the environment, with potentially devastating consequences for the regional and even global ecosystem.

The impact of these energy megaprojects on Canada is certain to be profound. No less significant, however, is the impact they will have on the United States. First, guaranteed access to Canadian energy resources will prolong the inefficient use of nonrenewable resources in the United States by offsetting declining energy reserves in that country. Second, by flooding the U.S. market with cheap natural gas and electricity, these projects will render conservation and efficiency investments relatively less cost effective. And, finally, an important impetus for conservationist policies in the United States will be removed if the environmental impact associated with large-scale energy developments occurs in remote regions of Canada rather than in the United States.

What is true for energy under CUFTA is true for all other natural resources. In fact, the first ruling to be handed down by CUFTA's dispute-resolution panel pertained to Canada's Fisheries Act, aspects of which were found to be "incompatible with the requirements of Article 407 of the FTA" (Canada-United States Trade Commission Panel, 1989). The particular regulation in question required that all fish caught commercially in Canadian waters first be landed in Canada for biological sampling in order to deter any false reporting. After this process, the fish could be exported to the United States. The measure was adopted to promote the conservation of herring and salmon in Canada's Pacific coast waters, where fishing stocks have been severely depleted as a consequence of inadequate fisheries management.

In deciding the case, the CUFTA dispute panel concluded that a conservation measure, if it had a trade-restricting effect, could be sustained only if it could be shown to be "primarily aimed at conservation." This is certainly a fair requirement. But the panel further stipulated that it had to be shown that the measure "was established for conservation reasons alone and that no other means were available to accomplish those objectives." Few conservation programs could ever satisfy such onerous criteria, given that most conservation initiatives yield at least some commercial benefits.

The salmon and herring case illustrates that in a contest between environmental and trade objectives, the former are not likely to come out the winner even when the effects on trade are negligible. Furthermore, because Article 407 applies to *all* natural resources, the implications of this precedent for other conservation programs are very serious. Yet the ruling hardly comes as a surprise, given the premium that CUFTA places on the unimpeded flow of goods and services and given that none of the institutions or agencies associated with the trade regime has a mandate or interest in promoting environmental objectives.

REDUCING IMPORT CONTROLS

Import controls are another target of trade liberalization efforts. Both GATT and CUFTA explicitly limit the right of governments to impose tariffs[4] and other restrictions, while GATT's Uruguay Round seeks to further inhibit sovereign authority. Yet there are several reasons why diminishing the right of governments to impose import controls may undermine important environmental protection measures in both the developing and the developed world.

For one thing, import controls allow a country to offset the advantage gained by countries that choose, in the interest of enhancing the competitiveness of their industries, not to adopt tough environmental standards. In the absence of either import controls or subsidies to underwrite the cost of environmental protection, a domestic manufacturer that must comply with strict and sometimes costly environmental standards is at a distinct disadvantage compared with the foreign manufacturer that has few or no pollution-control requirements to meet.

Restrictions on the use of import controls, together with pressures from the corporate sector to achieve a "level playing field," create a powerful disincentive for both northern and southern countries to regulate. Of course, deregulation or the absence of regulation is itself a form of subsidy, even though the various trade regimes do not recognize it as such, since it permits industry to freely externalize the environmental costs of production. And it is a subsidy that developing countries hard-pressed to attract foreign investment have often been willing to offer, even at the cost of serious damage to the environment and public health. The Brundtland Commission estimated that in 1980, developing nations would have had to spend over $14 billion in pollution control to establish the same standards that are in place in the United States (Walter and Loudon, 1986). For many an industry, this subsidy provides a very strong incentive to relocate. Critics of NAFTA in the United States have complained that lax enforcement of environmental regulations in Mexico promotes the relocation of polluting manufacturing plants south of the border.

Yet even if firms do not ultimately relocate, a climate that favors the elimination of import controls only encourages industry to use the threat of disinvestment to mobilize opposition to environmental protection. The Canadian Chemical Producer's Association (1981, Appendix C), for instance, warned several years ago that

> if unnecessary or excessive costs are introduced unilaterally by any country, innovation and development will simply cease or be transferred to jurisdictions with a more favorable business climate. Should this happen in Canada, it would quickly be reduced to a warehouse for chemicals.

Overt threats, of course, are often not necessary. Governments are keenly aware of the potential implications of new regulatory initiatives and have a strong inclination to accommodate corporate interests before the point of confrontation is reached. In many cases, governments will anticipate and avoid confrontation by choosing not to put forward initiatives that are likely to provoke a negative response from powerful corporations or business associations.

Finally, the elimination of import controls removes an important instrument that governments have at their disposal to enforce international environmental covenants. A GATT (1991) ruling striking down a U.S. embargo of tuna imports from Mexico provides a clear illustration of what is at stake. The embargo was enacted in accordance with provisions of the U.S. Marine Mammal Protection Act (MMPA), which regulates the fishing techniques used by the U.S. tuna fleet in order to limit, and ultimately eliminate, the "incidental" killing of dolphins and other sea animals. It also requires the U.S. government to ban the importation of fish caught by countries that allow fishing techniques proscribed by the MMPA. Although the MMPA is in some respects an imperfect instrument for achieving its stated goals (for instance, it allows the incidental killing of up to 20,500 dolphins each year by the U.S. tuna fleet), it nonetheless represents a good-faith effort to protect marine mammals from reckless destruction.

In August 1990, acting on allegations that Mexico and other Latin American countries were exceeding limits set by the MMPA, the U.S. government imposed an embargo on the importation of commercial yellowfin tuna from these countries. The Mexican government quickly challenged this action, and a dispute-resolution panel was convened under GATT. On 3 September 1991, the panel found the U.S. embargo and the provisions of the MMPA authorizing it to be in violation of the GATT agreement. In issuing its decision, the panel offered a broad interpretation of GATT rules, severely limiting the use of trade sanctions to accomplish resource-conservation objectives. No GATT member-nation, it argued, has the right to restrict trade for the purpose of protecting the environment beyond the country's borders, no matter how detrimental that trade might be for the environment.

The implications of this ruling for international environmental conventions are serious and far-reaching. For instance, the Montreal Protocol on Ozone Depleting Substances specifically allows countries that have endorsed the treaty to apply import restrictions to ozone-damaging products from countries that are not party to the accord; the GATT ruling could be used to challenge this practice. It also jeopardizes the worldwide ban on the importation of ivory made from the tusks of endangered African elephants. In effect, the GATT decision removes the only compliance mechanism—economic sanctions—that is available to a nation seeking to enforce international environmental norms.

Reinforcing this reading of GATT's rules, the panel also proscribed the adoption of domestic regulations that restrict trade in goods because of how those goods were made. Thus a country must treat like goods in the same manner, no matter how damaging to the environment the productive techniques used to harvest or manufacture them. This aspect of the panel's decision simply gives business a green light to seek out regions where environmental regulations are nonexistent or unenforced.

The panel also offered a very narrow interpretation of GATT's Article 20(b), which allows an exception from GATT rules where "necessary to protect human, animal, or plant life or health." The panel concluded that any country seeking to rely on this exemption would have to demonstrate that it had first exhausted all other means to achieve its environmental objective. Moreover, so narrow was the panel's qualification of the term "necessary" that it is difficult to imagine any trade sanction withstanding the test without the consensus of all 101 GATT nations.[5]

But perhaps the most controversial aspect of the panel's decision was its characterization of the U.S. embargo as a unilateral effort to impose U.S. environmental standards on other countries. Given the historical relationship of Mexico and the United States, it is not surprising that the charge of "ecological imperialism" would have found some support among GATT's arbitrators. The panel, however, grossly misinterpreted the purpose of trade sanctions authorized by the MMPA and similar legislation. Nothing in the statute entitles one country to dictate the internal regulations of another. It simply requires those who wish to sell in domestic markets to meet the same or similar obligations that domestic producers face. As noted earlier, without the authority to restrict imports, countries may have to choose between their commitments to the environment and their commitments to their domestic producers. In fact, the greater threat to a nation's sovereign ability to choose how to achieve environmental objectives is to be found not in measures such as those prescribed by the MMPA but, rather, in the GATT ruling that rejects both the embargo and the legislation that authorized it.

In its concluding remarks, the panel stated that if GATT parties wish to allow more room for environmental initiatives such as the MMPA, they will have to make that clear by amending the GATT treaty to describe precisely the ambit of environmental or resource-conservation exceptions to the trade agreement. In other words, if GATT parties want the trade agreement to be used to facilitate rather than undermine environmental objectives, they will have to explicitly say so. It is telling that the GATT parties have been unequivocal in their refusal to include the subject of environment in the present negotiations—even as a discussion point.[6] What this makes clear is that if the current Uruguay Round succeeds and a revised GATT is put into place, it will establish rules of international trade that are fundamentally incompatible with many national and international environmental initiatives. The ecological consequences could not be more disturbing.

ELIMINATING NONTARIFF TRADE BARRIERS

Environmental programs or regulations are increasingly coming under attack as nontariff trade barriers.[7] Opponents of strong regulation are now using trade-dispute-resolution mechanisms as a potent new weapon with which to undermine important environmental initiatives. By seizing upon this device, they can circumvent accountable and democratic institutions and instead take their case to trade-dispute panels, where they are likely to receive a more sympathetic hearing.

In 1988, for instance, the United Kingdom and the European Commission challenged a Danish law requiring all beer and soft drinks to be sold in reusable deposit containers. The law, its opponents argued, served to protect Denmark's beer industry because foreign producers would need to establish costly collection systems in order to compete in the Danish market.

In considering the complaint, the European Court of Justice noted the mandatory obligation established by the Treaty of Rome—the constitutional framework of the European Community—to preserve, protect, and improve the quality of the environment. It found the Danish regulations to be in keeping with this obligation and accepted them as a genuine and successful effort to accomplish environmental objectives. On these grounds, the court sustained the container deposit requirement but struck down the more important reuse regulations—more important because reuse is ecologically superior to recycling. Acknowledging that no actual restraint of trade had arisen as a result of these regulations, the court nonetheless argued that Denmark had failed to demonstrate that its measures were "not disproportionate to achieve a legitimate end." Even more problematic was the court's assertion that "there has to be a balancing of interests between the free movement of goods and environmental protection, even if in achieving the balance the high standard of the protection sought has to be reduced" (1988). It did not take long for U.S. and Canadian business interests, in similar fashion, to enlist the aid of CUFTA to attack environmental and work-place regulations in both countries as nontariff trade barriers. Putting the lie to the assertion that nothing in CUFTA would undermine environmental initiatives, in 1989 the Canadian government submitted an Amicus Brief challenging a U.S. ban on the production, import, and use of asbestos, a cancer-causing material.[8] The U.S. Environmental Protection Agency (EPA) estimated that the ban would save as many as 1,900 lives by the turn of the century.

No sooner was the ban announced than government and industry officials in Canada were denouncing the measure as insincere and politically motivated. Leading the charge was the government of Quebec, a Canadian province with a substantial stake in asbestos mining. This challenge represented more than an effort to overturn the U.S. law; it was aimed, as well, at preventing the establishment of a "dangerous precedent." As Quebec's Minister of Mines Raymond Savoie admitted at the time, "The biggest fear is that other countries will follow the U.S. example. The European Community . . . could follow the U.S. decision [and] adopt analogous regulations. We also fear the impact of the EPA decision on development projects in countries receiving American economic aid" (Dahl, 1989; also see Picard and Enchin, 1989).

On 18 October 1991, the U.S. Court of Appeals upheld the challenge on the grounds that the EPA had rejected alternatives less burdensome to industry and had failed to observe appropriate rule-making procedures. In what would seem to be the silver lining to this juridical cloud, the court ruled that the EPA was not under any obligation to consider the international effects of its policies. Should parties outside the United States wish to initiate a challenge of EPA regulatory actions, the court reasoned, then GATT was the appropriate forum. If the experience of the tuna embargo is any indication, however, this silver lining may prove to be illusory.

Efforts to harmonize standards on a global basis (the GATT's Uruguay Round, for instance) are another way in which trade agreements can weaken environmental regulations in the guise of eliminating nontariff barriers.

Certainly, the harmonization of standards makes good economic sense. After all, a producer forced to meet different specifications in several markets cannot take advantage of economies of scale and other efficiencies. The danger, however, is that standards will be harmonized at the level of a lower common denominator, thus undermining progressive environmental regulations. This has already occurred in the area of pesticides, where Canada has agreed to work toward "equivalence" with the U.S. regulatory approach. What this means, in effect, is that Canada will have to sacrifice its more stringent regulations in order to conform to weaker U.S. regulations. Canada currently requires that a pesticide be shown to be safe before it is approved, whereas in the United States a pesticide can be approved if the benefits of its use are shown to outweigh the risks. The difference between the two approaches is significant. In practical terms, it explains why there are 20 percent more active pesticide ingredients registered for use in the United States and over seven times as many pesticide products.

Moreover, the process of harmonization itself threatens the prospects for progressive environmental regulation. Traditionally, environmental progress in one jurisdiction has often created a "follow-the-leader" dynamic in which other jurisdictions are pressured to conform to the higher standard. This higher standard also frequently serves to provide policymakers with palpable evidence of what is possible and practical. Environmentalists can thus point, for example, to California's automobile emission standards, for example, or Sweden's air-pollution laws for waste incinerators, or Ontario's curbside recycling programs, or Germany's packaging laws in support of their claims that tougher environmental laws are viable. Harmonization as it is being pursued in current trade negotiations, however, would operate as a ceiling rather than a floor for environmental regulation. Thus any country that attempted to implement food-safety or environmental standards that were more stringent than international norms would risk retaliatory trade sanctions. This threatens to undermine the follow-the-leader dynamic, for a country could then move forward with environmental regulation only when all countries agreed that movement was necessary and only to the extent that a consensus could be forged.

Because harmonization proposals explicitly seek to relegate standard-setting to institutions—such as GATT—that are less accountable to the community and more amenable to corporate influence and control, the results are very different from a follow-the-leader effect. In general, we fail to recognize the extent to which trade deliberations are often inimical to democratic and consultative processes where full and public debate is allowed. It is highly unlikely that Canada's approach to pesticide regulation, for instance, would have been compromised to the degree that it was if the question had been subject to the customary parliamentary process. Yet in the context of trade negotiations, such a significant policy shift was less difficult to achieve.

NAFTA: THE ROAD NOT TAKEN

National governments and policymakers have been unable to entirely ignore the growing concern about current trade negotiations and their implications for the environment. The NAFTA negotiations mark a milestone in this respect. Pressured to consider the potential effects of NAFTA on the environment, the office of the U.S. trade representative undertook a comprehensive "Review of U.S.-Mexico Environmental Issues," which it released to the public in October 1991 and subsequently revised and published in February 1992. This review represented the Bush administration's definitive statement on environmental issues as they related to the NAFTA negotiations and, by extension, to trade liberalization generally. As such, it was not encouraging.

At the heart of the review was the belief that the only reliable path to environmental protection and resource conservation is that of economic growth, which free trade is expected to bring to both the United States and Mexico, especially the latter:

> Through its income and growth effects, the NAFTA should have a significant positive effect on the environment in the U.S. Mexico border region, in Mexico as a nation, and serve as an example to the world as to how two neighboring countries can address trade and environmental issues in parallel, mutually reinforcing fashion (USTR, 1991, pp. 190-191).

Environmentalists should be less than sanguine, however, about an assessment predicated on the assumption that increased economic activity is likely to translate into greater environmental protection. The rapid growth in *maquiladora* activity along the United States-Mexico border suggests a very different conclusion (on the *maquiladoras,* see chapter by Kopinak in this volume). The expansion of *maquiladora* activity has been accompanied by some of the worst environmental degradation Mexico has witnessed. A recent National Toxics Campaign study observed, "Seventy-five percent of the sites we visited were found to be discharging dangerous toxic chemicals which are in need of immediate monitoring. . . The violations we found in Mexico go far beyond what we expect at similar facilities in the United States" (Lewis et al., 1991). The release of toxic substances is but one of myriad environmental problems that have led many to describe the *maquiladora* zone as an ecological wasteland.

Impoverished nations, of course, have fewer resources than do developed countries to cope with serious environmental problems such as those produced by the *maquiladoras*. Redressing these problems often requires significant public and private expenditures. It is not obvious that any spur to the economy brought by free trade will increase the amount of attention paid to these problems. To the contrary, free trade may mean greater problems and diminished attention. The reason is simple: trade regimes do not strengthen environmental protection unless they are carefully and deliberately crafted to do so.

It is in this regard that the Bush administration's review was most disappointing. It recommended addressing environmental matters on a track parallel to the NAFTA negotiations rather than making the environment an integral component of the trade deal itself. Experience suggested, and the August 1992 agreement confirmed, that the practical result of this two-track approach would be a trade agreement with effective enforcement measures to ensure compliance and an environmental protocol with few enforcement mechanisms. Unlike trade agreements, international environmental agreements typically rely on little more than moral suasion to encourage compliance. The Great Lakes Water Quality Agreement is a prime example. Signed by the United States and Canada in 1972, this agreement commits both countries to work toward the "virtual elimination of the discharge of persistent toxic chemicals" into the Great Lakes. Yet neither country has recourse should the other fail to live up to its obligations under the agreement. And, predictably enough, in the absence of any threat of meaningful sanction, both countries have in fact failed to honor those obligations. As a consequence, in just about every year since the implementation of the agreement, the discharge of toxic pollutants by both countries into the Great Lakes has actually increased. No effective enforcement results in no meaningful compliance.

By contrast, trade agreements include the most potent enforcement mechanisms that exist in international law—retaliatory trade sanctions and countervailing measures. Indeed, it is difficult to find in any other regime, criminal or civil, sanctions as quick and effective as those in trade agreements. These mechanisms are particularly effective when wielded against nations that are heavily reliant on export trade, as are Canada and Mexico. This explains why, when countries are serious about enforcing environmental agreements, they include trade sanctions among the enforcement measures. Under the Montreal Protocol on Ozone Depleting Substances, for instance, a country may discriminate against, or even ban, the importation of goods from countries that are not signatories to the protocol or that do not respect its terms.

Whatever its limitations, however, the U.S. environmental review of NAFTA was a watershed in the debate about the environment-trade relationship. For environmentalists who have struggled to raise awareness of the importance of this relationship, the review represented a significant, though partial, victory. It will no longer be possible for governments to insist, as the Canadian government did not long ago, that trade agreements are strictly commercial agreements with no environmental consequences. The victory will ultimately be meaningless, however, if increased awareness is not translated into strong, enforceable measures.

Congress had a prominent role in promoting a commitment to moderate trade policy objectives in favor of environmental goals. The exchange between Senator Max Baucus and the U.S. administration raised the major issues involved.[9] On 3 June 1992, Senator Baucus wrote to the U.S. trade representative, Carla Hills, expressing his hope that environmental safeguards would be included in NAFTA. Senator Baucus was the chairman of both the Senate Finance Committee's International Trade Subcommittee and the Senate Environment and Public Works Committee's Environmental Protection Subcommittee. He was also a free trade proponent who vigorously supported President Bush's efforts to obtain fast-track authorization for NAFTA and GATT.

The character of this exchange between an influential senator and the Bush administration reveals a relatively sophisticated understanding of trade-environment interrelationships. It also makes clear that while the administration had become far more conciliatory in its tone on this subject, it continued to stonewall those who sought meaningful accommodation of environmental policy objectives in international trade agreements.

In his letter, Senator Baucus set out a list of environmental safeguards to be included in NAFTA if congressional support was to be assured. These fell into three general categories. The first was titled "Environmental laws and regulations should not be treated as trade barriers under the NAFTA." Environmental safeguards described under this heading, would require, first, that existing environmental legislation be grandfathered and made immune from challenge under NAFTA. Second, measures to comply with international environmental agreements would have to be similarly safeguarded. Further, any harmonization of environmental standards would have to result in their being raised. In addition, congressional approval would require any party challenging an environmental measure to prove that the measure has "no legitimate basis." Finally, the dispute-settlement process concerning environmental measures would have to facilitate comment by nongovernmental organizations and subnational governments.

In response to these proposals, the USTR offered few substantive commitments, but did express some rhetorical support for the need to preserve the integrity of commitments made in accordance with international environmental agreements—a kind of commitment, it is worth noting, the United States is notorious for avoiding. Similar conciliatory language was offered on the subjects of participatory rights and standard harmonization. On the more pointed demands, however, notably the request to grandfather existing environmental legislation, and to sustain environmental initiatives unless those challenging them can prove the absence of any legitimate basis, the administration's response was either negative or evasive.

The second general category of environmental safeguards demanded by Senator Baucus's letter concerned the need for NAFTA to include a "commitment . . . to ensure that future growth, trade, and investment take place in an environmentally sound and sustainable manner." Specifically, Baucus's letter required that all new manufacturing facilities in all three countries observe high environmental standards; that adequate funding be provided to support environmental protection measures, and to clean up the U.S.-Mexican border area; and that these commitments be made enforceable.

In response to these requests, the administration was even less forthcoming. On the key issue of providing sufficient funding to make meaningful the rhetoric of concern for environmental protection, the USTR offered only a reference to the financial commitments undertaken in the "Integrated Border Environmental Plan for the Mexican-U.S. Border Area" of February 1992. In that plan, the two governments commit themselves to spending approximately $900 million over a three-year period. Leaving aside the fact that a portion of this money is earmarked for nonenvironmental infrastructure ($168 million is designated for road improvement, for instance), the sums are trivial given the overwhelming need for even rudimentary sewer and water infrastructure in the border region. The cost of such basic infrastructure alone would be at least twice the amount the two governments have committed themselves to spending.[10]

The third category of environmental safeguard raised by Baucus was an "ongoing review of . . . environmental commitments and . . . the environmental impact of the agreement." This would require, according to the Senator's letter, the establishment of an advisory body to recommend the development and inclusion of further environmental measures. Somewhat surprisingly, the Bush administration declined this modest proposal, expressing concern about the proliferation of consultative committees. This response had to be considered disingenuous, given the plethora of trade advisory groups created to allow corporate participation in the trade negotiation process.

Any hope that the actual text of NAFTA would represent an improvement of the above-mentioned USTR positions was dashed when the final text of NAFTA was released by the three governments during September 1992. While the proposed NAFTA represents the first international trade agreement to explicitly address environmental matters, it does little to elevate environmental policy objectives above the status of rhetorical ideals to which only lip service will be paid.

Moreover, in sharp contrast to the vague and non-binding language that is used in the preamble to describe the virtues of "sustainable development" and "environmental regulation," and the need to "strengthen the development and enforcement of environmental laws and regulations," the substantive provisions of the text enshrine a regime of trade deregulation that will actually put these objectives even further out of reach. As described by consumer and environmental organizations opposed to NAFTA: "Several baby steps forward cannot overcome the sprint backwards in environmental and consumer protection the [NAFTA] text as a whole would cause" (*Public Citizen,* October 1992).

Not surprisingly, the three federal administrations flatly reject this assessment and, going even further, present NAFTA as an important tool for enhancing environmental protection throughout North America. In the words of a press statement representing the views of the three countries' most senior environmental officials:

> the Ministers endorse the view that the North American Free Trade Agreement is the most environmentally sensitive trade agreement ever negotiated. It was emphasized that NAFTA will promote both economic growth and strong environmental protection within the three countries. They noted especially the NAFTA preamble which includes a commitment to sustainable development and environmental conservation and protection (EPA Press Office, 17 September 1992).

In addition to the broad, purely rhetorical commitments of the NAFTA preamble, the ministers also emphasized the substantive provisions of the NAFTA text that would in their collective views ensure that:

> (a) the integrity of the Parties' domestic environmental regulatory regimes is maintained; (b) efforts are made towards enhancement of standards; (c) disputes

concerning environmental measures are resolved in an environmentally sensitive manner; (d) the trade provisions of key international environmental agreements are protected; and (e) Parties refrain from attracting or retaining investment by permitting the creation of pollution havens.

On closer examination, it is difficult to find the provisions of the NAFTA text that would support these rather grand claims. On the contrary, NAFTA appears to be the proverbial wolf clad, however scantily, in sheep's clothing.

On the first claim made by the administrations—that NAFTA will maintain existing health, safety and environmental stàndards—the governments point to provisions that will allow each government to prohibit the entry of goods that do not meet the country's standards. An examination of the text itself, and in particular the provisions of NAFTA that address consumer, health, and environmental standards, reveals that the agreement actually codifies current GATT and CUFTA jurisprudence—notably the Tuna case under GATT and the British Columbia Salmon and Herring case under CUFTA—that have been denounced by environmentalists. As mentioned earlier, this jurisprudence restricts the ambit of such regulation to purely domestic application. Thus, even where environmental regulations are entirely nondiscriminatory, they may not impose entry restrictions on imported goods (with the limited exceptions allowed by the international environmental agreements recognized by the text), if the purpose of that regulation is to protect the environment beyond the territorial limits of the regulating jurisdiction. This prohibition on import restrictions holds no matter how destructive those production or harvesting processes may be to the environment outside the territorial limits of the importing jurisdiction. It does not matter, in this regard, whether that extra-territorial environment is local, as in the case of the *maquiladora* regions of Mexico; regional, as in the case of acid rain in the northeastern United States and Canada;, or global, as in the case of marine mammal protection or global warming.

Rather than redress the adverse implications of the Tuna and Salmon and Herring decisions, NAFTA actually enshrines them within the text. The net effect is to create considerable economic and political pressure on all three governments to back away from creating or enforcing environmental regulations. The reason is that, given the inability to establish import restrictions, such regulations impose costs on domestic producers but not on their competitors operating in other jurisdictions. Thus, the elusive "level playing field" is tiled in favor of the non-regulating jurisdiction. Consequently, domestic producers will strongly oppose such regulations, threatening to move somewhere else.

The second claim made in support of NAFTA is that it will encourage efforts to enhance environmental standards. However, it is difficult to identify provisions that encourage environmental regulation. Perhaps the administrations are referring to the standard harmonization provisions in NAFTA. It was argued earlier that the standard harmonization provisions of CUFTA and those being proposed at GATT will likely undermine the "follow the leader" dynamics of progressive environmental regulation. The NAFTA harmonization provisions follow the CUFTA/GATT agenda by seeking to reduce issues of environmental regulation to judgments about science. These judgments would be delegated to international—and largely unaccountable—scientific agencies.

However, determining the appropriate measure of environmental regulation requires a complex balancing of often competing policy considerations—including scientific, economic, social, and ultimately ethical judgments. Here again, NAFTA reflects a myopic preoccupation with trade policy objectives whatever the environmental consequences of these objectives. There is no doubt that the harmonization provisions of NAFTA may ease the free flow of goods across international boundaries. But in the process, they will also curb the sovereign prerogative of governments to reflect and act upon their own societal need for, and type of, environmental regulation.

The third benefit touted is the set of provisions in NAFTA that will, it is asserted, improve the environmental sensitivity of trade dispute resolution. These provisions contemplate the establishment of scientific review boards for certain environmental, health, and safety issues that the parties agree to discuss. These provisions may improve the quality of dispute resolution under NAFTA, but they fall substantially short of the demands by environmental groups that dispute resolution become both public and accessible. In this respect, NAFTA is entirely unresponsive and, if anything, actually seeks to consolidate the regime of secrecy that attends trade dispute resolution. It would be unthinkable for the governments of Canada, Mexico, or the United States to propose a domestic judicial system that would operate in secret and entirely removed from any scrutiny by the public or the press. Yet such is the mystique and obscurity of the rules of international trade that these same governments can, without blinking, insist on just such a system for trade dispute adjudication. Such an adjudication system would be denounced in any other context as being more fitting to the ousted totalitarian regimes of Eastern Europe and the Soviet Union.

The fourth claim of environmental progress concerns the explicit recognition by NAFTA of named international and bilateral environmental conventions, including the Montreal Protocol on Ozone Depleting Substances and the Basel Convention on hazardous waste. By explicitly recognizing the right of the parties to honor their obligations under these agreements, even if the agreements are in violation of NAFTA or GATT rules, the governments are doing two things. The first is to make actions undertaken pursuant to these agreements far less vulnerable to challenge. The second, crucially important thing, is to warn each country that no actions taken under other current or future international agreements will be protected until those agreements are explicitly included in NAFTA. This implicitly asserts the paramountcy of trade over environmental policy objectives when conflicts arise between international commitments in these competing spheres. In these circumstances, it would be difficult for either Mexico or Canada to contemplate, in good faith, any new international environmental commitments (for example on global warming) unless the U.S. was also willing to become a signatory.

The final argument offered by the ministers in support of NAFTA refers to the investment provisions of NAFTA. These provisions direct each of the parties to refrain from attracting investment by creating pollution havens. In response to this claim, a number of points need to be noted. First, the provisions are not enforceable. Second, they miss the key problem of enforcing environmental regulations, even when they look perfectly respectable on the statute books. For example, a recent General Accounting Office study of six randomly selected, U.S.-owned *maquiladora* plants found that not a single one had prepared an environmental impact statement as required under Mexican law (U.S. General Accounting Office, 1992). Third, the NAFTA investment provisions ignore the likelihood of environmental disparities widening as one country enhances regulation while the others maintain the status quo. Once again, the ministers' claim appears to be much longer on rhetoric than it is on substance.

For those who were hoping to find in the proposed NAFTA meaningful and sincere efforts to reconcile trade and environmental policy objectives, the publication of the actual NAFTA text came as a serious disappointment. Given the sophistication of the debate about trade-environment linkages that took place during the NAFTA negotiation, it is not logical to attribute the U.S. administration's recalcitrance on this issue to ignorance about the potential environmental consequences of NAFTA. Rather, a more disturbing conclusion was suggested by the administration's failure to be more forthcoming in response to other, non-NAFTA proposals to ensure that trade policy objectives not be pursued at the expense of the environment.

The true agenda of the Bush administration in this area may be inferred from the role it played at the 1992 United Nations Conference on Environment and

Development. The Rio summit was the most important international meeting on the environment since the first summit in Stockholm on the same topic 20 years earlier. The Rio meeting's purpose was to test the willingness of governments to act on the principles of sustainable development that had been laid out by the Brundtland Commission in 1987. Expectations were high that the summit would yield international environmental agreements on several fronts, the most important (arguably) being global warming.

As anyone who followed the media coverage of this summit will know, it was a resounding failure. Many governments were unwilling to endorse, even at a rhetorical level, a meaningful environmental agenda. No government was more resistant to environmental initiatives than that of the United States, which consistently led opposition to multilateral accords on global warming and a host of other subjects. If President Bush's objective was to brand the United States as a rogue nation on environmental issues, he was thoroughly successful.

The invocation of the Brundtland Commission to integrate environmental and economic policy objectives has already been underscored. The Brundtland Report went much further, however, in describing a path toward sustainable development. This is a path the United States has belligerently rejected. In fact, the contrast between U.S. trade policy objectives and those advocated by Brundtland suggest that if NAFTA reflects current U.S. priorities, it will certainly and fundamentally undermine our prospects of achieving sustainable development. Consider the following examples.

Where Brundtland called for a 40 percent reduction of North America's enormous energy consumption by the year 2000, the provisions of NAFTA seek to promote energy consumption and actually encourage the three governments involved to subsidize oil and gas megaprojects.

Where Brundtland invited governments to advance equitable environmental and conservationist strategies, NAFTA would offer the United States and market forces preemptive rights in determining the allocation of North America's natural resources, for as long as those resources last.

Where Brundtland called upon the developed nations to break with past patterns that have threatened our planet's ecological viability and the lives of many species, including humanity, NAFTA intends to entrench as North America's "economic constitution" the very approaches to development and the environment that Brundtland identified as responsible for our present predicament.

In light of these examples, the Bush administration's response to the environmental concerns raised about its trade agenda cannot be seen as anything more than a smoke screen to appease its critics—while ensuring that its trade policy objectives are not obstructed by concern for the environment or sustainable development.

National and local perspectives all too often encourage myopic and parochial approaches to environmental degradation. Witness the different reactions that acid rain has elicited from the U.S. and the Canadian governments—a classic case of indifference on the part of one nation to the effects of its policies on another. It is critical, therefore, to work toward the establishment of bilateral and multilateral institutions that enshrine a global perspective on environmental problems. For in the absence of such institutions—whether they be concerned with trade, development, finance, or the like—we risk undermining the ecosystem that sustains us all.

NOTES

1. The federal minister for international trade, in response to a question on the House of Commons order paper during the fall of 1987. See Tester (1988, p. 197).
2. Article 904 of CUFTA explicitly prevents either government from restricting the export of energy resources for any other reasons than "national security," unless supplies are rationed to the same extent domestically.
3. See Article 906 of CUFTA. The only other category of government subsidy that is accorded this special status is defense spending.
4. GATT Article 11. There is no provision in the GATT rules that allows the imposition of a tariff to offset pollution-control costs.
5. Article 1 of the GATT agreement requires a party to GATT to accord most-favored-nation status to all other GATT parties.
6. At what was to have been the final meeting of the GATT Uruguay Round—in Brussels in 1990—the parties rejected a statement proposed by several Nordic countries, Switzerland, and Austria recognizing the importance of trade-environment relationships. See *EFTA Statement on Trade and the Environment* (1990).
7. For example, Canada and the European Community used GATT to challenge a U.S. tax on petroleum.
8. U.S. courts sometimes entertain interventions by interested non-parties to the proceedings as "friends of the court"—hence the term "Amicus Brief."
9. See correspondence between Senator Max Baucus (3 June 1992) and U.S. Trade Representative Carla Hills (12 June 1992) as reproduced in *Inside U.S. Trade, Special Report,* 12 June 1992.
10. For example, present estimates of the costs associated with rehabilitating sewer and water infrastructure for the province of Ontario are on the order of $6 billion. While

Ontario is not without water quality problems, its environment is positively pristine when compared to that of the *maquiladora* region on the Mexican-U.S. border.

REFERENCES

Brundtland, H., Chair, World Commission on Environment and Development. (1987). *Our Common Future*. Oxford: Oxford University Press.

Canada-United States Commission Panel. (16 October 1989). *In the Matter of Canada's Landing Requirement for Pacific Coast Salmon and Herring* (2TCT 7162).

Canadian Chemical Producers Association. (1981). Position paper on confidentiality. Appendix C in *Roundtable Discussion on to Chemicals Law and Policy in Canada*. Toronto: Canadian Law Research Foundation.

Dahl, J. (9 December 1989). "Perilous Policy: Canada Promotes Asbestos Mining, Sells Carcinogenic Mineral Heavily in Third World." *Wall Street Journal*.

Dillon, J. (1988). "Continental Energy Policy." In D. Cameron (ed.), *The Free Trade Deal*. Toronto: Lorimer.

EFTA Statement on Trade and the Environment. (3-7 December 1990). Brussels.

Environment Canada. (June 1988). "The Changing Atmosphere, Implications for Global Security." Toronto: Conference statement.

EPA Press Office, Press Release (untitled). (17 September 1992). Contact Luke Hester at EPA 202-260-4355.

European Court of Justice. (20 September 1988). *Re: Disposable Beer Cans: E.C. Commission v. Denmark*.

GATT. (3 September 1991). *United States—Restrictions on Imports of Tuna* (D621/R). Report of the Panel, General Agreement on Tariffs and Trade.

"James Bay: An Interview with the Chief of the Grand Council of the Cree." (May/June 1991). *Earthkeeper: Canada's Environmental Magazine*.

Lewis, S., et al. (May 1991). "Border Trouble: Rivers in Peril." *A Report on Water Pollution Due to Industrial Development in Northern Mexico*. National Toxics Campaign Fund.

National Energy Board [NEB]. (1 August 1989). *Reasons for Decision GH-10-88*.

Picard, A., and Enchin, H. (7 July 1989). "Quebec Planning to Fight U.S. Asbestos Ban." *Globe and Mail*.

Public Citizen. (October 1992). "The NAFTA Does Not Measure Up on the Environment and Consumer Health and Safety."

Summit of the Group of Seven. (16 July 1989). *Economic Declaration*.

Tester, F. (1988). "Free Trading the Environment." In D. Cameron (ed.), *The Free Trade Deal*. Toronto: Lorimer.

United States Circuit Court of Appeals for the Fifth Circuit. (18 October 1991). *Corrosion Proof Fittings, et al. v. Environmental Protection Agency, and William K. Reilly* (No. 89-4596).

United States Trade Representative [USTR]. (October 1991). *Review of U.S.-Mexico Environmental Issues.*

United States General Accounting Office. (August 1992). "U.S.-Mexico Trade: Assessment of Mexico's Environmental Controls for New Companies," (GAO/GGD-92-113), p. 13.

Walter, I., and Loudon, J. H. (1986). *Environmental Costs and the Patterns of North-South Trade.* Prepared for the Brundtland Commission (1987).

V

KEY SECTORS

Chapter 19

Continentalizing the North American Auto Industry

Lorraine Eden and *Maureen Appel Molot*

The automobile industry (defined here as autos and auto parts) is of enormous importance to the economies of Canada, the United States, and Mexico. In each of these countries it employs a significant number of people directly and, through its linkages with suppliers and buyers, another large percentage indirectly. The economic viability of the auto industry has a direct impact on the overall health of each of the three North American economies. Predicted substantial excess capacity and large numbers of plant closures over the next ten years threaten this economic health.

Even before the conclusion of the North American Free Trade Agreement (NAFTA), the economies of Canada, the United States, and Mexico were linked (Cameron, Eden, and Molot, 1992). The auto industry is one critical part of that linkage. Whereas in the early 1960s there were, in effect, three separate auto industries in North America, by the beginning of the 1990s the industry was well on its way toward integration along continental lines.

The explanation for the continentalizing character of North American auto production lies in the interrelationship between state policies and corporate production strategies. State policies in the three countries have facilitated integration, which has moved even more rapidly since the Mexican government's decision in the mid-1980s to open its economy. The 1965 Canada-U.S. Auto Pact, the 1989 Canada-U.S. Free Trade Agreement (CUFTA), and the Mexican auto decrees in the 1970s and 1980s are the relevant state policies that have affected North American auto industry location decisions. The trilateral agreement reached by the three states establishing NAFTA will further cement this continental integration.

Corporate production strategies, driven by technological change and the desire of North American auto firms to regain their competitiveness vis-à-vis their Japanese rivals, are also fostering integration. Recent corporate location choices by both auto assemblers and parts firms have been shaped by considerations of competitiveness within a globalized industry and by the introduction of "lean production" techniques based on just-in-time production and new information technologies. This continental organization for production characterizes not only the Big Three auto producers in the United States but also the Japanese transplants and Volkswagen. Auto industry investment, particularly since the mid-1980s, demonstrates the increasingly continental perspective of this industry.

What does continentalization mean for the auto industry? While the continuing evolution of the forces for and against further integration makes definitive answers impossible, a number of trends are now visible. Using trade data in autos and auto parts within North America, as well as evaluation of the shift to "lean production" techniques, we outline the extent to which there is a continental economy in this industry. We argue that the auto sector is the most globalized of the manufacturing industries and thus may serve as a bellwether for how other industries may respond to these kinds of state policy and technology changes in the 1990s.

What does continentalization mean for the Canadian auto industry? The Canadian auto industry, including components and assembly, now employs approximately 150,000 workers. This figure is lower than at the end of the 1980s, as restructuring and the relocation of some parts producers to either the United States or Mexico have reduced Canadian auto industry employment by some 24,000 jobs (Pritchard, 1991, p. B3). The assembly sector in Canada is totally foreign-owned. It includes the Big Three U.S.-based transnationals (TNCs), Volvo, and four Asian transplants (Honda, Toyota, Suzuki, and Hyundai). The great majority of their plants are in Ontario and Quebec.

The Canadian auto parts sector comprises some 600 firms. Slightly over half of the value added comes from a small number of captive plants—engine, transmission, and trim companies owned by, and vertically integrated into the production of, the Big Three. Canadian-owned components plants produce about 20 percent of Canadian parts shipments, with the remaining 30 percent accounted for by foreign-owned, primarily U.S. transnationals (Industry, Science and Technology Canada, 1990; Prosperity Secretariat, 1991, p. 98).

The Canadian state has historically had one concern about the auto industry—that it provide jobs, primarily assembly jobs, for Canadian workers (MacDonald, 1989; Reich, 1992). There was less attention to the nationality of ownership in the auto industry or to the level of Canadian value added that went into a vehicle. This policy orientation contrasts with that of the Mexican government, which has demanded high levels of domestic content in assembled vehicles and as much Mexican ownership as possible of parts producers. The U.S. state, as the home country of the Big Three, has, over the last decade, been preoccupied with the competition posed by the Japanese auto firms, many of which have moved assembly and now parts production to North America and are rapidly increasing their share of the U.S. market.

Because of its possible effects on the intra-North American distribution of production, employment, trade, and investment, the auto chapter was one of the most contentious in the NAFTA negotiations. The assemblers and parts firms in each of the three countries took very different stances on the NAFTA talks, positions that reflected their differing strengths within the global auto industry. Each government wanted to protect its share of North American production and investment. The U.S. state worried about the threat of Japanese competition, whereas both Mexico and Canada sought to increase their share of Asian transplant investment. Hence the three countries had different goals for their auto industries in the NAFTA talks. Whether Canada can maintain its historical share of Big Three production and trade in the 1990s is unclear. Although the NAFTA agreement preserves the Auto Pact and opens the Mexican market, the full impact of the accord, including the 62.5 percent North American content requirements, on the Canadian auto industry will not be known for some years. Canadian parts producers, in particular, worry about their future.

INTRA-NORTH AMERICAN TRADE AND INVESTMENT PATTERNS[1]

Trade Patterns

We have argued elsewhere (Eden and Molot, 1991a,b, 1992, 1993) that trade and investment linkages among the three North American economies are patterned like a hub and spoke, with two pairs of bilateral trading partners (Canada–United States, Mexico–United States) characterized by the asymmetric dependence of one party in each dyad on the United States. The United

States is the hub, the major trading partner, absorbing roughly 70 percent of merchandise exports from the two spokes, Canada and Mexico. The United States, in turn, sells about 20 percent of its exports to Canada and 6 percent to Mexico. Mexico and Canada trade very little with each other; Canada may rank sixth among Mexico's trade partners, but each country's exports account for less than five percent of the other's imports.

Although Mexico is a newly industrializing country, it sells a higher percentage of fully manufactured goods to Canada (69 percent) than Canada exports to it (24 percent). Close to 80 percent of Canadian exports to Mexico are in two categories: agricultural products (almost half of all exports) and machinery and transport equipment (a third). Fully two-thirds of Mexico's sales to Canada are in the machinery and transport equipment category. Indeed, engines constitute the most important single commodity traded between Canada and Mexico (Hart, 1990, p. 118).

Trade between affiliated companies, whether intrafirm or other forms of non-arm's-length transactions, accounts for a significant part of both United States–Mexico and United States–Canada trade. Approximately 35 to 40 percent of Canada-United States trade is intrafirm, and up to 70 percent is not at arm's length. While figures for Mexico are difficult to find, a significant percentage of Mexico-United States trade is also accounted for by the movement of goods between affiliated companies.[2] According to Sidney Weintraub, "because of the extensive trade that takes place between affiliates of the same company in Mexico and the United States, imports and exports have become part of the same process" (1988, p. 23). Much of this trade, and some Canada-Mexico trade, is in intermediate products, whether in autos, consumer electronics, or other manufactured end products, as well as some semifabricated goods. Intrafirm trade in autos and auto parts grew following the negotiation of the Auto Pact, and this intrafirm trade is the *raison d'être* for the *maquiladora* factories; rationalization of TNC operations is also increasingly frequent between Canadian and U.S. affiliates since the conclusion of the CUFTA.

Trade in automotive products between Canada and Mexico illustrates the way in which the activities of U.S. TNCs have linked the two economies, despite their limited formal economic connections. Because of the way in which the Auto Pact and the *maquiladora* industrialization program have facilitated rationalization of production, there is already something akin to free trade in automotive products among the three countries. For example, over 98 percent of automotive imports from Mexico into Canada already enter duty free under the terms of the Auto Pact.[3] Some statistics on the composition of 1989 intra-North American auto trade are provided

Table 19.1
Intra-North American Trade In Autos 1989

(all figures in thousands of U.S. dollars)

	CANADA TO MEXICO	CANADA TO U.S.	MEXICO TO CANADA	MEXICO TO U.S.	U.S. TO CANADA	U.S. TO MEXICO
Autos	0	13,516,841	62,568	1,174,841	7,014,122	17,198
Light Trucks	0	4,943,566	50	118,947	1,198,072	7,190
Engines	90	1,436,529	185,797	683,232	1,672,081	6,624
Engine Parts	18,983	548,660	29,404	110,014	1,009,978	390,333
Chassis with Engines	0	52,650	784	16,521	70,043	2,172
Auto Bodies	0	511	0	8,928	3,222	23,152
Auto Parts	62,745	6,151,602	192,403	1,044,745	9,069,855	1,973,304
TOTALS	**81,818**	**26,650,359**	**471,006**	**3,157,228**	**20,037,373**	**2,419,973**

Source: authors' calculations based on data from Statistics Canada and data supplied by the U.S. Bureau of the Census.

by Table 19.1, which breaks this trade into the following segments: autos, light trucks, engines, engine parts, chassis with engines, auto bodies, and auto parts, moving from the downstream output (cars and light trucks) to the upstream stages (original equipment parts).

As the table shows, Canada's exports to Mexico, which are very small, are heavily weighted toward auto parts. Mexican exports to Canada, while larger, are dominated by auto parts and engines. Half of all Canadian exports to the United States (the largest single category) are autos, while autos and auto parts together take three-quarters of all U.S. exports to Canada. Mexican exports to the United States are equally dominated by cars and auto parts, while over 80 percent of U.S. exports to Mexico consist of auto parts. In effect, the largest export classification from both of these spoke economies is auto parts and assembled vehicles.

This intracontinental composition of trade reflects the division of labor that resulted from the bilateral restructuring of production following the 1965 Auto Pact. Canada, because of its lower wage costs, became the site for the more labor-intensive industrial activities, final assembly, and the production of labor-intensive parts, while U.S. plants became the location for the production of components higher on the value chain—body stampings, engines, and drive train components. Big Three investment in Canada went to assembly production rather than more research-intensive areas, which remained with the parents in the United States.[4] As a result of this division of labor, Canadian assembly plants became dependent on the vehicle sourcing decisions of the Big Three and the particular demand for vehicles in the U.S. market (Holmes, 1993). While in the short term this division of labor has worked to the advantage of the Canadian auto industry, its longer-term implications may be less positive.

Investment Patterns

The above statistics illustrate the uneven character of trade concentration in both overall trade and auto trade. These patterns are also reflected in the investment flows and stocks linking the three economies. Approximately two-thirds of the foreign direct investment (FDI) stock in Canada and Mexico is controlled by U.S. transnationals. Canadians control about 25 percent of FDI in the United States. On the other hand, Canadian investment in Mexico is only about 1.5 percent of total FDI in Mexico. The dependence of both Canada and Mexico on the U.S. market and U.S. investment, and the limited nature of the economic ties between Canada and Mexico, again illustrate the hub-and-spoke nature of economic linkages within North America.

Transnationals based in the United States had investments of $67 billion in Canadian affiliates and $7 billion in Mexican affiliates by 1989.[5] In Canada, 48 percent of the FDI went into manufacturing operations; in Mexico, it was 82 percent. Similarly, in Mexico over 80 percent of all U.S. TNC sales and over 80 percent of assets were in the manufacturing sector, compared with 56 percent of U.S. TNC sales and 36 percent of assets in Canada. Thus U.S. transnationals used Mexico more heavily as a manufacturing location than they did their Canadian affiliates. The total dollar values of sales and assets, however, are much larger in Canada; Mexican sales in 1987 were 12 percent of Canadian sales of $145 billion, while Mexican assets were 11 percent of Canadian assets of $151 billion.

In the transportation sector, U.S. transnationals by 1989 had invested $7 billion in their Canadian affiliates and $1.5 billion in their Mexican affiliates. The transportation sector represented 24 percent of total U.S. transnational sales in both countries, even though sales in Mexico were only 12 percent of the Canadian levels. In terms of assets, however, U.S. transnationals were specialized much more heavily in Mexico, with almost 20 percent of all assets in this sector, compared to under 1 percent in Canada.

In summary, the trade and investment linkages within North America can be characterized as a hub-and-spoke relationship with the United States as the central hub, linked bilaterally to northern and southern spokes. This pattern is emphasized in the auto industry, where U.S. transnationals clearly dominate in each of the three countries. This integration is now being facilitated by the adoption of new technologies, the so-called lean production methods.

WORLDWIDE SOURCING AND LEAN PRODUCTION IN AUTOS

Worldwide Sourcing and Lean Production

U.S. transnationals have historically used FDI as a way to gain access to cheap natural resources in Canada and elsewhere. Since the 1960s, however, there has been a trend toward worldwide sourcing of cheap labor inputs. This trend has been facilitated by the spread of export processing zones (EPZs) throughout East Asia and Latin America. An EPZ is a form of free trade zone where components can be imported duty free for purposes of assembly and then reexported. By 1987, foreign components, frequently from offshore plants, were being used by close to 90 percent of U.S. manufacturers (Pastor and Castañeda, 1989, p. 210). Availability of cheap labor in the *maquila* factories worries labor unions in Canada and the United States, and is at the root of their opposition to NAFTA.

Having the opposite impact on TNC location decisions is the growing significance of knowledge-based or "lean" production. Lean production involves the joint use of information technologies (computer-aided design and manufacture, robotics, telecommunications hardware and software) and just-in-time manufacturing (just-in-time delivery of zero-defect-quality components). With lean production, the new factory is located near suppliers, accepts only defect-free components, utilizes mechanized production technology, can rapidly shift production from one product line to another, and employs a highly skilled and flexible work force (Eden, 1991; Hoffman and Kaplinsky, 1988; van Tulder and Junne, 1988; Womack et al., 1990).

As long as labor was a significant factor in overall manufacturing costs, TNCs had an incentive to locate in sites where labor was cheap, such as EPZs in developing countries. However, using lean production technologies reduces the importance of labor costs; as a result, many TNCs are relocating parts or all of their assembly activities closer to the final demand for the product in the developed market economies. In the North American environment, the adoption of the new production style should assuage some of the concerns of U.S. and Canadian labor with respect to the loss of manufacturing jobs to low-wage Mexican factories. On the other hand, because of their location on the U.S. border, Mexican factories are likely to attract FDI away from East Asia (Womack et al., 1990). If Mexican plants can be technologically upgraded—and there is some evidence that at least the Ford plant at Hermosillo functions on a comparable level with assembly plants in Canada and the United States (Womack et al., 1990, pp. 265-6)—and integrated into U.S. just-in-time delivery systems, Canadian plants may face more severe competition.

Whether transnationals will be induced to shift their investments among the three North American countries depends on several factors. The most important of these is the affiliate's role in the "value chain," the range of activities (extraction, processing, sub- and final assembly, sales and distribution, technology development, overhead functions) performed by the TNC. Affiliates can be classified according to three basic motives for foreign direct investment: resource-seeking, cost-reducing, and market-driven FDI (Eden, 1991). A resource-seeking affiliate is set up to extract and process raw materials at the upstream end of the value chain, a cost-reducing affiliate to manufacture parts and make sub- and final assemblies, and a market-driven affiliate to sell at the downstream end. Research and development and other overhead functions are usually assigned to the parent firm.

The choice of affiliate location therefore depends on the motive for FDI, the relative attractiveness of various host locations, and the availability and cost of alternative contractual arrangements. Whereas foreign plants in one location (for instance, Mexico) may be established in order to gain access to low-cost labor for subassembly, another affiliate may be located in a high-cost location (for instance, Canada) to gain access to the local market. The ability of plants in one country to withstand competition from TNC affiliates in another country depends very much on whether the plants are horizontally or vertically related to one another, on their adaptability to technological change, and on their ability to engineer new functions with the TNC's hierarchy (Eden, 1991).

Lean Production in the Auto Industry

Plants in the auto industry normally take on either a cost-reduction or a market-driven strategic function. The production of original equipment parts and their subassembly into chassis and engines is typically driven by the need to reduce costs. The more technologically sophisticated the component (engines, for example), the more likely that production will not be located in EPZs, but in areas where skilled labor is available. Final assembly of autos usually takes place in the consumer market, partly to ensure that the vehicle meets consumer preferences, but also often due to government regulations requiring domestic content. In North America, as noted above, the content requirements of the 1965 Auto Pact have been responsible for shifting assembly operations to Canada, while the manufacture of most sophisticated parts and the research and development functions have remained in the United States.

The shift to lean production methods in the 1990s is demonstrably changing the location of production within the North American auto industry. That Mexican workers are able to master lean production with the same speed as their U.S. and Canadian counterparts suggests that lean production will have a mixed impact on the evolving North American political economy.[6] On the one hand, lean production may preserve jobs in U.S. and Canadian factories (because labor costs become less important relative to knowledge-intensive functions) at the same time that it facilitates continental rationalization by U.S. transnationals. On the other hand, as affiliates are drawn more tightly into the TNC's overall strategic planning, the Canadian division may simply disappear into an integrated North American strategic business unit. Regardless of NAFTA, the changing nature of manufacturing will encourage a process that is already under way most notably, but not only, in the auto industry—namely, the rationalization of TNC production across North America as a whole.

The growing linkages in auto production across Canada, the United States, and Mexico are, in short, the result of the interplay of state policies and corporate investment decisions. The Big Three have been rationalizing production on a continental basis, and the transplants have followed this pattern (but so far only across two countries). Volkswagen produces all its North American output from its Puebla plant. Independent components producers have followed the location decisions of the major auto firms. It is this (together with labor costs) that explains the movement of Canadian and U.S. parts suppliers to new sites in the United States and Mexico.

Although a continental rationalization of production has begun, it is not clear how far and how quickly it will evolve. The push factors in this rationalization have just been discussed at length and some analysts (Womack et al., [1990, p. 226], for example) argue that auto producers are developing a "new configuration" for North America in which Mexico will be the production location for low-cost, entry-level cars and trucks for the continent while Ontario and the Midwest of the United States will supply larger trucks and cars for all of North America. The pull factors are the uncertain attraction of lower labor costs to the Big Three, higher transportation costs from Mexico, the less-developed state of Mexican infrastructure, and, perhaps most important, the contents of NAFTA, to which we now turn.

AUTOS AND THE NAFTA NEGOTIATIONS[7]

In a global economy in which trading blocks are becoming critical, all three countries in North America have an interest in creating a trading unit that will enhance their economic opportunities. The United States clearly sees NAFTA as a way to reassert its economic hegemony vis-à-vis Europe and Japan, as well as a way to broaden and deepen its economic empire within the Americas. The Mexican government views NAFTA as the means to consolidate its economic liberalization policies, guarantee unrestricted access to the U.S. market, and encourage the investment inflows necessary to promote long-run economic growth and employ its rapidly growing population. Given that a bilateral U.S.-Mexican accord would likely have worsened Canada's access to the U.S. market, the Canadian government decided to participate in the NAFTA talks primarily to preserve its U.S. market access. In addition, Mexico is perceived as a potential future market for Canadian exports. In short, U.S. motives for NAFTA are more geopolitical, Mexican more economic, and Canadian more defensive (Eden and Molot 1991a,b, 1992, 1993).

Despite the already high level of industrial integration, the auto provisions of the NAFTA agreement will have an impact on the future shape of the industry. A major point of contention in the negotiations was North American content rules.

Each of the players in the North American auto industry took a position that demonstrated its assessments of potential gains and losses from further continental integration. The Big Three auto producers, sensitive to their weakening competitive position, adopted a protectionist position on NAFTA, one that would effectively rewrite a key segment of CUFTA. Ford, Chrysler, and General Motors all demanded a higher regional content provision than the 50 percent extant under CUFTA; Ford and Chrysler advocated 70 percent while General Motors sought 60 percent North American (now including Mexican) content.[8] They argued, moreover, for the creation of a "Two Tier" system that would ensure that the five companies that are the major players in the Mexican auto industry (themselves plus Nissan and Volkswagen) would enjoy a privileged position in the Mexican market for 15 years (Hufbauer and Schott, 1992, Ch. 11). Under their proposal, performance and other requirements for the Big Three (plus Nissan and Volkswagen) would be reduced more quickly while those for newcomers to the Mexican market would have a 15-year transition period for these requirements and tariffs.[9]

What underlay this proposal was the concern that NAFTA would permit "Mexico to establish itself as a platform for major new automotive capacity from third-country producers for export to the U.S. market" (*Inside US Trade*, September 23, 1991, p. S-3). The result of the Big Three proposal would be the reservation of the domestic and import market for assembly firms already established in Mexico, while the tight rule of origin would make it more costly and more complex for non-North American companies to operate in Mexico.

The Canadian subsidiaries of the Big Three, not surprisingly, adopted the same position in the NAFTA talks as their U.S. parents, although the parent firms argued that their affiliates were nationally responsive in their trade-policy positioning. The Canadian parts industry, concerned about potential job losses to U.S. components producers as well as to Mexico, supported a higher North American content requirement under NAFTA. The Canadian parts industry advocated a 75 percent North American content requirement but, beyond that, wanted a 50 percent Canadian value added content rule to protect Canadian parts suppliers (Automotive Parts Manufacturer's Association, 1991).[10] The Mexican supplier industry opposed both the Two Tier proposal and that for higher North American content, preferring the transition period to be structured by the performance requirements of the 1989 Automotive Decree (Olea, 1993).[11]

Each of the three governments sought to protect its own auto industry. The United States was (and continues to be) concerned about the competitive strength of the Big Three producers. In the NAFTA talks it wanted Mexico to open its market more broadly to car imports,[12] simplified North American content rules, and a North American content level of at least 60 percent. Canada sought to preserve the auto assembly provisions of the Auto Pact,[13] which ensure the country assembly jobs, improved access to the Mexican market for Canadian auto parts and vehicles, and the resolution of some of the administrative difficulties with the CUFTA rules of origin. The Canadian government would have preferred a North American context requirement similar to that of CUFTA (i.e., 50 percent), which would have made Canada an attractive location for new auto industry, particularly transplant, investment, but was prepared to countenance a 60 percent content figure. Mexico wanted to maintain as many of the assembly provisions and domestic content requirements as it could to preserve its status as an attractive site for new TNC investment.

These differing state positions were resolved in a manner that was closest to U.S. demands. Under NAFTA cars must have 62.5 percent North American content to be shipped duty free from one country to the other. Mexico's 1989 Automotive Decree will be phased out in stages during the transition period and its restrictions on foreign investment reduced. There can be no new entrants to the Mexican assembly market for ten years; after that, new assemblers can have free access to North American markets if they meet the content requirements.

Canada was able to retain the assembly provisions of the Auto Pact; it was also able to negotiate some changes in how North American content is defined that are less stringent than under CUFTA. These changes may alleviate some of the content difficulties that resulted in U.S. Customs' charges that Honda Civics, assembled in Aliston, did not meet North American content requirements. On the other hand, the 62.5 percent North American content requirements will not do anything to enhance Canada's attractiveness as an investment location for transplant producers. Virtually all of the transplant investment in components production is in the United States, a fact that the new North American content rule will simply reinforce. Given the existing excess capacity in North American auto plants, the market sales plans of the Japanese firms, and the downscaling that has already started at General Motors,[14] the Canadian auto parts industry, in particular, has reason to worry about its long-run viability.

CONCLUSIONS

The auto industry is clearly the most integrated North American industry. TNC rationalization of production on a continent-wide basis, which has resulted in massive new investments in assembly and supplier capacity in both Mexico and the United States, has been promoted both by state policies and the new lean production technologies. Integration in the auto industry will continue regardless of NAFTA. What TNC positions on NAFTA demonstrated is that, although there is support for free trade, it is tempered by the realities of Asian offshore and transplant competition and fears about further erosion of North American market position.

State policies and the investment activities of the transnational auto makers have structured the Canadian auto industry and promoted its integration with the United States, and to a limited extent Mexican, auto industries. It has been argued (Womack et al., 1990) that continentalization will result in a spatial allocation whereby Mexico will be the site for low-cost entry vehicles (the least expensive cars), and the area from Indiana up through Ontario for medium and higher-priced cars. Although this assessment of future production sites might, at first glance, be reassuring in terms of the prospective health of the Canadian auto industry, this prediction is far too sanguine given the competitive stresses under which the industry is operating and the dramatic job losses that the Canadian industry has experienced since 1989.

What happens to the Canadian auto industry, and more particularly to the parts segment, will be determined by the interaction of state policies and corporate production strategies. Lean production methods are more closely linking the North American auto plants and their suppliers on a continental basis. As the three countries free up intra-North American trade and invest-ment, integration of auto production based on lean production techniques is likely to proceed rapidly.

NOTES

An earlier version of this paper was presented at the workshop "Critical Perspec-tives on North American Integration, York University," Toronto, Canada, 6-8 December 1991. This research was supported by the Social Sciences and Humanities Research Council of Canada, the Centre for Trade Policy and Law, and the Centre for International Trade and Investment Policy Studies at Carleton University. We would like to thank Bruce Wilkinson, Judith Teichman, Ken Thomas, Henry Nau, John McIntyre, and the editors for helpful comments. Research assistance was provided by Derek Baas.

1. Trade and investment statistics in this section are from Eden and Molot (1991a) and are explained in more detail there.
2. Exports of intermediate goods rose from 61 percent of Mexico's manufactured exports in 1980 to 70 percent in 1986; imports of intermediate goods were 65

percent of manufactured imports in 1986, up from 57 percent in 1980 (Weintraub, 1988, p. 23).

3. The remaining 2 percent are imported by non-Auto Pact companies and are imported at the Generalized Preferential Tariff rate of 6 percent (Standing Committee on External Affairs and International Trade, 1990, No. 61, p. 12). Under the Auto Pact, the United States admits duty free only cars assembled in Canada and made-in-Canada original equipment parts. Canada, on the other hand, admits, duty free, U.S.-made products and offshore imports from auto firms that meet Canadian content rules. Thus producers in Canada can bring in captive imports (vehicles they produce in third countries) without paying the Canadian duty (Morici, 1991, p. 114).

4. The exception to this is the 1980s General Motors investment in its Autoplex facility in Oshawa, which includes the first-ever stamping plant in Canada.

5. See Table 4 of Eden and Molot (1991a) for more details on the data in this paragraph and the next.

6. Ford's Hermosillo plant, which employs just-in-time production methods, was ranked second in the world in terms of quality (Womack cited in Olea, 1993).

7. On recent events in the North American auto industry see Automotive Parts Manufacturer's Association (1991), "Detroit South" (1992), Holmes (1991, 1993), Hufbauer & Schott (1992, Ch. 11), Industry Science and Technology Canada (1990), Molot (1993) and Reich (1992).

8. Regional content refers to the proportion of a car's content produced in a location required to allow the vehicle to move across a border duty free. The CUFTA established a tighter North American content requirement than had existed under the Auto Pact, changing the basis of the calculation of content to "direct cost of manufacturing" or "factory cost," which includes labor, materials and the direct costs of assembly, and excluding promotional and overhead costs.

9. To solidify their position in the Mexican market, and to facilitate the continental rationalization of the auto industry, the Big Three sought to reduce current Mexican government requirements, such as the percent of local purchases required. Retention of these requirements for Japanese transplant producers would make it more difficult for the latter to compete in the North American auto market from locations in Mexico. This is a strategy which employs the provisions of a free trade agreement to enhance the protection of those already producing inside the market.

10. The Japanese-owned Canadian auto assemblers wanted North American content rules of 50 percent. This group also wanted the 9.2 percent Canadian external tariff, which encourages domestic content, lowered at least to the United States' level of 2.5 to 3 percent.

11. The 1989 Mexican Automotive Decree, which came into effect on 1 November 1990, liberalized some of the conditions under which foreign auto companies operate in Mexico, but maintained local content requirements of at least 36 percent

for vehicles sold on the domestic market. For additional details on this Automotive Decree and previous ones see Hufbauer and Schott (1992, pp. 215-219).

12. Current Mexican regulations demand that two-and-a-half cars be built in Mexico for each one imported.

13. This provision requires U.S. assemblers to build in Canada one car for every one they sell in the country.

14. There is reason to worry about Canadian assembly jobs, given the necessity for the Big Three to downsize and restructure. As General Motors considers which plants it will close in the next few years, GM executives have made clear that even the new Autoplex in Oshawa is not exempt from possible closure.

REFERENCES

Automotive Parts Manufacturers' Association. (10 October 1991). *APMA Proposed Policy Positions for the Automotive Provisions of a North American Free Trade Agreement.*

Cameron, M. A., Eden, L., and Molot, M. A. (1992). "North American Free Trade: Conflict and Cooperation in Canada-Mexico Relations." In F. O. Hampson and C. J. Maule (eds.), *A New World Order? Canada Among Nations 1992-93.* Ottawa: Carleton University Press.

"Detroit South: Mexico's Auto Boom: Who Wins Who Loses?" (16 March 1992). *Business Week.*

Eden, L. (1991). "Multinational Responses to Trade and Technology Changes: Implications for Canada." In D. McFetridge (ed.), *Foreign Investment, Technology and Growth.* Ottawa: Investment Canada and University of Calgary Press.

Eden, L., and Molot, M. A. (1991a). "From Silent Integration to Strategic Alliance: The Political Economy of North American Free Trade." *Occasional Papers in International Trade Law and Policy,* Centre for Trade Policy and Law. Ottawa: Carleton University and University of Ottawa.

————. (1991b). "The Political Economy of a NAFTA: A Public Choice Approach." In W. Watson (ed.), *North American Free Trade Area.* Kingston: Queen's University, John Deutsch Institute.

————. (1992). "The View from the Spokes: Canada and Mexico Face the US." In S. Randall with V. Konrad and S. Silverman (eds.), *North America without Borders: Integrating Canada, the United States and Mexico.* Calgary: University of Calgary Press.

————. (1993). "Fortress or Free Market? NAFTA and its Implications for the Pacific Rim." In R. Higgott, J. Leaver and J. Ravenhill (eds.), *Pacific Economic Relations in the 1990s: Conflict or Cooperation?* London: Allen and Unwin.

Hart, M. (1990). *A North American Free Trade Agreement: The Strategic Implications for Canada*. Ottawa and Halifax: The Centre for Trade Policy and Law and the Institute for Research on Public Policy.

Hoffman K., and Kaplinsky, R. (1988). *Driving Force: The Global Restructuring of Technology, Labor and Investment in the Automobile and Components Industries*. Boulder: Westview Press.

Holmes, J. (1991). "The Globalization of Production and the Future of Canada's Mature Industries: The Case of the Automotive Industry." In D. Drache and M. S. Gertler (eds.), *The New Era of Global Competition: State Policy and Market Power*. Montreal and Kingston: McGill-Queen's University Press.

————. (1993). "From Three Industries to One: Towards an Integrated North American Automobile Industry." In M. A. Molot (ed.), *Driving Continentally: National Policies and the North American Auto Industry*. Ottawa: Carleton University Press.

Hufbauer, G. C., and Schott, J. J. (1992). *North American Free Trade: Issues and Recommendations*. Washington: Institute for International Economics.

Industry, Science and Technology Canada (ISTC). (1990). *Statistical Review of the Canadian Auto Industry: 1989*. Ottawa: Minister of Supply and Services Canada.

Inside US Trade. (September 23, 1991), p. S-3.

MacDonald, N. (1989). "Will the Free Trade Deal Drive a Gaping Hole Through the Auto Pact? *Policy Options*, 10 (1).

Molot, M. A. (1993). "Introduction." In M. A. Molot (ed.), *Driving Continentally: National Policies and the North American Auto Industry*. Ottawa: Carleton University Press.

Morici, P. (1991). *Trade Talks with Mexico: A Time for Realism*. Washington: National Planning Association.

Olea, M. A. (1993). "The Mexican Automotive Industry in the NAFTA Negotiations." In M. A. Molot (ed.), *Driving Continentally: National Policies and the North American Auto Industry*. Ottawa: Carleton University Press.

Pastor, R. A., and Castañeda, J. G. (1989). *Limits to Friendship: The United States and Mexico*. New York: Vintage Books.

Pritchard, T. (30 December 1991). "150,000 Canadians Watching." *Globe and Mail*, p. B3.

Prosperity Secretariat. (1991). *Industrial Competitiveness: A Sectoral Perspective*. Ottawa: Supply and Services Canada.

Reich, S. (31 March-4 April 1992). "NAFTA, Foreign Direct Investment in the Auto Industry: A Comparative Perspective." Paper presented to the International Studies Association, Atlanta.

Standing Committee on External Affairs and International Trade, House of Commons (SCEAIT). (1990). Hearings on Canada-U.S.-Mexico Trade Negotiations.

Van Tulder, R., and Junne, G. (1988). *European Multinationals in Core Technologies*. New York: John Wiley.

Weintraub, S. (1988). *Mexican Trade Policy and the North American Community*. Washington: The Center for Strategic and International Studies.

Womack, J. P., et al. (1990). *The Machine That Changed the World*. New York: Rawson Associates.

Chapter 20

The Petroleum Sector
under Continental Integration

John Dillon

Oil is at the very core of U.S. geopolitical interests in North American economic integration; a major U.S. objective in trade negotiations with Mexico and Canada has been to gain secure access to the petroleum resources of its neighbors. Unrestricted access to Canadian and Mexican petroleum reserves represents more than just one more "side payment" attached to a trade agreement. With crude oil reserves equivalent to only nine years of production, and dependence on imports growing, the Bush administration's energy strategy calls for greater reliance on imports from countries outside the Persian Gulf, such as Canada and Mexico. U.S. geopolitical interests demand that Mexico and Canada concede substantial control over energy as the price for a broad trade agreement.

This chapter provides a historical overview of continental oil issues. It analyzes the early domination of the petroleum industry in Mexico and Canada by U.S. transnational corporations (TNCs); the assertion of national control over the industry that culminated in the National Energy Program in Canada in the 1970s and the expropriation of the Mexican oil industry in 1938; and, finally, the return to U.S. control of the continental oil sector through the Canada-U.S. Free Trade Agreement (CUFTA) and the North American Free Trade Agreement (NAFTA).

A HISTORY OF U.S. DOMINATION

Mexico's oil industry took off after a 1901 decree by Porfirio Díaz made generous concessions to foreign companies, including S. Pearson & Son, later sold to Shell, and the Huasteca Petroleum Company, subsequently acquired by Standard Oil. That decree exempted foreign companies from nearly all Mexican taxes and allowed unlimited petroleum exports. By 1914, Mexico was host to 59 percent of all U.S. foreign direct investment in oil production. Canada was a distant second with 17 percent of that investment (Shaffer, 1983, p. 47). That same year, Mexico was the third largest oil producer in the world, following the United States and Russia, exporting two-thirds of its production to the United States.

During the Mexican revolution, British and U.S. oil interests financed factions they hoped would give them the best deal. Porfirio Díaz had angered U.S. oil companies with policies deemed to favor British investors. Accordingly, Standard Oil funded Francisco Madero, who overthrew Díaz. But Madero's attempt to institute a petroleum tax angered British interests, who in turn financed Victoriano Huerta.

President Woodrow Wilson refused to recognize Huerta, whom he tried to destabilize by landing troops at Veracruz and selling arms to Venustiano Carranza, who also received support from U.S. oil companies. Standard Oil and Shell also paid hundreds of thousands of dollars to Manuel Peláez, whose private army controlled extensive petroleum-producing areas between 1914 and 1920. Peláez's reign of terror forced landowners to sell their properties to foreign oil companies at ridiculously low prices (Castillo and Naranjo, 1984, p. 49).

After the 1917 Constitution asserted control over all subsurface mineral reserves, Mexico established a petroleum production tax and decreed that companies had to obtain permits before drilling and pay a 5 percent royalty (Castillo & Naranjo, 1984, p. 45). The U.S. government became very hostile when Mexico denied drilling permits to U.S. companies that held concessions granted by the old Porfirio Díaz dictatorship but had not commenced drilling. The United States sent Mexico a sharply worded diplomatic note insisting that every nation had certain "minimum duties" with regard to the treatment of foreigners, including the duty to refrain from confiscating their vested property rights.

Shaffer (1983, pp. 49-50) explains that the doctrine of

> minimum duty . . . in effect said that foreigners—or, more precisely, foreign investors—are a special, privileged class, not subject to the laws of the nation in

which they do business. Any nation could enact any legislation it wished regulating the business activities of its citizens as long as these laws did not apply to foreigners.

A decade later, the Calles government formally acceded to U.S. demands and recognized the doctrine of "minimum duty." But the U.S. victory was to be short-lived, as President Lázaro Cárdenas expropriated foreign oil properties in 1938.

EXPROPRIATION

The immediate reason for Cárdenas's bold expropriation was the refusal of foreign companies to obey an order made by the Mexican Supreme Court to settle a labor dispute. The companies claimed they could not afford to pay their Mexican workers more, despite the preferential treatment they gave to their expatriate employees. There was widespread resentment against the arrogant foreign oil companies depleting reserves and shifting investments to Venezuela. Mexican production had peaked at 193 million barrels in 1921. By 1937, production had declined to 27 million barrels, 60 percent of which was exported. Within Mexico the companies charged exorbitant prices (Castillo and Naranjo, 1984, pp. 70, 259).

Cárdenas's action received enthusiastic popular support. About $440,000 worth of money, jewels, and even pigs and chickens were collected from voluntary donations, demonstrating extensive political support for Cárdenas. The anniversary of the expropriation is still celebrated annually as a "day of national dignity."

The transnational oil companies fought the expropriation with a boycott of Mexico, refusing to buy petroleum or sell any production machinery. They made outlandish claims for compensation, counting the value of oil still in the ground as part of their losses (Engler, 1961, p. 195). The boycott caused economic hardship, but resisting the foreign companies became a point of national pride.

The companies tried to persuade President Franklin Roosevelt to retaliate by cutting Mexican import quotas, denying loans, or even using military force. Shaffer (1983) explains why Roosevelt took a conciliatory stance. The president did not want to jeopardize his Good Neighbor Policy toward Latin America. The U.S. ambassador to Mexico was very critical of the companies' ineptness. Mexico was no longer an important exporter. As Mexican production and exports fell, the companies moved on to Venezuela. Finally, in 1940, the oil companies settled their claims for $165 million in compensation.

CANADA'S OIL UNDER UNITED STATES CONTROL

The first productive oil well in North America was drilled in Lambton County, Ontario, in 1858, a year before Edwin Drake struck oil in Pennsylvania. In 1880, 16 small, independent Canadian companies joined together to form Imperial Oil to protect themselves against competition from Rockefeller's Standard Oil. However, they were unable to raise sufficient capital in Canada or England and finally sold a controlling interest in Imperial to Standard in 1898 (Shaffer, 1983, pp. 34-35).

Oil was discovered in the Turner Valley, Alberta, in 1914 by the Calgary Petroleum Products Company. This enterprise also ran into financial difficulties and turned to Imperial Oil for a bailout. By holding exclusive marketing arrangements with Calgary's gas utility and owning the only refineries, Imperial soon controlled production throughout the Turner Valley. Western Canada's oil industry boomed after 1947, when Imperial discovered the Leduc Field, near Edmonton. The rapid postwar development was dominated by major TNCs. Canadian ownership was concentrated in the smaller, junior players. By the end of 1979, 72 percent of Canada's petroleum industry was foreign-owned while 82 percent of revenues were foreign-controlled.

From 1961 through 1974, Canada maintained a National Oil Policy, which divided the domestic market into two areas: the land west of the Ottawa Valley was preserved for Canadian crude, while the area to the east used imported oil. A 1981 government study—*The State of Competition in the Canadian Petroleum Industry*—found that the National Oil Policy "did little more than recognize the supply pattern that had been developed by the leading firm—Exxon's Canadian subsidiary [Imperial Oil]" (Bertrand, 1981, p. 169).

The study, conducted under the Combines Investigation Act, concluded that the National Oil Policy had "increased the market power held by the... [TNCs] to enhance domestic crude prices and maintain 'unrealistic' transfer prices for crude oil by substantially isolating the Canadian market from declining world prices" (Bertrand, 1981, p. 12). As a result of these higher prices, the transnationals collected C$12.1 billion (in 1980 dollars) in extra revenues between 1958 and 1973.

One effect of the National Oil Policy was to lock Canada firmly into a continental marketing structure: importing supplies in the east while exporting from the west. Exports of oil rose from 185,000 barrels a day in 1961 to 1,175,000 barrels a day in 1973, the year of the "energy crisis." Prior to 1973, no Canadian government questioned the wisdom of exporting so much oil.

In December of 1969, Minister of Energy Joe Greene, declared his support for a continental energy policy at a news conference in Washington. Shortly thereafter, in February of 1970, the Nixon administration released the Shultz Report on oil import controls, which called for a "harmonized energy policy" with Canada (Laxer, 1974, p. 74).

James Laxer (1974, p. 75) recounts how at that time,

> the chief U.S. desire . . . was for large-scale increases [in imports] of Canadian natural gas on a long-term basis. The Nixon administration, not yet faced with oil supply problems, decided to cut the flow of Canadian crude to the U.S. market to bring the Canadian government speedily to terms. In March 1970, the U.S. imposed a quota on Canadian crude imports, cutting them back to 395,000 barrels a day. Two months later, the White House explained that the quota was aimed at pressuring Canada into a long-term energy arrangement.

After a polite diplomatic protest concerning the U.S. intervention in Canadian affairs, the Trudeau government acquiesced, establishing de facto continental energy sharing. In September 1970, while the U.S. oil import quota was still in place, Greene approved a deal that committed 6.3 trillion cubic feet of natural gas, equivalent to 34 percent of Canada's established reserves, to the United States.

Nixon's use of the oil quota to maneuver Canada into place occurred while the United States protected its own industry through mandatory quotas on oil imports from 1959 to 1973. The nominal purpose of the import control program was to protect U.S. "national security," which the Shultz Task Force defined as "the protection of military and essential civilian demand against . . . foreign supply interruptions . . . and the prevention of damage to domestic industry from excessive imports that would so weaken the national economy as to impair the national security" (Blair, 1978, p. 172).

Under this "national security" rationale, shipments by pipeline from Canada were exempt from the quotas that applied to vulnerable water-borne deliveries. In the case of Mexico, this loophole led to the bizarre "Brownsville turnaround." Some 30,000 barrels a day of Mexican crude were off-loaded from tanker ships into trucks at Brownsville, Texas.

> The trucks would then transport the oil under bond ten miles south across the Mexican border, where they would immediately turn around and reenter the United States carrying what was now transformed into 'exempt overland imports' (Blair, 1978, p. 176).

Blair explains that behind the facade of protecting national security, the mandatory quotas actually served the major oil companies, which received 57.3 percent of the exempt overland shipments from Canada and Mexico and charged higher than world prices for their domestic sales. The quota program seriously depleted U.S. reserves and resulted in higher prices for U.S. consumers. Blair (1978, p. 182) estimates that "the total cost of the import quota between 1959 and 1969 [was] over $50 billion, probably the largest subsidy to any single industry in U.S. history."

By 1971, Canada was exporting more oil to the United States than was consumed at home. At the time, Joe Greene boasted that Canada's oil supplies would last for 923 years while there was sufficient natural gas for 392 years. Later it became evident that Greene was citing supply estimates provided by the petroleum industry without any independent verification. An executive at Imperial Oil revealed that the companies had available to them a wide range of estimates of petroleum reserves that they used selectively according to their interests (Laxer, 1983, pp. 46-47).

The Canadian government was slow to come to grips with the 1973 "energy crisis." While oil exports to the United States were gradually reduced and an export tax was introduced in 1973, it was not until 1976 that the Trudeau government's Energy Strategy for Canada for the first time expressly rejected the concept of continental energy sharing. The export tax and the curtailment of Canadian oil sales prompted anger and threats of retaliation from Washington.

DEMANDS FOR A COMMON ENERGY MARKET

After the revolution in Iran in 1979 occasioned another round of price hikes, there was renewed U.S. interest in establishing a continental energy sharing arrangement. Presidential contenders from both the Democratic and Republican parties, including Jerry Brown, John Connally, and Ronald Reagan, pronounced themselves in favor of a common energy market involving Canada, the United States, and Mexico. Senator Edward Kennedy claimed that Mexico represented a new Saudi Arabia.

But the Carter administration listened to warnings that an overt grab for Mexican and Canadian petroleum might backfire. Others advised that the time was not yet ripe for a continental energy deal (Meyer, 1979). The chairman of Standard Oil of Indiana, John Swearingen, cautioned that "Americans must recognize that Canada and Mexico are separate nations" (Calgary CP, 1979). George Grayson (1981, p. 71) explained that

The idea of a continental energy common market evokes such adverse reaction in Canada and Mexico that to advance it as a serious policy option would jeopardize America's national interests in relations with its neighbors.

Publicly, President Carter played down notions of a formal energy sharing pact. Privately, Carter wrote to then Prime Minister Joe Clark encouraging him to imitate U.S. plans to develop synthetic fuels from oil sands, shale, and coal (Hall, 1979).

With regard to Mexico, President Carter took a long-term view, declaring,

we look upon Mexico as a very valuable present and future source of needed energy supplies for our country. We want to negotiate with them in good faith... over a long period of time (Halloran, 1979).

THE PETROLIZATION OF MEXICO

Heberto Castillo set the tone of the debate over petroleum that raged in Mexico during the López Portillo term (1976-1982). Castillo extolled Lázaro Cárdenas for recognizing that oil produces wealth where it is consumed, not where it is produced. Castillo emphasized that the capital-intensive nature of oil extraction creates few jobs and little development relative to the numbers of people employed when petroleum fuels domestic industry, agriculture, and transportation.

López Portillo came to power promising that Mexico would avoid overdependence on the export of unrefined crude. But he soon fell victim to external pressures to accelerate petroleum production and exports. At the end of 1976, Mexico faced a balance-of-payments crisis. López Portillo agreed to an austerity program in return for new credits from the International Monetary Fund. In addition, he moved to secure new private bank credits by declaring that Mexico had vastly greater petroleum reserves than had previously been announced.

In a series of dramatic pronouncements, López Portillo declared an elevenfold increase in Mexico's petroleum reserves. He claimed 72 billion barrels of proven reserves and another 300 billion barrels of potential holdings. The latter projection would have given Mexico more oil than Saudi Arabia. At the time both U.S. (Grayson, 1981, pp. 55-56) and Mexican (Castillo & Naranjo, 1984, p. 107) critics cast doubt on the accuracy of these projections. Recently, Francisco Inguanzo, a retired petroleum engineer from the Mexican Petroleum Company (PEMEX), confirmed that the data had indeed been falsified (del Rio, 1991). Nevertheless, López Portillo succeeded in creating the impression that Mexico had an immense pool of petroleum that could be exploited if only PEMEX could secure foreign loans.

In 1977, Mexico's finance minister journeyed to New York to declare, "Oil will be the turning point of the Mexican economy" (Koffman, 1977). The foreign loans to PEMEX that followed were a significant cause of Mexico's 1982 debt crisis. Three-quarters of the capital goods used by PEMEX were imported, mostly from the United States, at costs that rose twice as fast as the international price for crude (Hellman, 1983, p. 79). By the end of 1981, PEMEX owed foreign creditors $20 billion, up from $3 billion in 1977. Between 1976 and 1982, the cost of servicing Mexico's foreign debt more than swallowed up all petroleum export earnings.

The petrolization of Mexico's economy lowered the living standards of both the urban and rural poor. Capital-intensive investments increased employment in the oil sector by only 5 percent from 1973 to 1980. Peasant farmers suffered as food imports replaced domestic production. As capital inflows stimulated inflation, real earnings for minimum wage earners fell by 12 percent between 1977 and 1980 (Teichman, 1988, pp. 75-76). By 1981, oil had grown to account for three-quarters of Mexico's export earnings and one-third of government revenues. After world oil prices fell in 1981 and U.S. monetary authorities drove interest rates to exorbitant heights, Mexico could no longer make its external debt payments.

When the debt crisis hit, the Reagan administration demanded significant concessions from Mexico. The day after Mexico's insolvency became public, a leaked U.S. State Department memorandum revealed how U.S. officials wanted to use the new leverage offered by Mexico's financial difficulties. The memo said that Mexico "might sell more oil and gas to us at better prices." Mexico "with the wind out of its sails" would be more willing to ease restrictions on foreign investors, negotiate trade agreements, cooperate to control illegal immigration, and "be less adventuresome in its foreign policy," especially in Central America (*The New York Times*, 1982).

Mexican negotiators seeking bridge financing from the U.S. government almost walked out over the Treasury Department's insistence that they sell additional oil to the strategic petroleum reserve for $4.00 a barrel less than the prevailing world price. Eventually, the Mexicans caved in, agreeing to pay extra fees and higher interest on a $1 billion loan from the United States tied to an oil sale that contravened both the price and market diversification goals of Mexico's official energy plan.

CANADA'S NATIONAL ENERGY PROGRAM

Just as the Mexicans had found Reagan a tough bargainer, the Trudeau government encountered strong opposition to its 1980 National Energy Program (NEP). The NEP was designed to achieve energy self-sufficiency for Canada after that country had suffered a decade of buffeting by world oil price increases. The NEP also aimed to increase Canadian ownership over its petroleum industry and to give the federal government more revenue from petroleum development on the "Canada Lands," principally offshore in the Atlantic and Arctic oceans.

The part of the NEP that most upset U.S. corporations was a provision known as the "back-in," which required firms to give the federal government a 25 percent interest in every discovery made on the Canada Lands. In fact, the back-in was not so revolutionary as the Reaganites made out. Prior to 1976, Alberta had required that a 50 percent interest in oil and gas discoveries be returned to the provincial government. Nevertheless, the idea that U.S. companies that had invested in the Hibernia field off the coast of Newfoundland would have to surrender a 25 percent interest retroactively became the focus of opposition.

Ten days after the NEP was announced, a team of U.S. officials flew to Ottawa to express their "bitterness and outrage" at the prospect of such "withdrawal from the world." As Stephen Clarkson (1985, p. 23) explains,

> The American oil companies, finding their Canadian possessions under attack, screamed in outrage when they found out that the NEP had changed the rules of a continental game they had been playing profitably for decades . . . The new Reagan team of free enterprisers . . . supporting the practical complaints of their businessmen . . . launched a campaign to bring Ottawa to its ideological senses and political knees, calling on it to abandon its dirigiste policies.

U.S. corporations objected to provisions of the NEP on the grounds that they violated the principle of "national treatment" for foreign investors by treating them less favorably than they did domestic firms. To prevent any future discrimination against U.S. firms, U.S. negotiators insisted that national treatment for foreign investors be a cornerstone of CUFTA and also written into the General Agreement on Tariffs and Trade (GATT) and NAFTA. The challenge to the NEP was considered a test case by Washington. As one official told the Wall Street Journal, "If the U.S. allows Canada to get away with its new policies, what about Mexico?" (Clarkson, 1985, p. 35).

Just as declining world crude prices had led to a crisis in Mexico, by 1981 the NEP had to be revised. The assumption of constantly rising world oil prices had proven false, undermining the viability of both the NEP and the Canadian development strategy based on energy megaprojects.

The election of Brian Mulroney as prime minister in 1984 marked a definitive turn away from energy nationalism in Canada. Shortly after his election, Mulroney traveled to New York to announce the end of the National Energy Program, declaring that "Canada is open for business." Mulroney instituted an energy policy that the Canadian Petroleum Association, representing the largest transnationals, declared was "virtually identical" to its demands. After Mulroney conceded world prices, lower taxes, and permission for increased exports, it seemed redundant to include energy in the free trade agreement.

But the Reagan negotiators were looking far beyond the term of the Mulroney government. Their preoccupation was to make sure that no future Canadian government would ever again resort to interventionist policies like the NEP. A confidential assessment of CUFTA written by the State Department explained that "one of the reasons for considering energy . . . within the trade agreement is to ensure greater security of supply by reducing the risk of government intervention."[1]

In a sense, Chapter Nine of CUFTA is an exercise in overkill. Chapter Nine applies to the energy sector (broadly defined to include electricity, coal, and uranium, in addition to oil and gas) the same provisions that Chapter Four applies to all resource industries. Articles 902 and 903 mirror articles 407 and 408, which prohibit quantitative restrictions on exports, minimum prices, or export taxes. Articles 904 and 409, the proportional-sharing clauses, require Canada to allow continued exports of nonrenewable natural resources even during periods of national scarcity. If Canada were to declare a national emergency, it would still be obliged to allow the same proportion of its oil and gas production to be exported to the United States as was sold over the previous three years. Neither would Canada be allowed to substitute one type of resource for another—for example, a heavy crude for a lighter variety.

During the first three years after the signing of CUFTA, 1988 to 1990, Canadian oil exports to the United States averaged 56.2 percent of production, up from 41.1 percent in 1984 (before the Mulroney government deregulated the industry). Over the same period, natural gas exports averaged 32.9 percent of production, up from 23.2 percent in 1984. According to National Energy Board (NEB) projections, at the end of 1989 conventional oil reserves were equivalent to only 9.5 years of production and remaining natural gas reserves in western Canada were sufficient for 19.8 years. Before deregulation, the NEB applied a "surplus test" requiring that minimum supplies of nonrenewable hydrocarbons be available for Canadians before sanctioning exports. However, under CUFTA, the NEB has been reduced to a monitoring agency with limited ability to restrict exports.

The continued export of nonrenewable, conventional energy reserves at prices well below their replacement cost means that Canadians are subsidizing U.S. consumers. Canadian taxpayers further subsidize U.S. customers through generous government assistance to petroleum companies that cannot be recovered through export taxes, which are forbidden by CUFTA. While CUFTA generally disallows government subsidies to industry, Article 906 explicitly sanctions subsidies for petroleum exploration and development.

This short-sighted policy means that more expensive frontier reserves will be developed sooner than necessary, endangering fragile Arctic and Atlantic ecosystems and violating the rights of native peoples who have not yet settled their aboriginal land claims. Furthermore, the Mulroney government loosened the remaining limits on foreign takeovers of Canadian oil companies and abandoned the goal of 50 percent Canadian control of the petroleum industry even before the NAFTA negotiations were completed.

THE U.S. STRATEGY FOR NAFTA

While CUFTA was being negotiated with Canada, the Reagan administration was already anticipating similar talks with Mexico. A confidential assessment of CUFTA prepared by the U.S. State Department explicitly discussed the prospects for including Mexican petroleum in a North American common market. The memo advised that "the political climate in Mexico is not ready for a market-based energy trade arrangement at this time: the degree of government involvement in Mexico's energy sector has always been very large and is considered essential by many elements in Mexico."[2] This assessment changed dramatically under the government of Carlos Salinas de Gortari. In early 1990, Salinas's advisors began to discuss the possibility of a free trade agreement with top officials in the U.S. government. From the very beginning, despite the insistence of Mexican officials that this be kept secret until after the 1991 midterm elections, it was clear that energy was a major issue in the negotiations.

U.S. negotiators sought to avoid the appearance of an overt grab for Mexican oil. George Grayson cautions, "Oil can't be something the gringos pound the table on during free trade negotiations. That would be counterproductive" (Moffett, 1990). However, the United States did demand concessions, and energy was a major stumbling block in the negotiations. The Market Access chapter of the leaked Dallas Composite draft of NAFTA, dated 21 February 1992, showed that the Bush administration wanted Mexico to accept the same terms as Canada with regard to natural resources. Their proposal for a general proportional-sharing clause like Article 409 of CUFTA made no exception for oil or any other natural resource.

In the August 1992 NAFTA document, the Salinas negotiators scored an important public relations victory by exempting Mexico from the proportional-sharing clauses that still apply to Canadian energy supplies. But a specific commitment to the sharing of Mexican petroleum reserves during a supply shortage is not necessarily the greatest threat to Mexican sovereignty. Such a clause would only be invoked during an emergency. The Salinas government did accept provisions identical to those in CUFTA—provisions that outlaw the use of quotas, minimum prices, and special taxes on energy exports. These provisions could have a more devastating long-term effect on conservation of nonrenewable hydrocarbons than a proportional-sharing clause.

In order to win an exemption from the proportional-sharing clauses, the Salinas negotiators had to give ground on government procurement and investment rules allowing U.S. and Canadian corporations to participate in Mexican petroleum development. These rules were carefully crafted to allow all parties to claim that they respect the Mexican Constitution regarding formal ownership of petroleum reserves. As Adolfo Aguilar Zinser explains, formal ownership of hydrocarbons is an anachronism. The majority of petroleum producers, including countries of the Middle East [and the province of Alberta], incorporate into their basic laws arrangements similar to those of the Mexican Constitution (Aguilar Zinser, 1991).

For the United States, changes to Mexican investment laws and PEMEX rules regarding subcontracting are more important than questions of formal ownership of petroleum reserves. Accordingly, when presidents Bush and Salinas met in Washington in December 1991, the price that Bush demanded for reviving the stalled negotiations was a commitment that Mexico would open up its oil service industry to U.S. companies (Bradsher, 1991).

U.S. and Canadian oil supply companies won the right to bid on contracts from PEMEX and the Mexican Federal Electricity Commission. Initially, they can bid on half of the goods and service contracts tendered by Mexico's state energy firms worth more than $250,000. The share of contracts open to U.S. or Canadian bids rises to 70 percent after eight years and 100 percent after ten years. This concession is especially important for the U.S. oilfield equipment industry, which claims that it desperately needs access to the Mexican market in order to survive because of a diminishing U.S. market. Seventy percent of industry sales are now in the form of exports . . . [In June 1992] the number of rigs operating in the U.S. hit the lowest number ever since records have been kept (Granitsas, 1992).

The negotiators tried to give the appearance of respect for the Mexican Constitution by agreeing that U.S. and Canadian corporations could only bid for "performance" contracts that pay monetary bonuses for finding oil. "Risk" contracts that award a share of the oil found to a foreign company would be ruled out. However, U.S. industry sources insist that the language of this provision was purposely left vague to allow for each side to interpret it as it sees fit (*Inside U.S. Trade,* 1992). One U.S. company, Triton Production Systems, has already signed a precedent-setting contract allowing the use of U.S. crews on U.S. rigs drilling offshore in the Bay of Campeche.

A special $5 billion, five-year line of credit to PEMEX from the U.S. Export-Import Bank gives further leverage to the U.S. push for more business for its oil service industry. Canada's Export Development Corporation has offered a similar $500 million credit. These loans are tied to the purchase of U.S. and Canadian equipment and contracts for exploration. Edward J. Morse, publisher of *Petroleum Intelligence Weekly* and former U.S. deputy assistant secretary of state for international energy policy, explains that the Ex-Im Bank loan

could provide a wedge for the re-entry of US firms, which could be paid on a royalty type of arrangement for their services. And it is only a short step from 'pure service' to 'risk service' contracts—the cover by which Ecuador and other Latin American countries permit equity type investments in the oil sector (Morse, 1990, p. 2).

The U.S. and Canadian negotiators used the NAFTA talks to win more opportunities to invest in Mexico's petrochemical industry. In 1989, Mexico reclassified 36 petrochemical products from the "basic" category, reserved exclusively for the Mexican state, to the "secondary" category, in which private foreign investment is allowed. By June 1992, this effort had attracted only one new foreign investment (Lomas, 1991). During the NAFTA negotiations Mexico made 14 more petrochemical products eligible for foreign investment.

Liberalization of investment rules for petrochemicals was already anticipated by PEMEX in advance of NAFTA. A study written by PEMEX's finance department proposes that new petrochemical plants become turnkey operations where foreign corporations are contracted to build plants according to PEMEX specifications. The foreign partners would be responsible for financing the investments. PEMEX would then lease the plants from the builders, thus fulfilling the letter of the law which says that only PEMEX can operate basic petrochemical plants. Part of the production of these new plants will be dedicated to export sales to pay the leases (Ortega, 1991).

According to *Petroleum Intelligence Weekly,* PEMEX wants

> to open up the whole sector to foreign participation, including basic petrochemicals, the financing and the administration of plants . . . [producing for export, rejecting] the previous obsession with satisfying first internal needs (Ortega, 1991).

With most of PEMEX earnings going directly to the federal government, largely for payments on the external debt, the oil company lacks funds for developing the offshore and deep wells that contain 90 percent of Mexico's known petroleum reserves. Therefore PEMEX management wants to raise substantial amounts from international capital markets.

To make PEMEX more attractive to foreign lenders, the Salinas government laid off more than 70,000 workers and in June 1992 reorganized the enterprise into a holding company with four semi-autonomous divisions: exploration, refining, gas and basic petrochemicals, and secondary petrochemicals (Ortega, 1992). NAFTA's energy provisions complement these changes by opening up procurement and offering service contracts to U.S. and Canadian firms. Many Mexicans believe these measures represent an effective surrender of the control Mexico reclaimed when President Lázaro Cárdenas expropriated the petroleum industry in 1938.

Independent U.S. petroleum analysts and the U.S. Congressional Research Service agree with Mexican critics like Heberto Castillo and former PEMEX engineer Francisco Inguanzo that, at current market prices, Mexico's actual exploitable reserves are only about half as large as PEMEX claims.[3] In fact, unless there is new investment in costly deep wells and offshore development, Mexico's petroleum reserves will last for only about seven years.

CONCLUSION

Continental integration of the energy sector means that both Canada and Mexico face the premature depletion of their nonrenewable petroleum resources through exports that subsidize U.S. consumers. NAFTA incorporates the CUFTA provision allowing governments to subsidize petroleum exploration and development but disallows measures that would ensure that taxpaying citizens have first call on hydrocarbon discoveries.

In the NAFTA negotiations, President Bush sought to avoid awakening Mexican nationalist sentiments by downplaying the importance of ownership of Mexico's oil fields. However, it is clear that the Bush administration used all its negotiating leverage to secure unimpeded access to Mexican petroleum. Oil is not just a "side payment" to sweeten NAFTA for the United States. A historical perspective shows that NAFTA fulfills a major and long-standing geopolitical objective of the United States: to control continental energy resources.

NOTES

1. U.S. State Department. U.S.-Canada Free Trade Agreement Briefing Paper for Secretary Baker and Ambassador Yeutter. Excerpted in: "Confidential Appraisal of U.S.-Canada Pact Weighs Benefits, Shortfalls." (9 November 1987). *Inside U.S. Trade,* p. 16.
2. Ibid.
3. For more discussion of the actual extent of Mexican oil reserves, see B. López and M. A. Sánchez. (1991, October 7). "Controversy Grows on Extent of Mexico's Proven Reserves." *El Financiero International,* p. 26; H. Castillo. (1990, October 15). "Entegrar no es Integrar." *Proceso* (728), pp. 31-34; Beltrán del Río, op. cit.

REFERENCES

Aguilar Zinser, A. (22 February 1991). "Petróleo en el TLC." *El Financiero,* p. 8.

Bertrand, R. J. (1981). *Canada's Oil Monopoly.* Toronto: Lorimer.

Blair, J. M. (1978). *The Control of Oil.* New York: Vantage.

Bradsher, K. (15 December 1991). "Bush Tells Mexico He Wants a Free-Trade Pact Soon." *New York Times,* p. 18.

Calgary CP. (26 July 1979). "Canadians Warned by U.S. Oil Spokesman to be Cautious about Energy-Sharing Plan." *Globe & Mail,* p. B2.

Castillo, H., and Naranjo, R. (1984). *Cuando el Petróleo se Acaba.* Mexico: Ediciones Océano.

Castillo, H. (1981). *Los Energéticos y el Tercer Mundo.* Mexico: Editorial Mexicana.

Clarkson, S. (1985). *Canada and the Reagan Challenge.* Toronto: Lorimer.

del Río, P. Beltran. (9 December 1991). "Dato Oficial Sobre las Reservas Petroleras: 64,500 Millones de Barriles; Dato Real: 29,879 Millones." *Proceso* (788), pp. 16-21.

Engler, R. (1961). *The Politics of Oil*. Chicago: University of Chicago Press.

Granitsas. A. (10 July 1992). "U.S. Team on NAFTA Procurement Under Rising Pressure from Oilfield Industry." *Inside U.S. Trade,* p. 17.

Grayson, G. W. (1981). "The Maple Leaf, the Cactus, and the Eagle." *Inter-American Economic Affairs* (34).

Hall, J. (17 July 1979). "Carter's Plea to Ottawa: Back Our Energy Plan." *Toronto Star,* p. 1.

Halloran, R. (28 January 1979). "Carter Urged to Seek Pact on Mexican Natural Gas." *New York Times,* p. 16.

Hellman, J. A. (1983). *Mexico in Crisis* (2nd ed.). New York: Holmes & Meier.

Inside U.S. Trade. (24 July 1992). "NAFTA Energy Negotiators Narrow Differences on Petrochemical Sector," p. 18.

Koffman O'Reilly, A. (16 August 1977). "Oil Seen Turning Point of Mexican Economy." *Journal of Commerce.*

Laxer, J. (1974). *Canada's Energy Crisis*. Toronto: James Lewis and Samuel.

Laxer, J. (1983). *Oil and Gas*. Toronto: Lorimer.

Lomas, E. (28 October 1991). "La Reclasificación de Petroquímicos No Ha Atraído Más Inversiones." *La Jornada,* p. 1.

Meyer, H. E. (10 September 1979). "Why a North American Common Market Won't Work—Yet." *Fortune,* pp. 119-122.

Moffett, M. (26 November 1990). "Wells of Nationalism: Oil's Role in Mexico Raises Tricky Issues for a Free-Trade Pact." *Wall Street Journal,* p. 4.

Morse, E. J. (1990). "Gearing Up for an Oil Change." *Hemisfile: Perspectives on Political and Economic Trends in the Americas*. La Jolla, California: Institute of the Americas.

New York Times. (14 August 1982). "U.S. and Mexico: Major Rift Emerges." p. 2.

Ortega, F. (15 April 1991) "Punto de Vista de Pemex." *Proceso* (754), pp. 8-11.

———. (22 June 1992). "El Plan de Reestructuración de Pemex Elaborado por la Mackinsey, aún 'No Es Suficiente.' " *Proceso* (816), p. 8.

Shaffer, E. (1983). *Canada's Oil and the American Empire*. Edmonton: Hurtig.

Teichman, J. A. (1988). *Policymaking in Mexico*. Boston: Allen and Unwin.

United States General Accounting Office. (1992). *Mexican Oil: Issues Affecting Potential U.S. Trade and Investment.* Washington.

GLOSSARY OF TRADE TERMS

Adjustment
Financial, training, and reemployment technical assistance to firms and industries to help them cope with adjustment difficulties arising from increased import competition. The objective of the assistance is usually to help an industry to become more competitive in the same line of production, or to move into other economic activities.

Anti-dumping
Laws that provide relief from injurious imports sold at "less than fair value." This usually occurs when imports are priced at less than the "normal" price charged in the exporter's domestic market. The remedy is a punitive duty equal to the alleged dumping margin. The U.S. administrative authorities' methods for determining the "fair value" of a product are based on "constructed costs," which sometimes bear little relation to the actual costs and profit margins of the competitors of U.S. firms.

Article 19
That part of the GATT agreement which sets out special "safeguard" provisions for member nations. Under this Article, an importing country may increase tariffs or impose quantitative restrictions on an imported product, or take other appropriate measures to control imports, in circumstances where the imports are causing or threatening "serious injury" to domestic producers of similar goods.

Autopact
A sectoral trade agreement (the Automotive Products Trade Agreement) entered into by the United States and Canada in 1965 in order to encourage the rationalization and growth of their auto industries. It provides for duty-free movement between the two countries of new automobiles and original equipment parts.

Contingency Protection
Collective term referring to Anti-dumping, Countervailing duties and Safeguards.

Countervailing Duty (CVD)
These cases deal with charges of government subsidization. If imports are found to be subsidized and to cause or threaten material injury to any U.S. industry, for example, or materially retard its establishment, then they are actionable. The penalty is a duty on the allegedly subsidized imports to offset the estimated subsidy.

Dispute Settlement
Those institutional provisions in a trade mechanism agreement that provide the means by which differences of view between the parties can be settled.

Dumping
The sale of an imported commodity at a price lower than which it is sold within the exporting country or to third countries. Dumping is generally recognized as an unfair trade practice. Article VI of GATT permits the imposition of special anti-dumping duties against "dumped" goods equal to the difference between their export price and their normal value in the exporting country.

Establishment
One of the basic principles that comprise national treatment for investors. Right of establishment involves providing foreign investors the right to establish new businesses on the same basis as nationals.

Export Restraints
Quantitative restrictions imposed by exporting countries to limit exports to specific foreign markets, usually pursuant to a formal or informal agreement concluded at the request of the importing countries.

Export Subsidies
Government payments or other financially quantifiable benefits provided to domestic producers or exporters contingent on the export of their goods or services.

Fast-track
Legislative procedures set forth in Section 151 of the U.S. Trade Act of 1974. They stipulate that once the president formally submits to Congress a bill implementing an agreement negotiated under the act's authority, both houses must vote on the bill within 90 legislative days. No amendments are permitted. The purpose of these procedures is to assure foreign governments that Congress will act expeditiously on an agreement they negotiate with the U.S. government.

Framework Agreement
A trade agreement limited to a broad statement of objectives but including institutional arrangements to facilitate the attainment of these objectives.

Free Trade Area
A cooperative arrangement among two or more countries which agree to remove substantially all tariff and non-tariff barriers to trade with each other, while each maintains its differing schedule of tariffs applying to all other nations.

Generalized System of Preferences (GSP)
A concept developed within UNCTAD to encourage the expansion of manufactured and semi-manufactured exports from developing countries by making goods more competitive in developed country markets through tariff procedures.

Grandfather Clause
A GATT provision that allowed the original contracting parties to accept general GATT obligations despite the fact that some domestic legislation was otherwise inconsistent with GATT provisions. More generally, any clause in an agreement that provides that certain existing programs, practices and policies are exempt from an obligation.

Injury
The requirement, under GATT, that an industry seeking trade relief establish that it has been hurt by foreign competition. In the United States, a finding of injury has always been required for safeguard relief, and since 1979 for the bulk of CVD and anti-dumping cases.

Intellectual Property
A collective term used to refer to new ideas, inventions, designs, writings, films and so on, and protected by copyright, patents, trademarks, etc.

National Treatment
Refers to the extension to imported goods of a treatment no less favorable than that accorded to domestic products with respect to internal taxes, laws, regulations and requirements. GATT members are obliged to accord to one another "national treatment" with respect to internal measures that can affect trade in goods. Currently GATT does not require extending "national treatment" to trade in services or to foreign investment (transnational corporations).

Non-Tariff Barriers or Measures (NTBs)
Government measures or policies other than tariffs that restrict or distort international trade. Examples include import quotas, discriminatory government procurement practices, and measures to protect intellectual property. Such measures have become relatively more conspicuous impediments to trade as tariffs have been reduced during the period since World War II.

Orderly Marketing Arrangements (OMA)
International agreements negotiated between two or more governments in which the trading partners agree to restrain the growth of trade in specified "sensitive" products, usually through the imposition of import quotas.

Quantitative Restrictions
Explicit limits or quotas on the physical amounts of particular commodities that can be imported or exported during a specified time period. Article 19 of GATT permits quotas to safeguard certain industries from damage by rapidly rising imports.

Rules of Origin
The term for the set of measures used to differentiate between goods originating in one country from those in another for the purpose of the application of trade measures such as tariffs. For example, goods made up of components originating in various countries but which when assembled add 50 percent to their overall value may be considered to be goods originating in one country, whereas the addition of 25 percent in value would not qualify. Such rules are very important for countries establishing a free trade area.

Safeguards
Provide protection from fairly traded imports that seriously injure or threaten to seriously injure an industry. Safeguards include duties, quotas, adjustment assistance, or orderly marketing arrangements.

Section 301
A provision of the U.S. Trade Act of 1974 which creates sweeping powers to retaliate against foreign government practices that restrict the competitiveness of U.S. firms in foreign or domestic markets. In addition to enforcing the rights of the United States under any trade agreement, Section 301 allows the President, or in some instances the United States Trade Representative, to take action against any foreign government practice that "is unjustifiable, unreasonable, or discriminatory and burdens or restricts United States commerce."

Section 337
A provision of the same act (see above) that covers "alleged unfair practices in the importation and sale of imported products." This statute has been used mainly in disputes over intellectual property rights. An adverse ruling can result in an exclusion order against the disputed import.

Standards
A technical specification contained in a document that lays down characteristics of a product such as levels of quality, performance, safety or dimensions. It may include, or deal exclusively with, terminology, symbols, testing and test methods, packaging, marking, or labelling requirements as they apply to a product.

Subsidy
An economic benefit granted by a government to producers of goods—often to strengthen their competitive position. The subsidy may be direct (a cash grant) or indirect (low-interest export credits guaranteed by a government agency, for example).

Super 301
This phrase has been used to characterize provisions of the August 1988 U.S. Omnibus Trade and Competitiveness Act which broaden the scope of allowable U.S. retaliation under Section 301 (above). It mandates U.S. trade sanctions against countries which "violate" U.S. intellectual property rights. It also requires the U.S. administration to pressure major trading partners that have trade surpluses with the United States to eliminate their trade distorting practices under the threat of trade sanctions.

Uruguay Round
Eighth in a series of multilateral trade negotiations held under the auspices of GATT. This round was launched at Punta del Este, Uruguay in September, 1986.

USITC
U.S. International Trade Commission. A U.S. fact-finding and regulatory agency whose six members make determinations of injury and recommendations for relief for industries or workers seeking relief from increased import competition.

USTR
U.S. Trade Representative. An official in the Executive Office of the President, with cabinet-level and ambassadorial rank, charged with advising the President and leading and coordinating the U.S. government on international trade negotiations and the development of trade policy.

Voluntary Restraint Agreements (VRAs)–Voluntary Export Restraints (VERs)
Informal arrangements through which exporters voluntarily restrain certain exports, usually through export quotas, to avoid economic dislocation in an importing country.

INDEX

ABOUT THE CONTRIBUTORS

RICARDO GRINSPUN is an assistant professor of economics and a fellow of the Centre for Research on Latin America and the Caribbean (CERLAC) at York University, Toronto.

MAXWELL A. CAMERON is an assistant professor at the Norman Paterson School of International Affairs at Carleton University, Ottawa.

ADOLFO AGUILAR ZINSER is a researcher at the Autonomous University of Mexico's Center for U.S. Studies, and president of the Lázaro Cárdenas Foundation in Mexico City.

BRUCE CAMPBELL is a research fellow at the Canadian Centre for Policy Alternatives in Ottawa.

STEPHEN CLARKSON is a political economist at the University of Toronto who now concentrates on Canadian politics and U.S.-Canada relations.

STEPHEN DIAMOND is a student at Yale Law School who has received a doctorate in politics from Birkbeck College, University of London.

JOHN DILLON has been a researcher with the Ecumenical Coalition for Economic Justice (ECEJ) in Toronto since 1973.

DANIEL DRACHE is professor of political science at Atkinson College, York University, Toronto.

LORRAINE EDEN is a professor of international affairs at the Norman Paterson School of International Affairs at Carleton University, Ottawa.

JEFF FAUX is president of the Economic Policy Institute in Washington, D.C.

GERALD K. HELLEINER is a professor of economics at the University of Toronto.

JUDITH ADLER HELLMAN is a professor of political and social science at York University, Toronto.

KATHRYN KOPINAK is an associate professor in the Department of Sociology, University of Western Ontario, London, Ontario.

ROBERT KREKLEWICH is an international political economist completing a doctorate in social and political thought, York University.

ROBERT KUTTNER is co-editor of *The American Prospect,* a columnist for *Business Week* and the *Washington Post,* and the author of several books.

THEA LEE is an international trade economist at the Economic Policy Institute.

MAUREEN APPEL MOLOT is a professor in the Norman Paterson School of International Affairs and the Department of Political Science at Carleton University, Ottawa.

STEVEN SHRYBMAN is working as a policy advisor for the government of Ontario while on leave from the Canadian Environmental Law Association.

SCOTT SINCLAIR is a graduate of the University of Prince Edward Island and is completing a doctoral dissertation in the Department of Political Science at York University.

JUDITH TEICHMAN is an associate professor of political science at the University of Toronto.

EDUR VELASCO ARREGUI is a full-time researcher at the National Autonomous University of Azcapotzalco, in Mexico City.

MEL WATKINS is professor of economics and political science at University College, University of Toronto.

BRUCE WILKINSON is a professor of economics at the University of Alberta, Edmonton, Alberta, Canada.